THIS WAY MORE ADVENTURE

A journey of self-education in Africa

Janet Stuart

2QT Limited (Publishing)

First Edition published 2016 by

2QT Limited (Publishing)
Unit 5 Commercial Courtyard
Duke Street
Settle
North Yorkshire
BD24 9RH

All photographs in this book taken by J Stuart during the journey

Printed and bound in the UK by CMP (UK) Limited

A CIP catalogue record for this book is available
from the British Library

ISBN 978-1-910077-88-7

In memory of Aunt Mary and for our families.

CONTENTS

Review   Professor Keith Lewin

Foreword

PART ONE: GETTING THERE   1

Prologue   3

Chapter 1   The Voyage Across the Sea   7

In which we travel to Glasgow, are stranded in
Liverpool and eventually carried across the ocean
while being inducted into Nigerian life and history.

Chapter 2   The Voyage Along the Coast   18

In which we make landfall in Freetown and visit
Abidjan, Tema and Lomé, recognising traces of
colonial history.

Chapter 3   On the Threshold of Nigeria   27

In which we are adopted by the Delano family and
meet Aunt Mary's students, but otherwise find
Lagos hard to endure.

PART TWO : NIGERIA   37

Chapter 4   Exploring the North: Zaria and Kano   39

In which we secure a base camp, but find it
difficult to penetrate behind the local walls, in spite
of introductions to both traditional and colonial
elites.

Chapter 5   Exploring the North: Katsina and
Kwassam   52

In which we discover a life-long slogan, and
discuss the dilemmas of education, as well as
cycling into the bush to discover another aspect of
ancient Africa.

Chapter 6   Friends in the East: Umuahia and Enugu   61

In which we meet up with old friends, make some
new ones and compare life with novels.

Chapter 7   More Friends in the East: Justina Bello
and her Circle   71

In which we see development through Igbo eyes
and sympathise with returning exiles.

Chapter 8   Old and New in Benin   82
             In which the young of Benin show us their old
             traditions and look to the future.

Chapter 9   Ibadan: the Alalades and Ife   88
             In which we come to Ibadan, stay with another
             branch of the Delano family and visit ancient Ife.

Chapter 10   Ibadan: The Oguntoyinbos and Oyo   97
             In which we stay with the people who praise iron
             and visit Oyo old and new.

Chapter 11   Farewell to Nigeria   105
             In which we are rescued by Aunt Mary's students
             from the Nigerian health service and leave Nigeria
             with many questions about its future.

PART THREE: TANZANIA   111

Chapter 12   Arrival in Dar es Salaam   113
             In which we step into Tanzania, forge some new
             links in the chain and begin our quest for an
             ujamaa village.

Chapter 13   Moshi and Kilimanjaro   122
             In which we take a hard day's journey to Moshi
             and climb Kilimanjaro.

Chapter 14   Arusha and the Tourist Trail   133
             In which we look for handicrafts and, after a
             diversion into self-reliant education, actually see
             some animals. The countryside is baffling but the
             Christians are welcoming.

Chapter 15   Mvumi and Dodoma   140
             In which we move in Christian circles around
             hospitals and schools and find a depressing village.

Chapter 16   Mufindi   148
             In which we find an ujamaa village nestled up
             against a capitalist enclave.

Chapter 17   Morogoro   154
             In which I have a run-in with TANU, meet a
             different kind of teacher and we go climbing again
             with the Scandinavians.

| Chapter 18 | Korogwe and Ifakara | 164 |

In which we begin to feel the pull of South Africa, but first we visit an ex-Bath student, return to Morningside and visit Ifakara.

| Chapter 19 | Final Days in Dar | 172 |

In which we meet new friends, say goodbye to old ones and have some final tussles with the Tanzanian bureaucracy.

| Chapter 20 | Stopover in Lusaka | 180 |

In which we find an intermediate country and move comfortably between different social and racial worlds.

PART FOUR: SOUTH AFRICA   187

| Chapter 21 | First Views of the Republic of South Africa | 189 |

In which we explore our first contacts across the colour line and find possibilities emerging.

| Chapter 22 | First Interlude in Lesotho: April | 197 |

In which we settle into our base with the Hlaleles and buy a car; we are drawn to the mountains and meet some significant people.

| Chapter 23 | Exploring Johannesburg Through White Eyes | 209 |

In which we set up base in Jo'burg, are entertained by both British and Boer friends, visit the temples of Afrikanerdom and of gold and eventually reach Soweto.

| Chapter 24 | Exploring Johannesburg with Black Friends | 222 |

In which, pursuing all leads, we become involved with the Churches and visit Soweto again, this time as friends of a good doctor.

| Chapter 25 | Swaziland | 231 |

In which we pay a short visit to another independent country where we are welcomed by an old friend and make a new one.

| Chapter 26 | Nqutu and KwaZulu | 238 |

In which we remember some history, experience an appalling 'homeland' and visit an uplifting hospital.

Chapter 27   Second Interlude in Lesotho: May   246
              In which we come home to Lesotho, finding
              some more history on the way and ponder about
              education.

Chapter 28   Through the Ciskei   252
              In which we go where we should not have gone,
              visit missions and townships and meet a banned
              leader.

Chapter 29   White Settlers in the Eastern Cape   266
              In which we experience culture shock on a farm
              and are only partly restored by Grahamstown.

Chapter 30   East London and Transkei   272
              In which we explore the contradictions around
              border towns and Bantustans.

Chapter 31   Third Interlude in Lesotho: June   285
              In which we hear expatriate views on Lesotho and
              tour the mountains to see for ourselves.

Chapter 32   Exploring Capetown   295
              In which we drive through beautiful landscapes,
              meeting many different shades of colour and as
              many different opinions.

Chapter 33   The Underbelly of Capetown   310
              In which we are drawn into the work of the
              Christian Institute and become reporters of the
              darker side of Cape Town.

Chapter 34   Goodbye to Lesotho   323
              In which we stay in a different house but enjoy the
              same warm friendship.

Chapter 35   Final Return to Johannesburg   326
              In which we pick up old contacts, make a few new
              ones and visit Sharpeville.

Chapter 36   Farewell to South Africa   337
              In which we try to make sense of what we have
              learnt and decide what to do with it.

Afterword   349

Acknowledgements   353

Acronyms   355

The Author   356

Review

by Professor Keith Lewin

Janet and Patrick Stuart have written an engaging and evocative account of her personal journey through Sub-Saharan Africa in 1974-5 a decade after many countries became independent. The book is populated by the real characters that lived the experience of decolonisation and shared their space and thoughts with Janet and Patrick as they explored Sierra Leone, Ivory Coast, Ghana, Togo, Nigeria, Tanzania, Lesotho, Swaziland and South Africa. Anyone who had been travelling though these countries at that time will sense the authenticity and feel a resonance of the text with the sounds, scents and rhythms of the different countries and cultures.

They will also recognise the warmth and affection that transcends cultures, and the motives that led them to return to live and work in Southern Africa and subsequently contribute extensively to work on education and development at the University of Sussex. This is first and foremost a very readable memoir of a bygone time. But it also maps some of the events and the personalities that shaped the evolution of development and contributed to the social history of the times. This is a good read, especially for those contemplating a gap year travelling in Africa, and a welcome invitation to share two lives well lived.

Professor Keith Lewin. BSc; MSc; DPhil; FAcSS, C.Phys;
Emeritus Professor of International Development
Centre for International Education, University of Sussex

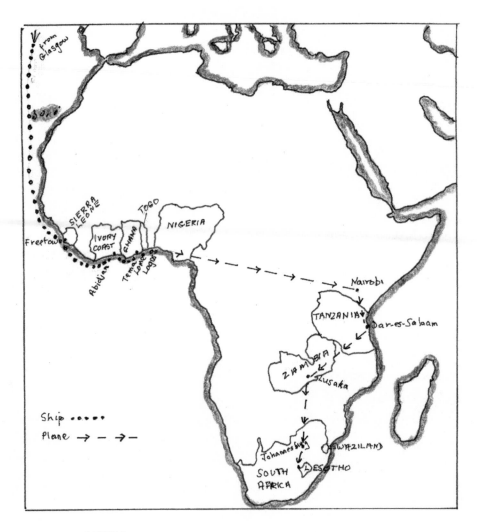

AFRICA
Routes taken by sea and air, with the countries visited.

Foreword

We travel not for trafficking alone
By hotter winds our fiery hearts are fanned
For lust of knowing what should not be known
We take the Golden Road to Samarkand.

We are the Pilgrims, master; we shall go
Always a little further: it may be
Beyond that last blue mountain barred with snow
Across that angry or that glimmering sea,
White on a throne or guarded in a cave
There lives a prophet who can understand
Why men were born: but surely we are brave
Who take the Golden Road to Samarkand.

(*J.Elroy Flecker, Hassan*)

This is a personal account of a journey through three contrasting African countries in 1974-5. My husband Patrick and I spent three months in Nigeria, two and a half months in Tanzania and three months in Southern Africa, based in Lesotho but making extended forays into what was then called the Republic of South Africa.

We went because we were curious. We went because in those days – some ten to fifteen years after the 'wind of change' swept through Africa, giving most of the former colonies independence from Britain and France – it seemed an exciting continent, full of promise, where new countries might pioneer new forms of social and economic development. For example, having decided to go to Nigeria with its avowedly capitalist ethos, we chose to visit Tanzania as a contrast, to see what Nyerere's 'African Socialism' might look like in practice.

i

But above all we went to meet people. We were extraordinarily fortunate in having personal contacts through Patrick's Aunt Mary and through the British Council of Churches. Other contacts came through family, friends and people returning from Voluntary Service Overseas. These allowed us to meet a wide range of people, mainly local, but also expatriates working in various aspects of development.

This is a joint story. Patrick kept a daily diary to which I added from time to time. The hand-written copy was sent home periodically as a letter to parents, so our families were the primary audience. It included, however, our own reflections and the debates we had with each other and with those we met, ranging over politics, economics, culture, education and all the fascinating aspects of social life we encountered. We also went bird-watching whenever we could and recorded our lists enthusiastically.

It is a very partial picture, seen through our personal and cultural lenses. It is also a snapshot of a moment in time. Travellers today would have very different experiences and see very different things. The Nigerian National Shipping Line, for example, no longer exists, yet the voyage out to Lagos, in company with the Nigerian officers and families who became our friends, was one of the most formative parts of our experience. Nigeria today is a much less optimistic and relaxed country, though surely its people, individually, remain as friendly and hospitable to strangers as they were to us. Tanzania has abandoned its path to socialism and is trying to develop along market lines. The debates we had then seem to come from a different world entirely.

The biggest change, of course, has been in South Africa. In 1975 it was still under white minority rule. The system of *apartheid*, or 'separate development', was being extended through the creation of ostensibly self-governing 'homelands', dubbed 'Bantustans'. Contact between people of so-called different racial groups was minimised.

Entering South Africa as we did, after six months of living in independent African countries, being welcomed and looked after by African friends, almost all with dark brown skins, we experienced cultural shock. No one greeted us in the streets. We could not meet up with our contacts and go to their homes unless they had pink skins like us. The 'Whites Only' signs warned us not to break the conventions of separation. Had we just jetted into Jan Smuts Airport from Heathrow, we might have not noticed where 80% of the population lived. It was a ridiculous, peculiar, unjust and inefficient system.

Eventually we found ways around it, and fortunately we could always retreat to the sanity and friendliness of Lesotho. At the time we recorded debates about: were white attitudes changing? What new forms of action might black people take? Was peaceful change possible? Was a racial bloodbath inevitable? A year after we left, school students marched in Soweto and were fired on by police. There followed fifteen years of action and counter-action, international pressure and internal debate until in 1990 Mandela walked free and in 1994 democratic elections were held. Miraculously, there was no civil war and although apartheid left a huge legacy of inequality and ignorance there is much to celebrate.

And what became of us? We looked, we questioned, we listened and what we learnt changed the course of our lives, separately and jointly. Patrick switched from analysing stocks and shares to investigating the role of British companies abroad and urging disinvestment in South Africa. My Lesotho contacts resulted, four years later, in an invitation to train teachers for Development Studies at the National University of Lesotho. There Patrick, described on his visa as 'accompanying spouse,' took a number of accountancy jobs, ranging from training bookkeepers to setting up new financial systems in both Catholic and Protestant mission hospitals – the only person to have managed to work for these competing organisations simultaneously!

After six years in Lesotho we returned to the UK. I wrote up my classroom research into a D.Phil thesis and worked for fifteen interesting years at Sussex University in education and development, while after a few years Patrick fulfilled his lifelong ambition to retire. At some point he had had the whole diary typed up and for years it sat in folders on the shelf, remembered anecdotally when friends and students gathered. My 1500 slides, having been enthusiastically shown to all and sundry until the audience fell asleep, likewise mouldered in their special chest.

In 1998 Patrick developed Parkinson's disease and eventually a form of intermittent dementia. As he could no longer focus clearly, we blew the dust from the folders and I began reading the diary to him. Whenever he got confused, violent, or stared into space, we found such reading brought him back to the present and set him chuckling over the memories.

Leaving academic work behind me, I began discussing with Patrick ways of editing the diary. We talked about what to include and who to omit; we met with a publisher and I started editing, summarising and reading it back to him. It was one of the things that brought us so close together in those last months. We hadn't got very far when he died, unexpectedly, but mercifully quickly, in September 2007.

> What we were, we are.
> What we had, we have.
> A conjoined past imperishably present.
> (*Nicholas Evans, The Smoke Jumper*)

This story, developed out of the diary, is part of our conjoined past.

PART ONE

Getting there

Prologue

On board the *MV River Gongola*, somewhere out beyond the Azores, the captain is throwing a party. Once the electrician has fixed the cassette player, the chief steward has broached the champagne and the rest of the guests have shuffled warily in, the captain rises.

'I bid you all welcome,' he booms. 'May this be a happy journey for all of you. May Mrs Uduku and her daughters come safely to Umuahia. May Mr Oguntoyinbo be soon reunited with his wife and daughter in Ibadan. May Mr and Mrs Stuart enjoy their time in our great country, Nigeria! Let my officers take care of you and make you feel at home on this flagship of the Nigerian National Line! Let the party commence!'

The music changes from British pop to Nigerian. Their favourite Afrobeat group is Fela Ransome Kuti's band, and my favourite song is 'She go say, I be Lady oh!' The noise level rises, with laughter and capping of stories. Enthusiasts take to the floor, mixing 'highlife' with traditional Igbo[1] steps.

I throw myself happily into highlife, but as dancing was never Patrick's forte, Ade Uduku teaches him the 'Duke of Edinburgh style'. Apparently when the Duke came on a state visit to Nigeria he went everywhere, including the dance floor, with his hands clasped behind his back. After he left, this style, suitably enlivened, was very fashionable for quite some time. Patrick's tall figure moves in this stately way around the floor until Chief Officer Alex, reeling drunk on Guinness, challenges him with the question: 'What is so special about going to Africa? Why you going there anyway? What will happen to you?'

'Well…' begins Patrick patiently, but Alex interrupts.

'Not like my going to the UK for the first time, huh? First night in

---

[1] This is pronounced *Ibo* in English. It refers to the language and culture of a group of peoples originating in South-Eastern Nigeria.

England, it was winter and I nearly froze to death. I sleep on top of the bed; I didn't know you had to get inside! What you think of that?'

We think this may be a traditional Nigerian tale. The party goes on till 2.30 am and we fall into our bunks absolutely worn out.

So why indeed were we going to Nigeria?

It was Aunt Mary's students who started it all. To which one might add a supper in Notting Hill Gate and a shared curiosity about what the 'wind of change' had brought to Africa.

Aunt Mary Anderson, or Mrs A as she was known at the Bath Domestic Science College, was a hostel warden with a particular sympathy for overseas students, and many kept in touch with her. On her retirement those from South-East Asia bought her an air ticket so she could visit them all. Having enjoyed this immensely, she suggested to her nephew Patrick that he help her plan a similar trip round Africa and come as her escort.

At this point, Patrick and I had recently met and he invited me to supper at 'The Ark' in Notting Hill Gate. Searching for a suitable subject of conversation, he told me about Aunt Mary and how he hoped to travel round Africa with her. I thought: 'What fun to join in! But do I want Aunt Mary playing gooseberry...?' A year later, we were married, and Aunt Mary had decided her travelling days were done. 'But you could always visit them on my behalf,' she suggested.

And so, eventually, we did. It was 1974, almost all the European colonies in Africa had become independent and we were intrigued by the different paths they were taking. On the west coast was Nigeria, flush with newly-found oil, and enthusiastically embracing Western capitalism. Here a good number of Aunt Mary's students were part of the rising middle class and happy to entertain us. In Tanzania, on the eastern plateau, the schoolmaster figure of Julius Nyerere was preaching African socialism under the slogan: 'A fair share of what little we have.' Only one Bath graduate could be located but we found other contacts. At the toe of the continent squatted the Republic of South Africa, still dominated by the descendants of European settlers, with all its other peoples locked into the caste-like system of apartheid. We wanted to explore it but didn't want to stay there. Fortunately within South Africa lies the tiny mountain kingdom of Lesotho and there Anna Hlalele, ex-Bath student and Stuart family friend, offered her home as our base.

We abandoned the idea of driving across the Sahara: we were mechanically illiterate and a car might bubble-wrap us against experiencing both people and places. We would travel by sea to Nigeria, by public transport within each country and by air between them.

Getting a boat to Nigeria wasn't that easy. The travel agency told us that the passenger liners were being phased out and the last one was fully booked. Cargo boats? 'Oh no, sir, there's only the Nigerian National Shipping Line and you won't want to go by that.'

'Why not?'

'You might be the only Europeans on board!'

We booked a cabin on the *MV River Gongola*, NNSL.

I gave notice to my school and Patrick asked for a year's leave of absence from his firm of stockbrokers. Most of his colleagues found the idea incomprehensible, but the managing partner wished him luck. The bemused reaction of the others was perhaps best illustrated by the gifts given at the final partners' lunch when, in a light-hearted mood, Patrick was presented with a fly swat for his enemies and a string of Woolworths beads for his friends – all wrapped up in a golliwog bag.

The response of many people was uncertain but well-meaning: 'How interesting, you'll be able to visit all the game parks.' Fortunately many others understood that we wanted to meet people and explore other societies, providing a wealth of practical help and useful contacts, but some of the riper remarks should be recorded.

'Africa is a country I have always wanted to visit.'

'Are you going to Nigeria to see the public executions?'

'In Black Africa make sure you have good political contacts or you might well end up in prison.'

'Are you going to see Ian Smith? I suppose it's alright if you keep away from the Blacks.'

'Miss, why do you want to go there? Mind you don't get eaten!' (from my Afro-Caribbean pupils in Brixton).

Finally, because of the debt we owed to Aunt Mary for the voyage, we adopted as our motto for its duration one of her favourite sayings: 'Everything will be for the best.'

We wondered if our voyage would have as great an impact on us as Aunt Mary expected. What would we learn? Would we become different people?

CHAPTER I
The Voyage Across the Sea

In which we travel to Glasgow, are stranded in Liverpool and eventually carried across the ocean while being inducted into Nigerian life and history.

The voyage, however, was slow in starting. The original sailing date was put back a week, giving us much-needed extra time to pack and hand over to our house-sitters. So on Tuesday October 1st 1974 we set off to Euston in our Pakistani neighbour's decrepit old taxi and took a dismal British Rail train to Glasgow, planning to stay overnight with our friends Tom and Susie Lawrie in Lanarkshire. The buffet cars were closed and there was an hour's delay but Tom met us saying cheerfully: 'Well, that's the worst of your journey over!' Not so.

We woke next day to the cold autumnal calm of Braehead, bade earnest farewells to the Lawrie family and headed to the docks. We found the *MV River Gongola* and wandered on board unchallenged until we met the chief steward, who exclaimed: 'Ah, the flowers must belong to you!' Patrick's parents had sent us a bunch of chrysanthemums, clearly unprecedented on a cargo ship.

Our cabin was small and snug with two bunks, a writing table, en-suite facilities and a small porthole. We unpacked and ventured cautiously down to the saloon for lunch. Patrick played safe with the European menu but I explored the 'yams and medium beef stew,' which scorched the roof off my mouth. We started chatting to the Nigerian officer at the table and asked him what time we sailed.

'I think it will not be till Thursday,' he said apologetically. 'We have difficulty with the refrigeration machinery.' So we returned to Braehead for another friendly and comfortable night.

When we got back to the ship cargo was being loaded: machinery, sugar and frozen lamb from New Zealand destined for the West African market. Suddenly the tempo changed and the dockers started throwing the packages of frozen meat into the hold at random. 'Are we about to sail?' we asked the steward.

'I think not, sir. The company, they say maybe Friday or Saturday.'

So next morning we went into Glasgow for a final shopping spree. Patrick had thrown my billycans out of our luggage but here I found a tiny compact camping stove, comprising a meths burner, a kettle, and two pans, which all packed inside each other. This proved to be a most valuable piece of travelling equipment which I was to use almost every day while on the move. So perhaps the delay was all for the best?

At lunch we sat opposite the chief officer. He looked rather like a black Peter Ustinov – trim beard, deep-set eyes, affable but able to switch instantly to severity and, as we found out, a little too fond of the drink to be promoted to captain. He introduced himself with his Igbo names but told us to call him Alex. 'Why are you coming to Nigeria?' he asked.

'To find out what is happening there and what the people think of it,' replied Patrick.

This set him off. 'Our military government is even worse than the politicians,' he said. 'They're all corrupt. All our wealth is going to them and their cronies, instead of being shared among hard-working people like us officers.' (We noticed he did not suggest they share it with the hard-working villagers.)

With a little prompting he revealed that his hero was Colonel Ojukwu. 'He was a strong leader, but mind you he did consult all the Igbos before calling for Biafra to secede.' Our first lesson in Nigerian politics was how the shadow of the Biafran war still hung over Nigeria, especially for those, like most of the officers, who came from the Igbo peoples of the Eastern Region and had suffered the most.

Nigeria had become independent in 1960, but the first few years were characterised by inter-ethnic rivalry, fuelled by disputed elections and a controversial census. In particular, the Igbos were seen as a threat because of their education and success in business. In 1966 there was a series of military coups, leading to the deaths of ruling politicians and to the massacre in the Northern Region of some 50,000 Igbos. Two million Igbos from all over the country fled back to the East and, after unsuccessful attempts to re-establish civilian rule, the Military Governor of the Eastern Region, Col. Ojukwu, declared that the region would secede from the Federation and become an independent country under the name of Biafra. The Federal Government declared war and soon recaptured the oil wells on which Biafra depended for revenue. Encircled and blockaded, the Igbos fought back with great determination, bravery and ingenuity for two and a half years, but with no external support – only a handful of African countries recognised the new state – they were eventually starved into unconditional surrender. Col. Gowon, Nigerian Head of State, immediately declared a programme of 'Reconciliation, Reconstruction and Rehabilitation' to bring the region back into Nigeria. By the time of our voyage, nearly five years later, much had been done, but memories were still bitter.

The *River Gongola* could carry twelve passengers, but on this trip there were only seven – and we were indeed the only Europeans. At supper that night we met our companions.

'My name is Ade Uduku.' The tall smiling woman introduced herself and her three daughters. 'We were studying overseas when war broke out and we couldn't go home to Umuahia, in the heart of Biafra, because I am a Yoruba, although my husband is Igbo. We went to Edinburgh, where he worked as a doctor; I am a nurse. We had these two girls, Chinwe and Ola, with us but their elder brother was at home. This one, Oluchi, was born in Edinburgh.'

'Mama says I'm a Scootish Aafrican!' five-year-old Oluchi trilled in a pure Morningside accent.

'When peace came my husband flew home to start up his practice again but we're travelling by ship so we can bring all our possessions with us. If we don't watch over them they might get stolen en route.'

Femi Oguntoyinbo, also a Yoruba, had lived in the UK for fifteen years, first studying for a degree in business administration and then working for an engineering company. He had sent his wife and daughter home by air and was accompanying fifty cubic metres of household goods to keep his eye on them. A quiet, pleasant man, Femi seemed to get on with all the Igbos on board, though we noticed he kept out of their political discussions.

We left Glasgow three days late, in the early hours of Saturday morning, and I was up on deck at dawn to see the rising sun on Ailsa Craig and the gannets dive-bombing for fish. During breakfast the engines stopped. 'Just minor repairs, no cause for alarm,' Alex explained. By lunch time we were moving again, but slowly, and listing somewhat to port. At dinner the rumour was that the pumps weren't working properly. Unable to influence affairs, we settled serenely down to play Monopoly with our fellow passengers and two young officer cadets, Chuks and Dotun.

Taking a last walk on deck before bedtime I said to Patrick: 'Last night the moon was astern. Now it's over the bows?'

'I think that means Liverpool,' he sighed.

And Liverpool it was. North Wales hove into sight after breakfast, we sailed slowly up the Mersey and were towed into a dock where fire engines came to pump out the tanks. We had been at sea for thirty-six hours and had progressed one port down the British coast.

As another delay seemed inevitable, we phoned our nearest friends and after a horrendous Sunday journey – pouring rain, closed docks, trains leaving from the wrong station – we were drinking whisky with Gillian and Michael on the edge of the Pennines. We argued about the coming election and tried to explain once more just why we were so eager to go to Africa in a dubious cargo ship.

'It's the openness of the continent with all its possibilities that attracts me,' Patrick emphasised. 'The newly independent countries are full of optimism and the future's exciting.'

'I'm writing a textbook for school kids on developing countries,' I explained. 'I want to see at first hand some of the problems and collect real-life examples to illustrate them.' Mike, as an economist, had more questions than answers but they wished us luck.

We arrived back on board to the news that one of the generators had been damaged by the salt water and we could be a further two days in port, so at supper there was general gloom. This time we sat with the captain, a tall flat-headed man with a smidgen of beard on the tip of his chin, who seemed less self-assured than the others and talked through clenched teeth. His pretty, fluffy little wife had brought her very noisy children on board so we retired to our cabin wondering when we would actually get under way.

Next morning we discovered that the leak was not yet fixed, the pumps were still not working properly, the damaged generator would have to be taken ashore for repairs and we might be in Liverpool for up to a week.

That was enough. Aunt Mary, the originator of this whole idea, lived in Leicestershire, in a small cottage without central heating but with a spare bedroom – who better to hibernate with? En route we called at the NNSL office, where they confirmed the week's delay and even offered to pay our travel expenses. Two trains later (both delayed) we arrived in Melton Mowbray to the warmest of welcomes.

It was a strange interlude. Our friends believed us to be steaming into the tropics and here we were, holed up in the heart of England, watching Harold Wilson (just) win his second General Election in six months. Patrick was disappointed that the Liberal vote had fallen below six million and I was disappointed at the small size of the Labour majority. We read the papers with foreboding: inflation was shooting up and the economic forecasts were gloomy.

Meanwhile I revised the first chapter of my book[2], and helped Mary cook while she chatted away about all the old students we were likely to meet. 'Wura Delano in Lagos is the most dependable,' she said. 'You'll be all right with her.' Four weeks later her words came true.

On Tuesday October 15th we went back on board for the fourth time, where the ship was beginning to feel like home. At supper we got talking to the chief engineer, Leo, who had an enormous black beard, curly eyebrows and a tremendous laugh even by Nigerian standards. A kind man, frequently smiling, he was married to an Irish Catholic wife and had a brood of very well disciplined children. 'Aye,' he said, 'There'll be a delay of several more days. We're waiting for spare parts for the pumps.'

Next day the local rumour industry was working overtime:

'Parts have to be sent from Germany'!

---

[2] I had been commissioned to write a book about 'the developing world' as part of a Social Studies series for junior secondary schools.

'The equipment connecting the generators to the switchboard is faulty.'

'You can ask the company to fly you to Lagos if it's urgent enough.'

What, and miss all this fun? We sat down and taught the Uduku girls some new card games.

Two more days passed. We took walks round the docks with the Uduku family. I drafted a historical chapter for my book; being poised between the First and the Third Worlds in Liverpool stimulated reflection on colonialism and the slave trade. Patrick went into town to collect our travel refunds and press for news. 'Yes, definitely today,' he was promised, but the ship remained immoveable. This was becoming a way of life.

On Friday October 18th Leo said: 'No more shore leave!' as his family disappeared down the gangplank in tears. A brisk southerly wind was blowing rain across the docks as a pilot came aboard, a tug was roped, the engines started up again – we were off!

We dropped the pilot off Anglesey – only to come to a dead halt again one hour later.

'Minor repairs.'

'No cause for alarm.'

'It is a fuel pump valve and we will be going again in an hour.'

Two hours later we were still stationary. BBC Wales was showing a programme on Freetown, our next port of call, but unfortunately it was in Welsh.

At 9.00 pm the night was fine, we were moving at one knot and the lights of the Lancashire coast were still in view.

At 9.45pm there was a different feeling to the ship - we ran out into the corridor and met Ade. 'Are we sailing?' The captain hastened down from the bridge with a big smile. 'We are sailing!

We were now fifteen days behind schedule, but our African education had advanced mightily.

At Sea

We were at sea for eight days. Conventionally – this was late October – the sea was rough down through Ushant and Biscay, with gales up to Force 9. Equally conventionally, we spent most of the first two days reading in our bunks, making valiant sorties for meals but sometimes having to abandon them in a hurry.

After this the weather got warmer, the seas calmer and the days took on a routine. Our cabin was cleaned for us, but we had to do our own laundry in the ship's washing machine. Patrick undertook his usual job of ironing – a challenge on a rolling ship and where the iron had no thermostat.

Once past Las Palmas, Alex showed us the 'Monkey Island,' which was a platform reached by a ladder, situated above the bridge and just in front of the funnel: perfect for quiet sunbathing. A faint smell of diesel tainted the salty air; the engine purred below us and the waves splashed past the bow. After his chores Patrick would take up residence there with book, sunglasses, binoculars, radio and sun tan oil: this was life in the tropics indeed. I would work on my book in the morning and join him after lunch. From here you could watch the flying fish, popping out of the water by the bows and skimming away over the waves, like giant dragonflies with red or grey wings and luminous blue-green bodies.

We read voraciously and – being both unemployed for the first time in our married life – had time to discuss the books and share views. I introduced Patrick to Marxist ideas via Isaiah Berlin's biography and he gave me Galbraith's *New Industrial State*, while we both read the iconoclast Ivan Illich[3]. As light relief we had novels, mostly by Africans or about the continent. We talked endlessly about these and other ideas: teasing, listening and – usually – appreciating each other's viewpoint.

But we had a rich source of other ideas at hand. Africa is still a land of story tellers and around the supper table our fellow passengers and the officers told us stories – if not the traditional ones, then deeply interesting ones about their lives.

Leo liked to reminisce about village life. 'The children used to run free and wherever they went they were treated by the adults as if they were their own; there was no need to go home to eat or even sleep. In the evenings groups of children would gather and the elders would tell them fables or fairy tales.'

Even in modern Nigeria children seemed to move easily between parents, grandparents and endless aunts and uncles. 'One of my aunts had

---

[3] Ivan Illich: *Deschooling Society*, Penguin 1973.

no children of her own,' the captain told us, 'but we were six. My mother felt so sorry for her sister that she sent me and my younger brother and sister to live with her and she brought us up.'

'Aye,' agreed Leo. 'Both my parents died when I was young so I stayed with my elder brother while he was training to be a teacher and he paid for me to start primary school. Then I moved to my grandmother's. I was her favourite and she called me Leo because that was the name she gave me at my christening – other people called me Chukwu. We often have lots of different names.'

'My elder brother, he paid for my education,' said the captain. 'Now I'm paying school fees for my nephews.'

'What about nieces?' I asked.

'Well, boys are more important to us, you know. The girls become part of their husband's family. But' – sensing my disapproval – 'nowadays we do give equal attention to girls.' I resolved to keep checking that out.

'Our parents bring us up, then we look after them when they are old,' Alex, the chief officer, challenged us. 'Not like in the UK, where you send them to care homes!'

Femi was listening, but shook his head. 'When we're back home I'll invite my father and my parents-in-law to visit us, but I don't want to go and live in the family compound – my elder brother would start ordering me about again!'

Some of the stories reminded us of Chinua Achebe's novels[4]. The position of chief, or *obi*, carries authority and prestige, albeit little direct political power. One can become an *osa* (lower rank) by paying money to other title holders and by giving a big feast, but to be a senior chief you must wait for a vacancy.

'In my home town, Onitsha,' Leo explained, 'the decision rests with the *obi*. But you can't become a chief unless your elder brother is already one so you might have to buy him a chieftainship first. Politicians always try and become chiefs; it makes the people believe in them more.'

The system seemed to combine elements of primogeniture, aristocracy and democracy. One could see it working in a small, stable, rural community,

---

[4] For example, *Things Fall Apart* (1958) and *No Longer at Ease* (1960), published in the Heinemann African Writers Series.

but transpose it to modern, urban society and bribery becomes endemic; perhaps this was where corruption started.

Modern politics kept recurring. We knew already that Nigeria was an artificial country, emerging out of Franco-British rivalries in West Africa and comprising three distinct groups of people: the Hausa and Fulani of the northern savannah, the Yorubas of the western coastal forests, and the Igbo peoples of the eastern coast and the Niger delta. These groups spoke completely different languages and shared little culture. Northerners had become Muslim through earlier Arab influences, while the coastal peoples were more or less Christianised by the missionaries. The three groups found themselves chained together and had been hitting out at each other ever since independence.

These Igbo officers made explicit their contempt and dislike for the Hausa and had horrifying tales of what happened to their Igbo relatives and friends in the North during the 'pogroms' of 1966–7. The better-educated and entrepreneurial Igbos had gone north to work, causing resentment among the Hausas. Many were killed, others mutilated and sent back south to beg. The current military government was dominated by northerners and, therefore, they criticised it.

'President Gowon's too soft,' complained Alex. 'He should copy Nkrumah, or perhaps Chairman Mao – he's a strong leader. I've got all Chairman Mao's books in my cabin, and I think we could learn a lot from his ideas.' At that time there seemed a wide array of global models to choose from and there was much discussion about which would be most useful to newly independent African states.

It was clear to us that these Nigerians felt enormous confidence in their own people and their own country, however much they complained of the present government. Yet they differed about how far they wanted to adopt European customs and culture.

The captain argued: 'We've got to become more European in our values and way of life. Only then can we become a powerful modern country.'

Leo, in many ways the most Europeanised and married to an Irishwoman, disagreed vociferously. 'No, no, we should hold to traditional Nigerian values. My brother has written a history of our district at home and edits a magazine about Nigerian traditions. We must teach these to our children.'

In some ways this reminded us of the Scotsman rhapsodising about life in the Western Isles who had lived for thirty years in London.

Ade said quietly, 'I don't want my daughters to grow up as European women. They must go to Nigerian universities and marry Nigerians.'

The saloon, however, was stocked with European games and we had uproarious rounds of Monopoly and Ratrace[5]. Patrick introduced the girls to chess and to all the Stuart family card games; the cadets taught us African draughts. The captain gave a party for the passengers; we gave a party for the officers. Envious of the comfortable, flowing clothes the Nigerians wear off duty, we decided to go native so Patrick borrowed a loose batik top from Femi, while I visited Ade's cabin to select a 'wrapper'. These are long pieces of brightly coloured cloth; the underskirt is tied quite tightly round the waist, and the top layer draped more loosely, secured with a tuck-in knot. A loose blouse of the same material completes the outfit.

'Are all these made in Nigeria?' I asked naively.

'Sadly not, we import them, mostly from Britain or France. Damask is the smartest, but it costs £15 a yard.'

Twice as much as my best curtain material, I reflected. 'I suppose you wear them many times, and give them to your daughters?'

'Oh no, patterns go out of date. We have to buy new ones to be fashionable! The well-dressed Nigerian woman is supposed to be the most expensive in Africa. She'll be wearing hundreds of pounds' worth of jewellery as well.'

I went quite cheaply to the party, with just a borrowed wrapper and my wedding ring, but the officers all clapped when we arrived as pale-skinned Nigerians.

All was indeed for the best on this voyage. We were lucky that we had missed the era of posh passenger liners and that we had caught a friendly cargo boat before they were made obsolete by container ships – which would make sailing to West Africa impossible. We had time and space to acclimatise in many senses: not only to tropical weather but much more importantly to Nigerian culture and even to the food. We

---

[5] Ratrace is a boardgame played with dice about getting rich, which seemed to strike a chord with the Nigerians.

were fortunate in the company on board – a group of tolerant, intelligent, amusing people who took pleasure in satisfying our curiosity and telling us about their country and its culture, yet who knew enough about the UK to understand where we were coming from. We, in turn, listened in to their own debates about politics and problems and our later agendas were in some ways shaped by these insights.

CHAPTER 2
The Voyage Along the Coast

In which we make landfall in Freetown and visit Abidjan, Tema and
Lomé, recognising traces of colonial history.

Sierra Leone: Freetown is where the slaves were settled.

We felt like Jim Hawkins approaching Treasure Island or Marlow
entering the 'heart of darkness' as we stared at the long line of high
cloud-capped hills that Portuguese explorers, around 1462, compared
with a lion's head. Sailing into the harbour between a long sandy beach
and low, red cliffs half-hidden by trees, we could have been the Knights
of the Joyous Venture from *Puck of Pook's Hill* – were those drums in the
distance? Low boats with bright orange triangular sails flitted moth-like
across the water and as we anchored for the pilot the dug-out canoes
swarmed out towards us. 'Best bananas!' 'Daggers for sale!' 'Sir, you want a
real African drum?' 'Madam, buy me monkey, only ten leone!'

Once berthed at the quay, we swayed down the gangplank and onto
the soil of Africa. The Uduku family followed hesitantly in fresh blouses
and their best Edinburgh tartan skirts, white socks and clean shoes, and
we explored together, inevitably finding ourselves at the slum end of
town. Chinwe, Ola and Oluchi stared at the wide open drains lining the
road, the muddy pools around the sparse water taps, at the vultures on
the rubbish heaps. Metaphorically holding up their skirts, wrinkling their
noses at the smells, not saying very much, perhaps they were thinking: is
this what 'home' will be like?

For us too, it was our first view of what would later become familiar to us. But with more adult and optimistic eyes we could see that beyond the dirty streets there was family life, energy and business. There were shacks but also more substantial stone houses and almost every home along the street had a stall – often just a bench or box – selling something, from toothpaste and cigarettes to vegetables and drinks. Most of the adults were well clothed, many of the women wearing gorgeous dresses and bright headscarves. Streams of modern cars, lorries, taxis and buses hooted their way along the road; this was very different from Edinburgh but it certainly wasn't primitive.

In the evening there was another party on board ship, this time including some gaily dressed young women from the shore. When we arrived on deck a senior port official approached Patrick. 'Captain, sir! Will you please turn down the music? You know there is a state of emergency[6] in Sierra Leone!'

Patrick assumed this was a joke but played for time just in case. 'Are you serious? It's not really that noisy.'

'Indeed I am serious, sir. You must have heard about the assassination attempt on the president. The treason trial is still ongoing and we are taking strict precautions.'

'I'm very sorry but I'm not the captain, just a passenger. You'll find the real captain in the saloon.' The traditions of Empire take time to disappear and the official could see no other white man.

Next morning a tour of Freetown by car was organised for the passengers. It was Sunday: the Christians were walking to church, their ladies wearing Tory conference hats, and the Muslim traders had taken their place at the roadside stalls. We paused at President Margai's grave and looked over the city spread out below. For three centuries Portuguese, French, Dutch and British traders competed in this great natural harbour, mainly for slaves. In 1792, the tides of opinion and of commerce having changed, Freetown was founded as a settlement for freed slaves under British authority and after abolition thousands more found their way there. They brought with them Western ways and Christian beliefs and settled along the coast,

---

[6] In October 1974 there really was a state of emergency. The story is evocatively told by Aminatta Forna in her memoir *The Devil that Danced on the Water*. From 1991–2002 Sierra Leone endured a bitter civil war, eventually ending with UN involvement and just as its politics seemed to be stabilising, the country was hit by the ebola epidemic

barely mixing with the indigenous peoples and their Arab inheritance from the interior.

In the centre of town there were modern, even multi-storey, buildings, alongside older ones in the 'Portuguese' style with their quasi-baroque cornices and pilasters. There were both churches and mosques and a modern Parliament building, impressively designed in local stone and tropical woodwork. A miniature House of Commons, with the Speaker's Chair and the clerks' tables separating government and opposition benches, it was now an anachronism since President Siaka Stevens ruled as dictator.

After lunch we drove to the Atlantic beach – miles of unbroken empty sand, hot sun, cool breeze, the mountains standing above us – where we had a blissful time surfing in the waves and sunning ourselves. Back in the town we tried to buy some oranges, which confirmed our worst fears about our bargaining powers. On the other side of the road there was a steady stream of men and boys off to the football match between a school team and a club called Blackpool; then came a herd of cattle being driven through the town by tall men with lighter skins and finer features, Mende perhaps, from the interior and behind them a huge school parade marking the beginning of the academic year.

All this mixing of traditional and modern, of faiths and cultures, business and leisure, felt like a good introduction to West Africa and sharpened our interest in learning more. And, as yet, it wasn't too hot.

Cote D'Ivoire: Abidjan tries to be a part of France

Two days later we reached the Ivory Coast. Above the flat, featureless coastline we could see the white tops of high-rise buildings. Gently the *River Gongola* rumbled along a canal cut through the sandspit and into the lagoon, a vast expanse of water with cargo ships clustered by shiny new port facilities, all gleaming in the setting sun. There was a feeling of bustle and prosperity.

The young cadets – Chuks, Doton and John - got evening passes and took us exploring into the French part of the city. It was a long hot walk through wide empty boulevards, the Place de la Republique and Rue Charles de Gaulle, asking directions in stumbling French. Finally we sat down in a pavement café, surrounded by tall, graceful, modern buildings, and ordered French beer. Mostly white faces were passing by, though the street girls and the odd body asleep in a doorway were black.

'Well,' said Dotun, 'what a splendid city! Clean and well-planned. Obviously the government here uses its money properly to help people live well. Not like Nigeria where it's all wasted.'

Chuks wasn't so impressed. 'People here aren't so well educated. I saw the harbour workers, all the bosses are white. I bet there aren't African officers in their merchant ships.'

'But look, they have colour TV!' cried John. Indeed they had and we rushed back to the ship where the radio officer had managed to link up the *Gongola's* TV for the Mohammed Ali/Joe Foreman boxing match in Kinshasa – the famous 'Rumble in the Jungle'. Patrick stayed up; I went to bed but was woken at 3 am by the enormous African cheer at Ali's win.

Next day we went with the Uduku family to Treichville, the 'African' part of town. Laid out on a grid pattern in French style with proper water and sewage systems, it too seemed much more prosperous, as well as more regulated than Freetown, and every street was full of little shops or workshops supplying a huge variety of goods.

The girls were much relieved by this appearance of European normality. 'I want a Coke!' declared Oluchi, so we went into a shop owned by a 'Syrian' as all people from the Middle East were called. It was stuffed with European goodies: tinned foods, British chocolates, French cheeses and of course the ubiquitous French bread batons. The girls got their fizzy drinks and we bought a nostalgic bottle of Cotes du Rhone.

Then we found our first African market and forgot our nostalgia. In a rambling building, partly two-storeyed and with a central courtyard, was a huge huddle of stalls so close together that there seemed to be no space to move between them. Women in bright wrappers and head ties presided over tables covered with fruit and vegetables in every shade of red, yellow, green and brown, some familiar to us, others strange. Some women sat on the ground beside pyramids of tubers and heaps of bananas. Others threaded their way around carrying large open basins of rice or meat on their heads. Children played, helped or hindered, while babies slept slung in shawls across their mothers' backs.

It was colourful, crowded, noisy and the warm air lapped our faces as we pushed from the dazzling sun thankfully into the shade. Scents tickled our noses: dust, spices, oranges, musky human smells of sweat and perfume. Vendors shouted, shoppers responded lustily in words we couldn't understand. Catching sight of us they'd call out in French and then in broken English if we replied.

While women sold food in one area, men sat at sewing machines in another, turning out dresses, shirts and jackets, or crafting bags and shoes from leather. 'Perhaps I can get trousers and shoes made to fit me at last,' murmured Patrick, who usually shunned all shopping expeditions. We found a row of batik tops, tie-dyed in soft colours, with machine embroidery round the neck and cuffs. He tried on the largest, a little tight but at least cooler than his shirt. 'Eighteen hundred francs,' said the trader. 'Large man, big shirt.' We dealt finally, in broken French, at Fr. 1200. Just over £2, so we were improving.

We returned to the harbour where tropical timber was being loaded into French ships along with coffee, cocoa and palm oil – the basis of its modern wealth. At that time, the Ivory Coast appeared to be flourishing, with close ties to Paris. In the future lay economic crises, a coup d'état and two civil wars, but for the moment Abidjan felt an exciting place to be.

Ghana: Tema is an embryonic port.

At supper the conversation turned to Ghana, admired by many Africans as having pioneered the path to independence from Britain in 1957. 'Nkrumah – ah, one of Africa's greatest men!' declared Alex. 'Look how he unified different tribes and created a real new nation! How different from Nigeria! We need a strong man like him!'

Third Officer Ekpo, usually so quiet, also felt inspired. 'I think his greatest contribution was to Pan Africanism. He helped found the Organisation of African Unity. It's given us a united voice in the world.'

The captain was more cautious. 'He was almost a communist, wasn't he? They gave him the Lenin Peace Prize.'

Alex responded with vigour. 'Capitalism can't deliver the development we need. Look, the Volta Dam is already finished and exporting electricity. He built the new port at Tema – you'll see all the factories there. They will soon be exporting as well.'

From the sea Tema did indeed give the impression of being an industrial town with factory chimneys and oil refinery spires punctuating the skyline. As the promised tour of Accra didn't materialise, the car having broken down, Leo took us into Tema instead. An official stopped us at the dock gates. 'Entry permit, sah, madam? 200 cedis each.' Leo found a police officer he knew; the dock official retreated and we passed through. 'They were just trying to make money from the passengers. This is Chukwu, an old friend from Enugu. He emigrated during the war and joined the Ghanaian police. Now we go to the Hotel Meridian. I want to buy jewellery for my wife.'

I spent a happy half hour in a smart Western boutique helping Leo choose a necklace for their wedding anniversary. His friend Chukwu took us all off to 'the best pub in town,' a drab, concrete building with an open centre, into which the rain was steadily falling. We found Ghanaian hospitality rather overwhelming, as the host kept filling up the glasses well before they were empty, and the local beer, brewed by a Ghana offshoot of Heineken, was very much stronger than UK beer. Luckily cold chicken with a strong pepper sauce was soon served and we staggered happily back to the ship. There didn't seem much activity in the docks, and there were vast empty spaces alongside the roads; we thought perhaps it would prove just a great white elephant, a fantasy of an over-enthusiastic dictator.

※

But we were wrong. After Nrukumah was overthrown in 1966, a series of alternating military and civilian governments took Ghana along a somewhat bumpy road but by 2000 elections had been restored and since then Ghana has flourished both economically and politically. Tema, like Ghana itself, took some time to get established but is now Ghana's largest port and handles international traffic for much of landlocked West Africa.

Togo: Lomé is still a Franco-German hybrid.

A few hours later we woke up in Lomé in a very small, very new harbour, and took a taxi into town with Leo. 'This would do well as a Mexican film set – where are the cowboys?' wondered Patrick, as we passed the low-rise buildings, faced with brownish-yellow plaster and dominated by a huge white Catholic church.

In the supermarket, where Leo was trying to buy some shorts, the staff spoke only French, but the restaurant was called 'Art München'. Patrick asked for beer. '*Ein kleines helles – hundert Franken, sah!*' The menu offered *Schnitzel mit Sauerkraut*. The rest of the clientele were German tourists from the big ship we'd seen in port, flying the German flag.

While Leo bought us quadruple whiskies in return for our interpreting, we rehearsed some history. At the Berlin Conference in 1884 Germany was palmed off with a slice of the old Slave Coast between British and French spheres of interest. After World War I it was split between the victors and the British half became part of Ghana. In 1960 France granted independence to the remaining sliver but the old influences persisted, amazingly strong after so many years. The Germans had built the port and our pilot was German, while the books and magazines in the bookshop suggested a significant German community remained.

Next morning we went swimming with the Udukus, Femi and a couple of crew members. Lomé's beaches were classic: golden sand fringed with palm trees and edged with pounding breakers. Each of us frolicked in the surf in our own way while Oluchi made sand pies. Femi got knocked down by a huge wave and seemed very grateful when Patrick pulled him back on shore – it turned out he couldn't swim.

When we went back to the ship for shade Leo took us on a tour of the engine room, where we eventually understood why the flooding had delayed us for so long in the UK. 'The leak was in a pipe system which we hardly ever used. Then, each of the three pumps had failed, but for different reasons. So we had to go into Liverpool. Somehow the flywheel splashed water into the generator coils and then we had to replace the generator!'

All that seemed a long time ago – but there were still delays ahead and at supper we learnt that we would not sail till the following afternoon. This so depressed Ade that she went into a decline and retreated to her cabin while the rest of us had a last hilarious games party in the lounge, ending in a very vocal and entertaining game of Ratrace. The other Patrick, the second officer, could get nowhere as he was continually being divorced, I nearly won but ran into heavy taxation and then got divorced and Chuks ended up the victor.

The delay gave us an opportunity to walk along the shore and examine both old and new ways of life. Close to the port stood a shimmering white building, its tall façade swept back into the shape of a wave – the newly opened Hotel de la Paix. As Femi wanted to know the price of a room we went inside to look around. The (French) interior design was delightfully imaginative, combining richness and sparkle that suited the ambience. But who would stay there? Certainly not the locals whom we met further along the beach.

There were large canoes drawn up on the sand, all brightly painted in primary colours, and a group of fishermen were pulling in their huge net. The women were collecting and sorting the fish, separating out the few large ones and spreading out the small fry – like sardines or whitebait – on the sand to dry before the children gathered them into baskets, lifted them on to their heads and trotted off to home or market. For many young Africans, childhood meant working for hours alongside the parents instead of going to school. At a rough guess the whole catch might have filled two barrels, which was hardly rewarding for the best part of a day's work for 150 or more people. We returned to the boat wondering how long it would take for the profits from the tourists to percolate down to the fisher-folk – if ever.

The final approach to Lagos

During the final days of the voyage there had been rumours that we would not be able to dock at Lagos.

'It's the oil boom,' said Leo gloomily. 'There's so much business going on. They say there are many ships queuing outside Lagos harbour to unload cement, cars, diggers, fridges, TVs, everything. We're just a cargo ship. We'll have to join the queue!'

We wondered when we would be able to get ashore. Days sitting outside Lagos in a hot ship on a painted sea under a burning sky did not appeal. But we had reckoned without the Nigerian extended family and friendship networks.

On the evening of November 4th we joined at least fifty ships outside

Lagos Harbour, all ablaze with lights, which suited our private calendar of celebrations. We had met four years before at a Guy Fawkes Party and November 6th is my birthday. All I wanted as a present now was a quick landing and somewhere to stay.

The rumour said we would not be allowed to dock so next morning we held a council of war and went to see the captain.

'My children are sick and very upset,' declared Ade. Femi explained he had a liver complaint and had run out of pills.

'Our visas are expiring,' said Patrick.

'Can we use the lifeboats to take us ashore?' I suggested.

The captain let us use the ship's radiophone to call the office about a launch but the agent was not answering. Ade then rang the harbour master, who just happened to be an uncle of hers, and he replied: 'Tell the captain that you will pick up the pilot at four o'clock.' We began to see how things were done in Nigeria.

Towards sunset we started to move towards the bar. Lagos lies on a swampy shore, rising dramatically on its islands from among the creeks and lagoons; the sparkling modern buildings glowed in the evening light against the dark green trees across the bay and all our friends, excited to be almost home, pointed out the sights as we anchored inside the Pool.

Meanwhile, we rang the agent from the bridge to ask him to fix us up with a hotel, wondering where in this maelstrom we could find a starting point. We had a last supper on board with our friends and were invited warmly to stay with the Udukus in Umuahia and with the Oguntoyinbos in Ibadan. Ade's uncle and one of her sisters came aboard and Ade introduced us, explaining about our trip and our contacts.

'Oh, I work at the General Hospital,' said the sister. 'I know Mrs Bisi Williams and Mrs Tina Lawson. I'll tell them you're here.' The bush telegraph had started whirring.

Then my birthday gift arrived, as a messenger brought a scrap of paper with a scribbled note saying, 'Welcome to Nigeria, ring me tomorrow. If you can't get me on the phone, come round to this address.' The name at the bottom had been torn off but it could only be Wura Delano. We were launched into our Nigerian Odyssey.

CHAPTER 3
On the Threshold of Nigeria

In which we are adopted by the Delano family and meet Aunt Mary's students, but otherwise find Lagos hard to endure.

So in what kind of country had we arrived? Nigeria is huge, complex and diverse, both geographically and culturally. The landscape ranges from tropical forest in the south to savanna in the north but all of it is accessible to human settlement and some of it is highly productive. By the same token its peoples have a long and complex history, especially in the North, where various empires swelled across the Sahel and receded again, leaving an Islamic legacy of culture and learning. In the forested areas of high population density smaller states fought over land and manpower and in the process developed their own forms of spiritual and temporal authority. Their metalworkers produced not only weapons but also the sculptures of Ife and Benin.

From 1500 onwards Europeans nosed along the coasts, looking for gold, slaves and tropical products but the climate held them at bay until quinine and steam power allowed a mixture of Christian and imperial missionaries to move inland. The actual takeover was relatively quick, from the establishment of a protectorate at Lagos in 1850 to stop the slave trade, to Lugard's conquest of Kano in 1903. By 1918, Hausa and Fulani, Yoruba and Igbo – along with many smaller groups – found themselves under British rule.

Between the two world wars the Nigerian economy stagnated but the Nigerians did not. Increasing numbers studied overseas and brought back new ideas and experiences; they became increasingly impatient with the laissez-faire policies of the Colonial Office and demanded self-rule.

Constitutions were drafted and redrafted, warnings about identity went unheeded, traditional leaders and new elites jostled for top positions. Doubtless many were fired by patriotism and altruism but others only wanted wealth and glory; all were being pressurised by their clans and home areas to ensure a bigger slice of the new cake went to them. And so, Nigeria became independent in 1960 as a federation of Northern (Hausa), Western (Yoruba) and Eastern (Igbo) Regions. This much we knew, and we planned to visit all three, looking, listening and finding out what we could about their past and present experiences.

Meanwhile it was my birthday and we were still waiting for the immigration officials. We were also hoping that the company would send some cash on board, as the captain had offered us a 'favourable' exchange rate, and we only had five naira[7] between us, but neither men nor money arrived. Eventually we were put on a launch and, seated on top of our suitcases proceeded up the harbour to the customs quay. The customs couldn't clear us until the immigration people came and by 5 pm they were still not there.

'We close at 5.30, sah,' they informed us politely. 'Your luggage will be safely locked in our shed until tomorrow.' Patrick scoured the quay unsuccessfully for a working telephone but at 5.20 the immigration officer arrived and was unexpectedly helpful.

'What are your plans? How much money do you have?' he asked, studying our passports. Nigeria was under military rule and we had visas for only one month.

'We're staying with friends in Lagos, but we're not sure after that; we want to travel,' murmured Patrick, producing documents which showed we were self-financing.

'It's obvious you'll need more than one month. Shall I extend it to three?' he said, and proceeded to do so. What a relief! A great worry had dissolved before our eyes.

The last hurdle was the taxi to Wura's. The driver offered to take us to Ayowemi Close in Surulere for N10, but we didn't have that much money so Patrick responded with a bold lie: 'Last time I went there it cost N2.50.' This worked and we settled for N4. It took well over an hour to

---

[7] 1 naira = 50p at that time

get there through the traffic jams and as the driver had no change we had to concede the fiver; outwitting taxi drivers would become a minor sport throughout our journey.

We knocked apprehensively on the door of No. 12. A shy teenager led us into the lounge where a plump man was asleep on the sofa. 'Dad, the English visitors are here.' Kunle Delano jumped up, exclaiming: 'How wonderful! We expected longer delays at the harbour! Wura is at evening class. Lanre, bring cold drinks! Would you like showers?'

By the time Wura arrived back with a couple of colleagues we were refreshed and unpacked. After much greeting intermingled with reminiscences the lights went out. 'The National Sports Stadium is using its floodlights,' Kunle explained, 'so they shed the load by switching out the local houses. It'll come back on.' It did and supper appeared about 10 pm but soon after eleven we retired, exhausted by the heat, the day's earlier frustrations and the overwhelming welcome we had received from the Delanos.

But our first night on African soil was not altogether comfortable. It was still very hot and the sheets stuck to our bodies. The windows, covered in fly screens, were permanently open and all the noises of the night flowed in. Patrick fell asleep but I lay listening to the unfamiliar sounds – insects, distant traffic, an irregular blowing of whistles and the sound of heavy sticks being thumped on the pavement by the night watchmen. Long before our alarm went off at 6.15 am our fitful sleep was broken by all the neighbourhood cocks crowing in chorus.

We spent a week under the wing of the Delano family and gathered a sense of how rising middle-class Nigerians might lead their lives. Wura was large, energetic and sociable, always in a whirlwind of activity. A schools inspector for domestic science, she left for work at seven, dropping the boys at school en route and returning mid-afternoon to shop, bake, visit friends and look after a large household. 'The Ministry won't put up our salaries,' she grumbled. 'I think I'll resign and set up my own business. I'd make cakes for birthdays and weddings or run a child-minding service.'

Kunle was a pudgy, jolly, kind man, who put us quickly at our ease and loved talking, especially about traditional customs. He had studied engineering in the UK and now worked for the government, but his main interests lay elsewhere: he was involved in basketball at the national level, active in Church affairs and in the YMCA. Most evenings he was out at meetings or visiting men friends and, as his father's eldest son, he was often busy with affairs of the extended family, as we were to see later.

Three of their children were away at university but Lanre and Tayo were still at home; as well-brought up boys they would wash and iron their own school uniforms, clean the cars and jump to attention when their father spoke. Then there were various relations: Tunde, who came here after his mother died to be reformed and educated; Kayode who helped out around the house in return for school fees, a cousin doing teacher training and a younger brother of Kunle's. This was the extended family in action: those who had modern jobs and money were helping poorer relatives to get education, apparently before spending much on themselves. The Delanos' lifestyle seemed quite spartan, with basic furniture and no air-conditioning, though Kunle planned to extend the house.

Surulere was one of the mainland suburbs where the government had built subsidised housing for civil servants but it seemed that most ran a business as well: walking round the streets, in front rooms or in the yards, we saw tailoring, a photo-agency and a private nursing home, while at the other end of the scale there were stalls selling bread, rice and cold drinks. In Awoyemi Close itself they were very discreet but No 11 sold cold beer in the afternoons if you knocked on the door and No 12 had chairs and tables for hire. Was trading second nature or did they need the money – perhaps both? In any case, with all this evidence of energy and hard work around us, we did wonder where the stereotype of the 'lazy African' came from.

In spite of this friendly family atmosphere a week in Lagos was long enough. We had a number of other contacts in the city but the congestion and the climate between them made every expedition a major feat of endurance and often people were hard to track down. For the first two days we went into town with Kunle; leaving at 7.00 am it still took us fifty minutes to cover the five miles into the city. Lagos spreads over four islands; already large multi-lane bridges with cloverleaf flyovers had been built to bring the traffic into the city centre but they couldn't cope with the volume of vehicles. The traffic was fearsome – either travelling at reckless speed with horns blaring or, more frequently, halted with horns still blaring in monster 'go slows' (Nigerian for traffic jam).

Lagos Island was the heart of the city, densely packed with government and commercial buildings but still with a certain amount of beauty. The tree-lined Marina, along the lagoon shore, we thought might have been charming without three lanes of traffic rushing one-way down it. The architecture of the 'Brazilian Quarter', settled by freed slaves from Latin America, was picturesque, with its baroque cornices and balconies poking out over the jumble of tin shanties that lined the streets at the northern end of the island. Some of the modern skyscrapers were pleasant if undistinguished and there were a couple of attractive remnants of colonial buildings. But the main impression was of noise, bustle and seething people. Sweating in thirty degree heat and with 90% humidity, we rapidly lost our enthusiasm for exploring and by the end of the week we had booked ourselves on to a long-distance overnight bus to Zaria in the hopefully cooler north.

Somehow Wura found time in her busy schedule to take us to see a few more of Aunt Mary's students. We had brought little gifts – carnelians gathered from Blakeney Beach and hand-crafted into jewellery by Patrick's stepmother Margaret – and they all seemed delighted to see us and to swap memories of their training time in Bath. Most of them were teachers of domestic science, showing off their modern teaching kitchens where students were learning to cook roast lamb, custard, spotted dick and sponge cakes. I thought of the delicious meals we were having at Wura's – yams in many forms, fresh fruit salads, spinach and okra, all sorts of beans and spicy stews – and I also wondered how many of the children would be able to afford electric stoves even when the power was on.

I tried to be tactful. 'What about Nigerian food?' I asked. 'We're really enjoying it and I'd like some recipes to take home.'

Wura shook her head. 'I'd love to teach them better ways of making *fufu*[8] and stews, and show them how to use their kerosene stoves more economically but the curriculum is still based on the British one.'

I groaned inwardly but, from the schools we visited, I could see how seriously Nigerians were taking education. In private nursery schools

---

[8] Mashed yam or cassava.

three-year-olds were studying the alphabet while in higher grades discipline was strict, with canes in evidence and learning was largely by rote. I began to wonder whether theories of progressive schooling had not yet reached Nigeria, or whether they were culturally inappropriate. This became a theme that would fascinate me for many years to come and lead eventually to my doctoral research in Lesotho.

The differences between rich and poor in Lagos were enormous. One ex-student, married to a consulting engineer who had furnished her with a substantial house, told us she often went to London to do her shopping and, when sympathising with us about the climate, sighed: 'Of course an air-conditioned car is a necessity in Lagos these days!'

As we had no such vehicle we went on foot to look (unsuccessfully) for Femi's father's house, which lay deep in the slums. We found ourselves in an area of narrow twisting streets with open drains, evil-smelling and slimy, where every square foot of land seemed used up. Looking down an alleyway into the compound beyond the front house, we saw how the raised stone benches along each side were utilised for drying peppers, for stacking pots, for a sleeping mat, by a mother suckling her child, by a group of men talking. There was no space at all; people lived in the courtyards rather than in the rooms and from the courtyards they overflowed onto the pavements and then onto the roads, kept at bay only by the traffic. After walking through the vast Jankara market with its streets of stalls we came out near the lagoon, where fishermen's families were living in squalor behind walls of woven mats held down with kerosene drums and old tyres, their hovels perched on precarious wooden jetties over the filthy water beneath.

In this pullulating city, rich and poor, traditional and modern, all existed side by side, competing for attention, for power and for a share of resources both human and financial. The traditional markets were on the streets but where were the modern industries? Through Patrick's father we had an introduction to the Nigerian branch of Reckitt and Colman, whose factory was producing Nivea, hairspray, and pharmaceuticals. 'Trade Unions aren't allowed,' they told us, 'but most of our workers are earning at least the minimum wage. Girls who can read and write might get a bit more.'

'We currently employ three expatriates,' explained the director, 'but soon there will be just one. About 40% of the shares have been sold to twenty-odd individual Nigerians, split up like this to prevent any one person exercising too much influence. The shares were bought on credit but the dividends (yield 30%) will cover the interest and capital repayments.' Some very rich men in the making, we thought. We would see some more examples of this in the East.

Kunle had found us a willing audience for his stories of traditional life and at the weekend invited us to his father's seventieth birthday party at their home village of Ifo. 'He has just retired from the University of Ife and they have bestowed on him the degree of D. Litt., which we will also celebrate,' Kunle explained. 'His full title is now Chief Dr Isaac Delano, Bajiki of Ake, and Baba Isale of Ifo – that means "Father" of the village.'

'Are these his hereditary titles?' I asked.

'Oh no. They are given by the *oba*, the traditional ruler. To get a title you have to be a man of standing and wealth; you have to entertain the other chiefs and make them "presents". It is a great responsibility to be the head of a village like this. That is why he lives out there, so he can carry out his duties.' Kunle went on enthusiastically to explain the family history. 'When the missionaries arrived in 1842 in Abeokuta my ancestor became a Christian. After the end of the civil wars in Yorubaland, about 1880, he came with Christian warriors to farm the land round Ifo and my family is still there.'

We drove out to Ifo on Saturday into a wonderfully colourful scene. The women were all in traditional Yoruba 'wrappers' – knee-length wrap-over skirts with matching blouses, made of heavy, embroidered damask – and elaborate head ties of silk so stiff that the ends stood up. The brilliant colours shimmered in the hot sunlight: gold, carmine, marine blue, emerald green, white or multi-patterned. Some women were dressed in identical material, a sign of solidarity between family members or close friends (known as *aso-ebi*). Because I hadn't brought a suitable outfit, Wura lent me a fairly simple blue-green cotton version of the dress and arranged my head tie for me. Everyone seemed to approve – anyway I felt the heat much less than Patrick who was in a suit, as were most of the Delanos. The village elders and other guests wore the *agbada* or 'pajama suit' with loose robes over it in white or pastel shades, complementing the flamboyance of their womenfolk.

Festivities started with a three-hour service in the big Anglican church, all in Yoruba except the speech celebrating the doctor's academic achievements. From this we learnt how, while working as a clerk, Isaac Delano began studying Yoruba language and lore as a hobby, how he published books and compiled the first Yoruba dictionary, and how this led first to a research fellowship at the London School of Oriental and African Studies and then to teaching at Nigerian universities. At the end of the service the priest called up groups of friends for blessing and the drums drowned the organ music as they made their way up singing, clapping and dancing to the altar rails. It was our first introduction to the liveliness of African church services, which we would come to appreciate in every country we visited.

Then we sat at long trestle tables under a palm branch shelter, between the old ancestral mud house and Dr Delano's three-storey modern home, while local schoolchildren handed round huge dishes of rice and yams accompanied by many kinds of meat, beans and vegetables. A couple of electric fans whirred away to keep me cool. According to the lady beside me, a cousin of Kunle's, the village had recently got electricity but there was apparently only one W.C. 'His children are clubbing together to buy one for their use when visiting Dad,' she whispered.

'My Uncle Isaac is a wonderful old man,' she continued, 'so fit and healthy. He had twelve children, you know, and three wives.' At my startled look she added laughingly, 'One after the other, not all together, because he's a Christian. Actually, I don't think he did marry the first one in church but that doesn't make any difference to Kunle, we all turn to him as the eldest son.'

Afterwards we wandered round the village. The houses were plastered over in yellow and ochre, while the roofs were of corrugated iron turned rusty, so the whole effect was one of tawny shades blending with the red earth and the green forest behind. Beside the earth road there was a deep, open, rather smelly drain, then a stretch of earth variously used for parking your car, repairing your car, talking to neighbours, cooking supper or tethering the goat, but most of all for trading – the little flimsy stalls were selling anything from a few oranges to dress materials and hardware. A constant hum of gossip permeated the village, goats bleating and cocks crowing, punctuated by car engines starting up as the guests left for Lagos and a different kind of civilisation. But here, that afternoon, the ancient and the modern seemed to have come happily together in Dr Isaac Delano. What tensions between old and new might arise within and between younger generations we had no way of knowing.

Before we left Wura said we must go and visit her brother Duro Alalade in Ibadan. Nigerian society is deeply rooted in family and kinship networks and we were fortunate to have tapped into this element, for in other ways the society struck us as competitive, individualistic and often ruthless towards others.

Was this typical of Nigeria? We headed north to find out.

PART TWO
Nigeria

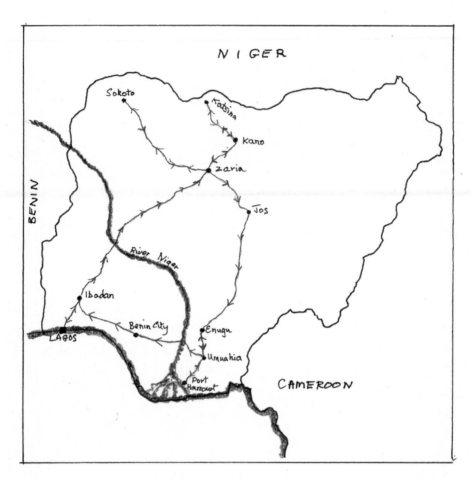

NIGERIA
Places visited by public transport.

CHAPTER 4
Exploring the North: Zaria and Kano

In which we secure a base camp, but find it difficult to penetrate behind the local walls, in spite of introductions to both traditional and colonial elites.

Zaria

Hot, thirsty and cramped by day, cooler, cramped and still thirsty by night: our journey to Zaria by National Bus Lines took seventeen hours and a lot of patience. Our seats were too small for Patrick's legs and his only comfortable position was curled up with his head on my shoulder. There was a loo, a stewardess who served beer, and women bustling up to the windows with basins of snacks on their heads every time we halted. We reckoned oranges and hard-boiled eggs were safe to buy.

Well after nightfall we crossed the Niger River on the one-track bridge used by both trains and cars and stopped on the other side for the drivers' supper in a lorry park. The rows of stalls were lit by little kerosene lamps; from the flickering braziers came the smell of roasting meat, the hiss of fat on fire and the chatter of punters. Beyond was the warm, soft, black envelope of the African night, lit occasionally by burning grass along the roadside.

We reached Zaria at 4 am and took a taxi to the Government Rest House, where the night watchman denied all knowledge of our booking. So, back to the deserted bus station. At 7 am we showed the Rest House our letter of introduction to the Sultan of Sokoto; they eventually promised us a room by noon and gave us a full English breakfast. Tentatively, we rang up our only contact in Zaria, Dr Hilton Whittle and his wife Anita. 'We're at the Rest House. Perhaps we could meet up and you could recommend a hotel?'

Within a few minutes Anita appeared and invited us to stay as long as we wanted. 'We've got a garden hut for you,' she explained. 'It'll be ready tomorrow.'

We slept off our journey in the Rest House's best suite and moved in next day. The hut had mud walls, a corrugated iron roof and a cement floor; a few days later a grass-roofed veranda was added, where we could sit to read and write. Anita provided camp beds, two chairs, a table, a food safe and a water pot; the outside loo was just a few yards away. This was perfect as we had our own sleeping bags and our precious little camping stove; we were independent from the family and for entertainment we had two haughty sacred ibises living by the duck pond. In return for hot baths, I cooked the Whittles the occasional meal, baby-sat when Anita went out and even helped run a children's birthday party. It was the cool season, when the *harmattan*[9] wind brought a haze that cut out the bright sunlight, so it was seldom over thirty degrees during the day and almost cold at night, a welcome change after the sticky heat of Lagos.

We based ourselves here for nearly a month while we explored the north, which is geographically, socially and culturally very different from the south and east. Less Westernised, more rural, with Islam as the predominant faith, it was much more difficult for us to get to know the people. None of Aunt Mary's students came from the north – itself indicative of the status of women and their lack of educational opportunities – so we had no invitations to stay in African homes and our contacts came from Britons who had worked there in various capacities. In particular, a retired colonial officer had provided us with letters of introduction to the Emir of Kano and the Sultan of Sokoto, which we hoped might open doors.

We planned the northern trip partly around these contacts, partly on the reputation and lure of the northern cities – Zaria, Kano, Sokoto, Katsina, old centres of the trans-Saharan trade – which sounded nearly as exciting as Samarkand and Bokhara. We were not as focused as we would become later on; we went where opportunities led and were interested in anything that came our way. In general we wanted to know: How do people live up

---

[9] The harmattan is a dry and dusty north-easterly trade wind which blows in from the Sahara towards the Gulf of Guinea between November and May.

here? What sort of development is going on? Inevitably our perceptions and insights were filtered through conversations with expatriates rather than being first hand. However, our European contacts were all in different ways deeply involved with the local society and through them we were able to meet a range of interesting people – from the Emir of Kano to the villagers of Kwassam.

We saw little of Hilton, who worked long hours at the university hospital researching meningitis, but Anita, who was interested in local crafts and spoke some Hausa, found time to give us an introductory tour of this ancient city state of Zaria.

'The old walled city contained the Emir's palace and the mosque,' she explained, 'but it was surrounded by open farming land, which was itself encircled by a further defensive ring of earthen walls. As the population increased houses spilt out into the farmland, creating a "new town" or Tudun Wada, and when traders from Europe or southern Nigeria arrived, they had to live in the Sabon Gari, or "foreigners' town" – that's where we are now. Why don't you hire bicycles and explore for yourselves?'

Rather dubiously we did and, once we got over our numb bums and aching legs, we found it a practical and interesting way of seeing both city and countryside.

We soon learnt how to be self-sufficient. At the Sabon Gari market, large, cheerful, unveiled Yoruba women traders sold garish cloth and brightly coloured enamelware alongside tourist trinkets, leatherware and baskets. Here we bought plates and cutlery and found 'euro food' in the shape of packets of soup and tins of meat, meths for our stove and even whisky, bottled in Nigeria. There was a chemist for antibiotics to treat my septic mosquito bites and the Tudun Wada market for fresh vegetables and fruit.

'Mind you wash them well and boil all your water,' warned Hilton. 'And don't buy meat in the market.' We only trusted the skewers of meat, coated in groundnuts and spices that had been already roasted over charcoal; I used them with the ubiquitous tomatoes to improvise stews in my little billycan and we remained fit and well-fed.

We cycled into the farmland area along sandy paths between fields of tobacco, cotton, cassava and corn dotted with family compounds. The adobe walls are built with balls of mud mixed with straw, then smoothed over with clay before decoration is added. The more prosperous the householder, the more decoration on the walls; the gateway to the Emir's palace, 500 years old, was covered with richly coloured arabesques, and many of the farming compounds were banded with white decorations. I became fascinated with these compounds. These silent, blank walls, topped with delightful little turrets like rabbits' ears, were frustrating: what sort of life went on behind them? Riding nearby we sometimes heard the thump, thump of grain being pounded with heavy bolts of wood in the mortars; there were women in there, living secluded lives like their grandmothers, cut off from the modern world. Equally, we were cut off from their world.

We watched the people outside for clues. Older women and young girls with calabashes balanced on their heads walking to market were not fully veiled but wore loose shawls over their heads that could be pulled across their faces; a few carried babies on their backs, nestling under shawls against the sun. Men rode by on horseback or drove donkeys carrying sacks of grain; the older ones were dressed in loose white robes with caps or turbans, while boys and the younger men wore jeans and shirts; here one cycled past with a basket of tomatoes on his head, there another rode a Vespa slung with bags of grain. People greeted us with smiles and often raised a clenched fist as a sign of respect. We smiled back, unable to communicate further.

We cycled into the old city and stopped at the mosque, where a new roof was being built by an Italian firm overseen by an Igbo called John. He took us up the minaret to look out over the Emir's palace, itself like a small village with its multiple compounds. We peered down but there was little to be seen.

John had been an officer in the Biafran army so we got chatting. 'After all those massacres up here, are you not scared?' we asked.

'They still need us,' John said. 'People up here simply haven't been educated. They don't have the skills to run the place and they don't speak English. We are well paid but we don't bring our families any more. It isn't safe.' Unfortunately his fears would prove only too well grounded in the coming years.

A Side Trip to Sokoto

Sokoto rhymes not with 'cockatoo', as we thought but with 'should we go?'
We went because we had a letter of introduction to the Sultan but what
we didn't realise in our naiveté was that there were two good reasons for
not going. Firstly, the Sultan, or Caliph, of Sokoto was still the spiritual
leader of all Nigerian Muslims and hardly interested in two wandering
Britons. Secondly, Sokoto was neither as old nor as interesting as Zaria,
Kano or Katsina. Fortunately, we also had an introduction to Jean Boyd,
who had lived in the area for twenty years and could throw some light on
life behind the walls.

Arriving after a long, hot and dusty journey in a second class bus – no
loo, no air-conditioning and even smaller seats – we found cheap beds at
a hostel run by the Sudan Interior Christian Mission, whose kind warden
drove us over to the Boyds.

Jean was very knowledgeable about local customs and had, in cooperation
with a Muslim scholar, translated into Hausa Arabic documents relating
to the history of the region. Over an excellent supper I quizzed her about
what went on inside these compound walls.

'The lives of Hausa women are still very restricted,' she explained. 'In
rich houses the women have no real work except looking after the young
children, as the husband is responsible for all outside the house activities
such as buying food and servants cope with the domestic chores. All
decisions are taken by the husband alone; he only meets with his wives for
relaxation and pleasure. The wives must obey the husband as long as his
commands are lawful. Some wives do become learned Muslim scholars
but they can only work if their husband gives them permission, which will
not be forthcoming while they are young. Many of the traditions are still
strictly kept; women and men do not eat together.'

'What about you, when you were working with them on the Hausa
history books?' I wanted to know.

'We sat together over the papers but I never ate with them. By the same
token, my husband has never been inside any of their family compounds,
while I could go in freely and get to know their wives.'

After supper she telephoned Gerry Summerhayes, Permanent Secretary to the Ministry of Local Government and the last expatriate in the Ministry, to find out if we could visit the Sultan.

'His Highness has just returned from medical treatment in the UK and is not receiving visitors,' he explained and then added obligingly, 'but I could take your friends with me when I go on tour tomorrow.'

Accordingly he drove us out next morning to Yabo, a small town nestling behind an ancient crumbling red wall in this wide, dry savanna land. While Gerry discussed the irregular appearance of the local accounts with the headman, we were taken round the village by his assistant, who spoke no English. It was all red-brown apart from the great evergreen trees, which threw welcome shade in the hot, dusty air as we wandered through the sandy streets lined with the same blank compound walls. Women and children were drawing water from the well and men were threshing grain to store in the large, bulbous clay granaries clustered behind each compound. There were a few meagre shops and an electricity cable was being laid, but we saw no cars or buses; this village seemed largely self-sufficient. It was too remote, too strange for us; we didn't have any keys to this world, to life behind the compound walls. What might 'development' mean here?

Back in the car we put this to Gerry. 'The village people are not looking for change,' he said, 'and the Federal Government means little to them. It is the Sultan they honour and obey; he has not only political power but also great influence as a religious leader.'

Islamic roots run deep here. Although now undeveloped by modern standards, two hundred years earlier this area of the Western Sahel was culturally advanced and important. Shehu Usman dan Fodio, an urbanised Fulani, was a religious scholar, mystic and revolutionary reformer at the start of the nineteenth century. He led a *jihad*, or holy war, against rulers he believed corrupt and set up the Caliphate of Sokoto in 1809. He then left his sons to rule and returned to a simple life of writing and teaching. We wanted to see his tomb but it was surrounded by such aggressive beggars that we panicked and left; in any case I would not have been allowed inside. A pity because the Shehu believed in education for all, including women, and if his advice had been followed northern Nigerian women might have been much better off.

Instead we cycled to an enormous exotic market, where we found goats, cattle, donkeys and camels, guarded by Fulani cattle herders with short cloaks and broad hats, and dark-skinned Touareg camel men in black turbans come in from the Sahara. Imported plastic was here replaced by piles of wooden calabashes, woven grass bowls and big-bellied brown clay pots. There were weavers and leather-workers, all men, from whom we bought a thick camel-hair blanket, with red and black stripes (which, faded, still covers my table), leather bags and brightly coloured tablecloths made of long hand-woven strips sewn together, to take home as gifts. Beyond the market the Sokoto River flowed through a wide, refreshingly green valley where we excitedly added some more exotic birds to our list, while passing troops of camels and donkeys trotted away into the dusty sunset.

At farewell drinks with the Boyds I met an old student acquaintance who was working out here for the British Council; he gave us a stress-free lift back to Zaria, where our little hut now felt like home. Mail had arrived, which assured us that our diary letters were reaching the parents. So the weekly battles with the post offices were proving worthwhile and we posted a further batch before setting off for Kano in yet another uncomfortable bus.

Kano

As the Kano bicycle renter told us when we protested at the higher charges: 'Zaria bush – Kano city!' and indeed everything was larger and more splendid than in Zaria. Settled for at least a thousand years, Kano was subordinate to Sokoto in Dan Fodio's time and in 1903 was captured by the British – with some difficulty because of its great walls. Now the capital of Kano State, it was crowded, bustling – and uneasy. Swinging between its ancient Muslim traditions and the pressures of modern Western development, which mainly came in secular or Christian forms, there were many tensions which at intervals exploded into riots. There was a huge army camp nearby, and the roads had been well tarred for military access.

Our networks in Kano were, again, entirely British. After a couple of nights at the grandly-named Hotel de France – the owner had once worked for a French colonial official and could turn out almost-dauphinois potatoes – we were invited to stay with Arthur and Issy Sanderson, contacts from another university friend, in their spacious modern bungalow. Arthur worked for the British Council while Issy alternated childcare and art work with looking after stray VSO volunteers. We seemed to fall into a similar category so we were offered home cooking, lifts into town and lots of informative talk, in return for which we did a bit of child-sitting and dog-walking.

Kano is impressive. Looking down on the Old City from the minaret, you see a maze of tiny streets with just a few broader thoroughfares full of buses and vans. The houses look as though they have grown out of the soil, with thick buttressed walls sloping slightly upwards to the partly-domed roofs whose ramparts are decorated with little pinnacles reminiscent of Fulani cattle horns. Behind these ramparts, on the flat parts of the roof, the women can work or sit and gossip in the evenings. As in Zaria the huge walls, once twenty-five feet high and still partly standing, encircled a great stretch of farmland. This was mostly now eaten up with swarming suburbs, though pyramids of groundnuts could be seen in the distance. Farming was in decline, we were told; it is hard work in this dry climate even with new irrigation schemes and school leavers wanted office jobs.

Even if they had wanted to work in factories there were few around, though informal workshops still existed. Exploring further on our 'expensive' bikes, we discovered a whole section of Kano market devoted to small-scale metal-working industries. Here they were beating out corrugated iron sheets to make boxes, trunks, buckets and watering cans. Pieces of old railway line were being used as anvils and the pattern was spray-painted on using a stencil and a flit-gun filled with paint. In a nearby smithy sickles were being made, while elsewhere they were melting down discarded milk tins and casting the three-legged cooking pots still used over open fires. All the tools used seemed improvised and the moulds were shaped by using old iron pots originally from Britain, so that the names 'Falkirk' or 'Eccleshall' were repeated on all the new castings.

For centuries Kano had been one of the great trading and manufacturing cities of the Western Sahara; they had been iron-workers for a thousand years and in the nineteenth century cloth and leatherware from Kano were sold as far north as Tripoli. But there were no modern industries in Kano now: no textile mills, no engineering and no technical training. All these men could do, in spite of their undoubted skills, ingenuity, entrepreneurship and hard work, was to recycle the left-overs of British goods, making a subsistence living by supplying the local market but never accumulating capital to develop further.

We began to understand what theorists meant by 'underdevelopment.' When the British took over the old Fulani Empire in the early twentieth century they brought peace and ended slavery; they left the culture alone and ruled relatively harmoniously through the Emirs. But in doing so they stopped economic progress in its tracks. British manufactured goods poured in, bringing clothes, shoes, tools and unimagined luxuries up the new railway line. All the profits of this new trade went to Falkirk, Eccleshall and other British cities and Kano's industrial heart gradually stopped beating. A major problem for Nigeria's development was to set it going again but to a different rhythm.

Another of our letters of introduction was to St Elmo Nelson, the Permanent Secretary to the Military Governor, and thus head of the civil service in Kano State. When we tracked him down in his office we found a traditional British colonial servant: very punctilious, rather formal, extremely knowledgeable as he had spent all his professional life in Nigeria, and quite extraordinarily helpful.

'I will see about your meeting the Emir,' he said. 'But tomorrow I am going to visit one of the district heads. Would you like to come with me?'

His car collected us promptly at eight and we drove out to the village of Dawakin Tofa. Alhaji Bello carried the high-ranking title of Makaman Kano and he was reputed to be the most efficient and respected of the district heads. A tall, distinguished-looking man, in magnificent pale blue robes and turban, he seemed kind and with a sense of humour; most courteous to us, we felt he could be fierce with his underlings. In his office, a room of concrete walls and metal-framed windows sitting incongruously inside his compound, we were offered tea and custard biscuits while we explained our trip. He talked of his many visits to London – in the 1960s he had accompanied the first Prime Minister of Nigeria, the late Sir Abubakar Tafawa Balewa – and asked us what we would like to know about his district.

Patrick wanted to understand the local tax system, which apparently went back to the days of the Fulani Empire. 'I have about 65,000 people rich enough to pay tax,' explained the Makaman. 'I need to raise about N400,000, so that's N6 a head. In October I call in the village heads, and tell them how much each village should raise. They can allocate the sums fairly, more from a rich man, less from a poor man. Last year there was such a drought that the government had to "forgive" some villages tax; we just couldn't collect it. But this year the rains have been good and we can raise the amount.' This seemed to us more feudal than bureaucratic, dependent on wise leaders exercising good judgement.

I asked him about education. 'I'll show you my schools,' he replied. 'I was once a teacher and that's a priority for me. I have two daughters who trained as teachers. Perhaps you would first like to meet my senior wife?'

At last I was inside the walls – though of course Patrick had to stay outside. A dark, twisting corridor led to an inner courtyard and the private apartments. Thump! Thump! Here were the women pounding grain, while other faces – other wives? – peered out of their doorways. 'Mrs Makaman,' looking about fifty, was smartly dressed in a yellow broderie anglaise wrapper, blouse and headscarf. A mattress on the floor and a large stack of enamel pots along the wall contrasted with a TV set and an array of cosmetics. She spoke no English, so through her husband I talked about our journey and she told me about her one visit to London. 'I wanted to see snow but I don't like the cold. Do you have children? No? How sad! My youngest are at school and two daughters are already married.'

She gave me a magnificent leather-bound feather fan as 'a momento of your visit,' and I left delighted but with many unanswered questions. What did she do all day? Would the college-trained daughters live so secluded a life?

The Makaman took us out into the village to show us his development projects. It was like a royal progress as people swarmed out to see him, crouching down with their clenched fist raised to signal their respect while shouting out greetings. He waved regally and occasionally muttered a reply, leaving his train of attendants to maintain a continual murmured acknowledgement. There was a wind-driven pump at the well, a play area with swings and a brand new secondary school of which he was very proud. The timetable and school rules, the duties of Head Boy and prefects, were all reminiscent of 1940s Britain. 'I hope many of these boys and girls will go to university,' he said confidently. He showed us the dispensary and the rising walls of a twelve-bed health centre.

'How do your people here earn money apart from farming?' Patrick asked.

'We make pots for the Kano market out of local clay and we dye cloth. Look!' The pots were piled high in open kilns, covered with grass ready for firing. In the dye pits white squares of cloth, tied with intricate knots to make patterns, were being sloshed and stirred in deep wells of indigo dye. Small-scale and useful but not an engine of economic growth.

Thanking him profusely, we said how much we would like to see him on his next visit to London. But I couldn't quite envisage his retinue in our terraced London house nor what his wife might be allowed to do while there.

We seemed to have passed the test and a visit to the Emir was arranged. His Highness Alhaji Dr Ado Bayero was educated in both Islamic and Western traditions; he served in the colonial administration before entering national politics and succeeding to his father's position. Mr Nelson clearly had a great deal of respect for his abilities and invited us to dinner in order to brief us properly. We ate in the beautiful garden of Gidan Dan Hausa, one of the old, decorated adobe houses appropriated by the British, while he talked us through the formalities. I asked about the dress code.

'You should wear a long skirt and cover your arms' he said, 'A pair of gloves is essential.'

This was an unforeseen problem. My scanty travel wardrobe included only two short-sleeved, knee-length dresses, so I put on the less revealing one and borrowed a shawl and gloves from Mrs Nelson. Patrick wore his creased jacket and tie and we were duly collected next morning in a huge Range Rover.

The Emir's palace covers over thirty acres and houses at least a thousand people. It was first built in the fifteenth century but, because adobe buildings decay in the rains, it has been constantly renewed and restored. The tall arched gateway in the surrounding wall leads on into a series of courtyards and gateways before you reach a smaller inner court with dark brown walls sculptured into decorative patterns. Here the Emir, dressed in creamy white robes and a turban sprouting 'rabbits ears', emerged to greet us, attended by bodyguards in red and green. As he came out attendants dressed in a variety of gorgeously coloured robes and splendid turbans started croaking out formal greetings – 'Go carefully! Mind where you step! Take care!' - or their approximate equivalents in Hausa, which they kept up wherever he went.

We followed the Emir into the audience chamber where he took his place on a skin-covered divan, his twin red and green spears being laid on the ground before him, while we sat with Mr Nelson in plush chairs on either side. Here a previous Emir had met Dr Heinrich Barth, one of the first European explorers to visit the Hausa kingdoms, in the 1850s. The walls were of heavily sculpted clay, with sparkling mica in the finishing plaster and the patterns were highlighted in red, gold and silver paint. Above us a high domed ceiling soared into the dimness. The air was heavy and quiet and we felt like interlopers amongst all this beautiful traditional grandeur.

We talked mainly about the Emir's recent visit to London – ostensibly for health reasons – and the gloom of all his friends there about the current state of affairs.

'London seems to have changed for the worse,' he said. 'All my friends say the country is declining. Why do you have so many strikes? The British don't seem to work as hard as they used to.'

Mr Nelson seemed to agree with him. Patrick answered hesitantly that Britain was undergoing a period of change and that we were still trying to modernise our industrial practices but the Emir appeared reluctant to get involved in an economic discussion. 'I still feel that we in Nigeria have a very close relationship with Britain,' he assured us. The interview was over, we were ushered out on a wave of attendants and Mr Nelson returned to talk business with the Emir. What that capable and intelligent ruler really thought about 'development', or indeed about the Military Government, we would never know.[10]

Before leaving Kano we devoted time to serious souvenir shopping. In the cloth market I wandered from stall to stall, unable to decide between the colours and designs, as the market women clamoured for my custom. Eventually I bought a length of blue, gold and red material for a long skirt in case I met another Emir. For presents I wanted tablecloths in the blue-and-white tie-dye we had seen in Dawakin Tofa, each one a different twirling pattern. But the traders sensed my eagerness and the prices I paid – N2, N1.50 – were certainly too high. Only when I'd got enough and was genuinely walking away, did the price fall to what it really was – N1.00.

---

[10] In 2013 he celebrated his Golden Jubilee after 50 years on the throne (clip available on YouTube). He died the following year aged 83, after the longest recorded reign of any Kano Emir.

CHAPTER 5

Exploring the North:
Katsina and Kwassam

In which we discover a life-long slogan, and discuss the dilemmas
of education, as well as cycling into the bush to discover another
aspect of ancient Africa.

Katsina

Since Sokoto had been mildly disappointing we thought we'd try Katsina. Reputedly founded in 1100 AD, Katsina was, in the seventeenth and eighteenth centuries, the commercial heart of Hausaland and became the largest of the seven Hausa city-states. It fell first to Dan Fodio, who ruled it from Sokoto, and then to the British. With little to offer the modern world its importance had dwindled, but it was the farthest north we could go. We didn't expect our visit to focus on schooling nor to give us a life-long slogan.

On Saturday morning Issy drove us down to the motor park, a market place for all sorts of transport – buses, taxis, kitcars (vans converted into minibuses) and mammy wagons. Most carry painted slogans such as: *Jesus saves! They shall not die! God is great! The fruits of hard labour!* A tout for a long-distance taxi soon collected us. 'N2 each,' said the driver and we climbed into the back seat of a large Peugeot estate with seven people already aboard. An altercation broke out which seemed to have something to do with us and a fellow passenger leant across smiling.

'They are saying he overcharged you – the price should be N1.20. But the driver says he's given you three seats for two people because of the gentleman's long legs.'

We thanked both sides. The passenger, whose name was Gideon Chile, turned out to be studying at secondary teacher-training college and we fell into educational conversation. The taxi leaving us somewhat stranded at the edge of Katsina, Gideon started walking us into town and then stopped at a primary school.

'These teachers are from England,' he explained to the startled head. 'Please show them your school and help them find a hotel.' Crowds of children flocked to pose for my camera, the girls in blue dresses and headscarves, the boys in mufti. To my surprise there were women teachers as well as men.

'How many pupils do you take?' I asked. 'There are supposed to be forty in each class,' he said hesitantly. 'But parents here, you know, they don't want to send their children to school. The girls help at home and then get married; the boys go to Koranic school.'

A trainee teacher was detailed to take us to the Magama Hotel, which was cheap, clean and comfortable, while their bicycles cost only 5k an hour. We rode off into the town which seemed to be drowsing in the sun, perhaps dreaming of its noble past and despising modern development. There was piped water but no big shops, few cars and hardly any modern buildings. People's clothes looked shabbier and although everyone we encountered was very friendly hardly anyone spoke English. But nor did the children come running for 'dash' or sweets and there weren't the beggars we saw in Kano. This was a truly traditional town and we were the only Europeans around.

Delighted, we cycled to the ancient Gobaru minaret, rising fifty feet high, four-square and unadorned, reputedly the earliest multi-storey building in West Africa. Its origin is unclear but it may date from the fifteenth century. At the height of Katsina's power this mosque was a famous institution of higher Islamic education.

The advanced students, their libraries and imams were long vanished but inside the huge gateway to the Emir's palace we found ourselves looking at today's Islamic education. There was a group of boys sitting on the sandy ground, each with a huge wooden tablet on which he had inscribed a verse from the Koran. Each was chanting his own verse over and over again till he had it by heart. As the babble rose and fell the *mallam*[11] moved among them swinging a long cord with knots at the end. Woe betide those who felt sleepy in the warm afternoon sunlight! We were to see several more of such *madrasas* around Katsina – much competition for our poor Western-educated headmaster.

Rather subdued by this we cycled out through one of the gates, along the old city wall – much mined now for building materials – and in again at another. The narrow streets twisted and turned. Unsure, I dismounted to photograph an elegantly decorated house while Patrick asked a passer-by how to get back to the city centre.

'That way main road,' he pointed left. And to the right, 'This way more adventure!'

Of course we took the right and got completely lost, but it brought us to a compound where a dignified old man sat weaving those long strips of cloth we had seen made up into blankets, his feet on the treadles, his hands guiding the shuttle. With no common language, we still became friends enough to be allowed to watch and take photographs. Eventually a man caught up with us. 'My boss, he say time finished now for bikes.' The only two *batures* (white people) in town mad enough to hire cycles were a source of great amusement and by now known to everyone.

On Sunday morning we took a last stroll around the town and met a gaggle of young ladies outside a Federal Teacher Training College and on their way to church. We walked a little way with them; these were Yoruba girls, and Christians, who had been sent north to study, perhaps partly to fill up the places, partly to engender a feeling of 'we are one Nigeria' by living alongside their Muslim sisters.

So could education bridge this cultural gap? Could Federal schools and colleges bring the two traditions together and educate Nigerian children to think of themselves as one nation, ready for an African future? We thought it would take a very long time.

After a late British-style breakfast – eggs, kidneys and potatoes – we met Gideon at the motor park. There were no taxis.

'What about the kitcar (a converted Ford van)?' I asked.

'I never travel in those, they are too dangerous,' Gideon warned us. But

---

[11] A *mallam* is an Islamic teacher; a *madrasa* is a school for Koranic studies

kitcar it had to be. We were crammed into the front seat as the driver set off slowly until a rival bus overtook him and they chased each other down the military road. Luckily I didn't know that every time we went over 60 mph the door Patrick was wedged against opened a crack further. We swore not to travel by kitcar again and travelled back next day from Kano to Zaria in a sober modern bus.

Into the bush to Kwassam

One evening soon after our arrival in Zaria Anita had invited us to supper to meet Barry and Pris Sharp, anthropologists working out in the bush not far from Zaria.

'In Kwassam there are four villages, three pagan and one Muslim,' Barry recounted. 'Each has its own language and social customs, even though there are only 120 people in the smallest community. I've learnt one language, Ruruma, which is spoken by about 5,000 people.'

'How do the people live?' Patrick wanted to know.

Barry was casual. 'There's plenty of land, so they grow crops and in a good year they can make money from the surplus.'

'So they could use this to develop the village?' Patrick persisted.

'They don't really use it for investment. They just brew more beer; beer's really important for their social life.' This led to a long involved discussion about the role of pubs in Britain versus mutual dependency in an African village while I asked Pris how she coped so far from shops. She grew vegetables, kept hens and bought 'bushmeat' – wild animals – from the local hunters.

I wondered how long they would be there. 'Probably about two years, till Barry's got enough material for his thesis. Would you like to come and visit us?'

Patrick and I looked at each other. This was something entirely new and therefore tempting.

'How can we get to you?'

'Well, in the wet season we're cut off but the road will soon open again. Or you can get a bus to Pambegua, pick up a taxi to Kauru and cycle from there. We'll leave a message for you.'

It all seemed a bit too vague and we put it to the back of our minds. But when we got back to Zaria from Kano and had a few days to spare, we thought: why not? That way more adventure!

There was no message about the road so we took an early minibus to Pambegua. There was no taxi to Kaura so we hired bicycles there from a man under a tree. We now had thirty-six miles in front of us rather than twenty-four and the day was already hot, but we set off, our bags bound fore and aft on the carriers by old inner tubes.

The first twelve miles to Kauru were a doddle, downhill most of the way on a half-made road and we reached the town in little over an hour; there was fried fish for sale but we had food with us and pushed on. Then the serious part of the journey started. There were stretches of hardish gravel then we would sink into soft sand. In places it was so rutted we had to get off and push. The path narrowed to a single rough track with grass growing eight or ten feet high on each side; it was hot and stuffy. Once, peddling uphill, I got so dizzy I begged for a halt but Patrick insisted we keep going. 'It will be dark by 6.30 and it's already past three. We've still got fifteen or twenty miles to go.' We compromised on forty-five minutes' cycling, followed by fifteen minutes' rest, rationing our water and oranges. We saw very few people and it became quite scary. Would we make it before the light, or our energies, gave out?

We arrived at the village just as the sun was sinking, quite exhausted and very saddle sore, but enormously relieved not to be spending the night in the bush. Barry and Pris, who had no idea we were actually coming, gave us a wonderful welcome. Barry went off to get a bucket of the local beer and Pris supervised the killing and cooking of their largest cockerel. We had a glorious wash in hot water in their outdoor 'shower' – screened off by grass matting – and slowly began to feel human again. After a great meal of chicken and rice we retired to the guest hut; Patrick slept like a log but I was too hot and the ground was too hard.

We spent two whole days in the village accompanying Barry on his rounds. Anthropologists seem to spend most of their time visiting and talking and we went with him. Every few yards we had to stop and greet people and be welcomed by them; strangers were rare and everyone wanted to meet us.

From the central market place the village spread out across the valley, the family compounds separated by fields and linked by a network of paths. Within each compound wives and other dependants each had their own separate hut, while the courtyards were filled with granaries standing on little legs. Everything was built of reddish clay and thatched with faded grey cornstalks. There was much social activity and visiting between compounds, which were too poor and primitive to have walls; visitors sat on mud benches in the cool of the thatched veranda and drank beer.

Ah, the beer! According to Barry it was the beer that kept the society ticking over. This was our first introduction to the traditional African kind, brewed throughout the continent from millet or sorghum, usually by women, for whom it is an important income source. Here they made it from guinea corn, cooked, pounded and fermented for three days. When fresh and well-made it was like a thin porridge with a slightly sour taste, refreshing in the heat and nutritious as well. Alcohol-wise, it felt about the same strength as English bitter.

Fortified by a mug of this which Barry had bought for us, we all set off for the fields, only to find the work party was taking a break in the shade. They shared their sweet potatoes with us, along with another pot of beer, before work resumed. Women cut the heads off the already felled guinea corn stalks while the men stacked them up ready to be carried back to the village. For a short time we joined the women and did a stint of harvesting with one of the sharp dagger-like knives which they used. It was hard work as the stalks were thick and tough and the leaves cut our inexperienced fingers.

Back at the Sharp compound we found two women had brought their sick children for medicine. Barry and Pris, using their own funds and advice from Hilton Whittle, were running an unofficial dispensary.

'It's really hard to get them to explain their symptoms,' Pris said. 'And then they don't follow our instructions. They also need to improve their diet by growing more vegetables and eating eggs, since many of the children are malnourished and of course succumb to infections.'

In a subsistence economy there is a fine line between survival and death; ignorance, stupidity or just bad luck can push you across. Pris had made an extensive vegetable garden as a model of what could be done but most of the women were too occupied with their fieldwork and with brewing to follow her example.

During our stay in the village we got to know some of the characters. There was Mallam Sali, the local fixer and a shrewd bargainer. He spoke quite good English and delighted in telling us about the local beliefs in death. Bad men would return and walk around at night with ropes around their necks, but if you gave people beer they would intercede for you with the gods. In return for these stories Patrick ordered some beer; as buyer he had to stir it up, then taste it, before filling up a bowl for the person on his right and so on round the circle, making sure he left enough for himself, before pouring the dregs on the floor – for whatever gods there might be around.

Surprisingly, we met a couple of Igbos here – blacksmiths whose skills were greatly valued in the surrounding villages. They had two charcoal hearths going as we watched them mending broken bicycle spokes. They showed us how they make 'dane guns' from the shaft of a car's steering wheel and how to muzzle-load them with powder and shot. People used them to shoot bushmeat and indeed next evening Pris told us that her tasty, if rather tough, kebabs were baboon meat bought from a local hunter.

In the gloaming Barry took us to visit a man who was ill with malaria; he was sitting in a room being heated by a wood fire with acrid smoke. We sat outside among the granaries being greeted by visitors and talking among ourselves. The bright stars of a moonless night shone above us, while the fire in the entrance hut cast a warm glow over the family and visitors gathered there. Insects chirruped, frogs croaked, the fire rustled and the soft Ruruma language echoed round the walls. We had gone back in time as, once, much of Africa was like this: a group of huts, neighbours and family together round a fire, with the warm wind and the white stars above.

Whither the North?

Our visit to the North had given us cultural and historical perspectives but provided few clues on how Nigeria might move forward. Sitting round the Whittles' table we quizzed their expatriate friends, all of them here in various ways to provide technical help and advice, as to why the North was lagging so far behind?

Pat, an agricultural advisor, thought priorities were wrong. 'There is still unused land up here. We're trialling new kinds of groundnuts and cotton and building irrigation schemes. But the Military Government isn't interested in the rural areas even though 70% of the people live there. They are focussed on the oil, which brings in the money, and on big visible projects like universities.'

Describing the metal workers of Kano market, Patrick asked how industry could develop. 'It will take a long time,' replied Steven, an economist. 'For starters, you need a much larger skilled workforce who can use modern technology. Then, where's the capital coming from? The government spends 50% of the budget on the army – and of course siphons some of it off for themselves. Foreign investors know there are still ethnic tensions and are cautious. They've put up some assembly plants – cars and so forth – but little else.'

Anita agreed. 'Sure, it's about education and skills. But it's also about culture. People up here are suspicious of change and accustomed to defer to their traditional rulers.'

'I do believe we can graft modern ideas onto the old structures,' said Renee, a sociologist. 'Three hundred years ago Zaria was one of the leading centres of learning in Hausaland and now they have built a new university here. I think the ideas of social change will percolate down as they modernise the curriculum. For example, the Federal Government has just decreed that 'social studies' will replace history and geography in primary and junior secondary schools.'

I explained I had been teaching social studies – a mixture of sociology, economics and politics – in London schools and wondered how I could find out more.

'My colleague Professor Udoh is in charge of the programme. I can arrange for you to meet him.'

Next day we visited Ahmadu Bello University and tracked down Professor Udoh, a little whirlwind of a man who appeared nearly single-handedly to be transforming Nigerian education.

'The government wants to use social studies as a vehicle for teaching tolerance of other life styles and to encourage unity and patriotism,' he told me. 'But it will also be a way of introducing new teaching methods. The children's own experiences should become the basis of lessons. Discussion will be encouraged – the child should not be told the answer!' From what I had seen, this would be revolutionary in Nigerian education.

He was busy training teachers in the new methods. 'I tell them to take their pupils outside and talk to the women who sell peanuts on the street. How do they fix their prices? If there are lots of groundnuts and no one wants them, the price falls. When groundnuts are scarce and there are many customers, they can raise the price. The children will understand this law of economics! But I only have sixteen post-graduate students and there are 800,000 primary pupils in the North.'

'What about the Koranic schools?' I asked.

'They are to be incorporated into the school system, and they will follow new curricula,' he said confidently. I thought of the *mallam* in Katsina and the head teacher in the nearby primary school, each bound to his own traditions, and wondered how this might happen. But I loved his enthusiasm and took away with me his *Guide for Primary Teachers of Social Studies*. Ten years later it would inspire me to work with Basotho teachers on similar booklets.

In spite of the so-obvious fault lines – Muslim and Christian, traditional and modern – the people we talked with were mostly optimistic. Education was the key to economic and social development and yes, it would come, eventually. No one at that time could possibly imagine the scenario, thirty-five years later, when an Islamic movement calling itself *boko haram* – '(Western) books are prohibited' – would sweep through Northern Nigeria, burning schools and kidnapping schoolgirls.

From Zaria we took the bus to Jos, where we stayed a couple of nights but finding little of interest we travelled on to Enugu.

CHAPTER 6
Friends in the East:
Umuahia and Enugu

In which we meet up with old friends, make some new ones, and
compare life with novels.

We spent three weeks in Eastern Nigeria. We could have been in a
different country; indeed, had Biafra won its war of independence
it would have been so. Instead of the wide open brown savannah lands of
the north with its military highways we travelled through rolling green
hills, interspersed with thick swathes of forest, on patched and worn-out
roads. Instead of guinea corn and groundnuts there were cassava and oil
palms. Instead of adobe the houses were more often concrete-walled and
tin-roofed. No mosques, but churches. And the people were different.
Most of the men wore European clothes, even suits and ties, while the
women, switching frequently between Western and traditional dress,
looked you in the face and chatted to you in English.

The differences were rooted in history and culture. Before colonial
times the Igbos had lived more or less quietly in small, self-contained
communities, run by the elders and subject only to the distant spiritual
suzerainty of the Oracle at Aro. 'Among the Igbos is no king,' the saying
went. They objected strongly to the warrant chiefs that the British imposed
on them and it took till 1918 to subdue the disturbances. As Chinua
Achebe described in his novels, 'things fell apart' but after a time the Igbo
found ways of putting them together again in a new form.

By independence the Igbos were busy, prosperous and pushing their luck
all over Nigeria. There might have been something in their self-sufficient,

relatively democratic way of life that gave the Igbo the confidence to confront the challenges of colonialism, taking up educational opportunities – and the Christianity that came with them – and adapting quickly to new ways of earning a living. At independence the first federal president, Dr Azikwe, was an Igbo. His fellow nationals had spread out over the whole country and, particularly in the north, were accused of taking all the best jobs and displacing the Hausa. Eventually this jealousy exploded into savage riots.

When we arrived less than five years had passed since the end of the Biafran war and it showed in the shabbiness of the houses, the many scaffolded sites and the shell-pocks on the administrative buildings; in some people's faces were traces left by famine. There seemed less money around; the markets were less exuberant and street traders were banned. Even the traffic moved more quietly and in a more orderly fashion.

To complete the contrast our travels here had a different focus: on people rather than places, on the present rather than the past, and most particularly on Aunt Mary's students. She was still in contact with a few; we were to gather news of them and to find out how many more were still alive in this bruised, post-war society. Since we only had work addresses, and the Christmas holidays had started, it took us a little time, but when word spread that 'Mrs A's' nephew was in town we became part of a social web in which we soon felt at home. With great generosity these families, many living in very reduced circumstances, invited us to their homes, drove us to events and shared us with their friends. For our part we went with the flow, enjoying the company and learning about their lives.

Umuahia

But we also had an invitation to visit the Udukus, our friends from the boat, and we tried them first. We had written to Ade c/o her husband at Umuahia hospital and, although we had had no reply, we had become sufficiently Nigerian to take the bus to Umuahia and present ourselves, bags and all, at their house, planning to use whatever hotel they recommended.

Chinwe and Ola gave us a tremendous welcome but it clearly wasn't the right time to come. 'Mum is still in Lagos with Oluchi waiting for the baggage to be unloaded. Dad is at the hospital. Please sit down and have a drink. No, we don't know any hotel – stay with us here.'

Rather embarrassed, we sat down and asked them how they were settling in.

'Well, we're supposed to be studying at home until Mum finds us good schools,' said Chinwe. 'It's not much fun. My old friends don't ask us round any more.'

'I miss fish and chips,' chimed in Ola. 'I really don't like Nigerian food. I wish we were back in Edinburgh. It's so hot here and there'd be snow there now!'

When Dr Uduku got home at 7 pm he was astonished to find two perfect strangers sitting in his lounge playing cards with his daughters. We repeated our request for a hotel but he insisted we have the master bedroom – there was but a single bed in the spare room – and that he take us out to dinner at the Rest House.

'Oh, we like Nigerian food…' I began and then saw Ola's face. We had a rather boring meal of steak and chips, to the girls' delight, while we tried to draw him out on the Military Government and its effects on the health service.

'We are going nowhere,' he growled. 'They are all incompetent and corrupt fools. How can Nigeria ever be one united country? We are all so different.'

Dr Uduku ran a clinic, including a small operating theatre, from his house as well as working in the local hospital as consultant, treating patients out in his father's village whenever needed and visiting two other hospitals. Working twelve or fourteen hours a day, he seemed to have little time to spend with his daughters and equally little understanding of their difficulties.

'Father says we must live like Nigerians now,' said Chinwe. 'We've been staying in the village but Grandad doesn't speak English and there's nothing to do out there. My cousins have their own friends. If we go into town here people stare at us as though we were foreigners. The kids shouted at us: "Go home, you Chinese!"'

We felt in a quandary. The girls obviously wanted us to stay, to have someone to talk to and entertain them. On the other hand we felt we were a burden to the good, busy doctor and probably a hindrance to his programme of re-Igboisation. We sent a telegram to Comfort Onwunyi in Enugu saying we'd be there on Saturday, three days hence.

Dr Uduku decided we should understand more about Biafran history so he sent a car and his driver to take us to Col. Ojukwu's bunker, from where he had directed the heroic defence of Biafra. It was a gloomy, sprawling set of rooms, twenty feet below the earth, and by torchlight it felt both sad and sinister. Our book about the Biafran war told us how the people had improved weapons and other materials: they refined oil in cooking pots for petrol, used coconut oil for brake fluid, built their own basic guns and very effective anti-personnel mines. Their belief that they would be the first really self-sufficient, truly independent, black African country gave them great strength but under the pressures of the blockade the administration broke down and corruption reasserted itself. Over a beer in the station cafe some railway workers gave their views: no, the railways hadn't recovered from the war; no, the most competent people don't get the top jobs. 'We keep it running from below,' they added, grinning. We thought Igbos would be good people to have on one's side in a crisis.

Back at the house we met Okechukwu, the eldest son, who had been brought up by his grandparents while his parents were overseas and was now studying medicine. Tall, handsome and fluent in Igbo, Yoruba and English, he was excellent company.

'Following in your father's footsteps?' Patrick enquired.

'I'll be a surgeon and live in a big town. I'll never practice in the village, you're at everyone's beck and call.'

'Would you take us to your village?'

'Sure, come with me tomorrow.'

It was like stepping into the pages of an Achebe novel. Two miles out of town the taxi dropped us at the end of the tarmac road and we followed a winding earthen path into the forest. The tall trees were well spaced-out and through the smaller trees light fell through onto patches of tilled soil. Here was a stand of bright green cassava, the food of last resort that kept them alive in the war. Here were clumps of beans, with fat pumpkins rolling along between them. Okechukwu pointed out the yam vines whose tubers lay growing beneath the soil. Palms with their feathery, fronded heads were everywhere – these bore coconuts, others palm-nuts, while

Above: MV River Gongola in Liverpool docks, with Patrick and the Uduku girls.

Above: Kunle and Wura Delano in traditional Nigerian dress.

Right: Officers and passengers during the voyage.

Right: Jankara market, Lagos.

Patrick reading in front of our garden hut in Zaria

A family compound in Zaria

Old compounds in Kano, seen from above

Alhaji Bello, Makaman Kano, at Dawakin Tofa with an
attendant and village children.

Firing clay pots at Dawakin Tofa.

Making new pots out of scrap metal at Kano.

Left: Katsina traditional house; here we were offered the route of 'this way more adventure'.

Below
Left: Weaver and his family in Katsina; the long strips are sewn together to make clothes and blankets.

Right: Boy at a koranic school, with his writing tablet.

Men threshing guinea corn.

A family outside their compound in Kwassam village; the main hut is flanked by granaries raised on stones.

The Stuarts preparing to cycle back from Kwassam through the bush.

Public transport: A long-distance bus surrounded by hawkers selling food and wares to the travellers.

Near Old Umuahia village a boy carries bucket of water from the river on his head.

Igbo ladies dressed in their best *akwete* cloth at the Oji River foundation-stone ceremony.

Omere Idah and his friend Philip in Benin; the terracotta statue was created by Omere's father.

Benin craftsman making a traditional brass statue using the 'lost wax' method.

Chiefs in Benin being filmed for the local TV.

Femi, Ayo and Toyosi Oguntoyinbo in traditional dress, outside their new house.

Ibadan old town with traditional compounds.

Public transport: a *danfo* waiting for passengers.

Traditional talking drums being played at Oyo.

The university of Ife.

others were tapped for palm wine. Growing between them we recognised the vivid green arches of banana trees and dark-leaved oranges. The whole forest was a farm, nourishing and sustainable.

The air was warm, smelling of earth and rotting leaves; it was still and quiet except for the call of a high-up bird, the cackle of hens and distant voices. Scattered through the forest were family compounds, concrete and tin predominating over mud and thatch. Chickens scratched outside the yards and we glimpsed pigs and the odd goat. 'The land is held by families,' Okechukwu explained. 'Each son gets a share; he can sell it, but only to a relative. If you want to build a house you need everyone's agreement.'

Okechukwu led us to his grandfather's compound and translated for us as we sat in his spacious, cool house on a comfortable old carved settee. One of his three wives served us European beer, cold from the fridge, alongside roasted nuts and slices of fresh pawpaw. Shy girls peeped at us through the door. Ola whispered: 'Everyone is so nosey! When we first came back they sat us on stools in the village while everyone came to look at us.'

Chinwe had memories from before the war. 'Let's show them the spring,' she said to Okechukwu, who inspected our footwear before agreeing.

It was in a deep stream bed some two hundred feet down a steep and twisting path, almost vertical in places. We clambered down using the cut-out footholds and hanging on to tree roots. At the bottom lay a pool of clear water reflecting back the surrounding palm trees. The evening water troop had just finished filling their pails and, balancing them carefully on their heads, they started back up the steep path.

'Can you still do it?' I asked.

Chinwe grabbed a bucket, placed it on her head and marched proudly along the stream. 'We used to go twice a day,' she said. 'In some ways it was quite fun. Downstream our mothers would do the washing and we'd bathe.'

Okechukwu added: 'It was rather like a youth club. We'd gossip and play and even flirt, there weren't any adults around.'

Patrick was surprised that there was still no modern water supply in a village with educated families. 'Oh, the elders had pipes laid long ago but the borehole was broken in the war and hasn't yet been repaired. Everyone neglects us here. The Federal Government doesn't care and State money has gone to elsewhere.'

When we got back into town there was great excitement as the luggage from the *River Gongola* had arrived, all forty-nine trunks, cases and tea-chests, but there was still neither sign nor word of Ade. The cook wanted to send the luggage direct to the village.

'No,' said Chinwe firmly. 'They'll all start helping themselves to presents! Put it in the back.'

Suddenly there was a burst of music outside – these were nurses from the hospital singing Igbo carols and collecting in aid of a new nurses' home. The cheerful voices soared away into the warm night sky reminding us that Christmas was coming.

We spent our last day catching up with our reading and writing or chatting with the girls. We asked them to guide us through the market, but when we got there it was as though we were the habitués and they the visitors; Ola looked completely lost, though Chinwe used her rusty Igbo to help me bargain over yet another piece of cloth. 'Nigeria seems a pretty hopeless place. They are so inefficient,' she said sadly in tones a European might have used. As they reminisced about Edinburgh and their school friends, we wondered how long it would take them to settle back in. When Dr Uduku insisted on taking us to supper at the Rest House again, we in turn insisted the girls come too, to have a break from yams. Halfway through the meal a messenger appeared: Ade and Oluchi had arrived!

Late as it was, Dr Uduku drove them off to the village to pay their respects to the family and so we only had a brief chat with Ade. She urged us to stay but we had, as we thought, committed ourselves to Enugu. 'We'll come again when you've got settled in,' we promised.

Enugu

On a hot, sticky, misty morning we rode an early bus back to Enugu. It did not seem a very prepossessing town, lying beneath a haze of smoke and dust, but we were searching for people not sights, so we took a taxi straight to Comfort Onwunyi's school. Once more the post office had let us down; she had not received our telegram and was astonished to see two white strangers on her doorstep. However, she took us to the Phoenix Hotel where for N9 a day we had a large bedroom with comfortable beds, lots of hot water in our own bathroom, plus air conditioning. There was a lobby with two easy chairs for entertaining visitors and even a writing table – what else could we want? It became our base for the next two weeks.

In the afternoon Comfort came calling, possibly to find out who we really were. After we had given her one of the carnelian rings and showed her pictures of Aunt Mary in her retirement, her reserve disappeared and she began telling us about the war.[12]

'I left Enugu just before it fell,' she said, 'and went to our other house in the village. But the Feds bombed our market and I got hurt by flying splinters, so we moved on to the next village until that was bombed too. In the end we were just living in the bush. It was the hunger that was the worst; there was nothing to eat but leaves. I got so reduced, so thin, my wedding ring fell off and I didn't find it again. My old father got really sick and never recovered fully; he died in the first year of peace.

'After the war we returned to Enugu but our house had been completely destroyed. Our big house in Port Harcourt was seized and we got no compensation; it's now a hotel and Igbos aren't allowed to own property down there any more. We had nothing! Then my husband was reappointed as a magistrate and I got my old school job back, so we began rebuilding our lives. I must say, although we feared a massacre, General Gowon ensured the Federal troops didn't get out of hand.

'It has affected my son Tobenna badly. He went back to school but didn't make it into university. He's applied to universities in the US to do engineering. There are so few jobs here and you simply can't get anywhere without a degree.'

From that point onwards we gave up planning our days, for Comfort lived up to her name and took charge of us, bringing us fruit to eat and gifts to send home to Mary, lending us her car and driver so we could do our shopping, taking us on visits and putting us in contact with as many

---

[12] The novel *Half of a Yellow Sun*, by Chimananda Ngozi Adichie (Harper 2007) gives a dramatic and authentic account of the Biafran war. The stories our friends told us were very similar.

of Mary's ex-students as she could – half a dozen in all. When we tried to thank her she simply said: 'I owe so much to Mrs A for what she did for me and Tobenna in Bath.'

When Christmas Day came they took us to church. The service was recognisably Anglican and, to our relief, in English. There were no Christmas decorations in the bleak, half-rebuilt church, but all the women were in gorgeously bright wrappers and head ties; they sat mainly on one side of the aisle and the men, some in suits, others in the loose Igbo tunic and trousers, on the other. The familiar Christmas anthems, sung with great African gusto, soared up to the iron girders of the nave.

Afterwards Comfort took us to her flat, poured some drinks and then turned to Patrick with something that looked like a brown head of garlic.

'You are the oldest man here. Please break the kola nut for us. Say a prayer and bid everyone welcome.'

Fortunately we had read enough Achebe novels to understand that this was a traditional welcoming ceremony; Patrick muttered a blessing and handed her back the nut, pleased and embarrassed at the same time.

Then we went back to the hotel as we had booked a Christmas lunch. This turned out to be what the Nigerian cook vaguely remembered used to be requested by homesick colonial officers between the world wars. Quite alone in the huge dining room, we were solemnly served tinned hors d'oeuvres, tinned turkey and sausages, tinned stuffing, savoury rice and tinned peas, a rather pallid fruitcake with brandy-flavoured custard and a wonderful dessert of fresh oranges, pawpaw and pineapple. We toasted family, absent friends and ourselves with tumblers of brandy in the deserted bar and went off for a siesta, for once rather missing traditional family tensions and the Queen's speech.

But not for long. Comfort picked us up again and took us to watch the masquerades. All through the town we heard the beat of the drums, the whistle of flutes and the shouts of the dancers. Then down the street came the chief dancer, covered from head to foot in loosely knitted raffia, coloured red and green; on his head was a carved figure. Alongside him danced his attendants, waving sticks and fans, singing, calling and shaking bells. From another street a group of youngsters appeared, their bodies painted with white and yellow markings, doing a war dance behind their masked and crowned leader. Crowds came out to watch and cheer – and obviously to drink and make merry in every possible way.

In traditional society a 'mask' was serious; it represented the local god and the priest wore it on solemn occasions, accompanied by drumming and dancing: to celebrate, to warn or to bring the community together. This seemed to us more like Halloween or Guy Fawkes Day and we wondered how much of the older meanings remained.

From the noise and merriment of the street Comfort took us to visit John Achebe, brother of the well-known author Chinua. The flat was comfortably furnished with plush chairs and patterned carpets, brown tables and a drinks cabinet. European prints hung on the walls; it was all rather reminiscent of post-war British lodgings.

We were introduced to several other guests. 'Here is David Ogbogu, he's one of the leaders in the Teachers' Union. This is Martin from Kwarra State. He has just qualified as a vet and is doing his National Service with us here. Now, let me welcome you in our traditional way.'

This time it was done properly. Martin, as the youngest, took the kola nuts round the circle; each person politely declined until they reached David, the eldest. He then broke the nuts into sections and addressed each of us in turn.

'Comfort, may your back salary soon be paid! Martin, we hope you have a pleasant stay in our town! Janet and Patrick, we wish you a good journey through Nigeria,' and so on, ending with 'God bless us all!' before we might nibble the nuts and raise our glasses.

John was a retired teacher and for my benefit he turned the conversation to educational matters. 'There's no doubt that the Eastern Region is far ahead, educationally, of the rest of the country,' he told us.

'Oh yes,' David agreed. 'Over three-quarters of our children attend primary school, much more than in the North or West.'

'How many go on to secondary school?' I asked.

'About half, but many drop out. We are trying to introduce comprehensive schools with technical streams to cater for everyone.'

'People really appreciate education here,' said John, pointing out of the window. 'See that new girls' school? It was totally destroyed during the war. When it reopened lessons were held in the open air and the teachers built shacks to sleep in with their own hands.'

We asked Martin to tell us about the National Youth Service. 'After the war there were so many ideas to try and reconcile the different national groups in Nigeria. This is one of them. All young Nigerians have to spend a year living and working in a different part of the country, to get to know people with different religions and customs.'

'Is it a good idea?'

'I'm enjoying myself here. Yes, most people think it's OK. Especially if you can't find a job.'

At the time of our visit, nobody knew how many Nigerians there were. Population statistics were too political, as they affected how votes and resources should be allocated, so the government kept the figures hidden. Certainly there were too many young Nigerians coming up through the expanding schools and burgeoning universities for the number of modern jobs available. They would become part of the future Nigerian world-wide diaspora.

CHAPTER 7

More Friends in the East: Justina Bello and her Circle

In which we see development through Igbo eyes and sympathise with returning exiles.

Justina, the obi's daughter

Justina Anazonwu Bello wasn't even on our list of ex-students but soon after our arrival this large, dynamic lady arrived in a chauffeur-driven car, dressed in vibrant colours and with a voice to match.

'How wonderful to meet Mrs A's nephew! I'd lost her address but I'm so pleased to meet you. Will you have supper with me? Good, I'll pick you up later.'

Justina turned out to be a typical Igbo entrepreneur. En route to her house she took us to her workplace where she was developing preserves from local fruits. 'During the war we couldn't get cooking ingredients from abroad, so I began experimenting with local plant products to see how we could make nourishing and tasty meals out of what was available. Now these are becoming quite fashionable. Did you see me on TV last night? I was demonstrating my new recipes. Try these ginger sweets. And this jam is made from a local wild fruit called *udola*.'

They were indeed delicious and so was supper: spiced chicken and rice cooked with coconut milk, accompanied by fried plantains, spinach with onion and tomato and a salad of grated carrot and coconut, finished off with fruit salad.

Over the meal she told us something of her life story.

'When I was studying in Bath I heard that my then husband, Mr Mba, was unfaithful to me. So I divorced him. I went to the US for further studies and when I returned I met a wonderful Yoruba man, Mr Bello, and we got married. Then Biafra declared independence and all the Yorubas had to leave. I would have gone, but my father was dying and I had to stay. One day the police came round.

'"Mrs Bello?" they said. "You are Yoruba. You must leave!" Just imagine my poor sick father struggling to prove I was his daughter, a true Igbo, and my place was here! When the war ended I went looking for Mr Bello but he was living with another lady. We're Christians so I couldn't let him do that and I divorced him.'

After Boxing Day Justina rang us up. 'Some friends of mine are building a new factory and I am attending the foundation stone-laying ceremony. Would you like to come?'

She arrived sumptuously decked out in a glittering brocade blouse and an *akwete*[13] cloth wrapper with the East Central State coat of arms woven into it. She clearly didn't think my denim trouser suit formal enough so I found myself once more in African dress: white cotton piqué blouse and heavy plum-coloured Akwete wrapper worn Igbo style, i.e. ankle length with a second piece draped round the hips. No head-tie this time.

The factory was the first to be built on a new industrial estate and would produce toilet paper and the like. The managing director, one Chief Okenwa, turned out to be an energetic character and a cousin of Justina's. Wearing his stockbroker's hat Patrick elicited from him the information that the government had a 50% stake in the enterprise and other shareholders, disguised behind a holding company, included the African Continental Bank of which Chief Okenwa was a director. These Nigerians seemed busy re-inventing capitalism for themselves.

We sat under a tin-roofed shelter in a red dusty field along with the local great and good, the men in flowing robes, their wives in multi-coloured wrappers and head-ties, jewellery glittering in the sunshine. An hour later the State Commissioner for Industry arrived and a wreath of flowers, made appropriately from multi-coloured Andrex, was hung around his neck. A stone was laid, a tree was planted, a cow was presented and long speeches

[13] Akwete is a traditional cloth, with heavy woven patterns of threads stretched across the fabric like embroidery.

were made. Chief Okenwa talked about enterprise and how it should be pursued; the commissioner said the state welcomed businessmen with good ideas; and a preacher emphasised the role of the individual, under God's guidance, in starting a successful business. The Protestant ethic had surely found fertile ground in Igboland.

With some relief the M-C announced the arrival of drinks, lunch and the dancing girls. It was champagne for the front row and then bottles of beer all round with plates of chicken, *jollof* [14] rice, English meat loaf, mixed salad and cake; we felt Justina's new recipes were sadly needed.

Then came the dancers: groups of children, youths or women, all in matching wrappers and head-ties, moving in unison to bands of drummers and pipers. Occasionally a dancer came forward to perform an energetic solo: they would dance up to the VIPs and chant praises of welcome; in return a naira note was stuck on their forehead. The preacher pronounced a last blessing and the party broke up laughing and talking. The setting sun glowed on the rich fabrics of the guests as they climbed into their gleaming cars while the drums sounded in the distance for the villagers walking home. The factory was modern but the cow, the dancing, the drinking and eating were surely traditional. Here the new grafts seemed to have taken and to be growing within the old social structure.

Justina was descended from the *obis* (rulers) of Onitsha and she was keen to tell us about her status and her Christian faith; both were clearly important to her. She recounted how in 1857, when the very first missionaries came up the River Niger and got stuck on the sandbanks outside Onitsha, the obi of the time offered them food and shelter. Later, when the mission schools opened, he sent his children along and so the family became Christians. She added: 'My father should have succeeded to the title but he refused, because it meant he would have to go through many pagan rituals and he felt it wasn't right. So the title moved to another branch of the family.' Justina and others of her circle now belonged to the Holy Church of the Apostle, headed by a charismatic preacher who, she claimed, had healed her with holy water.

On the Sunday she took us to her ancestral home in Onitsha. The great

---

[14] Rice cooked with palm oil, tomatoes, onions and spices, a dish common across West Africa.

Niger River stretched out before us, nearly a mile wide, but cluttered with great sandbanks in this dry season – no wonder the missionaries got stuck there. The sky was grey and a grey, half-repaired bridge led across into the haze. Onitsha, the lowest crossing point of the river, was in the front line for much of the war and most of the buildings were shabby, patched up from the shelling or still half-ruined. Troops were still billeted in the town.

At her uncle's place we met a doctor and his English wife who had stayed in Biafra throughout the war for the sake of her seven children. She told me: 'We didn't eat meat for eighteen months. It was hard but we survived.'

The doctor and his two brothers had just taken *ozo* titles. This used to be just a religious affair; members of the *Ozo* Society were considered to be moral leaders and the only people allowed to officiate at ceremonies honouring the ancestral spirits. It also acted as a mutual society; when a new member took the title, he had to pay a fee to all the older members.

'Today in Onitsha it costs more than £5,000, but less elsewhere,' the doctor told us. 'It's really a question of prestige nowadays, a way of ensuring your voice is heard in the community. No, the title doesn't make you a chief.' We began to see more clearly one of the roots of modern-day corruption: what in traditional society had been an insurance policy now looked like bribery.

Vicky Madiche, a survivor

Early in our stay Vicky Madiche called round. 'How splendid you are here! I am so sorry I don't have room in my house for you. Let me take you to lunch at the hotel.'

We saw a small, gentle-seeming lady, suffering from some shortness of breath and rather shaky on her feet. But when we heard her story we realised she was a person of enormous determination and courage.

'I had already got a teacher's certificate and I really wanted to go to Nsukka University to do a degree. But I was married by this time with a young child and that wasn't possible. So I stayed at home and studied for A levels while two more babies came along.

'Then Mr Madiche went to the London School of Economics to study social administration and I thought, this is my chance! When my last baby was old enough I left the children with my in-laws and joined him in London. I found out about the course in Bath and applied. But suddenly I heard that my baby had died! I was so sad but I was determined to do my studies. Mr Madiche finished his course and went home and I went on to Bath. You can imagine how lonely and miserable I was! But your dear aunt, she was like a mother to me. Now I'm working with Justina developing local dishes.

'We lost all our money in the war like everyone else. But my husband was in the civil service and he served the Biafran administration, he didn't have to fight. After the war they made him Resident in Umuahia and I can tell you, he made all the troops pay rent for the houses they were billeted in, not like in Onitsha!'

We spent a lot of time at the Madiches. Mr Madiche was a charming gentleman of the old-colonial school and almost embarrassingly pro-British. 'We do not have your sense of fairness,' he apologised. 'Nigeria is still among the less civilised – no, uncivilised! – nations.'

Just as we were about to leave one evening – it was New Year's Day – a group of people came singing into the house. 'Oh, is this how you celebrate New Year, is it a dance…?' I began, until Patrick shushed me. At that point everyone fell silent and one began to pray, asking Jesus to enter their hearts on that auspicious day. It was a group of elders from the Pentecostal Church bringing greetings to their members. Chief Okenwa, MD of the new factory, was there and other faces we recognised from the foundation ceremony.

Mr Madiche bade them welcome and introduced his visitors from the UK. The chief elder swayed forwards; clearly along the way alcohol had been taken, as the Irish would say.

'The British, how wonderful!' he shouted. 'It is the British who brought us the Light of the Gospel! You taught us how to live! We were cannibals before you came. Savages we were! Only through you have we learnt the Truth,' and more in the same vein. This was too much even for Mr Madiche and Chief Okenwa quietly drew the elder to one side, while we shook hands with everyone, thanked them for their good wishes and said goodnight. Christianity and capitalism appeared to go hand in hand in Eastern Nigeria.

Josephine Onwuku, from the next generation

Through the Madiches we met Josephine Onwuku, a primary school teacher. She belonged to a younger generation that had no need to go overseas for training and I found in her a kindred spirit.

'My husband Greg is an engineer,' she explained. 'We've got five children but we think that's enough now. I want to go back to university and study languages. We're building a block of flats here in Enugu, that'll give us some income and a home base here.'

'Most of the people we've met seem to be building houses in their villages,' I observed.

She looked at me shrewdly. 'This renewed attachment to the village, it's the war's fault; people feel insecure but it's a retrograde step. We Igbos, we're far too clannish. If you meet someone and he's from your village, he'll claim you like a blood-brother and you can't refuse him anything. You know why we stayed in Enugu over Christmas? Because if we went home all the relatives would demand "presents" and we'd end up broke! And it leads to corruption! Greg is provincial engineer and supposed to allocate all the contracts for the roads. But his boss, the commissioner, awards them to all his friends and village clansmen. No, we must move on.'

'Is it true that a man still has to pay the bride's family in order to marry her?' I asked.

She shrugged. 'Yes, officially. I'd cost about £300–400 today! But an educated girl will probably give her fiancé part of the money and anyway they always use it to furnish their house.'

Perhaps because she wasn't a 'been-to'[15], Josephine asked lots more questions about England and I had to tell her all about weddings and mortgages and in-laws. When I turned up next day at the Madiches she presented me with a short *akwete* cloth wrapper and head tie to match which I duly put on. 'Your blouse isn't right,' she said. 'Come to my place and I'll lend you a suitable one. Oh, and I want to show you that not all schools are like the one you saw in Lagos.'

---

[15] A common phrase at that time, used to describe someone who had been to the UK for study or work..

We left Patrick supervising our laundry being washed in Vicky's machine. On the way we visited the best (private) nursery school to which the Enugu elite send their children. The premises were a 'done-it-ourselves' tin shack but there were games, paints, plasticine, a 'shop' and so on, and although the top group were already doing words and numbers, it all felt much more relaxed and child-centred than the one in Lagos.

'We're bringing up our children the Western way,' the teacher said proudly. 'They should talk to their elders instead of being silent.'

'Just don't overdo it!' I retorted.

After this we got into one of those rounds of family visiting which Nigerians seem to delight in. First we went to her eldest sister, ostensibly to borrow the brother-in-law's car. At this point, seeing we were on another adventure, I phoned Patrick and told him to come over in a taxi. While we waited, I helped Jo make *moyin-moyin* for our supper. This is ground beans mixed with tomatoes, onions and peppers with egg or meat added; the mixture is then steamed in little moulds. The mixing was done in mortars with pestles, not in bowls even in this modern flat, and cooked on a kerosene stove. They tasted delicious.

The brother-in-law wasn't well, so *his* brother drove us to another sister's 'just to say hello'; the hallos turned into a bottle of beer apiece, so *that* brother-in-law took us on in *his* car to Jo's flat where we drank more beer, I was presented with a suitable blouse and we all returned to the first sister's for supper. We guessed they did a lot of this type of casual calling but having a couple of Britons in tow was an extra reason. In each place there were other callers besides us.

Justina insisted we spend our last night at her house so we packed up, paid our hotel bill – very modest thanks to the hospitality we'd received – and were collected luggage and all by her chauffeur. We made the most of our transport by going to the post office to post parcels home, to the Hotel Presidential for last Sunday's *Observer* and to the craft shop for a wonderful piece of cream and bronze akwete cloth, stopping every so often to take pictures. Each time I got out to take photographs the car followed me and when I'd finished there it was like a well-trained dog sitting at my heels.

When we arrived at Justina's all our bags were carried up and our ironing sent off to be done by the stewards – a welcome relief for Patrick! We spent the day visiting each of our friends and they loaded us with gifts for Mary and for us: more wonderful pieces of akwete cloth, a polished coconut mug and a thornwood carving. As we sat with them having a farewell drink at the bar of the Hotel Presidential we wondered where all this overwhelming hospitality had come from. Perhaps it was real gratitude for Aunt Mary's kindness in Bath; they knew what it is like to be alone among strangers. Perhaps it was partly pleasure that a British couple should turn up and take such an interest in their country; over the drinks and kola nuts we had asked a lot of questions and done a lot of listening. Maybe we were just tapping into an African tradition of welcome to anyone who could claim a tie of kin or friendship. But what could we do in return?

Before we set out, I had asked a well-travelled colleague how we could best repay hospitality from African friends. 'Think of it as a lake,' she said. 'You may not be able to repay them at that time. But what you have drawn from the lake of hospitality in one place and time, you can put back in another.' We resolved to do just this.

Back to Umuahia

But before we left we wanted to return to Umuahia and from there to go down to Port Harcourt, where we hoped to find the *MV River Gongola*, meet up with the officers and ask them to post our heavy parcels of gifts in the UK. In the absence of telephones we had learnt to use forked stick equivalents and sent three messages to Ade: by post, by government messenger and by the bus company. The reply came back next day by a cousin's hand: 'Yes, do come.'

But we found the household somewhat awry. Ade was in a social whirl of visiting relations rather than spending time with her children. Oluchi, like Ola, hated Nigerian food and seemed to be starving herself in spite of her father's threats. Chinwe was trying to get on with some studying and resented being at her mother's beck and call to help entertain guests. When we arrived Ola had gone to the local boarding school.

'She was in tears,' confided Chinwe. 'She still doesn't speak much Igbo and she doesn't have many friends there. The other girls ask horrible questions about where she has been and then laugh at her answers. She's been practising carrying water on her head, because at school the supply often fails and they have to collect it at the river.'

Next day we all went to fetch her back for the weekend. Founded by missionaries, the school was taken over by the government after the war and looked extremely spartan, with fifty bunk beds crammed into each dormitory. Ola had to take her own bedding, cutlery and even her own chair and desk. There seemed to be no pastoral care but Ola was more cheerful. 'A friend let me sleep in her dorm so it wasn't too bad.' Her mother started crying instead.

'Huh,' said her father. 'When I was at school we slept on bare boards and we had to wash the prefects' clothes. Once a month I walked home, no mini-buses then. These girls don't know how lucky they are!'

Ade felt far from lucky and was shocked at how run down everything was. 'Before the war the East was so much more prosperous than the West. We had good roads, good schools and hospitals. So much has been destroyed and it's going to take a long time to build things up again. In the meanwhile Lagos has forged ahead. Why, there isn't even a cold store in Umuahia!'

Dr Uduku's rather different slant showed his fears about Nigeria's future: 'You can build up the physical infrastructure but what worries me is how people in responsible positions are acting so irresponsibly. Look at my hospital – junior clerks aren't paid regularly, there's no rota for senior staff and it's chaotic! I'm supposed to be on leave but when I went in yesterday to see a particular patient none of my senior colleagues were there. And do you know where they'd gone? To a party celebrating the opening of a private hospital! That guy will make huge sums by charging high fees while our free hospitals will struggle on, surviving on crumbs from the state! All those at the top seem to care about are their own pockets and giving jobs to their relatives.'

We should have sent a forked stick to Port Harcourt but instead on Saturday we went down to the motor park, confident we could handle this wonderfully flexible local transport system. A large taxi had its engine running and looked ready to start so we got in, laden with our parcels. The driver turned off the engine and his accomplices got out so we transferred to a bus 'live-chicken class' i.e. no shock absorbers and full of market women. At the town of Aba we picked up a taxi whose driver appeared to have suicidal tendencies, leaping over the potholes into the path of oncoming cars until the other passengers calmed him down and we reached the docks safely, if rather shaken, only to find the *River Gongola* had sailed two days before. Sometimes not everything turns out for the best.

But we had had a heart-warming time in the East and a totally different experience from that in the North. The differences ran much deeper than landscape, houses and clothes. Here we had seen no expatriate advisors; the only Brits we had met were married to Igbos. Their society was picking itself up after the war, running their own schools and health services again and developing their own industries. Enterprise seemed deeply rooted in their culture; they grumbled the Military Government was holding them back and if given the resources they would do it all much more quickly themselves. They had not lost touch with traditions but adapted them and were, meanwhile, preparing to take on the Western world at their own game using Western methods.

We did wonder whether the old democratic checks and balances could prevent a growing gap between rich and poor. Would 'gifts' turn into 'bribes'? Chief Okenwu had published a pamphlet headed: *Don't envy others' success!* which urged personal effort - but would everyone be able to be successful in a larger, modern world?

We wondered too how the girls would fare. How long would it take before they felt 'proper Nigerians' again? Would Ade insist on moving to a town with supermarkets and cold stores? We exchanged a couple of letters but then lost touch.

※

Until, that is, I had finished this memoir and, googling to check spellings, found that most of the family were now living in the UK. Okechukwu had indeed become a city doctor and Ola was lecturing in tropical architecture at Edinburgh University. Sadly Chinwe had passed away, and so had the father, but Oluchi was working as a health administrator in London and Ade was being looked after, in true African fashion, by her children in the UK. We were able to meet and reminisce happily about our meetings over forty years earlier.

CHAPTER 8
Old and New in Benin

In which the young of Benin show us their old traditions and look to the future.

'Benin is a very native town,' Ade remarked dismissively as we caught a very early bus from Umuahia. That was just why we wanted to go there.

The powerful ancient kingdom of Benin was founded in the early fourteenth century by a chief, or *oba*, from Ife who brought with him craftsmen skilled in sculpture and metal-casting. As their wealth increased successive obas sponsored brass-workers to cast commemorative heads of the rulers and to decorate the palace walls with historic plaques. When the British entered Benin City in 1897 they were astonished at the technological skill and artistic power of these 'bronzes'[16] and, of course, carried many artworks off to European museums. We wanted to find out how far the artistic traditions continued.

At this time Benin was capital of the Mid-Western State, run by a well-respected military governor who was determined to bring it up to date with new roads, schools, modern shops and even a museum in a park. We established ourselves at the Edo Guest House, which offered a comfortable chalet with air-conditioning – but today there was no running water so we were given a large plastic tub of water with a bucket for washing and flushing the loo. The landlady also handed us canisters labelled *Doom* and *Prang*, 'in case of cockroaches,' she explained. Unfortunately these proved essential; after a mediocre supper of stew and rice in her restaurant we found our chalet crawling with the little brown beasts.

---

[16] Known as 'bronzes', most were made of a mixture of brass and other metals.

Our only contact in Benin was through Project Hand, a London-based organisation trying to help African craftspeople sell their products in Europe. Gudrun Ogbe, a German married to a Nigerian solicitor, ran a craft shop and we visited her on our first afternoon.

Gudrun was welcoming and informative. 'I was training in Germany as a, how do you say, "fashion designer", but when I come here with my husband I am interested in the local crafts. You know, they cast bronze statues here, still in the same way they have done it one thousand years ago. But they just copy the old models; I wish they can study new styles. I am helping them to improve the silver jewellery, so they can sell it in Europe.' The jewellery was indeed attractive and we took samples for Project Hand.

She gave us an introduction to the oba's secretary and next morning we walked through the old town to the palace. It felt more spacious than Kano; the hot sun beat down on wide streets edged with clusters of low houses, their walls of brown or ochre and the roofs of reddish pan[17]. A dusty breeze brought the smell of the open drains but we forgot this as we reached the oba's palace, shrunk from its eighteenth-century glory, with the towers gone, but still very much alive.

As we approached the gateway there appeared before us rows of venerable gentlemen clad in white wrappers with rows of coral adorning bare chests – and a TV camera. The local TV was shooting rehearsals of the ceremonies which were to be filmed the following week by the BBC for a programme called *Tribal Eye*, featuring Benin, Ife, Oyo and Oshogbo, all centres of ancient African art. What good luck for us!

Visitors were not allowed inside but the secretary asked one of the oba's sons to show us round the public courtyard where there were striking terracotta sculptures of past obas. 'These are done by Chief Idah,' he told us, 'you can take pictures,' so I joined the cameramen and presently a friendly young producer came over.

'Would you like to go inside and see the rest of the ceremonies?' he asked.

---

[17] Pan roofs are made from sheets of metal ridged to carry away water. Corrugated iron was used extensively for roofs in Africa and, either through weathering or from protective paint, was usually coloured red.

'Yes please, that would be most kind.'

'I'm not sure you'll be allowed. But I'll ask my father, the oba, I mean.'

So the producer was a prince! There were other boys around wearing similar brass ankle rings with their denim shorts – perhaps also princes? The royal wives also appeared from time to time, recognisable by their elaborate hair styles and coral beads.

As we waited outside another young man came up. 'Good morning, madam, sir. I saw you photographing my late father's sculptures. I am Omere Idah. Would you like to see some more of my father's works?'

We took down the address and said we'd come later. 'He probably just wants to sell us something,' muttered Patrick but I thought it sounded interesting.

Prince TV producer eventually got permission for us to watch the ceremony of installing a new chief. Inside the dim hall the candidate, dressed in white robes and coral beads, knelt in front of long rows of elderly men dancing to the beat of double drums and bells, until they raised him to his seat among his peers. Then all the chiefs processed down the forecourt and off to their homes in the town, but someone said the oba himself would come out into the forecourt soon, with dancers, to complete the ceremonies in public.[18]

Meanwhile I got chatting to the prince's girlfriend, a student teacher from Warri. 'That palace,' she said, 'it's quite creepy. People go inside there and never come out. They get eaten by the wild animals that live in the forest inside the compound.' Clearly the obas still liked to shroud themselves in mystery.

In the afternoon we visited Omere Idah, intending to return to the palace in case more dancing materialised. But he turned out to be so charming and so non-commercial that we spent the rest of the day with him.

First he showed us the great figures his father had carved out of the old city wall on which the house was built and inside the house many terracotta reliefs on the walls. Each had a story that went with it; some were

---

[18] Such ceremonies continue to this day. A 2013 YouTube clip showed similar dances while the Oba presented the royal coral beads to an eminent engineer; the equivalent of a knighthood from the Queen, perhaps.

historical, some parables, for this was traditional African oral literature. Omere acted parts of the story, repeated phrases and emphasised the important points; I could imagine children sitting round the evening fire listening to the stories of their people. When I asked if I might tape-record the stories to go with my photographs he re-told them almost word for word.

Then he showed us his own works, some heads and plaques and a box which he was carving for exhibition at the forthcoming All Black Festival of Arts in Lagos.

'I'd like to learn more skills,' he said. 'I want to study fine art in America, but I don't have the money.' In spite of his need Omere never pressed us to buy or donate, though he took enormous pleasure in explaining how the family skills and knowledge were passed on from generation to generation.

'Would you like to see some of the other crafts?' he asked tentatively. 'I can show you tomorrow.' We decided to stay another day.

Old Benin was still organised by its guilds: the brass workers lived and worked in one ward, the carvers in another, the goldsmiths in another. There were also whole streets given over to motor mechanics' workshops – one appropriately named James Watt Street. Omere, now joined by his friend Philip, seemed to have friends in all of them.

First they took us to a brass-workers' compound where we saw all the stages of the process by which they cast the classic bronzes and which they are still using. This is the so-called 'lost wax' method: they make a model in clay and cover it with a thick layer of wax. This in turn is covered with clay, a hole being left at the top. You pour in molten brass and when it is cold prise off the outer layer of clay. The brass has replaced the melted wax and you have your statue. It takes two months to model and cast a large figure which may sell for N200. Each is original although the style is copied from the traditional designs. The art is handed down from father to son and boys were working in their father's workshop after school hours, earning money for their education. We got chatting to some of them.

'What do you want to be?' asked Patrick, assuming the answer would be 'artists'.

'I want to be an engineer.'

'I'll be a lawyer!'

'I want to be a doctor – not for medicine, a doctor of book!' Was this a budding Ph.D. graduate or just a mistranslation?

Elsewhere we saw women making elaborately decorated traditional pots and a silversmith teaching his apprentices to make bracelets out of very fine wire. In the Carvers' Co-operative young men and boys were turning out ebony carvings of heads, elephants, obas' mothers, and so on, chipping away sweatshop fashion to radio music, while in the Idubor Gallery more serious artists were trying to sculpt statues out of marble as well as wood. Significant artworks and tourist tat were being produced side by side.

'I can show you a small palace if you like,' Omere offered, and took us to Chief Igiamen's house, one of the few compounds to survive the fire of 1897 and now preserved by the Department of Antiquities, who had employed the chief's daughter as a guide. It was a warren of red-walled rooms, with open spaces in the roof of each room to give light, while the floors had drains to carry away rainwater. Each room had a shrine, a large niche in the wall, full of strange, dusty objects. One seemed to be full of animal skulls, while another contained terracotta heads and a bottle of beer.

'This one for the god Olukun,' she said. 'These my ancestors. We give them presents, so they care for us.'

Her English was hard to follow but we suspected she still believed in them. We felt uneasy and were relieved when Omere took us off to see a man he called 'uncle', a primary school headmaster with whom we could talk about the modern world. A tall, bespectacled man with a benign smile, he welcomed us into his one-storey house and sat us down in his 'front room', with easy chairs set in a square, and small tables for the drinks. We recalled Chief Okenwa's house in Enugu, where we sat in a vast room with whisky bottles at our elbow; this room was small but friendlier and we were served cokes – at all levels of income there seemed to be a similar pattern for receiving guests. We decided hospitality was also one of the African arts.

Unusually, the teacher's room had a bookshelf with many history books. 'You've got a good library here,' I remarked.

'Oh, I took A levels in History and I would have gone on to university, but by then I was blessed with so many children that I had to get a job to keep them all.' We surmised that he was also acting father to Omere.

He told us he was sent on a headmaster's course, studying leadership, psychology, and sociology. 'A good head can make his staff work hard and be happy,' he explained. 'If they seem to be lazy, I talk to them and find out their problems. When a young teacher comes in I take a few lessons and make him watch me. In that way they learn, I don't have to reprimand them.'

I thought he understood 'leadership' already better than some of the London heads I'd had the misfortune to work under. 'What help do you get from the State Department of Education?' I asked.

'I wish they would build me a new school! I have very old buildings, and over one thousand children. We have to work two shifts: one lot comes from 7 am to noon, and the others from 1 pm till six. But the State has raised salaries, and gives teachers car allowances, so they are much more happy now.'

Finally we said goodbye to Omere and Philip. They got us a taxi but after a hundred yards we heard drums and saw dancing so we leapt out, paid him off and in the dusk watched three funeral processions parading round the streets. They were mostly women all dressed in the same cloth to show solidarity. Some men carried the drums, others huge umbrellas advertising State Express cigarettes. Does advertising help pay for the funeral rites, we wondered?

So we never saw the public dancing outside the oba's palace, but we'd had a wonderful introduction to the people of Benin and their arts. Exhausted by the heat, we sat down to bottles of beer and peanuts in our chalet before going across to supper. Alas, it seemed to be the same non-menu every night – rice and fish stew again. However, we had defeated the cockroaches.

CHAPTER 9
Ibadan: the Alalades and Ife

In which we come to Ibadan, stay with another branch of the Delano
family and visit ancient Ife.

At the bar of the Staff Club in Ibadan University we presented
ourselves to the secretary. 'Ah yes, your Yoruba friends have both
left messages to say you should stay with them,' she told us. 'But I could
book you into the Staff Guest House for a couple of nights if you like.' We
looked at the flowering shrubs and green lawns, the children splashing in
the swimming pool, the well-stocked bar and English newspapers laid
out on the coffee tables and thought we deserved some comfort after the
cockroaches.

When we returned to the bar we were introduced to a droopy-looking
Englishman with the words: 'These people have just travelled 4,000 miles
round Nigeria using public transport.' He gazed at us in astonishment
and muttered: 'You poor buggers!' before turning back to his drink. So we
rang up Duro Alalade and asked if we could stay with him instead. 'Of
course! My sister Wura has told me all about you. I will pick you up on
Saturday.'

We were now nearing the end of our time in Nigeria but we still wanted
to visit the Western Region, land of the Yoruba people. Geographically
it was part of the same tropical forest belt as the East, but culturally it
was different, with some of the oldest historic sites in the country. The
capital, Ibadan, had Nigeria's first modern university, where a couple of
Aunt Mary's students worked and, more importantly, new-made friends
had invited us to visit them here.

Ibadan was 'a village with a million inhabitants', they said. Founded about 1850 during the Yoruba civil wars, it grew to be a large commercial town before the British interfered. By 1975 there was a relatively small, compact business centre with offices, banks and European department stores but away from this intrusion the real Ibadan stretched out for several miles in a dense mass of traditional compounds, low and brown under a haze of *harmattan* and cooking smoke. On the outskirts were new residential areas of European-type houses set in spacious gardens for the elite, like Duro Alalade. When we went to visit his brother who lived near the family compound in the old area Duro joked, 'This is the native town where the indigenous live.'

Duro Alalade was a huge jovial man much given to jokes. 'Welcome to my little hut!' he exclaimed as we emerged from his Fiat sports car in front of a large two-storey house. A Peugeot and a Volvo stood in the drive. 'I've ordered an Audi with air-conditioning and stereo. I like cars.' He also enjoyed his two TVs, an electric organ and a superb hi-fi outfit.

As an accountant, he immediately began swapping stories with Patrick. 'I did my articles in the UK, working in the office all day for a pittance – thirty shillings a week in those days, wasn't it? But it was worth it. I have my own accountancy business now and a junior partner who's British. I'm doing OK, I get to travel to Britain and all over Africa.'

His wife had recently died and two of their daughters were at boarding school but Lola, who had just graduated from Ibadan University, was looking after her father. We had already met his son Tunde who was living with Wura in Lagos. 'She's a good mother to him,' said Duro. 'I think I'm a bit too soft as a dad.'

We were taken off to see the new house he was building and then to meet his British partner. There were other business colleagues there too, shaking their heads over the rising costs of building. 'It's Udoji,' they said. 'The workers are getting three rises this year, 25% each time, so they catch up with the new minimum wage.'

'What is this "Udoji" veryone is talking about?' we wondered.

'Well,' Duro answered, 'the Military Government set up a commission under Chief Jerome Udoji to report on "organisation, management and remuneration" in the civil service. I don't think they've done much reorganisation but this month all government employees got huge pay rises. The money's all coming from the oil – it's a way of spreading it round and keeping people content. Personally I think the government should use it to build better roads and schools.'

That evening we all pitched in to help get the house ready for a 'small' party for about twenty-five people. The first arrival was the permanent secretary in the Ministry of Lands and Housing, whose ease and charm of manner was good at warming up the party with very English (and probably Yoruba too) jokes. Once talking on serious matters he became very forceful and stimulating so I asked him about rural development and creating employment opportunities there. 'We should be developing labour intensive industries all over the country,' he said. 'But Nigerians like to work in modern businesses in the cities, even though that means less jobs. Our government doesn't really have a development policy.'

The talk turned to corruption and he shook his head. 'We all thought General Gowon was the one honest man. But now he has quashed the charges against the governor of the North-East State and imprisoned his accuser, even though everyone knows that the governor was lining his own pocket. Now people shout "thief" at Gowon in the street and university students are on strike in protest.'

Across the room I noticed a black-skinned couple who looked subtly different: their clothes, their stance and, when I spoke to them, their accent. Philip and Tandi were political exiles from South Africa who had found asylum in Nigeria. As I began to tell them excitedly about our trip, Tandi interrupted me. 'Oh, when you get to Maseru you must meet a very special person, who I met on a course here in Ibadan. She's called Anna Hlalele'

'But she's the very one we are going to stay with!' The world seemed extraordinarily small at that moment. Philip and Tandi had also stayed in Tanzania and gave us introductions to friends there. This was the next link in a chain of contacts which would take us across and down the continent and into places we had never thought to go.

We spent a relaxed week with the Alalades. Lola was happy to let me use the kitchen so we bought our own supplies and mostly cooked for ourselves. Duro came and went, gave us good advice and occasional lifts, but otherwise left us to organise our own programme.

Lola at twenty-one was an articulate and well-balanced young lady, more politically aware than many we had met. Her generation had had very different experiences from their parents who had struggled for their education in Britain in the 1940s and 1950s, enduring strange food, cold climate and often unsympathetic landladies – which was why Aunt Mary was remembered so fondly. Now their children were being packed off from an early age to the best, often expensive, local schools and by seventeen were studying at a Nigerian University.

'I'm lucky,' she said. 'Me and my sisters, we really have a nice relationship with our dad. He brings us up in an English way, not strict! He even let me walk out with a boy when I was sixteen – well, just to the end of the street. My aunts were so shocked. And once I got to uni he said I could do what I liked.'

I wondered aloud whether African teenagers went through the same sort of adolescent rebellion as British ones. 'Oh yes, we do. But we have to be quiet about it – we're not usually allowed to argue with our parents!'

It was time to plan the next stage of our trip. We hitched a lift with Duro into town to get air tickets to Tanzania. The only direct flight to Dar es Salaam from Lagos was a very expensive one with Pam Am so we settled for a more circuitous route: overnight flight with Ethiopian Airlines to Nairobi where we would change onto East African Airlines. The tickets had to be stamped by both airlines which meant they had to be sent to Lagos and back again, involving several anxious calls and visits before they were in our hands. Two weeks later we wished devoutly we'd taken the direct flight instead.

We went to the bank for cash, to the bookshop for a *Financial Times* so that Patrick could moan about the stock market, to the grocery so we could be self-sufficient, to the United Trading Company for new trousers for Patrick and finally to check out the British Council. Our contact there, one Peter Walton, took us through his exhibition of carved masks and invited us to supper.

It seemed to us that while the British Council was good at arranging cultural exchanges – masks versus Shakespeare – its officials were often cocooned from seeing Nigerian life as we had done. Over supper with Peter and his wife we discussed our respective experiences. 'I can't wait for my next posting,' he grumbled. 'The bureaucracy drives me mad. You wait all day and then something is missing so you have to come back. It takes so long to accomplish anything even with bribes. And in this heat one gets so exhausted.'

We could sympathise; it must be so difficult carrying on any normal business activity here to a European timetable. What was amusing for visitors with time to spare would feel very different if you had deadlines to meet. We too found the heat tiring but we could rest up between following unexpected trails through this complex, vibrant, bustling society.

Once again it was Justina Bello from Enugu, a Yoruba by marriage, who provided us with a couple of valuable contacts. Jean and Wes Weiderman, respectively a sociologist and an economist, offered us more sympathetic expatriate perspectives. Jean lent us a book on the Yoruba. 'I like them,' she assured us, 'but there is a saying: put two Igbos together and you have a cooperative enterprise; put two Yorubas together and you have a schism.' This well summed up some of the differences we'd experienced between the East and the West.

Wes gave us his gloss on the military government and Udoji. There was a need to rebalance wages between sectors, he explained, but it was also a move to buy popularity and it had backfired. 'All the teachers, doctors and lawyers are comparing notes and finding out someone is getting more than they are. Since civil servants have got rises of 30%, everyone in private firms wants the same and prices are just shooting up. The electricity goes off because the power corporation workers are on strike and next it's the water engineers, even though strikes are outlawed. The administrators in the military government are said to have taken the highest rises and no one trusts them any more.' Clearly the military were finding Nigeria as hard to govern as the civilians had done.

One day we split forces. Patrick went off to Lagos by bus to renew our visas for Tanzania and collect our mail from the Delanos. I decided to chase up the remainder of the Old Bathonians, as we still had letters and gifts to deliver, and took a taxi to the university campus to see Mrs Bisi Olusanya at the Food and Nutrition Unit. During the eight-minute ride I was propositioned, in a friendly way, by the taxi-driver – quick workers, these Yorubas! I was very glad I had Patrick at my side most of the time.

At Bisi's house like everywhere else I was made very welcome and reminiscences flowed. She looked up the rest of the contacts and drove me round to them but all were out or away so I just delivered the envelopes with photos and small gifts inside. Duty done. Bisi was on TV that night talking about child nutrition and I thought how proud Bath College of Domestic Science should be of how these good ladies had used their training.

Next I visited another cousin of Justina's, Mrs Gini Onuorah, who was librarian at the Nigerian Institute for Social and Economic Research. As her only task that morning was to write to the Udoji Commission complaining her revised salary wasn't high enough, we had time to talk about how I could access teaching sources on Nigeria and I invited her and her husband, an agricultural researcher, to supper that evening, assuming Patrick would be back.

But Patrick didn't get back till 8.45, hungry and tired; the bus was late and then traffic in Ibadan was gridlocked. Once revived with whisky, he told the usual tale of battles with taxi drivers and the Lagos traffic, but he'd managed to reach Awoyemi Close and pick up our Christmas mail from home, boxes of Kodak slides from films we'd posted in the north and a letter from Anna Hlalele in Lesotho. Best of all, the Tanzanian visas were now in order. Celebrating all this, we were halfway through a belated meal when Gini and Patrick Onuorah turned up. Truly time is elastic in Nigeria but so is food and we all had an extended supper together, during which Patrick Onuarah offered to arrange a visit to the International Institute for Tropical Agriculture.

Financed by the World Bank and Ford Foundation, it boasted a conference centre, shiny new laboratories and experimental plots full of different varieties of local crops – millet, yams, cassava, peppers and so on – at various stages of growth and under different conditions. We asked whether food production could keep up with Nigeria's fast-growing population but the American director was cautious.

'Don't expect a "green revolution" in Africa like there was in India,' he said. 'Here we aim to develop better varieties of local plants and to help the villagers improve cultivation techniques with their own tools. For example, we're studying weed growth to see when is the most effective time to weed so that farmers can extend their cropped areas. We're not short of land, it's manpower and techniques. We think food output could be doubled or more and the same for cocoa and palm oil.

'The real problem,' he added, 'is social status. Educated Nigerians don't want to have anything to do with agriculture. I've got lads from Botswana on my course who all want to be "proper farmers, like the Boers", they tell me. But Nigerians just want to work in offices.' This seemed to be a recurring story.

Ile-Ife

Becoming suddenly conscious of its history, in 1962 the newly independent Nigeria founded a university at Ile-Ife where, according to Yoruba legend, life itself originated. Here is a version of the story:

> Olodumare, the Supreme God, ordered Obatala to create the earth, but on his way he found palm wine, drank it and became intoxicated. Therefore his younger brother, Oduduwa, climbed down from the heavens on a chain carrying three precious items. The handful of earth he threw on the primordial ocean and the cockerel he placed on the earth to scatter it, thus creating land on which to build Ife. Finally Oduduwa planted the palm nut in a hole in this land, and from it there sprang a great tree with sixteen branches, symbolising the clans of the early Ife city-state.[19]

We set off early one morning to visit Ife. At the motor park we sat in a taxi for a while, but as it didn't fill up we switched to a *danfo* with our favourite slogan: *No Condition is Permanent*. A danfo, rather like the northern kitcar, is a roofed-in pick-up van, with seven-a-side benches built in the back, a central handrail giving you something to hold on to as it sways along the rutted roads while the driver tries to overtake everyone else. At once the taxi filled up and drove away, so we sat in the danfo eating our breakfast of slices of cold boiled yam and feeling that our white skins had put us at a definite disadvantage that day. In an unusually mutinous mood we decided that in Yoruba English 'Yes' meant 'I do not understand'

---

[19] Adapted from Wikipedia.

while 'Yes, sir' meant 'I do not understand and I don't really care.'

The *Ooni*, or King, of Ife still ranked as the first among the Yoruba traditional leaders and the current ruler, Sir Titus Adesoji Aderemi, had moved naturally into modern politics, becoming President of the Western House of Chiefs. His 'palace', a three-storey modernised house, had a broad forecourt thronged with people in both bright traditional robes and sober modern dress, standing, sitting, talking and waiting – for an audience, a job, a bribe? We went off to visit Yemi Delano, who was studying economics and by good luck we found her in the hall of residence.

A quiet, pleasant girl, Yemi offered to guide us round the various schools, including the prestigious Department of African Studies where her grandfather, Dr Delano, was a Fellow. The university campus had some of the most interesting modern architecture we had yet seen, while under the tall palm trees strolled students wearing short dresses or slacks and shirts – no African clothes, nor even an Afro hair-style like my African-Caribbean pupils in London. Their styles were definitely pro-Western.

Eventually Yemi admitted she should be in class, so we took a taxi back to the small, scruffy and dusty town and found the museum. There, from small, scruffy, dusty shelves, a magnificent row of terracotta and bronze heads stared out at us: the portraits of a generation of oonis.

The history of Ile-Ife is more prosaic than its myth. Between about 1100–1400 there flourished here a cosmopolitan city-state, grown rich by trade in cloth and kola nuts, gold, iron and ivory, as well as slaves. The kings promoted art and for a time commissioned their own likenesses in stone and metal. Then the fashion faded, the craftsmen migrated to Benin to set up a similar tradition and the royal heads lay forgotten. Some terracotta ones were taken to Europe in 1911, where few believed they could be African-made. But in 1938 builders dug up seventeen bronze heads in Ife town; one is in the British Museum and here were the rest: wonderful naturalistic heads of men and women gazing serenely into space and time.

On our last night with Duro he took us to supper with Tandi and Philip Mokeba, the South African exiles, where we met Todd Langa, another South African. Unlike the Mokebas she had a proper passport and could travel freely to and fro, but she told us how whenever she visited South Africa she had to inform Special Branch of her movements in advance and she knew they checked up on her.

'My sister once picked up some white friends of mine and took them home for a chat. Four months later Special Branch came nosing around to ask what they'd talked about! You're going to have to be very careful who you visit and what you say when you get to South Africa.'

In theory we knew this, but hearing it from someone who had been under surveillance made us realise that life in South Africa was not going to be as relaxed as this round of Nigerian visiting. Would we be under surveillance?

There was something subtly different in talking to black South Africans and we suddenly realised what it was – they were more like us, more European. It was not just the language but the outlook and the assumptions. Years later a black South African visitor to our London home told us: 'Yes, in the UK I feel at home and in Holland too, they are rather like the Boers. But in Nigeria – that's when I experienced culture shock!'

CHAPTER 10
Ibadan: The Oguntoyinbos and Oyo

In which we stay with the people who praise iron and visit Oyo old and new.

Our Nigerian friends did their best to shelter us from culture shock and when we moved to the Oguntoyinbos Ayo served us boiled eggs and toast for breakfast in spite of our protestations that we could eat yams and stew. They seemed to move in comfortable chameleon fashion between their different worlds and little Toyosi was playing happily with the neighbours' children, although she was heard to remark that Nigerians weren't sometimes very nice to each other. We were fitted into their large modern flat, crammed to bursting with the goods Femi had been guarding on the boat: three-piece suites, tables, lamps and pictures galore. Our share was a rather small double bed in a rather stuffy room and our sleep wasn't helped by the watchman proclaiming loudly through the night that he was still awake.

Femi had a plethora of schemes for making money. 'I might invest my savings in property,' he mused. 'I'm building a house in a new development. Or perhaps I'll breed dogs, Alsatians are popular here as guard dogs. Or I might buy second-hand sewage tankers in the UK, ship them out here and hire them to Ibadan City Council to collect the night soil in the old city.' There seemed no end to Yoruba enterprise.

As I did our laundry in her British washing machine Ayo chatted away about Yoruba marriage customs. 'You know, in the old days, we were polygamous. Nowadays, wealthy Muslim men usually have more than one wife. If you're a Christian, if you can afford it, you have a string of mistresses. So nothing much has changed, really!'

African names usually have meanings. 'Oguntoyinbo' means 'Ogun (god of iron) is worthy of praise' and the clan were, naturally, blacksmiths. But the family story went beyond that and Femi enjoyed retelling it:

'My grandfather came from the Sudan. He was captured there sometime in the mid-nineteenth century and brought as a slave to join the Oguntoyinbo household. In time he was freed and adopted into the clan. My own father was born in 1869, we believe, the youngest of the family. He didn't train as a blacksmith, he ran away to Lagos when he found he was the child of a slave. He worked for a while as a houseboy, then as a "chainboy" for a surveyor and on the railways. One of his masters offered to send him to school but he never went. He became a government messenger though, and when he retired from that aged fifty-five, he became boss of a stevedore gang on the docks; he was over seventy when he retired! He took a second wife and I'm her youngest son. He's still going strong at a hundred and six!'

We didn't meet the father, who lived in Lagos, but Femi took us on a round of family visits. First we drove to Awe, traditional home of those who praise iron. The old smithy had recently been rebuilt with a pan roof, the forge was lit and an axe-head was being beaten into shape, the sparks flying and the hammer clanging.

Across the road a door opened and an elderly, dignified man came out. 'Greetings, Uncle,' said Femi and prostrated himself briefly – right down, full-length on his hands like a quick press-up – before he rose again to introduce us. 'These are my English friends; this is my cousin but I call him Uncle out of respect.'

'Please take some refreshment with us,' said Uncle and to their delight we chose palm wine rather than cola. I took a family picture and Femi distributed small gifts of money to the ladies as was customary.

The road to his sisters' village of Fiditi lay through fairly open and rolling countryside, lit to brilliant green by the setting sun. While supper was being prepared Patrick and I strolled round the village. Its wide dusty red-brown streets were clean but untidy, with chickens, goats and children each following their own pursuits, clucking, bleating and chattering. The low houses were scattered along the sides, rusty pan roofs stretching out on their wooden poles to give shade. The newest homes were built of concrete blocks but most were still faced with the same red-brown soil over lathe and plaster, with only the large Catholic church standing out white against the umber background. The warm, humid evening air was tinged with wood smoke from the cooking fires overlain by a faint potpourri of people and animals. By the end of our circuit we had collected a tail of small children calling out '*Odabo* (goodbye) Mummy, *odabo* Daddy.' Children use 'Mother' and 'Father' to all senior adults as a title of respect and this was their translation.

In the courtyard long mud benches ran along the sides and here we all settled down for a supper of stew, rice and fried plantains: visitors from the city in high Yoruba fashion, the local family in more muted wrappers and blouses, us in European clothes, and Toyosi running around with her village cousins talking pidgin Yoruba. The rising moon added a silver gleam to the low lamp-light, while the occasional chicken, goat or dog wandered in through the house. 'The Irish would feel at home here,' whispered Patrick.

The brother-in-law had a farm nearby but also ran a building materials business. 'Did you see our new public water taps?' he asked proudly. 'When people used the stream they got guinea-worm but now we're safe. We've got the concrete poles up for the electricity, but no wires yet,' he grinned. 'We've got to pay for it ourselves and it takes time.'

However, when we got back to Femi's flat the electricity was off and our supply of candles was running low. So much for installing electricity.

Fakeye and the old town

'I'd really like to buy a nice carving,' I said to Femi.

'You should go to Fakeye, he is the very best in the West,' was the answer. We borrowed a car and driver from Femi's pharmacist cousin, a quiet, smiling, generous man who lived nearby and set off. En route we picked up our Tanzanian tickets and booked seats at the Mid-West Lines bus station for our return to Lagos the following week; the use of a car was a precious resource to be fully exploited.

Fakeye lived in the heart of the old town and it took us a long time. Once off the tarred roads we entered a spider's web of narrow, rough streets with further paths and drains winding in between the buildings.

Made of mud blocks, they were faced with cement and often two storeys high with pillared balconies and brown tin roofs. There were no walled enclosures as in the North but each 'compound' was made up of many little rectangular houses inhabited by members of the same clan, perhaps several hundred, densely packed together. Women worked and gossiped outside, children played, goats and chickens scratched around for food. It all looked very sociable and very unsanitary. The car worked its way down the centre of the road between street traders selling everything from watches and cassettes to shirts and shoes. Where pavements might have been, women sat frying bean cakes or toasting plantains and serving them to passers-by.

When we got to Fakeye's compound he was out and there were no finished pieces for sale but one of his apprentices took us to a brother, Ganiye Fakeye, less famous but carving in the same tradition. We were so taken by some of his work that we ordered a pair of figures – a drummer and a dancing woman. But we would be long gone by the time they were ready – could we trust him to send them to us? We decided yes; we paid and he promised to deliver them to the Oguntoyinbos for posting to England.

We doubted we would ever see them. But a year later a parcel arrived for us and there were our figures; they stand today on my bookshelf. We never knew who brought or posted them to London but Ganiye Fakeye kept his word.

Yoking the independent Yorubas to other historic peoples was clearly not one of Britain's best colonial ideas. We were having supper with Bisi Olusanya, looking – by lamplight as the electricity was off yet again – through the collection of photograph albums that invariably appeared at such times to help the conversation along. 'Here I am in Bath,' she said proudly. And there too was a much younger Aunt Mary, surrounded by students.

Bisi's husband was a jolly, rotund and energetic doctor, who arrived late for supper after his hospital rounds. Listening to our accounts of the trip so far, he shook his head when we praised the Mid-West State. 'Brigadier Ogbemudia is a dictator,' he said. 'He runs a police state and you can't criticise him. We really don't want to be joined up with such people or with the Hausas. We Yorubas need our own independent country like Oyo was in the past.'

Ah, Oyo – another of the historic places of the West! 'You must really go to Oyo,' enthused Bisi. 'It was the capital of the great Yoruba Empire. Go and visit the Alaafin, I'm sure he'll see you.'

Oyo

We took another danfo to Oyo, this time with the slogan *May God Protect Us* above its windscreen. We thought it referred to the Christian god but it might well have been a prayer to Ogun, or one of the other deities of the forest along our road, to protect us against the taxis trying to prove they could drive faster than any danfo.

The Oyo Empire, established in the fourteenth century, grew to become one of the largest West African states south of the Sahara. Its people acted as middlemen between the trans-Saharan caravans and the coastal traders. Salt, leather, kola nuts, ivory, cloth and of course slaves passed through their hands and the state thrived on the taxes. This funded a standing army, including cavalry from the tsetse-free north and infantry from the forest areas. The leader, known as the *alaafin* or 'owner of the palace', ruled over a sophisticated and complex society. He was not an absolute monarch as he was held in check by two other groups, the warriors and the priests. An alaafin who failed in his duties could be forced to commit suicide; the succession went to one of the royal clan, though not always the son.

Of course we did not see the Alaafin that day. 'You should have asked for an appointment,' scolded his secretary in an upper-class English accent as he took us around the palace. At that moment the talking drums started up: '*kabo oyinbo, kabo oyinbo*! Welcome white people!' A series of wide courtyards with low, thatched, one-storey brown houses stretched in every direction, with one new, white-pillared hall for ceremonies, built by the current ruler who was an Oxford graduate. The inner courtyards, where we had to take off our shoes, held some wonderful carved pillars but the shrines were empty.

'Come back on Saturday week, there will be ceremonies that afternoon for the making of new chiefs,' said the secretary, beckoning to a waiting boy to take us to the craft workshops and so we met the weaver's son,

Waheed Salaam.

We were disappointed at the quality of the wood and leather work so, after buying a leather bag and some antique beads, we took Waheed to a 'beer parlour' for cool drinks and joloff rice. Alert to any chance of a deal, he invited us to his father's house. 'He is a weaver and so am I,' he boasted. The cloth was beautiful: woven in long narrow strips in strong colours, heavy with a fine pattern. I coveted a finished set of wrapper, head tie and stole but it was expensive and the weaver refused to bargain or to sell the pieces separately.

'I'll weave a piece for you,' offered Waheed. 'Come back next week. Now I've got to go to school this afternoon but I'll drop you off.' He changed into a crisp school uniform, hailed a taxi and took us back to the centre of town. That was one very self-assured and smart sixteen-year-old.

The following weekend Femi and Ayo drove us to Oyo but, since we left late, visited cousins on the way and got caught up in traffic, we arrived too late for the ceremony itself. However the whole of the outer courtyard of the palace was still full of visitors wearing brilliant Yoruba robes. Under large gaudy umbrellas sat the Alaafin and other notables, with army officers prominent, watching traditional dances being performed to the sound of drums and calabash rattles.

The Alaafin rose; he wore heavy ceremonial robes and an elaborate crown with beads hanging over his face. He processed on a wave of drumming and trumpet calls, his great red umbrella held over him as he moved forward in short running bursts, attendants fanning him the whole time. The chiefs who had just been created – including one woman and those who had achieved success in the modern sector – assembled with their families and friends and to the sound of dane-guns firing and preceded by drummers, moved off to their own compounds to feast their retinues.

I met up with Waheed who proudly delivered a length of lovely dark blue cloth, enough for a long skirt; I paid the agreed N10 and persuaded him to talk into my tape recorder. 'I go to commercial high school,' he intoned. 'My father and grandfather were weavers. I have six brothers and sisters. I want to be big businessman and make lots of money.'

This was a theme that ran through many conversations that we had with Nigerians.

On our last weekend we invited all the friends we had made in Ibadan to drop in at the Oguntoyinbos, who seemed delighted to meet new people. The Weidermans arrived and Toyosi took charge of their little daughter. Then came Bisi Olusanya, Aunt Mary's student, and her doctor husband. There were the Onuorahs, cousins of Justina's, and the South African exiles, who gave us some more addresses in South Africa along with warnings to be careful. Only the Waltons from the British Council never turned up. Conversations ebbed and flowed over politics, economics and development, but unlike in Zaria, it was mainly Nigerians talking.

'So what do you see happening next in Nigeria?' Patrick started the ball rolling.

'The military government must go,' declared Femi. 'The politicians are ready to come back. The army is too much influenced by the Hausas, and the North gets more than its fair share.'

'The problem is the oil money,' said Patrick Onuarah. 'It's going on government salaries and prestige projects. It needs to be spread more widely to help farmers and rural people.'

'As an outsider, I'd invest in infrastructure – roads, electricity, schools and clinics,' responded Wes Weiderman. 'The government needs to think long-term about the country's future needs and draw up some plans. At the moment it's just a free-for-all.'

A heated debate arose among the Nigerians about the role of public servants.

'Doctors are now on go-slow, because they think the Udoji Commission has not been fair to them. The doctors are civil servants. They shouldn't be so greedy. They ought to be more dedicated to serving the community.'

'But if you don't pay them enough they'll leave and set up private practices. Then there won't be hospitals for the poor.'

'Why shouldn't they set up private practices and earn more money? That's only human. Good ones will prosper, the others will go bankrupt. That's how the market works.'

Our friends might have black skins and wear Yoruba robes but they seemed to have been well inducted into the Western capitalist system. Did their own culture predispose them to want to accumulate wealth and compete with each other? From what we understood of Yoruba society it was never as egalitarian as that of the Igbos. But in the past there was less opportunity to amass wealth, while obligations to family and clan led to redistribution. Or perhaps selfishness and greed is the default position of humanity? We wondered if Tanzania, with its philosophy of 'African Socialism', would offer us new perspectives.

CHAPTER 11
Farewell to Nigeria

In which we are rescued by Aunt Mary's students from the Nigerian health service and leave Nigeria with many questions about its future.

Nigerians are among the world's most reckless drivers and on the road from Ibadan to Lagos we had a grandstand view from our front bus seats of the wrecked vehicles littering the roadsides. We felt lucky to have survived this far and quite ready to give up our forays to the motor parks.

Lagos seemed even hotter than before. As we needed cholera boosters Kunle dropped us off at the vaccination centre but afterwards I felt so sick and dizzy that I collapsed onto a seat outside. In Lagos it is, of course, who you know that matters so Patrick, realising that Ade's sister Nicki and a couple of Aunt Mary's old students worked there, dashed off to the nearby General Hospital. During a frantic hour of searching, explaining and telephoning, between them they organised a car and driver to pick me up, an air-conditioned room in which to lay me, a doctor to diagnose 'collapse with low blood pressure' and tea and biscuits to fortify Patrick.

After a few hours in the cool I felt well enough to be driven home but it took a couple of days to shake off the high temperature and diarrhoea which followed. The cholera jabs? The heat? Travel fatigue? Probably a combination but thankfully it was a one-off, and it gave us an insight into how Nigerian health services operate.

At the Surulere Health Centre next day there were long queues, but fortunately Mercy Dare, yet another ex-Bath student, was working nearby and told the receptionist we were Very Important People. We paid the standard fee of 50k, and were taken straight in to a doctor who was smoking a cigarette and reading the newspaper despite the queue waiting outside. Although by this time I was almost recovered he gave me a – free – prescription for three drugs; none of which were available at the dispensary. Mercy drove us to a 'good' chemist which sold us the two important ones.

At home we found Dr Delano there, equally angry at the medical profession. 'My car has broken down, so I came into Lagos by danfo today for my weekly medical treatment,' he explained. 'But no doctor was available; I'm told they were all in an "Udoji" meeting, discussing salary levels! Why do Nigerians only work hard for themselves, never for the public good?' he fumed. It was not the first time we had heard that question.

When I went back to thank Mercy for her help, I got chatting to a paediatrician, Dr Adekoposi. She wore a thin, light shawl over her head and I realised she was Muslim. I told her of our experiences in the North.

'Oh, I'm Yoruba,' she said as though that explained it all. 'My family converted to Islam but we don't live in seclusion down here. That's all Hausa cultural nonsense; my girls all went to school and university. My husband supports my professional career – we need the money.'

Next day she took me round a series of special schools, for the blind, for the deaf, and for the physically handicapped. All three were still run by churches as state education did not cater for special needs. 'Now that would be a good use for the oil money,' I thought.

Meanwhile Patrick was having the first of his airport luggage experiences. To save on excess baggage, we were trying to send one suitcase by Pan Am freight direct to Dar es Salaam. As he later told me, 'Wura dropped me at the International Terminal, but the offices are in the other one, so I carried that damned suitcase, all 18kg of it, 600 yards, to the Pan Am office, which was shut. Another 200 yards to the Ethiopian Airlines, but that was shut too. No left luggage office, no passenger lounge in sight, so this time I took a taxi back to International and had a beer. Finally the Ethiopians opened, they confirmed the tickets, and offered a concession on freight charges, so I agreed, even though it doesn't go by direct flight.

'They took me to the cargo office, which gave me endless forms to fill in and kept referring to a customs declaration I should have got from

Central Bank. Finally they just took the forms and I paid the charge. Then I had to see the senior officer. He made me open the suitcase, and finally – what a relief! – said OK, you don't need the customs declaration. As I left, the man from Ethiopian Airlines said "The cargo office want N5 to pass the suitcase; you must give him something." I coughed up N2 for Nigerian Airways and gave another N1 to the helpful Ethiopian guy. So I just hope the suitcase will get there safe and sound and be waiting for us in Dar.'

It didn't and wasn't, but that is another story.

We relaxed by reading the newspapers, whose headlines epitomised the current concerns:

> 'Student teachers' college in Port Harcourt closed by an Udoji strike!'
> 'Banks re-open as union leaders are released from jail.'
> 'Five armed robbers were executed at Port Harcourt recreation ground before more than 20,000 people. Several were hurt as the crowd surged onto the field to have a glimpse of the dying robbers'.
> 'Mr Daddoh, (who had forced a state commissioner to resign because of allegations of corruption) was himself arraigned in court accused of blackmail and extortion and despite assertions of police brutality was remanded for several days.'

We would not know the ends of these particular stories but as straws in the wind they were not very encouraging.

On our last evening Kunle took us to a cousin's birthday party. At first we all sat round in a circle of chairs on the lawn in virtual silence until Kunle stood up. He made a short speech of welcome, prayed for the family's wealth and happiness, then took a bottle of beer and poured a generous libation onto the grass. Everyone relaxed, the cake was cut and the women brought round plates of fufu, rice and stew, beer flowed and the circle broke up into noisy, laughing groups. A drummer began his vibrant, rolling beat and Wura, as senior wife, danced up to the head of each branch of the family in turn in formal greeting. Later each of their wives came up to her and pressed a small amount of money into her hand. Government rank, amount of salary, size of house or car – these didn't seem to matter as much as the respect due to her position in the family.

I'd been 'interviewing' family members with a small tape recorder and afterwards Lanre said: 'Can I ask *you* a question now? Were you scared when coming to Nigeria?'

We assured him we weren't and it was true: nervous at the start, perhaps, but our hosts soon put us at our ease and on our journeying we had met only kindness from strangers. We had appreciated their energy, exuberance and enterprise, and their loyalty to family and friends, among whom we were fortunate to have been counted.

But we wondered, as we said goodbye at the airport, what the future would hold for this huge, unruly, adolescent giant of a nation, free at last from British dependency and seeking a role in the world. Would its diverse peoples, so uncomfortably yoked together by colonialism, stay together? What would happen to the oil wealth? What form of government could mesh the individual enterprise with a sense of public responsibility towards the less well-off?

＊

Since then Nigeria has been through traumatic times but the nation has stuck together so far in spite of Islamic movements in the North which want to set up *sharia* law. There have been long periods of military dictatorship, interspersed with weak civilian governments, until in 2011 President Goodluck Jonathan was elected in what was deemed to be a reasonably free and fair way. The dependence on oil has been problematic and much of the money was squandered but by 2014 Nigeria had become Africa's largest economy and was considered to have 'taken off' in economic terms, on the way to becoming a middle-income country. Differences between rich and poor remain huge and corruption flourishes still. Many Nigerians have emigrated and, for good or ill, brought some of their cultural characteristics with them.

PART THREE

Tanzania

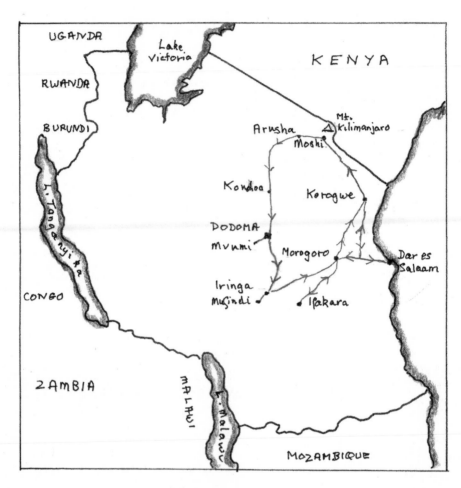

TANZANIA
Places visited by bus and car.

CHAPTER 12
Arrival in Dar es Salaam

In which we step into Tanzania, forge some new links in the chain
and begin our quest for an ujamaa village.

'On the other side, quick!' I flung myself across the gangway as the
plane banked just over the snowfield. The crater of Kilimanjaro,
deep, grey and smoky, was encircled by a necklace of short blue-green ice-
cliffs, from which the slopes of black grit fell steeply some 3,000 feet to
the forest below. 'It looks gruesome to climb! Do we really want to try it?'

Tanzania was going to be different. There was only one ex-Bath student
to visit; otherwise we had a few British contacts at the university and
one on a tea plantation. Some German friends of mine, Karola and Gero
Jentsch, were stationed in Dar es Salaam and were acting as our post office.
In Ibadan we had been given the Dar address of Nobambo Socenywa, a
black South African nursing sister here in exile. Beyond that we knew we
wanted to climb Kilimanjaro and visit a game park, but mainly we were
here out of political curiosity.

What was Julius Nyerere's 'African socialism' like in practice? Was this
an alternative to the 'African capitalism' we'd seen in Nigeria? Could
Africans develop a modern way of life by building on their 'communalist'
roots, and taking lessons from European socialism as well? Could they
make a virtue out of poverty – giving everyone *a fair share of what little
we have,* in Nyerere's words, and prevent a few grabbing all the benefits
of development that really belonged to the many? We hoped for some
answers.

Dar es Salaam airport was cool and calm. The officials seemed slim
and light-boned compared to the heavily-built Yorubas; they were polite,

quiet and efficient. We passed easily through customs and immigration but when we reached the freight office to pick up the suitcase sent in advance there was no sign of it. 'Maybe it's held up in Addis Ababa?' they suggested. 'Try Ethiopian Airlines offices in town.'

Gero Jentsch had booked a room for us at the Mawenzi Hotel – clean, if cramped, with – oh joy in this steamy place! – a partially functioning air-conditioner. We showered, lunched, slept and then wandered out into the city.

Could this be the same continent as Lagos? Dar seemed so neat, so clean, so quiet by comparison. The air was just as hot and damp, but a fresh evening breeze swept in from the sea as we strolled through broad tree-lined streets, where traffic islands were studded with flowering shrubs, past modern offices and shops. There were no open drains here and little traffic; no hawkers or stalls on the pavements, no honking or shouting – so much more subdued than in Lagos. Down by the harbour wall the promenade was busy with families, mostly Indians, the men in smart Western suits, the children in bright outfits, many of the women covering their heads and their brilliant saris with loose, flowing black gowns known as *buibuis*. The gulls were calling above the chatter and laughter and the tug-boats were hooting; we found a way down to the shore and dipped our toes in the Indian Ocean. The sun was setting behind us and the light stretched low over the water, tipping the wavelets pink. The air smelt warm and salty with a hint of incense somewhere on the breeze. We were in a new country.

Lying just south of the equator, Tanzania rises from a small coastal plain to the highest mountain in Africa and to the ranges along the Great Rift Valley, where Lakes Tanganyika and Malawi form part of the western boundary. Much of the land is savannah – wide plains of grass and scrubby bush, fine for grazing where there is water but too dry for easy farming. The mountain ranges catch the rain and are thickly forested, some being planted with tea and coffee.

Famously, skeletons of some of the earliest human ancestors were found in Tanzania and it seems to be one of the areas from which *homo sapiens* set out to settle the rest of the globe. In historical times many tribes passed through the high plains, or settled there as farmers and iron-workers, but no large states grew up; trade routes crossed the plains but most of the wealth was drained down to the coast. When Vasco da Gama arrived there in 1498 he found a chain of substantial, prosperous cities which he and his followers promptly plundered.

From around 700 AD onwards Arabs had traded down the coast and intermarried with Africans; their descendants became known as 'Swahili,' with a distinctive language and culture, many following Islam. They were the market middlemen, organising exports of gold, ivory and slaves from the interior in exchange for imports of cloth, porcelain and metals from Asia; later on mercantile castes from India settled in the cities. After a while the Arabs beat the Portuguese back down the coast to Mozambique and in 1840 Sultan Seyyid Said of Oman moved his capital to the island of Zanzibar.

During the late nineteenth-century scramble for Africa, Imperial Germany found some unconquered land between British Kenya and Portuguese East Africa, pushed the Arabs out of Dar es Salaam and annexed a large slice of territory up to the Rift Valley. When Germany lost all its colonies as a result of World War I, the League of Nations made Tanganyika a British Protectorate. One consequence was that land could not be alienated to European settlers; another was the lack of any incentive to develop the country economically. Tanganiyka came therefore to independence in 1961, poor but relatively free of racial conflict and vested interests. There was a chance to do something different.

The next two days were spent chasing up our contacts – and our missing suitcase. The Jentsches – Gero worked for German overseas aid[20] – lived in a large breezy house among the diplomats in Oyster Bay, and over an excellent lunch of fillet steak and vegetables we began asking questions. 'I find it interesting and I am glad to be here,' said Karola. 'But there are difficulties; sometimes we have no water, sometimes no electricity. And food – now there is no butter in the shops and last year there was no wheat flour, so no bread; we must eat rice.'

'Do you think that Tanzania will succeed in developing a different path?'

Gero was diplomatically cautious. 'It is too early to say. We find the idea

---

[20] Gero was a civil servant in the *Bundesministerium für wirtschaftliche Zusammenarbeit und Entwicklung.*

of rural development appealing, but the economic situation is not good and not much progress has been made since independence thirteen years ago. Exports of coffee and tea are stagnant. The oil price rise has hit them hard and the government have now to import food because of the drought. The minimum wage has been increased, but inflation is hurting everyone.'

'What do Tanzanians really think about Nyerere and his policies?'

'That is a difficult question. We do not easily make contact with the Tanzanians. They are sometimes suspicious of *wazungu* – that is white people. They don't always want to speak English – they learn Swahili in school and that is enough.'

'Do you think we will have problems travelling around?'

'You should be careful. Do not photograph dams or the new railway. Janet, you are wearing slacks, that is good, or buy a long skirt, not shorts.' At that moment my main problem was that half my clothes were in our missing suitcase.

Whatever their problems with Europeans, Tanzanians welcomed South African political refugees. We rang Nobambo Socenwya and invited her to lunch. A short, stout woman, wearing blue sunglasses with her floral frock and with a somewhat nervous smile, she began talking at us as though we were students, but after we had given her news of her friends in Nigeria she became more relaxed, describing her work as a nurse-tutor at the Muhumbili Hospital.

'The medical standards here are worse than in South Africa, but treatment is free for all.' She paused. 'Well, if you can pay you go to private wards where the care is better!'

'So there are still differences here between rich and poor?'

'Yes, but not like in other countries. Nyerere cut ministers' salaries and he changes them round every two years to stop corruption. And if you are a civil servant you're not allowed to build your own house and then rent it out.' She laughed. 'But they build them in their children's names!'

We found ourselves doing a lot of walking in Dar. We walked from the hotel to the Ethiopian Airlines, where the staff said they were looking for our suitcase in Nairobi. We walked to the Tourist Office marked on our map to find out about Kilimanjaro and game parks and found it was the East African Community Political Information Office. We walked down the road to a putative bus station which turned out to be a heap of rubble being redeveloped. Finally we trudged back to the hotel, which was burning up our cash. There the phone rang and it was Nobambo. 'I do have a spare room here. Would you like to stay with me while you are in Dar? It is rather small but you can share my kitchen.'

We celebrated this splendid unexpected link in the chain of hospitality with the last of our whisky and a meal in the best restaurant we could find. Next morning Nobambo turned up in the hospital Land Rover to fetch me and our luggage, while Patrick went off to the airport in a last desperate attempt to find the missing suitcase.

Although land was nationally owned, private occupancy was permitted and Nobambo had built herself a bungalow in a new estate just behind Oyster Bay. Set within a strong thorn fence, it was surrounded by bananas and pawpaw trees shading rows of vegetables. There was a large living room and a kitchen off it, two bedrooms and a bathroom. To my initial horror, the spare room had only one 3ft bed in it, but she soon produced a Put-U-Up as well. Cupboard space was limited but then we'd lost half our stuff. 'How am I going to climb Kilimanjaro without my boots?' I moaned.

I shared lunch with Nobambo and her friend, although our agreement was 'separate feeding', and while they snoozed I sat sleepily on the porch, determined to be brave and sensible if I never saw my belongings again – until late in the afternoon a very sweaty blue-shirted figure appeared on the road, carrying the famous lost blue suitcase on his shoulder. Nobambo took one look and hauled cold bottles out of the fridge.

Once restored, Patrick told his second airport story. 'When I got to the airport the freight office had just closed. I explained, I swore, I pleaded and kept on pressing till the senior cargo officer there agreed to release the suitcase if I could produce a customs man. So I went over to the passenger arrival section. The senior customs officer said that it was quite impossible without permission from the commissioner, but suggested I see the chief security officer. As I entered his office he was busy reading the *Dandy* but he listened patiently to my story. First he said no way could a passenger terminal customs man deal with freight. Then he remembered he knew a cargo customs man who lived nearby whom he might be able to fetch in his car. After waiting for about twenty minutes they both returned and we went to the cargo shed and there was the suitcase! No wonder they hadn't identified it – the handle to which the label had been tied had been torn off. They didn't even ask for a tip; I had to call them back to thank them for their great kindness.'

'That's right,' said Nobambo. 'Tipping is considered immoral if not illegal in this country.' We began to feel kindly towards Tanzania.

We stayed at Nobambo's for a week. She was enormously hospitable, but the nights were hot and stuffy and it was hard to sleep under the jury-rigged mosquito nets, even though we'd fixed up an old fan and netted the open window.

I shared the kitchen stove with Luciano, the cook, but although I'd reached Chapter 16 in *Teach Yourself Swahili* we had to communicate with signs and laughter, especially when the local rice defeated my efforts to cook it properly. Buying familiar food was more difficult than in Nigeria; we didn't trust the meat and fish in the market and there were no expatriate stores, though at the local 'supermarket' I found tinned mackerel and pork luncheon meat – from China. But there was an abundance of vegetables and the fruit was gorgeous: pawpaw, passion fruit and mangoes.

Nobambo gave us a preview of South African reality by explaining how she came to be here. 'When I was training as a nurse in South Africa we were all taught together – Black, White, Coloured[21] – and took the same exams. But when they developed the policies of apartheid in the early sixties, they separated us into racial groups and the exams were of different standards. Some of us, both Black and White, set up a committee to oppose this division. It was illegal, of course, and the police searched my house.

'Then we heard that the Tanzanian hospitals were in trouble because so many European nurses left after independence. Julius Nyerere was appealing to all African nurses to come and help. That decided us. About twenty of us, people on the committee and others under political pressure, we hired a bus and left secretly in the middle of the night. We crossed into Botswana and then flew to Dar.

---

[21] Under the South African apartheid system people of mixed race were separated out from Whites, Blacks and Indians and classified as 'Coloureds'. In this book I have used capitals for 'White', 'Black' and 'Coloured' when indicating groups of people artificially kept separate.

'It was the right thing to do. But when my mother died they had to send the letter via London, because the South African police intercept letters addressed to Tanzania. I couldn't go to the funeral, of course, which was terribly sad. When you get to Johannesburg please take a letter to my sister. Letters from here don't reach her.'

The next links in the chain were being forged.

Meanwhile we learnt the local bus routes, browsed in the markets and tried to orient ourselves politically. The obvious place for that was the University of Dar es Salaam, founded at Independence.

Unusually for an African head of state, Nyerere was himself an intellectual. His speeches and writings had been collected in books such as *Socialism and Rural Development* and *Education for Self-reliance,* which we had read in London. He wanted the university to play its part in building the new African Socialism and left-wingers from America and UK found a spiritual home here, along with exiles from Rhodesia and South Africa.

A six-mile bus journey took us out to the new campus of flaring modern buildings set in wide tree-lined avenues where an imposing if elderly English lady (who turned out to be the famous Marxist economist Joan Robinson from Cambridge) directed us to Andrew Coulson's flat. It was a long walk across the campus in the midday sun and we paused in the shade to watch sunbirds drinking nectar from the flowers. Andrew and Judy were completely mystified by the unannounced arrival on their doorstep of two unknown sweaty and sun-scorched *wazungu,* but nevertheless they invited us in and poured cold drinks, until the penny dropped. 'Oh, you're friends of *that* Judith!' Andrew exclaimed. 'Do stay to lunch.' [22]

We shared our sandwiches and Judy produced a huge salad while Andrew told us about *ujamaa* villages. 'The word ujamaa derives from Swahili meaning "familyhood,"' he explained, waving a dictionary in our direction. 'For years Nyerere has had this vision of people living and working cooperatively for the good of all. They would live in a village, farm together, share the work and the produce, build and run cooperative

---

[22] Andrew had been working in Tanzania for eight years, first as an economic planner for the Ministry of Agriculture and then as an economics lecturer. In 1982 he published *Tanzania: a political economy,* a comprehensive survey of the history and development of Tanzania up to 1980. The second edition, with a survey bringing the story up to 2012, has helped me to reconstruct what was happening while we were there.

enterprises, help each other build houses and so on. It derives from a rather idealistic idea of what African communities might have been like before colonialism disrupted them and capitalism encouraged a desire for wealth and consumer goods.'

'Is this a sort of communism?' we wondered.

'No,' said Judy. 'He's not a Marxist. I think he was influenced more by Christian Socialism when studying in the UK. You know they call him "*Mwalimu*", the teacher? He truly believes that the right policies can change people.'

'By 1967,' Andrew went on, 'Nyerere was unhappy that development in the rural areas was allowing the rich peasants to take over more and more land, leaving the rest as landless labourers. So he promulgated the Arusha Declaration, announcing the creation of a socialist state and nationalising the nascent industries. It prioritised agriculture and rural development, curbed privileges and demanded that people work hard for the common good. Villages would be established on ujamaa lines, and "education for self-reliance" would ensure children were prepared for life as socialist farmers, not ambitious clerks.'

By the time we reached coffee, we felt we had a good grasp of Nyerere's vision and its rationale. 'But how is it being implemented?' we asked.

Andrew sighed. 'There are some villages that really are committed to these ideals, but only a few. In other places the government has been bargaining with the peasants: if you move into a village we'll provide famine relief, a school, a shop. But I'm afraid that recently the government has lost patience and announced over a year ago that everyone has got to move into villages.'

They gave us a long list of contacts in Dar, Moshi and Dodoma and wished us luck.

Wanting to know what they taught under the title 'development studies,' I visited Dr Frank Mbengu, a South African exile recommended by a London friend. In an office full of papers on Vietnam, Russia and China he treated us to a lecture on why the Moscow brand of communism was so superior to the Chinese form and therefore why he was opposed to Nyerere's kind of socialism. We sighed: there seemed little agreement. But later, teaching development studies in Lesotho, I would discuss with my students some of the ideas that came out of this theoretical hot-house.

We had been in Dar for a week. The heavy damp heat, the cramped living conditions and the rounds of rather inconclusive meetings made us eager to move on. We discovered long-distance buses which would take us to all the main towns and our plans began to take shape.

Dodoma, where the new capital was being built, sounded interesting. The Coulsons had introduced us to the Anglican minister at St Albans Church in Dar, whose wife had worked with the Church Missionary Society in Dodoma.

'The central area is where most of the villagisation has taken place so far,' she said. 'The Church has reorganised itself to match. Huge numbers of people have moved into new villages from their scattered settlements and the Church has had to follow.'

'Do you think we could learn about the ujamaa villages up there and perhaps visit one?

'Perhaps. Diana Stroud works at the Diocesan Centre; you can contact her and you can probably stay at the Christian Conference Centre.' And that's what we did.

We decided to start in the north, climb Kilimanjaro if we could, spend a little time looking at animals and then head off south to Dodoma before going on still further south to the Iringa plateau, where we had invited ourselves to stay with the Hesters on their Brooke Bond tea plantation.

We planned to be away for about three weeks but in the event it was over a month before we came back to Dar.

CHAPTER 13
Moshi and Kilimanjaro

In which we take a hard day's journey to Moshi and climb
Kilimanjaro.

On Friday 14th February – St Valentine's Day, but Patrick never thought much of pink-hearted cards so as usual I didn't get one – we set off on our first journey by Tanzanian public bus. It left promptly at 6.30 am, our reserved seats were right in the front with a panoramic view out over the landscape and all seemed set fair, even though there was a diversion and we had to go the long way round via Morogoro. What we didn't know was that the bus companies were all subject to import restrictions, so they were short of spare parts, and that they employed few maintenance engineers. In blissful ignorance of problems ahead we tried to interpret the landscape.

At first we travelled through a rolling hilly countryside, green with grass and trees, amongst which were scattered huts with small plots of cultivated ground being made ready for the rains. The huts were mostly built of mud and poles and the roofs were thatched with grass or palm leaves. Some farms had small patches of sisal, or crops of cassava, rice and maize, and there were many mango, cashew and banana trees.

Then we came to a wide flat valley bare of houses and trees. Large herds of cattle were grazing there and many people were working with long-handled hoes, preparing the ground for planting. There was no sign of villages – was this a government farm? If so there was no mechanisation.

As we approached Morogoro, mountains lined the horizon and we passed huge sisal plantations, dating from colonial times but now government-owned. The long straight rows of spiky dark green sisal plants spread far into the distance and near the processing factory racks of sisal fibres were drying in the sun. In several places we saw groups of Maasai, dignified and impressive with their traditional bead collars, ear decorations and copper or silver coloured armbands. Later in the day two young dandified Maasai got on the bus and appeared to find everybody else very amusing.

Morogoro lies on a plateau, surrounded by mountains which rise sharply from the level plain to nearly 7,000 feet right over the town, with dramatic crags and sharp peaks. For lunch we bought hard-boiled eggs and skewers of chicken, freshly grilled over charcoal, and fruit, glad to find roadside vendors as good as in Nigeria.

After we turned north we passed through long stretches of monotonous hilly forest with frequent signs of bush burning; it looked as though large new settlements were being established in virgin country – were these ujamaa villages?

Gradually the going got harder. The sun shone straight into our faces, and the engine casing below our knees became too hot to touch. In spite of the open window the thermometer above the driver read forty degrees Celsius. We must have had one of the oldest British Leyland buses in the entire fleet; the suspension was packing up and the engine noise was horrific. Towards evening the fuel pump gave out and the bus stopped. After two hours stranded in a remote cafe, we were transferred to another bus and travelled on into the darkness. Suddenly the lights failed and the bus ground to a halt, its nose in the bushes. After desperate fiddling the driver brought the lights back on, but the self-starter no longer worked. The passengers pushed the bus back onto the road and down the hill, flinging themselves in as it gathered speed. We reached the Moshi bus station at midnight and hailed a taxi, whose starter didn't work either, but fellow drivers shoved it into life and eventually we reached the sanctuary of the YMCA hostel, at the limits of our endurance.

Through sign language the night watchman understood our plight and found us a comfortable little room on the top floor, with hot showers down the corridor. I boiled up a packet of soup on the wonderful little meths stove and we ate the rest of our hard-boiled eggs before dropping into the first really cool sleep for days.

At six I woke with cramp in my toe and walked over to the still-dark window to ease it. Sure that couldn't be…? A huge massive hump, grey against the black night sky – it was Kibo, the main peak of Kilimanjaro. In the dawn light it brightened, little by little, till the sun came up, the ice-crown glowed a flamingo pink and the sky turned blue behind it. Magic!

After breakfast Kibo had faded from sight, wrapped in its daily scarf of cloud, but now we were determined to conquer it. At the YMCA tours office we met a slim, fair girl speaking excellent English with a faint accent. Her name was Leena Japilla, from Finland, and she was making her second attempt on the mountain but the clerk was being unhelpful.

'These people were not so good when I went last time,' she confided. 'I was very ill and I could not get to the top. But I hear the Marangu Hotel takes more trouble over its clients. I think I will telephone them.'

In an hour it was settled; we were all three booked for a climb starting from the Marangu Hotel some twenty miles away on Monday, and Leena's sister Raija would drive us there. We had forty-eight hours to prepare for the expeditions, buy food, get fit and sort out our clothes. I had boots with me, Patrick only his heavy shoes.

Food was to figure prominently in the experience. 'I'll take fruit,' said Leena. We bought tins of Chinese meat, cheese, packets of rice and soup, eggs, cabbage and boiled sweets. There was no Kendal Mint Cake – just nasty Chinese chocolate. Vaseline for our faces, Anadin for the headaches.

Were we fit enough? We improvised some swimming gear and beat our way solemnly up and down the YMCA swimming pool, hoping this would teach our lungs to cope with the thin air, and then took a long walk out into the countryside.

On arrival at the hotel on Monday morning the Swiss *Frau* in charge inspected our clothing with horror. 'We'll put nails in those shoes for you,' she instructed Patrick. 'And you madam, shorts are no use, we'll lend you thick trousers. You'll all take fur-lined mittens and balaclavas as well as sunhats, walking sticks and a thermos for hot tea. Water bottles will freeze.

'The climb takes five days, three up and two down,' she explained. 'You stay in huts with bunks. The porters will carry bedding and your stores; you may only carry small rucksacks yourself. At the edge of the crater is Gilman's Point, then, if you want, you can carry on to Uhuru Peak which is the summit. Good luck!'

'Well,' Patrick announced. 'Maybe I'll make the second hut. That'll do.'

'I'll just see how far I can get,' I murmured.

Leena said firmly: 'It will be all right if we go *pole pole* – that's Swahili for slowly.'

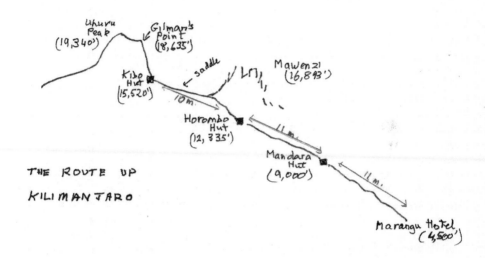

THE ROUTE UP KILIMANJARO
Huts, heights and distances

Day 1: Up the Forest Path

We set off with our guide Mattei and three porters, one of whom, Melchiore, was designated to go to the summit as assistant guide if needed. Streams of people were going to their coffee farms: women in brightly coloured *khangas*[23] and headscarves, carrying hoes or bunches of bananas on their heads; men in shirts and trousers, everyone calling out greetings. Leena, who spoke quite good Swahili, taught us the basic phrases: *jambo*, (hallo) *habari?* (how's things?), *mzuri* (good) and so on.

---

[23] *Khangas* are large pieces of thin, factory-made cotton cloth, printed in bright colours, which served as long skirts, shawls, head coverings and baby-slings. At that time, many women wore khangas printed with party slogans, or with Nyerere's head, to show their loyalty to the party.

After a couple of hot hours on the dusty road we came to the Park Gate and entered the forest, glad of the shade, but the path became ever steeper and rougher. When we stopped by a stream for lunch another would-be mountaineer, whom we christened the Alpinist, gave us a lecture on the inadvisability of eating and drinking on a climb. More of him later.

Other groups on their way down were passing us, some cheerful ones who'd made it, others saying 'tough,' 'terrible,' 'cold.' By the time we reached Mandara Hut at 9,000 feet the sun was sinking and we put on the first layer of sweaters. There was a bar, beer and comfortable double-decker bunkbeds. The guides cooked rice for us and we heated up our tinned stew to put with it; raw cabbage and raisins served as a salad. Sharing our room was the Alpinist – a German called Peter – Paul from Sweden and two Americans: Meale, a tough fifty-eight-year-old, and his godson Scott, aged twenty. After a token wash in the freezing stream, the sun set and we retired to bed by the light of our meths stove while Leena played her recorder.

'I think I might make the Saddle above the second hut,' I prophesied.

Day 2: Through the flames and into the clouds

At 6.30 next morning there was a glowing pink sky with white clouds flowing past *below* us, till the sun rose red over the mountain to light up the forest and meadow in front of the hut. The guides cooked our porridge – few lumps, I noted approvingly over Patrick's glowering face – and we supplemented this with hardboiled eggs.

By 7.45 the kitbags were packed again, hoisted on to the porters' heads and we were off on another steep path, flanked by giant tree heathers. After a couple of hours we reached an extraordinary meadow: above the grasses were giant groundsel, looking like candelabras the size of telegraph poles, and huge ten-foot high lobelia with spikes of blue flowers being visited by flitting sunbirds. Unfortunately, part of it was on fire and dense clouds of smoke blew across the path. Suddenly we got our first clear views of both major peaks: Kibo, rounded, capped with snow, and Mawenzi, a fistful of jagged peaks which are only for rock-climbers.

The air was thinning now and we breathed more deeply. The guides made us halt at regular intervals while cameras clicked, porters smoked and we all told each other to take it *pole pole*. We reached Horambo Hut, ten miles away, in the standard five hours.

Horambo was much more primitive, with tin shacks and two filthy loos. We were now over 12,000 feet and it was much colder. We spent the afternoon acclimatising by walking out along an old lava flow to look at Kibo peeping through the cloud.

'I don't think I'll make the top,' said Patrick.

The other groups comprised three athletic young Germans, two tough Dutch girls, the American pair and another American. Paul the Swede was fit and relaxed. Peter (the Alpinist) arrived long after everyone else, feeling very sorry for himself. These two shared our hut and we found Peter's descriptions of his intestinal problems even more distasteful than his earlier arrogance about alpine eating habits. We were thirteen in all – but for how long?

We spread our foam mattresses on the hard wooden bunks and sorted out our essential stuff: from now on the porters had to carry firewood and water, so all unnecessary weight must be left behind. Our supper didn't somehow taste very good and we both had slight headaches. I couldn't get warm until I put on more socks and the hired warm trousers. Patrick kept waking every now and then with heavy bouts of shivering. We had flashing lights behind our eyelids, the first effects of altitude.

Day 3: 'Pole pole': slowly does it

We woke at 6.30 to another beautiful red sunrise over a sea of milky clouds. The porridge was lumpy this time and Patrick swore that an Irishman shouldn't have to eat such stuff.

The path started steeply up through more scrubby bushes mixed with giant lobelia. We were walking with Paul, as Peter the Alpinist had wisely taken himself and his intestines downhill – the first casualty. At the ominous sign '*Last Water*' the porters filled the containers and on we went.

'This was the day that made me ill,' warned Leena, so we walked as though taking a two-year-old for a stroll, climbing gradually below a long lava cliff on our left, Mawenzi's peaks wreathed in mist above us to the right. The path became stonier and steeper and clouds rolled in behind us. We stopped to eat pineapple while the chattering Dutch girls passed us waving cheerfully.

Suddenly the peaks began clearing and at last we could see Kibo full and clear: the hut twinkling at the foot, then the gigantic wall rising up to the snow cap. And the path! For the first half it twisted among rocky shoulders and then went vertically up a grey scree corridor. With glasses we could see faint zigzags across the scree and the shadow of the Cave Shelter. Near the crest the track disappeared: there was just rock to Gilman's Point.

'I'd like to get to that cave, halfway up,' Patrick enthused.

'That's too ambitious for me,' I replied.

Leena just smiled.

Meanwhile, in front of us stretched the Saddle, a broad featureless expanse between Kibo and Mawenzi, dotted with boulders. This was where we must not hurry, though the path was level and we felt OK. Leena stuck to her toddler's walk. I practised deep breathing, which eased the tight feeling in my forehead. We could see the others strung out along the path, Germans far in the lead, then the USA. Our porters had passed us too. But Mattei patiently followed our snail's pace.

Every hour we stopped for a rest against the warm boulders, drinking tea from Mattei's thermos, eating cheese biscuits (me), cabbage and raisins (Patrick) or mango (Leena). Food became very personal on the mountain. As the path got steeper we halted more often and waited for Paul, who was groggy. At 3.40 we walked up to Kibo Hut – three small buildings and an outhouse.

Our porters had bagged us the best bunks. Others were occupied by the young athletic Germans, all in various stages of nausea and headaches, having done the journey in five hours while we had taken eight. Two of them clearly couldn't go any further.

But we thought we could. We sat drinking tea and staring at the face of Kibo which we would have to climb in the dark. We selected stuff we could cram into our pockets next morning – chocolate, raisins, oranges, boiled sweets – as only the guides would carry rucksacks with thermoses of tea. Then an American produced what we'd yearned for: Kendal Mint Cake, and gave us huge pieces. I took my little camera, the tiny binoculars, dark glasses.

At 5.15 pm the guides brought us supper of soup, crackers and a little cheese. It was so cold that by six we were in bed, wearing five or six layers of clothing, our heads aching. The bunks were hard and no one slept much. With my rucksack as a pillow I felt I was balancing my head on Gilman's Point. Patrick's shivers came back. 'I'm not going further than this bunk,' he whispered.

Day 4: Uhuru Peak or bust

It was a relief to be called at 1 am. We gulped down tea with Anadin for the splitting headaches. The porridge was saltless and even I was defeated. We put on balaclavas, fur mittens and all our anoraks and, following Mattei's lantern, started up the path *pole pole*.

It was starlight and very still. My head cleared and I felt slightly better. We overtook the USA, who were obviously in trouble, and soon Paul turned back too. We reached the loose ash and gravel where for each step you slipped back half the distance and your rhythm was lost. Using the sticks, we hauled ourselves onwards till we reached the shallow Cave Shelter and sat in silence, panting and nibbling Kendal Mint cake. Melchiore tried cracking jokes but no one laughed. The remaining German was there, and the two Dutch girls, but one turned back soon after.

The next stage was hell. I counted the zigzags, struggling for breath in the thin air. Patrick kept calling halts. I needed them too, but Leena was too cold and went on ahead with Mattei. It was getting light. We took it in turns to lead. Behind us the sky got red. At a sitting halt I photographed Mawenzi peaks against an apricot sunrise. The path got narrower and began twisting between the high, grey, gritty rocks. Patrick got his second wind; he was leading a fraction too fast and Melchiore was helpfully pushing me from behind when my breath gave out – this was what I'd dreaded – and I had to sit and pant and pant.

So I went on very slowly, trying to match my breaths with my steps again. The sun had risen behind us. Suddenly, looking up, I could see flags, only 100 yards away. Patrick was above me; we scrambled on and then, as I was hanging onto a rock, feeling sick, a cry of 'Look there.' Ten feet more and I was sitting on the rock in the sun, looking down onto ice-cliffs in the crater. Mattei was holding out a cup of tea, I thrust my camera into the nearest pair of hands and said, 'Take our group.' It was 7.30 and we were at Gilman's Point.

'Shall we go on to Uhuru Peak?' asked Patrick.

Mattei said: 'No, *Mama* is feeling bad.'

I said: 'Yes!' It was too cold to rest for long, so we set off for the Peak.

It was only another mile and a half, an easy ridge walk in the Scottish Highlands, but at 19,000 feet every step was an effort and it took us two hours. First the path led along the inside of the crater rim, looking down on a mound of smoking green ash fringed with fields of spiky ice pinnacles. Then, as we picked our way across a glacier, we saw the great ice-cliffs that hung over the outer edge. Beyond them we looked out over space; there were puffy clouds far below but it was too hazy to see more. Only Mawenzi's peaks stood up solid against the sun, while plumes of smoke from its base reminded us of the bush fire and the world we'd left behind.

We halted frequently, all feeling slightly sick. The lone surviving American, Arnold, was close behind us but the Dutch girl and the German had gone down. The last haul up a gentle but persistent slope almost made me turn back, but Mattei put his arm round my shoulders to urge me on and at last the four of us, plus three guides, arrived at Uhuru Peak, 19,340 feet, at 9.20. We shook hands, took photos and signed the book kept in an old tin.

It was too cold to stay and we started off back along the ridge, our triumph dulled by tiredness, panting at the least slope. The men were both sick, although Leena and I survived —women are said to cope better with altitude, or perhaps photographing ice-cliffs took my mind off the nausea. When we reached Gilman's, Melchiore explained: 'Now you can start running,' and began leaping down the scree. We followed more slowly; I managed a few slides in my boots but Patrick's shoes filled with stones. Even so it took only an hour to get down the slope we had spent six painful hours climbing up.

At Kibo hut we dropped onto the bunks while the ever-caring Mattei made us tea. It was wonderful to be lying down, warm and no longer sick, with bright sunshine all round, but Mattei soon had us up again.

Back across the Saddle we went, laughing and chatting this time. Arnold told us he was fifty-three and had come over from Washington just to climb Kilimanjaro and Mt. Kenya. So we computed that the average age of those who had reached Uhuru Peak was thirty-nine – all the youngsters started far too fast, while we went *pole pole* all the way.

But by the time we reached Horombo Hut we were all slipping and stumbling, with blistered feet and aching muscles; we had been walking for nineteen hours. Patrick had a splitting headache and I was convinced my toe was broken, but even the flashing lights behind our lids couldn't keep us awake.

Day 5: Tip the world, I want to walk up!

The good Frau warned us the last day was the worst and she was right – twenty-two miles downhill showed how unfit we conquerors really were.

We set off at brisk pace over ashy, burnt and devastated meadow, for in the last two days the bush fire had swept right across the mountain and the giant groundsels were blackened stumps. Downwards, always downwards, would the path never flatten out? Our legs ached and our toes were bruised from the bumping. After a brief stop at Mandara Hut – which was full of firefighters – the guides urged us onward. The path was rougher than we remembered it and we were reduced to hobbling over the rocks almost as slowly as we came up, sweating in the heat again. At the park gate it was our turn to give good advice to all the clean, healthy groups on their way up as they stared at our red-faces, blistered noses and grimy clothes.

Even the road, dipping steeply downhill, was torture to our sore feet, till a lorry lifted us along for about a mile. Tottering and exhausted, we paused to buy mangoes to quench our thirst and eventually reached the hotel after eight hours of solid downhill. We checked in our gear, bought beer all round and took leave of our wonderful porters, who had made it possible for us. Mattei told us he was sixty-nine and then went off home – running! – to do the whole thing again next day.

There was one final stage: to get back to Moshi. We sat under the banana trees beside the road, hardly able to move, waiting for the bus which didn't come. A taxi demanded an exorbitant fee. Should we book into the hotel? Patrick ate the last of the cabbage. We were almost at the end of our tether.

When the bus arrived it was so full we had to stand on our tortured feet in the aisle, clinging on in agony till it deposited us back at the YMCA, to clean clothes, hot showers and soft beds. We could see a storm out over the plain and Kibo was hidden in menacing clouds. Other people were up there, lying on bunks with headaches and all their clothes on. We were drinking whisky, celebrating with Leena over the best meal the canteen could offer, and telling each other, 'I never want to walk another step.'

CHAPTER 14
Arusha and the Tourist Trail

In which we look for handicrafts and, after a diversion into self-reliant education, actually see some animals. The countryside is baffling but the Christians are welcoming.

'Happy birthday, Patrick!' I said next morning, congratulating myself on having remembered.

'Forget it. I feel eighty-nine rather than thirty-nine,' he muttered into the pillows.

I put one blistered foot to the floor, trying to stand upright. Even my hands were cramped from the sticks and it took ages to make coffee. Every step was agony as we crept down the stairs. However, after another grumpy breakfast – this time there wasn't any bread so even Patrick had to eat porridge – we felt able to stagger down into the town and sit in the Kibo Coffee Hut watching the world go by.

Under the brilliant sun Moshi was neat and colourful. At one end of the single long shopping street stood a blindingly white mosque, with an equally glaring Hindu temple at the other. Arabs and Indians pioneered trade into the interior – first for slaves and then for skins, ivory and other produce and now their descendants still run most of the commercial life, mistrusted by locals but tolerated by the government. An Indian greeted us and we limped over to sit with him.

'Life is very uncertain for us. There is a new edict every day,' he complained. 'Why should I, a businessman, have to farm? And I don't like the education system for my children – they spend too much time on gardening and too little on academic subjects.' We had the feeling he might not stay around for long in the new Tanzania.

We spent the afternoon trying to get Kilimanjaro grime out of our clothes and I had a final swim; Patrick's toes were black and blue from the climb and not for public display. We had both lost several pounds in weight. Next morning, still limping, we took the bus to Arusha.

'Psst – you got dollar?'

'Spears, sir? A necklace for you, madam?'

Arusha was full of tourist stalls and itinerant peddlers thrusting long knives and other nonsense at us. Maasai strolled by in flowing cloaks and bangles and Chagga women bustled around in bright orange or yellow headscarves. It was supposedly a growth point, with the headquarters of the East African community and an industrial area down by the railway, but the centre of the town with its little Indian shops seemed run-down and dowdy.

We stayed at the YMCA while pursuing our two objectives in Arusha: one was to follow up contacts for Project Hand, the London charity for marketing African crafts, and the other was to organise a quiet couple of days in one of the game parks. In neither were we fully successful.

Harry Adams, our Project Hand contact, was a short, talkative and energetic character, originally from London's East End. There he fell in love with a visiting Chagga lady and followed her out to Tanzania where they'd been married for twenty years.

'Chaggas are business-minded,' he confirmed. 'More Jewish than the Jews – I can say that, I'm one myself! And they are wonderful people at home, so clean and tidy. When they were in London, my wife and her friend wanted a bath every day and their landlady said: "What for?" No, there's not a lot of corruption, but the government officials are pretty incompetent.'

He took us to a batik shop with wonderful wall hangings. I bought one but the owner was not interested in exporting them. Then he introduced us to Ali Sherriff, tall, dark-skinned and a born entrepreneur. His family used to sell seeds to farmers but, when that was taken over by the government marketing boards, he turned to cottage industries: pottery, weaving, wooden toys and coconut shell trinkets.

'Importing is so restricted that I have to make everything myself,' he explained. 'I made my own mills for grinding the clays and I'm experimenting with new glazes. I send apprentices to India to study pottery and I'm building kilns in the villages.'

The designs were not particularly original and the finishes not always perfect but his drive, energy and skills were highly impressive. It seemed a shame the government did nothing to support these initiatives which, as tourism increased, would bring at least some income into the rural areas.

Of course most tourists come to Tanzania to see wild animals and we did eventually go to a game park. Not one of the big, famous reserves, which would have taken a lot of time and money, but to a small, beautiful local one, Mt. Meru; not a dramatic self-drive safari as we'd first planned, but a day's expedition with Thomas in an ancient Toyota. He was very knowledgeable, with fluent English, but we were difficult clients with unusual priorities.

'I hope you will see elephant, giraffe and rhino,' he explained as we drove out of town. But I was pointing at a long row of children flailing with hoes in a nearby field.

'Please stop,' I cried.

'Madam, we are not yet at the park!'

'But this is important. Will you interpret for me if I talk to the children?'

With Thomas's help we introduced ourselves to the teachers, who spoke good English, and I explained I wanted to find out about modern Africa. They seemed pleased and after a chat I asked if I might photograph the children. They were digging a ditch to carry off surplus water when the rains came and laughed delightedly when we tried a few hacks with the *jembes* (hoes); the ground was very hard. We'd just read in the local paper that the country was importing three million hoes – and now we knew what they felt like to use.

It was officially a primary school but many of the 300 children were into their early teens, having started late. I bought a little wooden figure from their carving workshop while the headmaster explained how they were trying to implement 'education for self-reliance'.

'We cultivated the field first with the hired tractor; the children will help by weeding and harvesting the maize. This is our staple food; we make it into porridge. The surplus we will sell to buy paper and books. We are trying to be self-sufficient, like Mwalimu says.'

This visit cut three-quarters of an hour off our park tour, but then we'd come to Africa to meet people rather than to see animals.

Mt Meru is an old volcano that blew out its eastern side some millions of years ago; the park stretches up into the dramatic crescent of the big crater that is left and includes swamps and woodland around a chain of lakes – a perfect habitat for interesting birds and beasts.

As we entered, a giraffe loped gently away. Thomas pointed out waterbuck and warthog then stopped the car saying excitedly, 'Colobus monkey.' Way up in a tall tree a white face surrounded by long white and black hair peered at us. As Kipling said: 'Brother thy tail hangs down behind!' and so it did, like a long thick white bell-pull. Nearby was a whole family – big, beautiful animals with thick, shaggy, black and white coats.

'There will be big game at the crater lakes,' he promised.

'Thomas, actually we are interested in birds. Could you show us those too?'

'Of course, sir.' He stopped the car. 'Look up there.' Big eagles and hawks were soaring overhead – all totally unidentifiable, of course.

Round the lakes there were buffalo grazing. We saw a lot of waterbuck, about the size of red deer with grey coats, white rings on the rump, big ears and slightly curved horns; bushbuck, much redder and smaller, and a tiny dik-dik. Then a party of hippo heaved themselves out of their glorious mud beds and lumbered into the water, sinking again until we could see only their eyes.

As we rounded the next corner, it looked as though pink rose petals had fallen on the water and drifted in masses along the shores; these were the flamingos. As the car came close they set up a murmuring, beginning to walk away, before the outer ones strode across the water and took off, followed by the next wave till the whole flock had lifted into the air. Every bay of the lake had its flamingos and I photographed my fill until the sun went in. By the time we stopped for lunch in a hide the rain was sweeping across the bleak landscape and Mt Meru was half hidden by cloud. We could have been picnicking in a Scottish bothy. Not a typical African safari but it made us feel at home, particularly when the radiator boiled over and we had to help fill it from a puddle with our picnic mugs.

Thomas patiently stopped the car every time we saw a new bird, though only the bee-eaters with their gorgeous colours elicited any interest from him. In the end he found us half a dozen elephants as well as zebra and lots more gorgeous giraffes with babies, so honour was satisfied on both sides.

Back at the YMCA in Arusha we felt everything had 'turned out for the best', as Aunt Mary would have said. Our guide had helped us see fourteen different kinds of animals and more than thirty different species of birds, many of them new to us, and we didn't have to drive ourselves on those terrible forest tracks. In addition we'd been into a school and looked at 'self-reliance' in practice. Whether this practice could help increase food production or change children's attitudes to farming would be a question for another day.

After a long wrestle with the cork – neither we nor the bar had a corkscrew – we had a very drinkable bottle of Dodoma red wine to celebrate but alas! the shortages had reached the main menu. There were no 'bananas and meat' (local speciality) and no 'crams' for the 'cramed' steak (fried *Schnitzel*), so we settled for the excellent fillet and liver.

Next morning as we shopped for picnic supplies and postcards the air felt quite different, cool and moist, smelling of damp earth and wet pavements. The rains had come at last, so that crops could be planted and the farming cycle move on. And how lucky for us that we had climbed the great mountain before fresh snow made Kibo peak impassable! We turned our faces southwards and prepared for Dodoma.

This was our earliest start yet: we got up at 4.15 am in order to queue for tickets for the 6 am bus. The night watchman fetched us hot coffee with bread and marge and the taxi arrived promptly at five. The ticket queue at the railway station was very orderly and we got 'superior' class, with headrests and more room for Patrick's long legs. As the luggage was being loaded we watched the full moon fade in the dawn light and heard the sound of the muezzin calling the faithful to prayer. It seemed an auspicious beginning and we looked forward to arriving in Dodoma at about 4 pm. Unfortunately, that was not to be.

It was a particularly frustrating journey in many ways. Imprisoned in the bus with no one to ask we watched great tantalising chunks of the country roll past, mysterious and unexplained. Those large tractor-cultivated fields outside Arusha, were they government farms? Far across the brown dry grassy plains, could those be Maasai villages, with square huts and large cattle enclosures? We'd been told in Arusha how their grazing lands were being restricted and how over-grazing was destroying the soil. We wondered how they fitted into Nyerere's – or anyone else's – policies of rural development.

Beyond the plains the land rose into green well-watered hills where the maize was already showing cobs. That new settlement, all tidily laid out, was that a real ujamaa village? In the centre, under poles carrying the national and party flags, a meeting seemed to be in progress. Political lectures or community discussions?

The sun got hotter as we climbed through the mountains and we nodded off. Suddenly we woke up; an overturned lorry had blocked the road in the middle of a bridge. Undaunted, the driver took a detour, crossed the river at a ford and brought us into Kondoa, a smart clean little town dating from German colonial times. Here we bought hard-boiled eggs, chapattis and oranges before leaping back on the bus.

However, we needn't have hurried, as this bus too had broken down; perhaps crossing the ford had been too much for it. An hour went by and then another. Would we have to spend the night here? Eventually another mechanic arrived and by five o'clock we were under way.

We finally reached Dodoma at 8.40 pm, a journey of 270 miles that had taken fourteen hours. The Christian Conference Centre was, mercifully, still open and they gave us a perfect room, plain and puritan, with our own shower. Once more we cooked up soup on the little stove to go with our remaining bread, cheese and raisins, and fell into our beds dreaming of muddy roads and overturned buses.

The CCC clearly believed in plain living and high thinking. Breakfast was self-service and we ate at a common table. My neighbour watched me putting salt on my maize-meal porridge. 'Even that won't make it taste like oatmeal,' he commented. 'Are you from Scotland? I'm Sandy Maver, by the way. I do the books for the Church offices in Dar, but I'm up here for two months teaching elementary book-keeping for the diocesan clerks.' Patrick was delighted to find a fellow accountant and we exchanged experiences.

After breakfast Patrick went off to persuade the bank that he had arranged credit facilities in Dodoma – it took him one and a half hours plus an interview with the accountant before they found his letter – while I went to see Diana Stroud, the diocesan administrator, whose name we were given in Dar. She was clearly a busy lady and hardly had we begun when the radio telephone came on.

'It's Mvumi Hospital, Theo Kitchen here. I want to talk to you about...' I realised that Andrew Coulson had told us to contact Theo so, when Diana finished, I borrowed the phone and asked him if we might visit the hospital, where he was the medical superintendent.

'Certainly, come out today and stay over the weekend. You can take the nurses' bus. It leaves in an hour.'

I fetched Patrick from the bank; we threw things into the rucksack and, with seconds to spare, joined a group of giggling nurses on the hospital bus.

CHAPTER 15
Mvumi and Dodoma

In which we move in Christian circles around hospitals and schools and find a depressing village.

Mvumi lay some 30km west of Dodoma in a huge shallow bowl painted in primary colours; the earth was red, with bright green trees sprinkled across it, and blue wooded hills peeked up in the distance. Clouds rolled over the plain bringing darker shadows and occasional showers. The air was damp and we found it pleasantly fresh, but the two shy young nurses who took us to the Kitchens' house assured us: 'It is very cold today.'

'You are welcome,' said Liz Kitchen quietly. 'Which church are you from?'

'Er, well, we met Father Watson at St. Albans in Dar,' I began, haltingly, explaining our trip.

'Sit here, lunch is ready. Lord, bless this food and all who share in it.'

Conversation was stilted until Patrick began quizzing Theo about the hospital, how it worked and how it was financed.

'The hospital is run by the Anglican Diocese of Central Tanganyika to serve the people of Dodoma Rural District,' Theo explained enthusiastically. 'We have a full operating theatre and a specialist eye unit. We are a teaching hospital; we train nurses, lab assistants and all grades of medical auxiliaries who can supplement the doctors. We make small charges for all treatment but it doesn't cover the costs. The government pays local staff and makes grants for each student; our expatriate staff are paid by their sponsoring bodies, usually one of the missionary societies.' His vision for the future, he told us, was to staff clinics in each village with a midwife, a dispenser and a medical worker.

Of course at this time we had no idea that ten years later Patrick would be reorganising the finances of a similar mission hospital in Morija, Lesotho, and discussing very similar visions.

Theo took us past long, low, white-washed buildings with shady verandas, set in the shade of tall evergreen trees and surrounded by red, well-swept, sandy ground. White-overalled nurses moved between buildings and a woman plodded round to the kitchen with a load of firewood on her head. Somewhere a radio was playing Tanzanian pop music with a low insistent beat. A few women, wrapped in several layers of colourful khangas, were sitting out on the veranda, suckling babies or feeding small children out of bowls.

'It's the quiet season now; it's the lean time of year when people have little money to pay doctors. That's our mother and child unit, where we take in malnourished children and try to show the mothers how to cook more nourishing food. This is one of the poorest parts of the country and this is the second year that the rains have failed, so there is much malnutrition, especially among the very old and the very young.'

The village spread out haphazardly on a gentle slope leading down to the river. Sandy paths criss-crossed between the houses, which were mostly of poles plastered with mud, under flat thatched roofs. Patches of maize grew here and there but the plants were small, yellow and weak. Towards one end of the settlement the houses were bigger, faced with concrete and roofed with tin; here was a large white rectangular building with a flag flying over it.

'That's the TANU[24] administrative building.'

'Oh, so this is an ujamaa village?' Had we found one at last?

'No, not really,' replied Theo. 'They just brought people from four old villages, so we've got about 10,000 people here, mostly from the Gogo tribe. They elect a chairman and committee annually, who organise the communal services: the borehole water, the shop, the distribution of famine relief. But the Party is really in charge. They send us a ward executive officer who reports up the line, eventually to the president himself, I suppose.'

---

[24] Office of the Tanzania African National Union, the only party allowed.

An air of depression hung over the whole village. Nearby a few men were drinking at the 'hotel' – just a bar really – and some women were sitting outside a small shop furnished with only a few tins of food, matches, bars of soap and brooms.

'There used to be several shops,' said Theo, 'but they were closed down so as not to compete with the "cooperative" one. But it's badly run, as you can see, and there was financial mismanagement. There isn't even any flour and that's bad, because there is famine here.'

'Doesn't the government help?'

'They're importing grain, I believe, but the retail system just doesn't work and famine relief isn't always as fairly distributed as it should be. These old men here, they say they're not allowed to drink *pombe* – that's the local sorghum beer – except at weekends, because of the grain shortage, and they can't afford bottled beer. Of course they blame the government for disturbing their drinking habits!'

We thought of Nigeria: the ubiquitous hawkers and roadside markets, the private lorries and mammy wagons carrying people and goods all over the country. That was one aspect of free market capitalism that worked and was efficient. The flip side was that Nigeria had a lot of rich men in Mercedes and beggars on the streets; Tanzania had neither.

In the evening we sat round the dinner table with the Kitchens and an Australian couple, Bob and Jane, and asked them tentatively what they really thought of African socialism.

'I think they are right to focus on rural development,' replied Bob. 'And you can't provide schools and clinics so well if people are scattered all over the countryside.'

'But if that's their tradition, if people like prefer to live in small groups near to their fields and their cattle, how can you justify using force to move them?' asked Patrick.

Jane suggested it was just for one generation. 'Their children will grow up in a village and accept it as normal. Within a generation society will have changed.'

'Only if their new life is demonstrably better than their old,' retorted Theo. 'And that isn't true here. The land isn't suitable for intensive agriculture.'

Next day being Sunday we dutifully accompanied Liz to the Swahili service in the small stone church. She translated the main points of the sermon, which seemed to be about helping your neighbour, a maxim embraced by both socialism and Christianity.

'Nyerere's writings are so idealistic,' I reflected. 'How far is he, as a politician, aware of how difficult it is to implement those fine ideas?'

'He spends much time touring the country,' replied Theo. 'He does talk informally to people, including those who protest, so we have to assume he knows something of the hardships involved.'

'The trouble is,' said Liz thoughtfully, 'he is trying to change human nature through political means. People are naturally selfish and they'll always work for their own advantage. You need a religious belief that transcends the human. You know,' she told us, pleased with the evidence, 'in last year's famine the only people who really looked after the poor were the Christians, not the Party members!'

Theo took us to visit his houseboy's family. The parents lived in a traditional house, a long low building, divided into three rooms with walls of mud brick and a flat roof of poles and mud. We stooped to enter the reception room, shared at night with the goats. Next was the kitchen, where a woman was grinding maize on a stone while smoke trickled out of the one tiny window as there was no chimney. 'Terribly bad for chests,' muttered Theo. The only furniture was a stool; they slept on mats on the floor; on the walls hung a bow and sheaf of arrows with fearsome iron points. 'I use them to chase the hyenas away from my animals,' explained the old man.

The son's more modern house, built of blocks with a sloping iron roof, was furnished with a table, chairs and a bed, while the cement walls were decorated with old calendars, pictures and woven baskets. Inside the door stood his bicycle, of which he was very proud. The family posed for a group photograph and then the host escorted us a little way along the path as was the polite custom here.

'The peasants of Ireland were living much like this when famine struck,' mused Patrick. 'But they had an escape route over the sea. There is no such magic road here.'

Mvumi was a depressing place. How could you build the New Jerusalem

143

here, against the harsh realities of unproductive land and insufficient rainfall, for people who had been traditionally pastoralists and shifting cultivators and who didn't share your dream?

On Monday we took an early bus back to Dodoma. The urge to build a new capital after independence was understandable and Dodoma was well-placed at the country's heart, but right now it looked nothing like a capital city. There was one main street, full of potholes which merged at intervals into building sites, and so far only a couple of government offices had moved up here. The small scruffy market also served as the bus depot; apart from that there were a couple of shops stocked with tinned foods, whisky and other essentials of expatriate life, some Asian stores and a 'cooperative' which had the monopoly of selling flour, rice and sugar. The party headquarters of TANU had appropriated the old colonial offices across the road from a modern bank; they glared at each other like the rival systems they symbolised.

As the Conference Centre was now full we booked ourselves into the only hotel, a blend of German colonial and British Rail styles, with comfortable netted beds and huge baths. I seemed to hear a turbaned servant sliding up muttering, '*Chota peg, memsahib?*' but it was only Patrick offering me a dram of the locally blended whisky – surprisingly good.

Now we began our search for the elusive ujamaa village in earnest. We marched up the steps of the TANU office and asked to see the area commissioner. To our surprise we were shown straight in.

'Welcome,' he said, shaking hands. 'How can I help?'

We summarised our trip. 'We are very interested in Nyerere's philosophy of African Socialism. We would like to visit an ujamaa village, so we can understand more fully how it is being implemented. If we could go with a TANU official, maybe he could explain the policy to us?'

'Of course, that should be no problem. I'll just telephone the prime minister's office, down the road.'

After a few minutes he returned shaking his head. 'I'm sorry. It seems that British visitors have to apply at the High Commission in Dar for permission to visit a village.' He seemed so friendly that we asked him to explain more about TANU.

'I am the District Secretary of the Party, as well as Area Commissioner.

Dar es Salaam.

Village with old huts and a new cement house.

Giant heather, with Kibo peak in the distance.

The Stuarts dressed for climbing Kilimanjaro.

Kibo seen from across the Saddle.

Leena and the guides at Gilman's Point.

Ice cliffs, looking out over space and bush fires far below.

Walking along the crater edge, Mawenzi peak in the background.

The group at Uhuru summit.

Giraffe at Mt Meru Park.

Flamingoes flying along the shore of the lake.

Mvumi Village.

A family at Mvumi.

Igowole Village.

Mr Thawe (*centre*) and his family.

Shambas on the slopes of the Uluguru Mountains.

A *ngoma* at Shangazi's.

Mothers dressed in *khangas* at Bikwa Clinic.

Mother and baby at the clinic.

Schoolgirls hoeing their *shamba*.

This is to ensure that the policies being carried out reflect those of the Party. TANU is the most important organisation in Tanzania and it is the true representative of the people. We devise the policies, Parliament puts them into legal form and the government carries them out. A new law will soon be passed, amending the constitution so that TANU becomes the supreme power in the country.'

'What about Parliament? Are other parties allowed there?'

'No, all MPs have to be party members. But several members may contest a seat. And even ministers may be unseated.'

Cogitating over this apparent combination of democracy with party dictatorship, we went shopping. There still wasn't any bread so we bought some more whisky and a bottle of red wine, just in case Sandy and Diana, the two good Christians we'd invited to supper, were drinkers too.

The supper went well. After days of frugal living we enjoyed our five courses: soup, prawns in a very hot sauce, slightly tough lamb, jelly, excellent crumbly cheddar (imported from Kenya) and poor coffee (grown up the road, why so bad?). The bottle of *Chateau Bihawana* was perhaps a little sweet, but Diana relaxed under its influence and even teetotal Sandy entered energetically into the conversation.

'What did you think of Mvumi?' Diana asked.

'Depressing,' answered Patrick. 'They have just forced people to move into a village by offering famine relief and now they are trying to indoctrinate them to work for the common good. How long will they have to renounce personal freedom while they're learning to love the community above themselves?'

Loyal to Nyerere, I suggested the party was trying to build on the sense of communal duty found in traditional society.

'That's a myth,' said Sandy firmly. 'A kinship group, or perhaps a hamlet, might care for its own, but how can you transfer that kind of loyalty to the nation or even to a township of 10,000 people?'

'Well,' replied Diana, 'in Victorian England you had lots of philanthropists who worried about the poor and set up orphanages and hospitals.' I didn't somehow feel this was a good comparison.

After supper Sandy offered us hospitality in return. 'My flat at the Conference Centre has a spare annex. You're welcome to use it for the rest of your stay.'

This was perfect. With two iron beds, two desks and a little scullery in which we set up our stove, we had all we needed – and no rent! If we wanted we could eat in the canteen. And that was where we found our next clue to ujamaa villages.

The tall, burly African sitting opposite us at lunch was shrouded in a heavy sweater and we exchanged remarks about feeling cold. He introduced himself as Emil Ndonde and told us he was doing an external degree at the London School of Economics. I shared my experience of studying economics there and then found out he was working at the TANU office, with special responsibility for ujamaa villages. Was this another chance? Cautiously, I asked him about his work.

'Sadly, people in Central Region aren't so politically aware. Where I used to work in the south, the village people themselves often took the initiative and those villages are working well. Here most of the villages are 'villages of settlement', not ujamaa villages.'

'Please, can you explain the difference?'

'In the settlement villages there isn't any change in economic or political organisation. People just go on cultivating their own fields and they don't work together to change anything. They don't feel part of the nation. In ujamaa villages we set up communal activities and we try to make them feel part of something bigger. Members of the local committee go off to regional meetings, for example, or for training.'

'Could you get us permission to visit a good ujamaa village?'

He shook his head. 'I'm sorry, I don't think so. There are a lot of regulations about foreigners visiting because often they are very critical.'

So instead of ujamaa we followed up the other slogan: *education for self-reliance*. Through Diana we met a couple of British teachers working in local secondary schools who were happy to show us round.

At Msalato Girls' Secondary all the girls had assembled for marching practice, with heavy sticks as make-believe rifles. 'If they complete Sixth Form they will have military training during five months national service,' said the British volunteer showing us round.

'When I was at school,' Patrick reminisced, 'we had to drill twice a week with a real rifle!' I don't think the volunteer believed him.

All pupils were also supposed to learn practical agriculture but the school *shamba* (garden) at Msalato demonstrated just how hard it was to combine study and farming in a semi-desert land. The maize they planted before Christmas had died in the drought and the next planting was looking very feeble. So they had carefully planted a field of vines and every girl carried water to her vine each day. Perhaps their successors would be harvesting grapes, but it seemed unlikely and the expatriate teachers thought the time would be better spent studying. Though primary school numbers were rising fast – perhaps three-quarters of the age group – less than 1% were getting to A levels. Where would the future professional cadres come from?

In Sandy's flat we had time to write up the diary, read a book of papers on Tanzanian Socialism and rest for a while. We had managed to telephone through to the Hesters who were expecting us at the end of the week. In a way, it was a relief to be leaving the mission circuit; they had been enormously friendly and helpful, but we did have to take our *chota pegs* surreptitiously. And the canteen still didn't serve decent porridge for breakfast.

CHAPTER 16
Mufindi

In which we find an ujamaa village nestled up against a capitalist enclave.

Mufindi was a lucky shot in the dark. Patrick had a tenuous introduction to a Mr Hester, chairman of the Brooke Bond Tea Company in Mufindi; I thought it sounded interesting and from Dar wrote off to the Hesters asking if we might visit in early March. We then left for the north. A friendly reply reached us in Dar c/o Jentsches; when we phoned them from Dodoma, Karola read it out to us. We rang Mrs Hester directly and, amazingly, the dates fitted.

'It'll take you two days by bus,' she said. 'Best stay overnight at Cat Lodge in Iringa and take the morning bus to Mufindi where we'll meet you.'

On Friday morning we were up at 5.30 and even then we got the last two tickets for the 8 am bus. We shared a three-person seat with a nursing tutor who was going home to Mbeya, in the far south, for her two weeks' leave; the journey would take her three days but she couldn't afford to fly. She was delightful, but large, and Patrick had to perch on the edge of the seat for most of the time.

Apart from that the journey was uneventful. Around midday we finally confronted the mountains which had been lying close on our right-hand side for much of the journey and climbed onto a plateau where scattered huts gave way to more planned villages, this time with well-grown fields of maize and tobacco. We arrived in Iringa in a soft Scottish drizzle.

Cat Lodge was decidedly European in atmosphere. The bar served many kinds of beer and sandwiches to the sound of Bavarian drinking songs, for

Iringa was an old German colonial base. We were to find more traces of German occupation soon.

Next morning we had a smooth bus ride along the road known – before it was tarmacked – as the 'Hell Run', built with international aid to bring copper out of Zambia after Southern Rhodesia declared independence. First there were rolling plains with cattle and homesteads thatched neatly with the local grass, but soon we were moving ever upwards into great green forests with mist blowing through the treetops.

At Mufindi we were met by the company car and – unkempt, travel-stained, with battered luggage and bursting bags, Patrick sprouting a half-grown beard since Kilimanjaro – we were wafted up to a huge rambling bungalow set in an English garden. In the sitting room there was a great log fire to take the chill out of the air. Mrs Hester, a warm, friendly and energetic woman, whose slightly scatty manner belied her organising ability, was politely oblivious to our appearance and ushered us into the 'chairman's guests wing', as it said on the key tags, and into luxury that we had become totally unaccustomed to. There were big comfortable beds with bedside lights, masses of hanging space, carpets on parquet floors, a writing desk, a dressing table and our own bathroom and loo, with lashings of hot water.

The Hesters seemed genuinely interested in our quest. June Hester turned out to have a social science degree and was hoping for a work permit so she could become the company's social worker. 'When we first came out here,' she reminisced, 'the expatriates lived their lives quite remote from the Africans. Frankly, there weren't many people to talk to. But now with education and Africanisation of our management it's much easier. I started a sewing circle with the wives and I'm now secretary of the parish council because our company church has become open to the whole community. I meet all sorts of people there.'

There was also quite a variety of people at the Mufindi Club where they took us for drinks, supper and the weekly film, which happened to be *Blue Max*, about a German flyer in World War I. Was it chosen because of the old German connections? We found ourselves talking to an elderly German who told us how he started a coffee farm here in 1926, lost it when the British interned him during the war and started again with tea.

Now he wanted to sell up and retire to Germany but no one would buy land that might soon be nationalised.

Mr Hester thought it tactful to introduce us to the area development officer, who was also the senior TANU representative and doubtless keeping an eye on all strangers. After chatting politely for a few minutes, I asked him about visiting an ujamaa village. 'Oh, you'll need permission from Dar for that,' he replied and moved away.

On Sunday morning Mrs Hester cajoled us into coming to church by saying we might meet some local people. After the Swahili service, which was even more difficult to follow than the Mvumi one, she introduced us to a tall, dignified, grey-haired man, Mr Thawe, TANU district chairman.

When we explained our quest he immediately responded: 'Well, I live in an ujamaa village! You must come and see it.'

At last! But after last night's forbidding diktat we felt in a quandary. 'We would like to, but we don't have permission from Dar. We don't want to make trouble for anyone.'

'That's all right,' said Mrs Hester decisively. 'They will be visiting you personally, won't they?' We were invited for tea the following afternoon.

The Sunday rituals included lunch-time drinks at the Club. There were plenty of golf-playing expatriates – Mufindi had a splendid golf course – but we also got talking to an African tea-factory manager who had been with the company for twenty years. What did he think of the new regime?

'The problem really is education,' he said. 'I want my son to go further than I have but only two or three from our village school can go on to secondary education. So I'm paying for him to go to a private school in Iringa. He'll maybe get to university that way.'

The deputy manager, a younger bouncy man, nodded in agreement. 'I was ill in secondary school and missed university. I'm trying hard to catch up now and earn enough money so I can give my children a good start.'

We didn't think either of them was much concerned with building a socialist society. They had found their own way upwards out of poverty and it was natural enough that they wanted their children to go further.

But how had this island of capitalism managed to survive? After the Arusha Declaration the 'commanding heights' of the economy were nationalised, but not smaller companies like Brooke Bond. They were allowed to go on as private firms, earning precious foreign exchange for the country, under certain conditions, including paying taxes, speeding up the Africanisation of management and respecting the government's policies.

'For example,' explained Mr Hester, 'we have to ensure that every worker has a *shamba*[25] to grow his own food and time to work on it. We negotiate with the Ministry over wages; our workers get the national minimum along with free housing, water and wood. Of course, there's also a TANU committee on the estate but they are actually quite useful to us in dealing with political problems.'

We were driven around a bit of the vast plantation which covered hundreds of acres. Tea bushes are grown in dense rows and kept at waist height so that they look like flat, green tables, separated at intervals by shelter belts of taller trees. The pickers, wearing bright yellow oilskins against the rain and wet bushes, moved swiftly along, nipping off just the bud and first two leaves before throwing them into their sacks. When I got out my camera Mrs Hester hesitated.

'Please be careful that you choose a well-dressed woman. There was a bad press report about Brooke Bond workers in South Africa. I know that we look after our people quite well but I don't want a torn skirt being construed as poor labour conditions! Our political position here is sensitive enough.'

On Monday Mrs Hester took us to Igwole village to visit Mr Thawe. Was this the real thing? It looked much more prosperous than most we'd seen, with neat brick houses set around a central area.

Mr Thawe showed us round and explained how the system worked. Every ten houses formed a 'cell' that elected a leader to represent them on the village committee; these leaders then transmitted party directives back again. Mr Thawe had been elected to the post of district chairman by all the 300 or so 'ten-cell leaders' in the five neighbouring villages. He was responsible for 'political education' and spent much time visiting the committees and discussing party policies.

---

[25] A *shamba* is a farm or garden. In keeping with the doctrine of self-reliance, all workers, including those in towns, were supposed to have access to a piece of land where they would grow their own food.

We stopped at the school, which held 325 children and seven teachers. Nearby villagers were building a brick house for a new teacher. Patrick asked one of the older staff how he felt about the changes.

'They are good,' the man replied. 'People like living together. The best thing is that we have a good clean water supply. All the children can go to school and older people come as well, to learn to read and write.'

We wondered if this was just the party line but Mrs Hester thought the women definitely gained from the mutual help and company provided by the village. 'The clinic has a nurse/midwife, a dispenser and a dresser. They really appreciate that. I've just found out that they are starting a pre-school group in response to a directive from the centre. When I get my work permit, that's one of the things I'll focus on for our employees.'

At Mr Thawe's home we met his wife, a quiet, dignified lady in a green and gold outfit and a bright headscarf, who offered us tea and slices of omelette.

I told Mr Thawe I was writing a book about African development for schools. 'Could you please tell me what are the most important things British schoolchildren should know about Tanzania?'

He paused, and then began: 'We are trying to build a society of equals so that all shall have equal freedom. We do not want a society in which a few will be at the top of Kilimanjaro while most are down at sea level. We know that people have different capacities and talents but we wish to ensure that all have the opportunity to get a fair share of the country's wealth through hard work. The ujamaa village will make sure that everyone can have a house, some land and a role to play in the community, provided that they are prepared to work. As long as we have enough land, we can give everyone security.

'We don't try to give everyone equal shares, just the equal opportunity to prosper by hard work. If you cultivate with your family one acre rather than half an acre, your family benefits; if you work twice as many days as somebody else on the communal farm you get twice as big a share of the produce. That is our idea of fairness!' he concluded.

Patrick asked whether there was any opposition to these ideas and Mr Thawe admitted some people did dislike the system. 'Those that had large farms lost them. We have gone back to the traditional African system of "right to use", not "right to own" land. We have a large communal area here; we have tractors and harvesters. We grow maize and potatoes for food, and wheat and pyrethrum for sale. The produce and the profit are divided up between the workers proportionate to their input. Some of the cash is set aside for investment.

'Of course the output varies from year to year, the weather perhaps, or just stupidity! In some years people elect a good committee and do well, in others they elect a bad one and do worse. We in TANU don't interfere; people must learn from their mistakes.'

We could have been talking to Nyerere. Mr Thawe had the same quiet authority, a similar idealism rooted in his sympathy for humanity and a certainty that people could, with support, organise themselves in unselfish ways. And it seemed to be working here. Mufindi had plentiful land, good rainfall, not too many people and some external sources of cash from Brooke Bond wages. But what about less-favoured places? And would the children educated in that school be content to stay as farmers?

CHAPTER 17
Morogoro

In which I have a run-in with TANU, meet a different kind of teacher and we go climbing again with the Scandinavians.

Kilimanjaro was directly responsible for our visit to Morogoro. As we hobbled away from the mountain Leena invited us to stay with her near Morogoro where her brother-in-law was working at the university's faculty of agriculture. So we agreed we would stop off there on our way back to Dar.

The road from Iringa was the most dramatic yet. There was mist round the hilltops and it was raining as we set off through the rocky countryside and plunged over the edge of the plateau alongside a roaring red-brown river which kept disappearing into a deep ravine below the road. Sharp spiny ridges ran down from the surrounding hills towards us as we twisted along the valley. Convoys of lorries carrying copper plates ground their way along the road in front of us, providing our driver with continual challenges as he tried to overtake them, while we shut our eyes. Towards us came Chinese-made lorries carrying materials to the Great Uhuru Railway.[26]

Once down in the hot damp plain we found ourselves willy-nilly on safari again; the road ran straight through Mikumi Game Park, where elephant and giraffe ambled along beside the road, impala and bushbuck ran away from the bus, buffalo and gnu grazed in the distance and we even glimpsed a lion. Baboons were everywhere, running around with tails held

---

[26] Also called the Tazara railway (*Uhuru* means freedom in Swahili) this was being built with Chinese aid between Kapiri Moshi and Dar es Salaam, in order to reduce landlocked Zambia's dependence on Rhodesia, still under white-minority rule.

stiffly upright and babies clinging to their backs.

We arrived in Morogoro, punctually for once, at 2 pm and took a taxi to the Golf Club – seemingly the sport of choice for expatriates here – where we were expecting a lift. It was closed. The heat was sweltering. We tossed up for who should telephone; I lost, and after some effort reached a voice that promised to tell the Salonens we'd arrived. We waited in a patch of shade. Around 4 pm, as it began to get cooler, Leena and Raija turned up, on the off-chance we'd arrived – the message never reached her. Ah well, that's Africa, but somehow you get there in the end.

So all was well and we were soon sitting in their house eating meatballs with a special cabbage salad prepared by Leena in memory of our favourite food on The Mountain. We shared our memories, laughed over our injuries – Patrick's toenails were now hanging loose – and made plans for the next few days.

'What would you like: the game park, a clinic, our local school, or a weekend at Morningside?

'Where's that?'

'One of the most beautiful places in the world, and easier to reach than Gilman's Peak.'

'That sounds great, but I'd like to see the clinic and the school too.'

The clinic at Bikwa was run by Dutch Catholics and supported entirely from Holland so as to be independent of the government. They trained local women in childcare, handicrafts, typing, and nutrition so they could return to their villages to pass on their skills. I accompanied Raija on her weekly visit to the mother-and-baby clinic, where there were about a hundred women, all in those cheerful khangas, bringing their babies slung across their backs to be weighed, checked and medicated if necessary. I helped bag up the soya bean flour and distributed the soya bean oil, donated by the US and sold very cheaply onwards. Such centres seemed potentially to target aid just where it was needed most, supporting women and children in their own homes with the hope that knowledge and good practice would spread.

Kilikala School was also founded by Catholics but like all schools was now under government authority, as I was to find out. My visit was arranged by a friend of the Salonens, Sally Wylie, who was teaching

English there.

The (Tanzanian) headmistress was quite happy for me to sit in classes and to tape interviews with students if they were willing. Sally's O-level students were doing Chinua Achebe's novel *Things Fall Apart* and we had agreed I would talk about Nigeria to give them some background. I told them about the modern version of the kola nut ceremony and that masquerades were still danced. I tried to stress the essential cultural continuity among the Igbos, as well as the changes brought by the Western education which they so eagerly embraced, because it seemed to me that Tanzania was finding such a fusion more difficult. They were a bright bunch and asked many questions, including how I would compare Nigeria and Tanzania. Fortunately the bell went at that moment.

After break I went to a political history lesson given by Mr Kyomo. The topic was Ghana under colonialism but my presence seemed to be making him uneasy about criticising Europeans, and the lesson lost direction. I was relieved to be taken off to talk to the Sixth Form.

'What do you think I should teach English kids about Tanzania?' I asked.

One girl eventually came up with: 'ujamaa – it's so nice because people live together and help each other.'

'About the beautiful mountains and game parks,' said another.

'Do you have to work on a shamba?'

'How do people get jobs?'

'Have you got many old people in your village?'

It seemed very hard for them to envisage an urban way of life where one might not wish to have children and where old people lived on their own. When the bell went the conversation had become very lively and a couple volunteered to come back at lunch time and talk into my tape recorder.

Back in the staffroom Mr Kyomo came up to me. 'I must apologise to you for speaking against the Western countries. You see, I am the TANU representative here and I am responsible for teaching children about socialism.'

I told him not to worry. 'In our universities there are many Marxists and other radicals who say just the same sort of things. I'll see you later when I come back to tape-record the girls.'

That was my big mistake. When I returned to the school that afternoon he was lying in wait for me and invited me into his office. I guessed what was coming but it took him fifteen minutes to get to the point. First he apologised again even though I assured him I was not offended. Then he wanted to know our exact names and the nature of our journey. I reiterated my teaching plans and showed him the list of questions I wanted to ask the girls, offering to let him hear the tape. It was no use.

'I hope you will not go on with this project. If I'd known you did not have permission from the government I would not have allowed you into my class. I should not have given you my name. Please tear that page out of your notebook. You must not write to the students. You must not discuss this with anyone. Please leave the school!'

Of course I found his panic even more interesting than taping the girls. As the headmistress explained as she took me back into town, he felt he couldn't do anything without orders from above. 'I don't mind at all if you arrange pen friendships for our students with girls in London,' she assured me.

Leena grinned when she heard the story. 'I have a friend John Mkalimoto, who is a different kind of teacher. He works with unalphabetics – how do you say – illiterates?

John's paid employment was as a 'houseboy' for a professor of agriculture but he was inspired by Nyerere and wanted to be a teacher. A young man of great personality, with a flair for leadership, he did political work among the local villages and through him Leena had got to know a number of families.

Under the eaves of the village meeting house a blackboard was propped up against the wall. The growing maize stalks rustled nearby and behind the trees the mountains loomed against the evening sky. On the concrete step sat a man and six women, one suckling her baby. We were greeted by the sound of chanting – *a, b, c, d*. Then they identified each letter on the blackboard and suggested words that began with it. Swahili is a phonetic language, so this went well. After that they took up their readers and the more advanced stumbled through a few paragraphs. Finally they practised some simple arithmetic. John encouraged, listened patiently and made them laugh.

'Mwalimu Nyerere wrote all the readers himself. They make it easy for beginners to read, and they teach good practice as well. This one is about good ways of preparing food and what to grow in your shamba. This one is on political education; it explains about TANU and tells people how to behave and work to build the nation.'

'Are the classes voluntary?'

'Well, we do push people to come. The really keen ones can learn to read in about three months but some don't take trouble. That grandmother there, she has trouble with her eyes and I don't think she will succeed.'

'Do you get paid?'

'Oh no. But if I keep on doing it the Party will give me a good report.'

Next morning we packed heavy rucksacks with food and clothing for three days in preparation for a weekend up another mountain – no porters this time.

Morningside

The Uluguru mountains, patched with forest and shambas, rise up behind Morogoro. At eight o'clock it was already hot. There was a gravel road but we took a path which climbed steeply on to one of the main ridges. There was no breeze and with a thin mist hovering above us it was like walking in a Turkish bath; the sweat poured off us.

For the real inhabitants of the mountains neither the steepness nor the heat seemed a problem. From the villages strung out along the ridges people were continually trotting up and down to fetch water, to cultivate their shambas on the mountain side or to work on the communal lands down in the plain. There was a constant murmur of greetings as they passed and paused:

Jambo! (Hello!)

Habari? (How are you?)

Mzuri (Well.)

Habari … la kazi? (How is … your work … your family? … your children?... your home? … your crops?)

Asante sana (Thank you very much.)

Raija and Leena responded fluently and at equal length; I stammered out a few exchanges. Patrick merely grunted *jambo* and *asante*, grudging the breath required until he discovered that one of the greetings included 'How is your tiredness?' 'Ah, that's the one for me!' he announced, and proceeded to use it for the next twenty years.

After an hour we stopped to rest in a village called Mwongo where Leena had made friends with an elderly lady whom she addressed as *Shangazi* or 'Aunt.' We sat for a while as Leena and Raija chatted with the women who gathered round to greet us, their babies sleeping peacefully in khanga slings over their backs.

Later we stopped by a stream to paddle but Patrick didn't dare risk his toenails. The last part was an even steeper zigzag, often using steps cut out of the rock. Sweat dripped off us. Then, suddenly, we were on the ridge and Morningside lay before us.

Built in 1911 as a Lutheran mission house, it now belonged to the university and was used as a weekend retreat for homesick European staff. There was a huge old-fashioned kitchen and scullery where visitors cooked their own food, a spacious sitting/dining room with an open fireplace and a supply of wood, multiple bedrooms and even hot showers.

In front was a broad veranda giving a marvellous view down over Morogoro and to the plain beyond with the main road snaking into the distance. Immediately below we looked down on the thatched roofs of the houses along the ridges and the cultivated areas plunging down to the stream at the bottom of the valley. Upwards, sharper rocky ridges led through the forest belt to the summit. Around the house were old gardens full of flowering shrubs, roses and tropical flowers.

We lunched off soup and toasted cheese sandwiches – which became the staple fare for the weekend – before a wonderful long siesta.

When we got up there were American voices among the Finnish ones asking if there was a room for the night. Ellie and Shelton had driven up the road looking to buy fresh vegetables and fruit and stumbled on Morningside. We all helped cook a huge vegetable stew and then ate mangoes and roasted peanuts round the fire.

Shelton explained he farmed maize and cattle in Missouri and was here to help develop improved maize seed.

'Before that we were in Ethiopia. Boy, that was like living in Biblical times! They sure did need a revolution!'

The conversation turned again to the feasibility of socialism in a selfish world and somewhat to our surprise our corn-belt friends said they felt the need for a basic change in American society.

'Do you think the people in the villages here are happy?' someone asked.

'We can't really tell,' answered Leena. 'When I visit there is always some excitement, or we go to a *ngoma* (dance) when everyone is celebrating.'

Ellie said softly: 'They are more relaxed than we are, they are content with so much less. And look how they resist attempts to move them even when the government offers modern facilities. That says something about how they value their present way of life.'

The next day we participated briefly in that way of life. We walked back down to Mwongo village to meet John, the adult education tutor, and his wife, Mama Lukinga, who was from that village. A number of men were passing through on their way to a TANU meeting and had stopped to talk with John. They greeted us courteously.

'Can women go to meetings too?' I asked.

'Of course they can and they often speak. But sometimes they are too busy looking after the children and doing the cooking.'

'Ha!' I muttered. 'The whole world over! Anyway, what is the meeting about?'

John looked grave. 'You see how the people here have cut down much of the forest to cultivate the slopes. This is dangerous. The rain no longer soaks into the ground through the trees; it runs off and washes the soil away. Even the water supplies in Morogoro are being threatened by this. We have told the people they should move down to the plain and let the trees grow again on the mountains.'

A much older man cut in. 'Excuse me, but we do not want to go down to that desert there. Before Independence the British had the same idea and tried to make us move down to the plains. We made great protests; we rioted. Then TANU came and took our side, so we supported TANU. Now you are saying the same thing? I cannot believe Mwalimu means that.'

John looked embarrassed and the discussion moved back into Swahili. We wondered whether in this case the people would win again or whether their own government, with somewhat more legitimacy, would persuade them. Rationally, the slopes were not the best place to grow crops – but 'democracy is the right to make the wrong choice'.

We went to talk to the women gathered outside Shangazi's hut. Leena persuaded the old woman to sing while I took a photo. Younger women joined in and began swaying to the music; Shangazi fetched an old tin basin, turned it upside down and started drumming – a small ngoma was under way! We placed money on the drum – a traditional 'thank you' – and all joined in. Then Leena was persuaded to do a Cossack-style dance and finally I contributed a sort of Highland fling while Patrick grabbed the camera.

When we were all exhausted the women brought us tea and soft fluffy cocoyams. The younger kids came up shyly and showed Patrick their football, made of banana leaves tightly wrapped in paper and tied up with strips of rubber. It hardly bounced but was splendid for barefoot kicking.

Sitting sipping our tea, we looked more closely at the houses. The uprights of the walls were of good thick timbers; on both sides bamboo poles were laid across and tied together with a type of bark which was very strong and pliable when used fresh, but which hardened with age. The gaps in this cross hatching of wood were filled with mud. In rare cases a surface coating of more weather-resistant clay mixed with ground stone was put over the whole wall, giving a smooth finish. Inside the hut, which was divided into three sections by mud walls, there was a ceiling of bamboo poles. They told us the huts lasted about fifty years.

'Why are some huts square and some circular?' we asked John.

'Ah, the round ones are from my people, the Ngoni. They came up many years ago from the south and drove the people into the mountains here. We are related to the Zulus and they build their houses that way. My grandfather was a great warrior called Lukinga and I call my son after him. That's why my wife is called Mama Lukinga! My father was a chief but he wanted to get paid by the Europeans, so he took a job as a watchman. I wanted to go to secondary school and become a teacher but there wasn't a place for me. That's why I am a houseboy.'

There was a huge variety of crops growing in the fields around the huts, much maize, but also bananas, groundnuts, pumpkins, beans, cassava, spinach and others we didn't recognise. A healthy diet, but even so we had seen some children with the lighter hair and swollen bellies that signal malnutrition. The hillsides were intensively cultivated, but were perhaps unable to support the growing population.

On our last morning, as we were sitting on the balcony watching the pattern of the clouds on the green hills below, John came past again. 'There's going to be a ngoma in Chomo village to celebrate a girl who has reached puberty. Would you like to go?'

As we reached the ridge we could already hear the music from the village below – insistent drumming and clinking notes. In the open space between the huts people had gathered from all the villages around, the women draped in their best khangas, the men in their smartest trousers and tops, many wearing hats or berets. Some of the youths carried slim metal walking sticks spiral painted in bright colours. The band consisted of two home-made xylophones, maracas made of seeds in old tin cans, and two drummers (one playing three drums). They stood in the centre while the younger children danced around them in a ring. Then the youths joined in, forming an outer circle and dancing more vigorously. Now came the girl, carried on her father's shoulders, with a sword in one hand and a fly-whisk in the other, her eyes downcast, her face unsmiling in this serious moment. As she was danced around the band, people reached up to tuck money into her dress or to throw it into the baskets held high beside her. Finally she was taken into a hut; the band packed up their instruments and marched off down the hill to the next village where they were needed.

We didn't stay for the party that followed but wandered slowly back to Morningside, getting better views of the birds and pondering once more the problems of development. If the villagers moved down to the plains and new villages were built, the kinship groups might be broken up and what would happen then to their dances, their ceremonies, their way of life?

It was time to go home down the steep path that shook up our Kilimanjaro muscles once more. We were soon soaked by both rain and sweat and thankful for the strong drinks and hot showers when we got back. We managed to telephone our base in Dar es Salaam, only to find that Nobambo was in hospital for gall stones, but that her friend Edith had moved into the house and was expecting us back.

Before we left, the Salonens gave a small party for us to meet their friends and neighbours. The group here seemed much more positive about the country and its problems than many expatriates; perhaps Scandinavians are more used to accepting a strong state, providing it is democratic. While acknowledging the criticisms, they seemed to be saying that it was all a question of what price you think is reasonable to pay to solve the country's terrible problems.

CHAPTER 18
Korogwe and Ifakara

In which we begin to feel the pull of South Africa, but first we visit an
ex-Bath student, return to Morningside and visit Ifakara.

It poured all the way to Dar but it was good to see the countryside
greening up and the maize growing. Nobambo's friend Edith, another
South African nurse, welcomed us back to the hot little house and we
sent Luciano out for basic supplies – beer, bread, jam and eggs; marge had
apparently disappeared from the shops as well as butter. It was worryingly
easy to get used to having a servant.

Just as we were sitting down to our skimpy lunch a tall white-haired
African appeared at the door. He must have been well into his sixties but
held himself very upright and walked with a vigorous stride. His deep-set
eyes appraised us for a moment and then he smiled and held out his hand.
'I am called Hononu. You must be the Stuarts. When I am in Dar I always
eat lunch at Nobambo's. Luciano, I am ready for the meal.'

Over the next few days we got to know and like Mr Hononu very well.
Exiled from South Africa, he was employed full time in South African
liberation politics, moving between political centres in Dar, Addis
Ababa and Lusaka, expenses paid, but otherwise surviving mainly on the
hospitality of fellow-exiles, like Nobambo, who fed him daily. He took
our South African education a step further by telling us his story.

'I was born in the Transkei and went to the mission school, where my
best friend was the minister's son; there was no distinction made between
Black and White then. In 1924 I started training as a primary school
teacher. After a few years I went back to school and in 1933 I got my
matric and went to Fort Hare University. It was started by missionaries,

mainly for Blacks, but there were Whites and Coloured there too; it was famous all over Southern Africa.

'What makes me sad now is how the quality of education available to Africans has deteriorated. Do you know about the Bantu Education Act of 1954? It forced Black and White to be educated separately. Both the Roman Catholic Church and the Anglicans under Bishop Reeves closed their schools rather than have them operate in this way.

'I fought against it. I was chairman of the Cape Province African Teachers' Union, and all we teachers who opposed the Act were sacked. We fought them in the courts for wrongful dismissal, and when we won the government changed the law retrospectively!

'In 1964 I was placed under house arrest. That meant I could go out to work but people had to get permission to visit me – even my relatives. I think I would rather have been in prison! I had to report daily to the police and they checked my house at night when it was dark – but if I left my study light on all night they did not come in. That's how I escaped – I left the lights on and got to Swaziland before they realised.'

We asked him how he saw the South African situation developing, and he gave us a gloomy picture.

'As time goes by, there is less and less likelihood that the black community will respond positively to any reform instituted by the white regime. The apartheid laws are being applied more and more harshly and I think there will be violence and bloodshed. Blacks have been so effectively isolated from white contacts that the young militants see the struggle as one against Whites themselves rather than one against an unjust economic, legal and political system.'

South Africa was the final goal of this trip and here was a hint that we should be moving on. But among our month's pile of mail was an invitation from Christine Mbaruka in Korogwe, Aunt Mary's only Tanzanian student, which we accepted with delight; that would be our final commitment here. There was no reply from Anna Chipimo, whom we wanted to visit in Lusaka, so we thought we might skip Zambia and go straight on to South Africa. We wrote to Anna Halele in Maseru and asked if we could arrive in early April.

Meanwhile, we went off to Korogwe, a six-hour bus journey north of Dar. Christina met us at the bus stop with family in tow: her two daughters, her son and a man whom she introduced as her fiancé. She was slim and elegant in a long red skirt and cream blouse, her hair neatly braided. At first a little wary, she soon became her usual lively, amusing and chatty self and seemed genuinely pleased to have these unknown foreign visitors to stay.

'Your aunt was so kind to me. What a lovely ring she has sent me! I wasn't in Bath very long, because after a year I went home to visit my children and found my husband had left me for another woman, so I had to stay. Then I met Bill here, and as soon as the divorce comes through we are going to get married.'

They lived in a spacious three-bedroom bungalow provided by the school and we were made very comfortable in the boy's room; we guessed he had to sleep on the sofa but, as an African child, he made no complaint.

Later Christina walked us round the school. Like all those we had seen it comprised lines of long white buildings with verandas; classrooms at this end, dormitories at that one. Like others, it was founded by missionaries but had been taken over by the government. The emphasis here was on agriculture, so they kept pigs and chickens and were planning a small dairy herd.

Although it was Saturday the girls were out in the shambas; the maize here was growing well and they were using the long, heavy hoes to weed between the plants. The evening sun lit up their bright non-uniform khangas; they were chattering and singing as they worked.

'Grace, my daughter, should be there too,' Christina said, 'but she got the night off because we had visitors; I pretended you were family. They make her board because they say they have to assess how well she behaves in the community; it's not just about exam success here!'

'What brought you to this school?'

'I was sent! We can't choose where we go. But it's a good school, well-staffed, with an efficient headteacher. At the moment she is away on a nine-month political education course, where they have to do military training as well. I'm glad I'm not a head!'

After supper we talked to Bill, who trained as a vet in the US and had a job with the livestock marketing board. He was a quiet, serious character, whom we found kind and interesting. He began by expressing patriotic belief in Nyerere's policies but it soon became apparent he was no socialist.

'I think they should allow individuals to use their own initiative much more. For example, we have a housing shortage. Now, Christina and I, we have saved some money, but as government employees we cannot use it to build a house to rent out – that would be called exploitation! But what happens if I lose my job? Most of us are employed by the government and if I were sacked – perhaps for saying the wrong thing – I'd not find another. I'd have to go back to my village and live as a peasant!'

It crossed my mind that his veterinary training would be very useful in an ujamaa village but I kept quiet.

It was Palm Sunday and yes, we went to church again, to a High Anglican mass conducted, of course, in Swahili. On entering we were given tall branches and, as we processed round the church with waving palms, the bright shawls covering the women's heads and the chanting, I could easily imagine the streets of Jerusalem.

Bill and Christina seemed eager to introduce us to their friends, which gave us our first real opportunity to talk with middle-class Tanzanians. Mr Muongo was a partner in one of the few remaining privately-owned sisal estates and appeared delighted to meet some Western capitalists.

'I fear they will nationalise us all soon,' he lamented. 'The government is stifling private initiative. They must get off our backs! We should be like Kenya, where people can make money. They are much happier there.'

I said how impressed I was with the school.

'Oh yes, but they should not teach children in such beautiful surroundings because they will never want to go back to the villages! They should build more schools, with just basic amenities. It's all oral!'

We gathered this meant there was a wide gap between government policies and their implementation. But the contrast with Nigeria was interesting; whereas Chief Okenwa had a Mercedes with a TV in the back, Mr Muongo drove a battered old Peugeot and Christina didn't even have a car.

'Can you eat *ugali?*' asked Christina as we sat down to lunch. She had provided us with salad, omelette and cheese but there was also a huge mound of stiff, white maize porridge. 'This is our staple food.' It wasn't unpleasant and the accompanying beans and vegetables were very tasty, but it was all very filling and we needed a long siesta to digest it.

I was rather nervous when told that her neighbour, Mr Kimbono, was responsible for the TANU Youth League and wanted to meet us, but he turned out to be much more intelligent and open to discussion than my frightened friend from Kilikala.

'The League is for everyone under eighteen and we organise different activities depending on age: the youngest girls learn patriotic songs, we teach the older ones about socialism and nation-building, or about other political systems like yours. Then they do voluntary work, like cleaning up the grounds of the hospital, cleaning the market place or helping the local ujamaa villages with their cultivation or harvesting. We are certainly building socialism! This is a much better way forward than Kenya or Uganda. But I am interested in other countries too. How are things in Britain?'

He struck us rather like a public schoolboy who *knows* his school is better than anyone else's. Indeed, Mwalimu Nyerere's speeches so often sounded to us like those of an earnest public school headmaster, extolling the virtues of loyalty, hard work, sacrifice and leadership, exhorting them to high standards and clean living. We decided TANU could be the prefects, whose job it was to pass the message on and keep discipline but who were not always so kind or effective.

Next day, laden with presents from Christina, we returned to Dar. We were finding the sticky heat ever more oppressive and, in spite of drinking lots of salt and water, I often felt groggy. Nobambo was still in hospital and there was no word yet from Maseru. We decided to take ourselves back to Morningside for a breath of fresher and cooler air.

There were now political shadows over our mountain paradise. 'They asked me questions about you when I made the booking,' said Raija. 'It may be because of the government's plans to move the villages down to the plain. There was a whole page in the *Daily News* last week, which accused the villagers of being very selfish in not agreeing to move down. We think perhaps the government will move very quickly and just force them to move before they have time to organise protests, like they did against the British in the 1950s.'

Ignoring the politics this time, we spent four days at Morningside, reading, writing, watching birds and admiring the sunsets – it was a real holiday. The air was gloriously cool and the intermittent rain provided a good alibi for inactivity. From the balcony we watched the clouds build ever higher over the plains, while along the ridges the sun lit up the fields into brilliant green patterns, till the storm swept in from the north-east and the huge clouds dissolved into rain, an endlessly fascinating spectacle.

One evening we were joined by Ursula and Sigismund Hadelich, from Germany. We exchanged some of the strawberries we'd bought on the mountain for a glass of their Chianti, and conversation flowed.

'We are working on an agricultural project in the Kilombero Valley. Few people lived there because communications were poor, but now the new railway is being built through it and we are helping the people to develop better farming methods. The FAO[27] thinks that if the floodplains were properly managed, they could support far more people. Would you like to visit for a couple of days?'

So we found ourselves packed into their overloaded estate car travelling southwards on rough dirt roads. At an apparently deserted railway line we stopped.

'This is the Great Uhuru Railway', Sigismund explained. 'They've reached the Zambian end and it's due to open this year. But there are still a lot of Chinese projects going on, like engineering shops, quarries and a hydroelectric power station.'

'People have told us that Tanzanians see China as a role model in terms of development. How do they get on with them?'

Ursula smiled. 'Well, the Tanzanians admire their capacity for hard work, but they can't fraternise, as the Chinese seldom speak either Swahili or English and are strictly supervised. It is said that the Chinese are never allowed to travel in groups of less than three. It follows, therefore, if you see three Chinese together they are ordinary people; if you see two Chinese it must be Chairman Mao and one other, and a single Chinese on his own must be Chairman Mao!' At that point we saw a solitary figure walking down the track under a green umbrella – perhaps that was the Chairman himself?

---

[27] Food and Agricultural Organisation of the United Nations

The Hadelichs had a staff bungalow in the grounds of the Agricultural Research Institute and next morning we were introduced to the director, whose speech was suitably optimistic and politically correct.

'We are doing applied research, mainly on rice and citrus fruits. We experiment with different methods of cultivation and we are cross-breeding to improve local strains. We are supporting the villagisation policy; with their communal labour they will be able to produce cash crops for both internal and external markets.'

Sigismund's job was to organise demonstration plots in the surrounding villages and to train agricultural extension officers – trying to put the research results into practice so that food production would increase. Ursula worked on the public relations side and soon realised we had a limited interest in citrus.

'I think you might like the river,' she said, driving out through a mosaic of swamps and rice paddies, threaded with little creeks and alive with birds. Finally we came out on the banks of – yes indeed! – a great, grey-green, greasy river, at least 300 yards broad, swollen with the recent rains and laden with debris as it rushed along. We saw neither crocodiles nor the Elephant's Child, but probably they were both nearby, as the Kilombero Valley is the largest freshwater wetland in East Africa, a huge network of channels that rise and fall with the seasons, flooding the land with rich alluvial soil, and internationally important for both birds and animals.[28]

We hired a dug-out canoe and climbed rather nervously inside. It was remarkably stable, at least twenty-five feet long and broad enough for us to sit comfortably in the bottom. We opened our red and black umbrellas against the sun and pretended we were Victorian explorers, while the boatman pushed us upstream with paddle and pole, keeping close to the bank where the current was weakest. This was wonderful for bird-watching. A brilliant flash of blue – that was the pygmy kingfisher, similar to the British one, while its larger pied cousin was striped in black and white. There were, as always, yellow weaver birds building in the reeds and a little scarlet bishop nearby. Overhead sailed the magnificent African fish

---

[28] Since we were there, people have migrated on to the floodplains and there is now a great conflict between the demands of human development and the conservation of the birds and animals. The elephants from the nearby Selous National Park can no longer find their old migration paths across it and the endemic *puku* antelope is nearly extinct.

eagles, calling like wild gulls to each other. The African darter – a kind of cormorant – flew by, looking like a prehistoric relic with its long tail and kinked neck.

After a large lunch and a long siesta, we reckoned it was time to offer our services on the shamba. As an old Swahili proverb says: 'When a guest comes to your home, on the first day you feed him, on the second day you let him rest and on the third day you give him a hoe.'

At the Institute each member of staff had a plot on which to cultivate rice. The Hadelichs had sown theirs broadcast and experimented with using no herbicide, so we spent an hour or so weeding. It was very hard going.

'Now you understand why weeding can be the factor which limits how much land a family can cultivate,' said Sigismund. 'And when weeds get entrenched you move your shamba on to new land. That's one reason for the shifting cultivation you see around here. And that's a problem they've got to solve if they set up permanent fields.'

We found the Hadelichs delightfully easy and congenial company and we pressed them strongly to come and visit us in London. They never did but I recently found a reference in a travellers' blog to their organic farm in Tuscany, where thirty years on Ursula was still welcoming in stray visitors, plying them with wonderful meals and then giving them a hoe on the third day...

CHAPTER 19
Final Days in Dar

In which we meet new friends, say good bye to old ones and have some final tussles with the Tanzanian bureaucracy.

The Silver Sands Hotel charged five shillings for access to the beach, but this included a table and chairs under a thatched roof as shelter from the fierce sun. The white sand was almost too hot to walk on and the wavelets on the incoming tide were bath-water hot. Further out it was cooler but very salty where I floated on my back watching huge cumulus clouds pile up in the east. The sea turned from green through myriad shades out to brilliant blue, and along the distant reef was a necklace of green islands ringed with sparkling white beaches. There was Indian pop music in the background from the hotel and gulls calling along the shore. A warm, spicy wind cooled our wet backs; we swam some more, drank beer, ate peppery meat grilled over charcoal and swam again – it was a brilliant antidote to the Dar es Salaam blues. The last of Patrick's Kilimanjaro-blackened toenails was washed away, along with memories of hot, uncomfortable bus journeys.

We had found some newspapers and searched for international news. The Kenyan headlines trumpeted:

'*Vorster is optimistic about the future of South Africa*'; '*Many children are killed by Vietcong attacks*'.

The Tanzanian ones, however, took a different slant:

'*Vorster says he will never drop racism*'; '*China hails victories for FRELIMO in Mozambique*'.

The Times informed us that there was a gathering political crisis over the Common Market. 'Maybe the Labour Party will at last break up and give us Liberals a chance,' wondered Patrick lazily. It all seemed very far away.

Meanwhile, we were not quite sure what to do next. Anna Hlalele's letter said she wouldn't be home in Maseru till April 16th – two weeks away. (She was in fact visiting her daughter Mary who was living in our London house.) But we'd had no reply from Anna Chipimo, who lived in Lusaka. Abortive telephone calls via the Zambian High Commission elicited confused information that she had moved, or was in London, or both. Flights from Dar to Lusaka were infrequent and there were no onward flights from Lusaka to Johannesburg for political reasons, we'd have to go via Botswana. So perhaps we should skip Zambia?

It was the black South African connection that took us there in the end: Mr Hononu's sister Tamara was married to an Englishman, Brian Bowers, and they were living in Lusaka. 'You'll be very welcome with them,' he assured us. So we decided to fly to Lusaka on Thursday April 10th, and on to Johannesburg via Francistown in Botswana the following Monday, giving us two days in the 'City of Gold' before going on to Lesotho.

It was now time to tie up all the loose ends in Dar. We had so far failed to meet up with Godfrey Urassa, a chartered accountant with the international firm of Cooper Lybrands, but to Patrick's delight a dinner date was now finally fixed.

Godfrey moved in very different circles from our other contacts and took us to a smart hotel where he seemed well-known. We were introduced to the Aga Khan's representative – appropriately, a jeweller. Full of quiet charm, if a little reserved, Godfrey was soon discussing the iniquities of the Tanzanian tax system with Patrick. His wife Mary was impeccably groomed and looked every bit the upper-class lady; it turned out that her father was Lonrho's representative in Tanzania and I found conversation difficult until I mentioned Kilimanjaro. It turned out they both came from Chagga families – the local tribe – and still had land up there. 'Town property is held on lease from the government,' he explained, 'but agricultural land is still held under tribal custom and with us it's from father to son.'

'Yes, we're very go-ahead people,' he added. 'Did you know we tried to establish our own country once? When Princess Margaret came to Tanganyika before independence we managed to arrange that her car flew a Chagga flag!'

Mischievously I asked him if he had to cultivate a shamba in Dar as well. 'No,' he laughed. 'I bought exemption for all my office staff! But the poor senior officers at the Central Bank, who I see quite often, they have to go and dig their shambas, even though there are millions of shillings of transactions awaiting their signature.' We wonder if that accounted for the delays at the bank.

After dinner they took us back to their large modern house for brandy and we asked them what people really thought of Nyerere.

'He's unpopular, they blame him for the inflation. But there isn't an alternative in view; there's no group around which an opposition can coalesce. He's moved the government up to Dodoma to get away from the influence of the coastal Arabs and Indians. There's no chance of a change of regime in the foreseeable future.'

We took Andrew and Judy Coulson out to dinner at their favourite Indian restaurant to thank them for all their help and to discuss our impressions.

Andrew said: 'When I came here eight years ago, I could see what Nyerere was trying to do. I do believe the original ujamaa policy was right. But it's gone off course. The policy now is to create development villages as fast as possible. To do this they have resorted to force in some cases. That's totally wrong and against the original vision. Decisions are now being made centrally instead of locally.'

'We met Emil Ndonde in Dodoma, and he said something similar.'

'I'm glad you met him, he is one of the old school. He has fought many battles in TANU circles in favour of ujamaa and self-reliance and against the increasing power of the central authorities.'

We told them about Mr Thawe in Mufindi.

'They must have taken their ideas from the first phase villages in Ruvuma, in the south, where the villages were pioneers. It took time, but people were really involved. In the second phase, the villages were set up with a certain amount of bribery: if you will move into a compact village and do some communal work, we will give you water, a school and a dispensary. Now we are into a third phase: they are compelling the villagers to move. It's all about providing services efficiently, and about the benefits of larger scale farming, not about self-reliance at all.'

'But, ideology aside, surely such villages can indeed be justified in terms of economies of scale?' suggested Patrick. 'If this country is to feed itself, output per farmer must be raised, and this can most rapidly be done by larger scale farming using mechanical aids, tractors, fertilizer and so. To increase productivity, one needs capital and I can't see where that's coming from; there isn't enough saving within the country and foreign capital would obviously be unacceptable. There aren't any large estates to take over, like in Russia.'

Andrew shook his head. 'The economies of large-scale farming here aren't proven; machines might help at harvest time, but planting and weeding are labour-intensive anyway, and you need people to feel involved in the outcome, which they won't be if all they've got is a strip in a collective field. What we need is for people to get together voluntarily and have the government provide technical advice, training and enough capital to get them started. But that would take a long time and time is what we don't have.'

Andrew's final recommendation was more personal and more cheerful: 'In Lesotho you must visit my sister Janet Taylor. Her husband Don teaches development studies at the university.'

This was yet another link in the ever-lengthening chain of friendship and one that was to have career-changing consequences for us.

Next evening we entertained the Jentsches to supper at the Oyster Bay Hotel, a step back into Euroland, where we drank G & Ts on the terrace before supper and a bottle of Mosel with the wonderful seafood. They had been immensely kind, receiving our mail, lending us their car and generally supporting our ventures. Over coffee they asked us what were our conclusions about Tanzania.

'I'm with Nyerere,' I said. 'If they can really achieve an egalitarian, just and fundamentally democratic society, the present rather dictatorial policies will have been justified.'

Patrick disagreed. 'I have found myself becoming steadily more laissez-faire in my attitudes! Can a government really be justified in compelling a people to make such major changes in their way of life? I fear that having resorted to compulsion in moving people into villages, the government will find it increasingly easy to justify further compulsion in order to attain their objectives – and those objectives aren't necessarily those of the people they govern.'

Gero said diplomatically: 'I can see both sides. What worries me most is that the government does not really have the administrative capacity to ensure their plans – which in many ways are admirable – are carried out properly, or to check the results.'

On Monday we went into town again to confirm the tickets and Patrick went off to the bank to draw out some more cash; thanks to the great generosity of everyone we'd stayed with we still had plenty of funds, even though it took an hour for the bank to ascertain that fact and produce some. Meanwhile, I went to the post office to post our last parcels back to England and entered a Kafkaesque world.

At the parcels office I was directed to the customs man. I had three parcels, one of them labelled 'gift', so I was told to get an 'export licence' from the Bank of Tanzania. He gave me three sets of forms to be filled in in triplicate (but only one piece of carbon paper). I trotted off to the Bank of Tanzania, some ten minutes away and joined the queue. When I reached the window the clerk asked where were my passport and currency forms? Patrick had these at the other bank so off I dashed, still lugging the parcels, and brought him along. Another queue. Then the clerk sent us to reception with a note. We waved the note and quite quickly got escorted to the second floor, where six or seven clerks were shuffling paper. Our forms were taken off elsewhere and we sat for at least half an hour. Perhaps it was tea-break? When they came back they still had to be stamped and signed. All this time no one ever looked at the actual contents of the parcels.

Then we were escorted downstairs and back to the counter where we signed a register enumerating our parcels, and – two and a half hours later – we were able to return to the post office clutching the stamped forms. My friend in the customs office actually did search the parcel I'd kept open and when he was satisfied all it contained were some grass bowls and wooden animals wrapped up in Patrick's old pants, he allowed the others to go through unchecked.

All through everyone had been very quiet and courteous; no throwing of weight around, slowly but helpfully pushing us through the bureaucracy. Finally when I reached the posting counter the clerk looked at the name and said, 'I have a message from the head postmaster about Stuart.' He went off to check and returned saying, 'Your parcels are to go through.' In the end, someone had bothered to make sure there was no hitch but it had still taken us three and a half hours.

Finally it was our last morning. We packed everything very carefully, using a rucksack in place of the old suitcase and, surprisingly, it all went in. This time it was Patrick fighting diarrhoea and he went back to bed – these things seemed always to hit us as we left a country. I went to the post office, armed this time with the right forms, to post our last parcel; they recognised me and all was well.

But it seemed we were destined to have more luggage problems at Dar airport. We arrived promptly, an hour before departure, took our baggage to the customs area and then went to change money. This took rather a long time and when we returned our bags had been placed in a side office.

'These your bags, sir?' There was no explanation given and we didn't dare ask, as a large silent man with two smaller but equally silent assistants proceeded to remove every single item from our carefully packed bags. They took out the socks stuffed into Patrick's shoes and opened the tiny kettle inside our pack-away cooking set. They even inspected my Tampax. Two ladies stood by and we expected to be strip-searched, but they stopped at our pockets. It was getting closer and closer to take-off time and we were sweating already in the Dar heat. Then they opened Patrick's briefcase and started reading all our papers.

'That's a draft of my book for schools', I said. 'You can see it's about African history'.

Patrick's notebook was there with its torn-off pages and the officer spotted the name Nyerere, but fortunately the remainder was pretty illegible. 'Where is the rest?'

'I sent it home.'

'Where are your films?'

'I sent them to be processed.'

'Hm. You can pack up again.'

Hurriedly we crammed everything back in and rushed off to complete formalities; fortunately the plane's departure had been delayed for Lord Pitt, the then Leader of the Greater London Council.

We sighed a great sigh of relief at take-off and celebrated with double whiskies while we pondered why we had been subjected to such a detailed search. Just a spot check? Suspicion because our money-changing took so long? Or did the knapsack coupled with Patrick's half-grown beard spell hippies and drugs?

Perhaps it was just a salutary reminder of Tanzanian tensions and the fact that we were heading south, where people were going to be even more suspicious. We decided Patrick had better shave off that beard.

Watching the featureless brown landscape far below us, we pondered where Tanzania's future might lie. With Emil Ndonde and Mr Thawe, who wanted to give all farmers a decent standard of living? With Bill and Christine and the ambitious factory managers, who wanted to become comfortably-off, property-owning bourgeois citizens? With the radical theorists at the university, who wanted Tanzania to challenge the system of global capitalism? Or with the Godfrey Ucassas, who already had links into that system?

❖

It was to lie with the salaried elites and their international links, for Nyerere's vision was not realised. As we had learnt during our brief stay, too few were attracted to the ujamaa ideals of cooperative living, and there was little evidence that villagisation, whether voluntary or enforced, would rapidly increase people's wealth and happiness. On the contrary, it seems to have held back food production.

In the 1970s the price of oil and other imports rose, while the prices of tea and coffee fell on the world market. Tanzania became deeply indebted, inflation increased, shortages became more acute and corruption grew. In 1985 Nyerere stood down and his successor Mwinyi agreed with the IMF (International Monetary Fund) to devalue the shilling, free up trade and cut government expenditure. Though this stimulated the economy, Nyerere's real achievements in education and health care went backwards.

In 1995 multiparty elections returned President Mkapa and by the turn of the century the Arusha Declaration was largely forgotten; the country was on a capitalist path to development. State businesses were privatised, debt written off and foreign investment encouraged. Discoveries of gold, gas and other minerals boosted exports, along with tourists, who appreciated the country's openness and stability. The economy grew fast and in 2012 President Kikwete said Tanzania would be a 'middle-income' country by 2025, though many doubted this would happen.

Education has expanded hugely; transport has been improved (though the Uhuru railway fell into disrepair for a time; it now runs about one train a day!), there is internet access and a lively press. While most of the benefits have gone to the rising middle class and the city-dwellers, there was some evidence that by 2015 farmers in well-watered areas were also doing better. Nyerere's vision – of equality, relevant education, state intervention to ensure services are available to all, rural development and good leadership – remains as a reminder of what needs to be done in Tanzania and elsewhere.

There is another sadly visible change: because the world's climate is getting warmer the glaciers on Kilimanjaro have greatly diminished and one day it will lose its snowy cap.

CHAPTER 20
Stopover in Lusaka

*In which we find an intermediate country and move comfortably
between different social and racial worlds.*

Our short, casual visit to Lusaka provided a useful breathing space and
a bridge – geographically, culturally, politically – between Eastern
and Southern Africa, between new countries testing out independence
and one that was as yet denied that freedom. We found it interestingly
hybrid.

Modern Zambia lies like two clenched fists up on the central African
plateau, just west of the Great Rift Valley. A crossroads area in early times,
it contains African peoples from many tribes; Europeans arrived in the
1890s when Cecil Rhodes' British South Africa Company started mining
copper along the Kafue River. In 1923 the company ceded Northern
Rhodesia to the Crown, while Southern Rhodesia became a self-
governing colony dominated by white settlers. Then in 1953 the two quite
different units, together with Nyasaland, were forced into a Federation,
which was hugely unpopular with Africans because the Rhodesian
settler government opposed black majority rule. At the end of 1963 the
Federation was dissolved and Kenneth Kaunda was elected President of
a new independent country known as Zambia. He proclaimed a policy of
'African Socialism', nationalised the copper mines, and by 1975 made it a
one-party state. However, Zambia remained open to Western investment
and there were many expatriates there providing technical expertise.

Lusaka itself seemed much more Western than either Lagos or Dar,
with wide streets and mostly low, irregular, square-topped buildings, an
occasional high block rising into the arching blue sky; the heat of the sun

was tempered by the dry breeze. In the centre we found small but well-stocked specialist shops, even a boutique playing pop music, while the market area was surprisingly prim, selling vegetables in plastic bags.

Yet if there was a European stamp on Lusaka, middle-class Zambians were now making it their own; Africans (and a few Asians) were running the shops, young black teenagers were walking down the street in miniskirts and bell-bottomed trousers. When an African woman, dressed in a modern short skirt and jumper, got out of a car and tied her baby securely to her back with a shawl, I felt confused by the cultural mix.

To our dismay all hotels were full, so in desperation we rang the Chipimo home, only to find Anna was indeed there but with a houseful of guests after a family funeral. Enormously concerned for us, she telephoned around till she found sofas for us at the flat of her friend Sonia Kidson, a parliamentary administrator. Next morning Anna herself, a tall elegant woman in smart Western clothes, picked us up and took us to her sister's beauty salon, which specialised in modern African hairstyles: long 'extensions' were being braided into the natural hair and then arranged in wonderfully intricate plaits and loops. I felt extremely scruffy by contrast with my long straight brown hair inexpertly trimmed by Patrick.

Anna's husband Elias had recently returned from diplomatic service in London. 'We've let our big house in Lusaka to an embassy,' Anna explained, 'and we've bought a twenty-acre plot in the country. We've started up an intensive poultry-rearing business – I've got hundreds of hens! Of course I remember your dear aunt very well and I'm so sorry I can't put you up. But you must come out and visit us on Sunday.'

So we activated our other, South African, chain of links. Brian Bowers was married to Tamara, Mr Hononu's sister, and ran a sports shop in central Lusaka. They fixed us up with an empty student-warden flat out at the university where we could rest and re-organise ourselves. In preparation for South Africa, I posted home all books that might be banned and Patrick did indeed shave off his Kilimanjaro beard so as to look more conformist.

On Saturday evening we had supper with the Bowers and their two little brown-skinned children, who were very polite but much more talkative than the African children we'd met so far, chatting away about the wildlife programme they were watching on TV. Brian was a cheerful, balding character with white fluffy sideboards, at first glance an unlikely-looking person to be married to a black South African militant's sister. He had come out to Rhodesia from London to work as a white hunter but, as he told us, his political views didn't fit with those who feared African advancement would threaten their white status.

'When I invited black university graduates to dinner and my neighbours told the police, I thought it was time to leave. I was finally declared a "prohibited immigrant", and I came up to Northern Rhodesia just before independence. I didn't want to get involved in politics. I only wanted to live in a more just society.

'Then I met Tamara. She had fled South Africa and was working here as a nurse, with none of her family around. So I wrote a long letter to Chuchu – that's her brother in Dar whom you met – asking him if he would let his sister marry a white man. I was really worried! Of course he's the least racist person in the world and he said yes, so that's when we got married.'

Tamara, who had much of her brother's air of quiet authority, was pessimistic about returning to South Africa. 'At least our children can grow up here without suffering discrimination. They go to the International School and learn to live in a multiracial society.'

Brian spoke of serious economic problems for Zambia. 'Kaunda supports the liberation movements in Rhodesia and South Africa, and the country suffers for this. The border with Rhodesia is closed and importing goods for my shop is problematic. Our copper exports have to go by road via Tanzania until the new railway opens. Meanwhile the shops are full of Chinese goods to help pay for it – because even fellow-socialists tie up their aid with strings.'

On Sunday Sonia took us out to have lunch with one of her friends and then to visit the Chipimo family. We seemed to pass miles of garden suburbs, some with massive new villas, others with more modest homes, but all fringed with colourful trees and awash with rainbow bougainvillea. European girls on ponies were riding along the wide grass verge and buying ice-creams from the Kentucky Fried Chicken stall. Indian and African families were driving up to shop at the supermarket. It was comfortingly relaxed, comfortably multiracial. Sonia's friend was a teacher and ran a large chaotic household full of animals and children; we might have been back in an English hippy community.

By contrast, at Anna's large country home we were led straight into a solemn family conclave, where about twenty people were sitting quietly listening to an elderly man who was speaking into a tape recorder. The modern chairs and settees were ranged four-square along the walls and we felt we were back in African society, not just because many of the women were wearing traditional dress and some were suckling infants, but also because of the whole feeling of family respect, the silence in which they listened and the quietness of the children.

Elias, with perfect manners and ease, switched off the tape recorder and introduced us. 'This is my uncle, he is talking about our family history and we are taping it for future generations. Please sit down. How was your trip?'

I felt we were intruding and took an opportunity to visit Anna in the kitchen, where she was roasting maize. Other people arrived to express their condolences over the death. Soon there were two groups: the European and non-family on the porch, drinking beer and eating roasted cobs, the family still sitting inside, while Anna and Elias moved serenely between the two. Somehow she found time to gather all her children together for a photograph to take back to Aunt Mary.

We left at sunset, under a flaming red sky, with mauve and purple clouds to the north. Was this a good augury? Would this apparently relaxed, tolerant society keep its peaceful sanity in spite of the tensions around them in Mozambique and Angola, in Rhodesia and South Africa?

※

The answer to the above seems yes, comparatively speaking, and with blips. Over the next fifteen years, copper prices fell, Zambia accumulated huge debts, and, globally speaking, socialism fell out of fashion. In 1991 Kaunda was forced to reinstate multiparty democracy and free elections brought the 'Movement for Multiparty Democracy' to power. Our friend Elias Chipimo was a strong supporter and held office under the new President, Chiluba. Cautiously, they began to liberalise the economy and by 2002 even the copper mines were privatised. Global institutions approved, some debt was forgiven, and Zambia entered a period of economic growth. In 2015, many people were still poor and the economy was too reliant on minerals, but regular elections had been held and the country had been peaceful. Elias Chipimo Jnr – ten years old when we met him – was leading a new party ostensibly dedicated to human values and honest government.

I visited the University of Zambia a couple of times in the mid-1990s, as part of link programmes with Sussex University. Most of the senior positions in the education field were now held by very competent Zambians, many of them women. One of them invited me to stay at their home, where I encountered a strange contradiction. Greeting an older male relative, she would kneel before him. When I remonstrated in the name of feminism, she told me, eyes twinkling: 'It is amazing how assertive one can be while speaking on one's knees!' Zambians, it seems, are good at finding constructive compromises and working things out in their own way.

PART FOUR
South Africa

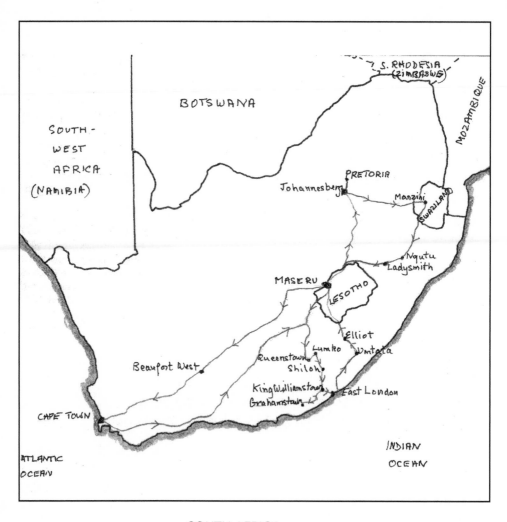

SOUTH AFRICA
Places visited by car.

CHAPTER 21

First Views of the Republic of South Africa

In which we explore our first contacts across the colour line and find possibilities emerging.

Flying over the high veld, the hazy brown ground below us resolved itself into large farms, patched with dark ploughed fields, and then merged into the suburbs. Every other house seemed to have a swimming pool, a blue eye winking up from clusters of trees; these must be rich – and therefore white – areas. Cooling towers on the horizon, slowly puffing out steam, reminded us we were returning to an industrial world. Here the African bush had been banished and replaced with motorways and buildings, with concrete, glass and smoke. A glimpse of yellow, flat-topped hillocks – the gold-mine dumps – and we settled among the jets at Jan Smuts Airport. At immigration there was no search and little questioning from the dour official. As he stamped my passport I remembered this would prevent us from ever re-entering Tanzania. So the way back was barred now: for good or ill we were in South Africa.

Towards the southern end of the continent, the vast and ancient rocky plates of Africa are tipped up, rising towards the south-east to the 10,000 foot peaks of the Drakensberg. From here short rivers tumble down into the warm but narrow coastal plains of Natal and Transkei. North-westward stretches the great grassy plateau – the high veld – drying out eventually into the Kalahari and Nambian deserts. It is a beautiful landscape, veined with precious minerals but hard to farm.

The first known inhabitants were the hunting San and the herding

Khoikhoi. Then Bantu-speaking peoples spread down from the north, along the eastern coast and onto the plateau, bringing iron-working and crops with them. In 1652 the Dutch East India Company set up a trading settlement at the Cape which, over the next 150 years, spread north and eastward; as fertile land was scarce, many Dutch-speaking farmers (known as *boers*) became pastoralists too, taking their flocks up over the hills into the interior. After Britain annexed the Cape in 1806, and thirty years later abolished slavery, this movement turned into a great exodus of Boers who then set up their own republics on the high veld. Meanwhile, the African kingdoms such as the Zulu and Ndebele were expanding and consolidating their power. The scene was set for clashes of race and culture.

After decades of political struggles and several wars, first between the immigrants from Europe and the indigenous Africans and then between the Boers and the British, the Union of South Africa was established in 1910 with the Whites firmly in power. There were still tensions between the English-speaking and Afrikaans-speaking groups but gradually they drew together to protect their privileged position against the black majority.

By 1913 black Africans were beginning to adjust to their loss of independence and to engage with new ways of farming. Some rented land from the Europeans, paying in cash, labour or by '50/50' share-cropping; some even bought their own farms. This did not suit the rising class of white commercial farmers nor the industrial barons who needed workers for mines and factories. So in 1913 they passed a Land Act forbidding Africans to own or rent land except in the Native Reserves, which comprised then about 7% of the country. In the remaining 93%, they could only be employed as labourers. This held back the rise of a black peasant farming class, which was threatening the Europeans, and provided a source of cheap labour for the towns.

In 1948 the Afrikaner-supported National Party led by Dr Malan came to power and under the label 'apartheid' began legislating for complete separation of the racial groups in all aspects of life – formalising what was already accepted practice. The keystone of this policy was the 1959 'Promotion of Bantu Self-Government Act,' which set up ten supposedly independent 'homelands', one for each of the ten tribal groups. These were to be farming communities, and would also act as dormitories and retirement homes for the black men labouring in the white towns. When they were unemployed or no longer fit for work, they had to return to their 'ethnic homeland' even if they were not born there.

This gave the government a pretext, over the next twenty years, for moving over 3,000,000 black people from farms, towns or so-called 'black spots' into their designated 'homelands'. Not only were these areas – just 13% of the country – far too small to accommodate all their 'citizens,' they were also the least productive areas, being dry, rocky, or already overgrazed and eroded. Furthermore, most of these 'Bantustans' as they were named, were made up of separate 'islands' or pockets of land, only Transkei being geographically coherent. As the flagship 'homeland' it was given 'internal self-government' in 1963 with Chief Kaiser Matanzima as 'Prime Minister'.

On arrival we booked into the Holiday Inn at the airport, an 'international,' or integrated, hotel. There were no 'Whites Only' signs, but also very few black guests. The receptionist was white while the porters were African, and we noticed they didn't catch our eyes to share a laugh as a child chased a football down the corridor. Our room had every comfort except TV; there was as yet no television in South Africa for fear of foreign influences. Beside the bed *Die Bybel* was laid out in English and Afrikaans. We thought it might be open at the passage saying that the '*Sons of Ham should be hewers of wood and drawers of water for ever*', but it wasn't.

Downstairs in Ouma's Koffie Huis we gloated over European food: toasted cheese sandwiches, real butter, apples and even Cadbury's chocolate from the automat. Only the milk tasted of preservative; this was not quite Europe. But it didn't seem like Africa either; the black hotel staff walking home were dressed in tweed skirts, jackets and berets, looking rather like Edinburgh ladies – except for the knee-length woollen wrappers over their skirts. It was cool, with stormy skies and I put on the sweaters I had not worn since Kilimanjaro.

We began calling our contacts, tentatively since we knew none of them in person. The phone was less efficient than we expected; the service was desperately under-manned because some of the jobs were White-reserved, for example Blacks couldn't install phones. This was South Africa.

Friends of friends first: Beryl Unterhalter responded warmly and arranged to meet us in town. Then business: we left a message for Mr Henwood of Anglo-American. Finally the South African Council of Churches: Harry Makumbire came on the line. 'We bring greetings from Rakhetla Tsehlana in London,' I began unthinkingly. 'Please come to the office, it's better than talking like this. I'll be there at three this afternoon,' Harry said quickly and the phone went click. It was only later we discovered the phones to the SACC were tapped. This was South Africa.

We took the airport bus into town, intensely curious to experience this strange country more directly. At the city terminal we saw our first 'Whites Only' notice, and two black men promptly walked through it. But transport was indeed segregated: buses took Blacks or Whites but never both. One railway entrance was almost deserted, through the other flowed the stream of black faces, in at breakfast time and out again in the evening, of workers who serviced Johannesburg. Yet all races could enter the shops if they had the money; in the posh department stores sales assistants were white or, in cheaper places, 'Coloured'; only the man in the photo shop selling cheap films was black. South Africa was divided by class as well as race.

In the heart of the city vast square towers rose about us into the hazy blue sky, above wide bustling streets full of cars and buses. The air was fresh and invigorating in spite of the sun, for Johannesburg lies at 6,000 feet above sea level. Black faces mingled with white on the pavements, all wearing European dress; women didn't carry babies and there were no street traders, though on the pavements there were Africans sitting on the ground resting or eating. People walked as though intent on their own business – and then it struck us: there were no greetings, no smiles, no eye contact between white and black people. We didn't need to learn the local phrase for 'Good morning, how are you, how is your family, your work, your tiredness,' because there was an invisible pane of glass between us and them. We wondered how, even if, we could break through the barriers in this strange South Africa.

Our first sally was to a foundation stone of South Africa's wealth and power: the Anglo-American Corporation. Founded by Ernest

Oppenheimer in 1917, it grew to be the world's largest mining company with interests in gold and copper, coal and diamonds. We walked down Main Street to its massive granite headquarters and found Mr Henwood in a spacious office, furnished with teakwood desk, leather armchairs and nineteenth-century prints on the walls. A robust figure, with greying hair and sharp eyes, he greeted us warily but once our credentials were established by Patrick mentioning his stockbroking background, the reserve vanished. 'What are you doing in this country?' he asked.

'We want to find out more about the political and economic situation,' said Patrick. I added I was interested in education. Obviously surprised we didn't mention game parks, Mr Henwood picked up one of the easier threads.

'You will find the work of the Oppenheimer Trust most interesting,' he said enthusiastically. 'We provide bursaries for black students. Recently the government has vastly increased the amount spent on black education: it has risen from 13 million rand a year to over 100 million. That's good progress, isn't it? I can take you into Soweto and show you some schools if you like.'

'That would be wonderful,' I responded, wondering about the statistics.

'Do come to lunch with us one weekend. My wife would be delighted to meet you. She can tell you about the "Centre for Concern" she runs, where black domestic servants in white areas can learn housecraft, sewing or typing. Some people are opposed to this, since the women might no longer wish to be servants, but we think one should teach them to be proud of being servants. Not everyone can be a Chief, there must be some Indians, don't you think?'

We took the first of our deep breaths and accepted his invitation.

As an antidote, we went off to find the Institute of Race Relations and its bookshop. Asking the way at a hotel, we heard an English-sounding voice behind us: 'I can take you there.'

'Elliott, what on earth are you doing here?'

'I'm just here on one of my routine visits. They let me in again – I'm on the blacklist, so I never know if I'll be barred.'

Elliott Kendall was originally a Methodist missionary; he was now African Affairs Secretary to the British Council of Churches and an ardent opponent of apartheid.

We exchanged family news; it was his daughter Alison who had told us about the lake of hospitality. He had just come from Mozambique and in typical Elliott fashion, kept dropping interesting remarks.

'There's a Marxist revolution in progress there. It seems to be taking much the same form as the Chinese Revolution in 1949… We had to leave China then, of course, but I can see many similarities… The whole country is participating. Half the Portuguese have fled, so the services are undermanned, and since so few Mozambicans got any education, we don't know how they will manage. If only people here would take a good look and learn some lessons… Anyway, best of luck with your trip. Don't forget to call at the South African Council of Churches.'

That was our next stop. Harry Makubire was a wiry man of intense energy and intelligence, barely containable within his small poky office. This time we established our credentials with a message from his exiled friend in London and told him we wanted to know about apartheid. Phones kept ringing and people were constantly at his door asking questions, but finally he sat down long enough to tell us about his role.

'I do family and welfare work for the Council. My main task nowadays is looking after the dependents of the political prisoners, and in particular I try to help educate the youngsters. I want to send the high-flyers overseas for further training so they can return and be leaders in their own communities.'

'We understand that they can get scholarships from charities like the Oppenheimer Trust to study at white universities,' I said.

'But there are very few bursaries and it is so difficult for them there! The white staff are prejudiced against them. And they don't always pass – imagine having to travel in from Soweto and then studying evenings in an overcrowded shack with no electricity! Much better to get them overseas' scholarships where they live in congenial surroundings and are treated as equals.'

'Mr Henwood was saying that much more money is spent on black education nowadays,' Patrick offered.

'Rubbish! The Department of Bantu Education[29] spends R40[30] on each black child, while R400 is spent on each white child – a tenfold difference! And those 'bush' colleges' – (he was referring to the new black universities in the 'homelands') – 'they're all staffed by white professors. No real advancement for black academics even there.' We began to see how many different perspectives there might be in South Africa.

'First Elliott turns up, now you – how splendid that the British Churches haven't forgotten us,' said Harry. 'We do feel very isolated sometimes.'

Rather embarrassed, we hastened to explain that we were not part of any church group but had more secular interests in economics and politics. We gave him the names of the black people we had introductions to in Soweto; of course, he knew them too and promised to help us to get in touch. When Beryl Unterhalter came to pick us up at the SACC we found they knew each other well and even worked on the same committees.

We took a different deep breath. So it *would* be possible to meet and talk with black people, much as we had done for the last six months! So there *was* some possibility of multiracial cooperation and friendship, however much disapproved of by the authorities! Just how difficult – and how magnificently rewarding – this was to be, we had yet to find out.

Beryl proved equally energetic and welcoming. Dark-haired, svelte and smartly dressed, she lectured in sociology at Witwatersrand University, at that time one of the most liberal of South African universities. She rushed us round the campus in pouring rain, allowing us a few glimpses of neo-classical architecture straddling the hilltop looking north – sunwards, of course – over the rich suburbs below, and took us down there to her home.

The 'Northern Suburbs' of Johannesburg are a synonym for white wealth. Large houses stand in shady gardens, each with its winking swimming pool, behind iron gates and guard dogs. Over a welcome cup of tea we explained our quest to try and understand South Africa.

She rose and fetched a pile of large, paper-bound volumes. 'These are some of the publications of SPRO-CAS. That's the *Study Project on*

---

[29] Bantu, properly speaking, distinguishes a group of African languages. The term was used by the apartheid regime to denote Africans and acquired a derogatory meaning. In particular, Bantu Education was a designedly inferior form of schooling for Blacks.

[30] At that time £1 = approx. R1.50

Christianity in Apartheid Society, published by a group called the Christian Institute. They are looking at the possibilities of peaceful change. Take these; they will help you.' This was our introduction to what would become a central thread in our visit.

'And what prospects do you see for peaceful change?' Patrick asked.

Beryl shook her head. 'Not a lot. Our daughters are at university in the UK and our son David is doing sixth form studies at Bedales. We want them to have the option of working in a free society.'

Now, for once, we became the questioned. 'Do tell me about Nigeria and Tanzania. I would so love to go there but as South African citizens we can't travel to the north. Won't you stay to supper? My husband Jack will want to know all about President Nyerere's policies.'

Jack was the South African equivalent of a QC and had defended certain political cases in the Republic and Lesotho; he and Patrick were soon immersed in a discussion of ujamaa. Beryl drew everyone in turn into the conversation and our discussions flowed through a splendid meal accompanied by local wines and liqueurs. As we left she said: 'I have a permit to visit Soweto and I'd be happy to take you there. Oh, and next time you come, do bring your slides of Nigeria!'

As Jack drove us back to the airport hotel, right across the city and out the other side, the skyscrapers were all lit up and it did look like a 'City of Gold'[31]. The abiding impression was of wealth and power – but how strong were the foundations?

A cartoon in the *Rand Daily Mail* summed it up for us: a white man is painting a slogan on the wall: 'RSA has the richest economy in the world'. He is standing on a plank resting on the shoulders of some black men, then looks round and says: 'Right, boys, put me down now.'

How long would *they* keep holding *them* up? We were to pose this question again and again, and get as many different answers.

---

[31] This nickname for Johannesburg has even been Africanised as 'Egoli'.

CHAPTER 22
First Interlude in Lesotho: April

In which we settle into our base with the Hlaleles and buy a car; we
are drawn to the mountains and meet some significant people.

Lesotho is the land that neither Zulus, Boers nor Britons could conquer.
After Shaka's wars in the 1820s, remnants of defeated tribes came up
from Natal over the Drakensberg Mountains and sought refuge in the
wide plains beyond. Those settling near the western foothills came under
the leadership of an able young chief known as Moshoeshoe; through
limited warfare and much diplomacy, including marrying many wives
from different clans, his authority became recognised over a wide area.
Intellectually curious and anxious to make the best of new opportunities,
Moshoeshoe sent for missionaries to educate his people in Western ways.
The first to respond was the Paris Evangelical Mission Society, followed
by Anglicans and Roman Catholics; these religious fault lines still run
through Basotho[32] society, exacerbated by clan and class. They all built
different churches and schools, trading stores opened, ploughs, guns and
European clothes were imported and the Basotho flourished.

It was the 'white tribes', however, sweeping north in search of land, gold
and diamonds, who drove them out of the richer agricultural plateaux
and back into the mountains. In 1867 Moshoeshoe appealed to Queen
Victoria. 'As a flea creeps into a blanket, may my people find protection
from our enemies under your rule,' he wrote. So Basutoland became a
protectorate and escaped incorporation into the Union of South Africa;
within its boundaries no white people could own land and there was no

---

[32] The country is *Lesotho*, the people are called collectively *Basotho* (sing. *Mosotho*) and they
speak *Sesotho*.

apartheid. In 1966 it became independent under the name of Lesotho with a constitutional monarch – Moshoeshoe II – a House of Chiefs and an elected Parliament. It was to this singular country we had come: about the size of Wales, but as mountainous as Switzerland, politically free, yet landlocked into the Republic of South Africa and economically dependent on it. For the next three months, it would be the base from which we explored the strange world of apartheid and to which we kept returning for interludes of peace and sanity.

Here we were among friends. Anna Hlalele, in her student days, had spent holidays with the Stuarts and read bedtime stories to Patrick's young half-brothers, Robert and James, so that as small children, they would call any black woman 'Anna-lady'. Her own children, Victor and Mary, had done A levels in the UK and Mary was now living in our own house while studying microbiology at London University.

At Maseru's tiny airport the Hlaleles were waiting for us. Anna was a petite, smiling lady, neatly dressed European-style, who chatted easily to everyone, while Wilson was more reserved. 'We're living in our posh house in Qoqolosing Road, alongside the diplomats,' joked Anna. 'After independence we were the first Basotho to build in the "white" area of Maseru West, and move out of the "African location[33]"'. Their house was a large roomy brick-built bungalow, standing in its own garden, with the obligatory 'servants' quarters' at the back, now home to members of the extended family. Over champagne and a huge meal we recounted some of our adventures so far. Anna had visited Nigeria and had not been impressed.

'Their cities are so dirty,' she complained. 'They just don't seem to care. Every time I came back from shopping I took a shower! I couldn't possibly live there.'

Enormously considerate and kind, with many social and professional commitments, Anna lived in a social whirl; while she saw to it that we were well looked-after, she mostly left us to our own devices. It was exactly what we needed.

---

[33] In pre-apartheid and colonial days there was already de facto segregation in white-settled Southern Africa. Most Africans lived in areas known as 'locations', usually outside the white towns.

Maseru lies 5,000 feet above sea level, thirty degrees south, and winter was coming on. From Anna's garden we looked across the River Caledon to the 'lost territories' now in South Africa, where the wide sweeping grasslands, broken by *koppies* – flat-topped, steep-sided hills – glowed in the evening sun. As the light faded the sky turned pink, then amethyst and darkened to a million stars. We scrambled into our comfortable bed and snuggled down underneath a pile of bedclothes, with chilly feet, glad to have reached a haven to rest up for a while.

Maseru had a peaceful, remote feeling; it lies in a sloping hollow between low, rounded and rocky hills, whose sandstone cliffs fall in layers to brown grassy slopes. Next day we walked along the gravelled roads lined with large houses, past the trees hiding the royal palace and down onto Kingsway, tarred and named for the visit of George VI in 1947. The sky was cloudy and a cool breeze zipped down from the mountains. There were few cars and the traffic was mainly minibus taxis hooting up and down for fares; most people were on foot, occasionally on horseback.

But this was Africa again: there was a buzz of conversation on the streets, shouted greetings, warm handclasps, people gathering in knots to talk. Our white faces stood out and people looked to see if they knew us, nodded and passed on. Almost everyone was wearing a 'blanket' of some kind over their European clothes; the men wore them fastened over the shoulder, the women wrapped them like huge, thick shawls over their backs, sometimes with their babies peeking out from underneath. These were not traditional; nineteenth-century Basotho found the traders' woollen blankets far more comfortable than antelope-skin *karosses* and Yorkshire weaving mills flourished on the trade, bringing out particular designs such as 'Prince of Wales Feathers' or 'Spitfire' to suit the times. Only the conical grass hats with their distinctive topknot are truly traditional, but most people were wearing woollen berets – much warmer against the cold winter wind!

Maseru at that time was hardly more than a large village. We passed solid, sandstone buildings: government offices, a church, the post office and a sprawling hospital. In the market, which sold mainly cheap manufactured goods and processed foodstuffs, vendors sat huddled over charcoal braziers, or clustered in the shelter of a north-facing wall seeking the pale winter sunshine. Outside the Mines Recruiting Office there were groups of men in drab blankets leaning on their shepherds' sticks, waiting their turn to go to work in the gold mines of Johannesburg.

For this was the other face of Lesotho. The census recorded two million people, but at any given time half of them were away working in the Republic – as miners, factory workers, or domestic servants. In general, Basotho were better educated than black South Africans and were in demand as workers – but under apartheid law they could not bring their families with them nor settle in the country. They lived in hostels and sent their money home to pay for rebuilding their houses, for school fees, for their parents' medical costs or even for someone to plough their land for next year's crop of mealies. Migrant earnings kept Lesotho's economy afloat; there was not enough land for everyone and so they were dependent on the Republic.

There was hardly any industry. Well-meaning expatriates had helped set up knitting and weaving workshops among the women which produced wall hangings, ties, shawls and so on for tourists at inflated prices; they were sold in a shop built to resemble a Basotho hat and crowned by the inconic topknot. From a sheepskin workshop Patrick bought a warm jerkin to keep out the cold and I got bedroom slippers.

We spent nearly two weeks in Maseru, relaxing and catching up on chores and answering our UK mail. There was laundry to be done, repairs to make and two weeks of the diary to write up; I summarised some of our adventures in a round-robin letter which I stencilled and ran off in Anna's office to send to friends. Everything seemed easier in the invigorating air: the clothes dried quicker, one's hand didn't stick to the page with sweat and even the post office was friendly, eventually producing the parcel of winter clothes we'd posted in Lagos. Anna let us use her kitchen so we could cater for ourselves and Patrick learnt that eggs take longer to boil at 5,000 feet above sea level. (They say Lesotho has the highest *lowest* point of any country – apparently Tibet and Bhutan have deeper gorges!)

We decided to buy a car to give us maximum flexibility within the Republic's segregated systems and soon we'd acquired a four-year-old blue VW Beetle from a departing expatriate. It was to give us a few headaches but the Lesotho number plate brought unexpected benefits.

After we'd been there a couple of days people starting calling round in the evenings, curious to meet us. Anna knew everyone; she had run a radio programme on nutrition and had worked in the Ministry of Agriculture in Chief Leabua Jonathan's first government. When Jonathan's Basotho National Party lost the next elections, in 1970, he refused to accept the result, imprisoned the leaders of the opposition Basotho Congress Party and carried on ruling with military support. Since then, politics had become somewhat toxic and our friends preferred to discuss South Africa.

Vincent Malebo, Director of Broadcasting, asked us what we thought of Johannesburg and we said how horrified we were at the racial segregation.

'Oh, petty apartheid has much improved,' Vincent replied. 'I can eat and sleep in most Johannesburg hotels, but not restaurants. The Group Areas Act says – I quote: "It is a punishable offence for anyone, in an area allocated to persons of another racial group, to partake of refreshments that involve the use of seating in a restaurant or tea room".'

'So that's why we saw black South Africans sitting out on the street kerbs at lunchtime!' exclaimed Patrick.

'Yes, but I think that it's now up to the black people themselves to show the confidence to demand equal treatment. I well remember when I went with the Ghanaian Robert Gardiner to Bloemfontein Airport. He simply ignored the "Whites Only" notices and breezed straight through and nobody tried to stop him!'

'They probably recognised him and didn't want a diplomatic incident,' I suggested.

'No, I think it's the confidence. I don't have it – I sat on a "Whites Only" bench once, after I'd been in the UK, but I could feel their eyes boring into me and oh, I just got up and left.'

A couple of days later, there were African guests from another quarter. It was Saturday, the Hlaleles were away and Hlomi, who lived in the back quarters and helped out betimes, was to look after us. We'd just finished supper when there was a knock on the door. A contact of Anna's, with three friends, had arrived from the Republic asking to stay the night; they had a puncture and couldn't travel further. Hlomi, looking at us warningly, said there were already guests. 'Well, this is Africa,' we thought and smiled welcomingly before disappearing and leaving Hlomi to sort out the beds.

When we got up next morning they had gone to church. I'd just made a small stew for our lunch when they reappeared and produced a huge cold leg of lamb. Mr and Mrs Ukwe, with their friends Alice and Grace, told us they'd come from Sharpeville to sing with a church choir and spend the weekend in a free country, whereupon we pooled all the food, opened a bottle of whisky and sat down together.

'Sharpeville? Isn't that where the massacre was in 1960[34]?' I asked.

'Yes, our church is just across the street from where it happened. We can still remember the peaceful march, everyone showing their passes, and then the police opening fire. It was terrible. Several of our friends were killed or hurt.'

Mr Ukwe told us he worked as a long-distance lorry driver, making good money with overtime. His wife had just been taken on as sales lady in a store which until recently had only white staff, so they felt things were changing, if slowly. Three children were at boarding school and they'd just bought a big second-hand Chrysler. Clearly this was an independent and upwardly mobile group.

'We like travelling so much! Now we can manage to go to nearby countries which aren't segregated. We went to Gaborone for Christmas. Our friend Alice here, she has even visited Lourenco Marques.'

'We've been to Nigeria and Tanzania,' I began and the next hour passed quickly. While Patrick and Mr Ukwe went off to fix the puncture, I brought out my slides and regaled the ladies with pictures of Nigerian fashions, as well as with our Kilimanjaro adventures. Then they asked for a photo of us all together.

'This has been such a nice visit,' they said. 'Please visit us in Sharpeville. Our priest, Father Molapo, would be so pleased to see you. And it is permitted to meet you in a church.'

We wrote down the address, uncertain of being able to keep the promise. But we did and that was to lead to a final wonderfully warming experience.

There was another of Aunt Mary's students in Maseru, whom we had not presumed to contact directly – Queen 'Mamohato. Halfway through

---

[34] Under apartheid all black men had to carry a 'pass book' for identification, so that their movement, jobs and places of residence could be controlled. In 1959 this was extended to women. On 21st March 1960 there was a peaceful demonstration against the 'pass laws' outside Sharpeville police station. The police opened fire, killing 69 and wounding 180.

her course at Bath she was summoned back to be married to the heir to the throne. She kept in touch with Mary and we'd once met them both for tea at a London hotel but that seemed a tenuous connection.

'Nonsense,' said Anna briskly. 'I know her well. She'll be delighted to see you. I'll get you an invitation to the garden party she's giving for Women's Day next week.'

Patrick, who wasn't at all sure he should be there at all, put on his only suit and this time I was demurely attired in a long red and gold dress I'd made out of Tanzanian cloth. Anna, like most of the Basotho women, wore the so-called 'traditional' skirt and head tie, made from 'German print': cotton patterned in brown, red or blue, showing scenes of animals and plants. The first missionaries imported this cloth so their converts could cover up their breasts and it had become a kind of national dress.

The palace had once been the governor's residence, the building less impressive than the spacious garden designed by some homesick colonial. In marched the band of the Police Military Unit, followed by uniformed youth bands with drum majorettes leading a procession of schoolchildren. The sun shone, the air was warm for once, the scent of pine and gum trees drifted on the breeze, while the martial music echoed out to the distant cliffs.

Suddenly all the women broke into ululations – expressions of joy – as the Queen arrived, wearing the special chieftain's blanket; taller than most, she looked distinctly regal and assured. Anna was mistress of ceremonies, which started with a prayer, a hymn and a praise-song to the Queen. Then came the boys' dance in the stamping style made famous by the Zulus. The girls' dance was quite different: they knelt and gently swayed their head, shoulders and torso, never rising from the ground – rather too submissive for Women's Day, I thought. There were gifts and speeches, followed by tea and cake with more music and dancing, till the national anthem brought it to a close. While the official photographs were being taken we were summoned by Anna to meet the Queen, who, doubtless well briefed, said she remembered us and would we come to supper at the palace on Tuesday.

The royal supper party was a modest and sombre affair and, as I was suffering from backache, a rather uncomfortable one for me. We were escorted by guards into a large, dimly-lit room dominated by a portrait of King Moshoeshoe I. The King, who kept strictly to his ceremonial role, often pursuing his own academic interests back in Oxford, was away at the time. The Queen herself seemed rather shy, but the King's private secretary, an extremely bright and sophisticated talker, kept the conversation going through the meal.

'So you visited Tanzania? His Majesty and I were very impressed with much of what we saw when visiting there.' It turned out that Mr. Phafane had worked in the Ministry of Education and that he and the King wanted to encourage a more practical curriculum in local schools.

'What do you think about the "homeland" policy in South Africa?' we asked, having heard that the Lesotho government was making overtures to the 'homeland' leaders.

Diplomatically he avoided a direct answer. 'The South African government wants to divide and rule. You know, they deliberately foment fights between Basotho and Xhosas in the mine compounds to stop the Transkei getting too friendly with Lesotho when it gets more independence.' Conspiracy theory was obviously alive and well in Lesotho.

There was a large expatriate community in Lesotho at this time, since the small embattled country – one of those later known as the 'front-line' states[35] – was considered a worthy recipient of aid. In Tanzania Andrew Coulson had told us to visit his sister Janet as her husband Don Taylor was teaching at the university in Roma, and a London friend had recommended Bridget and Jasper Selwyn. So we sent off letters.

Typically, Bridget was the first to reply and, being an old Africa hand, bustled round in person to Anna's house to organise us.

'I just picked up your message,' she said. 'Are you free for dinner on Sunday? Jasper teaches maths at Lesotho High School and I'm running a nursery school.'

At dinner, Jasper and I began a conversation about education which has continued on and off for forty years while Bridget enlightened us about local politics.

'The leaders seem more concerned with staying in power than improving

---

[35] So called, because the apartheid forces took their war against the liberation movements into the neighbouring countries.

the country,' she said. 'There are good civil servants but they just get frustrated. Even though many people still respect the chiefs, they want Leabua Jonathan to hold elections, but so far he hasn't.'

Next day we set off for the university. The road lifts gently out of the Maseru suburbs and passes between two rocky hills lying like crouching beasts guarding the town. Beyond, across the flat, gullied fields rise the blue-purple peaks of the Maluti, the western side of what South Africans call the Drakensberg, looking hazy in the morning sunshine. It was harvest time; thin stalks of tawny yellow maize swayed in the wind or were being cut by women with sickles. When the horse-drawn carts had taken away the cobs the scrawny herds of cattle moved in to find what nourishment they could from the stalks and weeds. All summer the cattle, sheep and angora goats had been up in the mountain pastures, looked after by herdboys in crude summer camps. Now they were back in the lowlands, but as there were no fences the boys still had to guard them with swinging sticks and high-pitched calls, ragged blankets pulled around their shoulders against the chilly morning.

'That's why women are better educated in Lesotho than men,' Anna had explained to us. 'Girls go to school all year round, the boys only when they can be spared from herding. You see, cattle can only be handled by men and since the fathers are away in the mines, the boys must take over. Women plant, weed and harvest but if there is no man around to harness the oxen to the plough, the land lies fallow.' That might well be true, but this lopsided education had become a cultural norm even in the towns; Anna herself was better educated than her husband and we met several such couples.

The road, still tarred, swung onwards till it cut through a ridge of rock and we looked into a wide semi-circle of peaks, dropping in layered ridges formed by ancient lava, towards the wooded settlement lying in the dip. Here the Catholic fathers had founded their first mission station – known as Roma – and in 1945 built a training college for priests which had now become a constituent part of the University of Botswana, Lesotho and Swaziland.

Handsome new sandstone buildings were arranged round open tree-lined spaces, while students warmed themselves in the sun, scorning blankets in favour of European jeans and anoraks. Two buildings stood out from the others; one was an ultra-modern Catholic chapel, built rather like the conical Basotho hat in white stucco with a crown on top; the other was a two-storeyed set of shabby concrete offices built round a courtyard – the Oppenheimer Building – which housed the education department and was obviously part of Mr Henwood's outreach work.

Staff houses lay in crescents to the north, each sandstone bungalow standing in a substantial garden. Over coffee we sat on the Taylors' porch, shaded by a climbing rose, and looked out to the magnificent sandstone cliffs and the peak of Mount Makhetha beyond. The long bluegum leaves rustled in the wind amid the soft fluting of red-winged starlings.

We raked over our respective memories of Kilimanjaro – Don and Janet had also reached Uhuru peak – and then listened to their accounts of teaching in Botswana.

'I taught at Swaneng Hill,' said Don. 'It was founded in Serowe by Patrick van Rensburg, a renegade Afrikaner who wanted to integrate academic and non-academic schooling in South Africa and got exiled for his pains. They tried to teach practical skills alongside academic ones, to make education relevant to the likely future needs of the students.'

'What did you teach?' I asked.

'Development studies. It teaches the students about their own society and how they can participate in changing it. We used practical work to ram home some of the lessons. Lesotho wants to introduce this into their schools and that's why I'm here training teachers to teach it.'

'But that's the sort of thing I've been teaching in London...' Another conversation started that would lead, in 1979, to my taking up Don's job and to an office in that shabby Oppenheimer Building, which was still there, un-refurbished, in 2012.

Reluctantly we left the Taylors and, leaving the tar behind, took the mountain road leading upwards into the heart of Lesotho to visit the Bushman rock paintings at Ha Khotso. Each bend or hill brought another magnificent panorama into sight and we had a fine view of the sharp ridge of Machache rising to nearly 10,000 feet. Sometimes horsemen would come riding down the ridges or children run alongside the car calling out 'dibongbong', asking for sweets in corrupted missionary French.

In the lowlands many houses were just little rectangular brick boxes with one-slope roofs, but up in the mountains they built square or round huts out of quarried stone with thatched roofs and elaborate porches that kept out the wind. It was all much more substantial than anything we had seen in Tanzania. Of course the harsh climate called for a higher standard of building but they looked less drab and suggested more prosperity. The real problem seemed to be agriculture. Erosion was a major problem and we saw fields of maize and sorghum with deep gullies running through them. Over-grazing, over-population and a disinclination to terrace the fields seemed to be responsible.

We had our picnic lunch sitting in the warm sun on the ridge above the gorge. Cow bells were ringing across the fields and people were threshing beans down by the village. We followed the path down to where a sandstone cliff jutted out over the stream, its base eroded away to form a great cave-like shelter. Here the Bushmen, as the San people were nicknamed, had used white, red and ochre to create paintings full of life and movement. There were eland, lion and birds accompanied by figures of people standing, dancing, hunting and running. They had survived perhaps a thousand years of wind and weather and some were faint now; the watchman sprayed them with water to sharpen up the colours so I could take pictures. The San once hunted and gathered food all over Southern Africa, but when the pastoralists and farmers, first Bantu and then European, chased them off the land, they found their last refuges in the mountains and deserts. They are gone from Lesotho now but sometimes a square yellowish face, or substantial buttocks, reminds one that their genes live on.

We bought a road atlas and started planning trips into the Republic.

'Look how difficult it is to get round Lesotho – whether you go south or the north, the Drakensberg block the way. I'd like to see Durban, though.'

'We must go back to Johannesburg, there's so much to do there.'

'That telegram from Francina saying come to Swaziland, it didn't actually give us her address!'

'Capetown would be good, but it looks an awfully long drive – maybe just to Grahamstown and Port Elizabeth?'

'What about Transkei and Umtata?'

We decided to go back to Johannesburg, then on to Swaziland and Nqutu in KwaZulu, returning through the north of Lesotho; we thought it would take three to four weeks. After that we would decide on a southern loop. We would cast ourselves out on the tide and let fate decide; it took us on to some very strange and interesting roads that we would never have found on our own.

The Maseru craft shop built like a Basotho Hat.

Anna and Wilson Hlalele at
their country home.

A Mosotho horseman wearing a
traditional blanket.

Our Volkswagen Beetle entering Lesotho at the northern border.

Small herdboys selling Basotho hats at Bushman's Pass.

Queen 'Mamahato (wearing blanket) and her ladies; Anna Hlalele is on the far right.

Rural women carrying their goods on their heads.

Roma: the University chapel.

Roma: a sandstone staff house on campus.

Ha Khotso cave paintings.

St Charles Mission against the Maluti mountains.

Orange River valley in the highlands.

Homesteads at Thaba Bosiu.

Traditional village with rondavels.

Wilson's trading store at Ha Ntlamas.

Sledge drawn by oxen.

The road towards the Maluti with aloes and riders.

View over the lowlands from Morija.

CHAPTER 23

Exploring Johannesburg Through White Eyes

In which we set up base in Jo'burg, are entertained by both British and Boer friends, visit the temples of Afrikanerdom and of gold and eventually reach Soweto.

In Europe it was May Day but we were going into South Africa and all thoughts of singing *The Red Flag* must be strictly banished.

The River Caledon here separates Lesotho and South Africa, winding sleepily along through grey-green willows and golden-tinted poplars. The border posts were at either end of Maseru Bridge and on the South African side there were, of course, separate queues for Black and White. Our names were twice carefully checked on a large revolving file against the list of undesirables, while a large notice asked: 'Have you any books which may be banned in South Africa?' But our baggage wasn't searched and, after all the forms were carefully processed, we were waved through to start exploring the Republic.

The high veld has a stark, proud beauty, with its rolling open land and little flat-topped steep-sided hills adding a sense of drama. As we turned north, leaving the foothills behind, it flattened out into huge well-ordered fields of maize and sorghum, the heavy heads hanging down, like adverts on cornflake packets, while herds of red-brown well-built cattle grazed in the pastures.

It was extraordinarily empty of people and even of traffic. Every so often we glimpsed a neat white-gabled farmhouse set in its clump of trees – there lived the *baas* and his family. Discretely separate would be a jumble of low mud-brick huts for the workers. Occasionally we'd pass a black figure walking along the road, who'd look up hopefully at the chance of a lift, or a pony and trap carrying a black family. Where did the children go to school? Was there any social life at all – for Black or White?

We passed through a couple of little towns, each dominated by thick fingers of grain silos, reminiscent of the American Mid-West. We stopped at one of the picnic lay-bys: the air was very still and cool in the shade with that sharp edge that comes with altitude; it smelt of dust and gum-trees. Little stoat-like animals scurried across the road, watched by a solitary buzzard on the telegraph wires. Silence dominated the empty landscape.

Just south of the Vaal River a great bank of smog rose over industrial areas; here were factories and a huge refinery making oil out of coal. Here were townships too and we began to puzzle out who might be living there. The first had endless rows of exactly similar houses covering acres of ground, one row following another, with no changes to break the monotony as they went over the rise and up the next hill to the horizon; that was surely for Blacks. The next was densely packed, but with bigger houses, some with garages. Was this a Coloured location? It was hard to interpret things.

Suddenly over a rise we came face to face with the jagged skyline of Johannesburg, while the road turned into a motorway swooping up and around the old mine dumps and across flyovers. Following Janet Taylor's tip off, we found our way to Hillbrow and the Hawthorne Residential Hotel, where we rented a large en-suite room for a modest weekly sum (R48). Importantly, there was a battered telephone kiosk in the hall.

We'd driven 450km, so we unpacked the whisky first. 'What about peanuts?' I enquired from the depths of a hot bath. Ten minutes later Patrick reappeared bringing not only high-quality nuts but also Mars Bars, dried apricots and Gold Blend Instant Coffee. We were back in the land of our own comfort food.

Later we wandered out in search of supper. Hillbrow was at that time a relaxed, somewhat bohemian, residential area with large blocks of flats. There were plenty of cheap eateries where we could choose pizzas, pancakes, even ice cream, and little shops selling newspapers, groceries and toiletries. Best of all, we found a large bookshop where classical music was playing as we browsed the shelves before buying some South African novels and the classic *Field Guide to the Birds of Southern Africa*. It felt cosily European and we thought it would be a comfortable base for the next two weeks. But as Trevor Huddleston had written[36], there was little comfort in South Africa.

Once we'd conquered the telephone – while the handset was at eye-level, you had to kneel to read the instructions – we began to set up meetings with as many people on our lists as we could find. Unsurprisingly, the white contacts were easiest and we started off with the English-speaking business world, where Patrick thought he might find some common ground.

Mr Henwood immediately renewed his invitation to spend Sunday at his home in the most opulent area of the northern suburbs. By the time we arrived in the rain, the tennis players had retired and the pool looked uninviting, so they took us out to pick roses and to admire the huge wooded garden.

Before we sat down to lunch, grace was said. 'It's communism, not racialism, that's the main problem in the world,' said Mr Henwood. 'They want to drive out Christianity, like in Mozambique. But I think we're strong enough here, we will keep the communists out. You see, we South Africans, we know our Blacks. They're not ready for one man, one vote.'

The talk, over roast meat and two veg with apple crumble to follow, ranged widely and although it was a friendly discussion, the supposed common ground began to feel like a treacherous swamp shaking dangerously beneath our feet.

'Mind you, we don't support the Nationalist government,' Henwood assured us. 'They set up these crass regulations that prevent the Blacks developing a middle class. Sometimes we feel we're living under a dictatorship.'

'Which party would you like to see in power?' I asked him.

'I've always voted for the United Party, but next time I might support the Progressives. I wish the outside world would leave us alone – all those sports boycotts and disinvestment campaigns, they hinder rather than help.'

---

[36] *In Naught for your Comfort*, published in 1956, Fr Huddleston described his work in the shanty towns of Johannesburg; it was the first ringing denunciation of apartheid.

Patrick said carefully: 'Some of the exiled groups, like the ANC[37], think that military force will eventually be the only option. They know how terrible the costs would be but they believe that nothing will change without it.'

Mr Henwood looked shocked. 'Oh no, that's wrong. If only we had good leaders we could work it out. Like Smith in Rhodesia, he's got the right ideas. Given a stable society we can solve our own problems.'

Mrs Henwood told me the younger generation were different. 'They've rejected apartheid,' she said. 'Our son brought an African student home to stay. He was a real peasant, probably never been in a dining room before, but behaved like a natural gent. And Mr Kambule, the headmaster from Soweto, came to dinner. Mind you, we had to tell the servants beforehand or they might have objected to serving a black man.'

'You must stay to tea,' she invited us. 'We have Anglican friends from Cape Town.' Slightly bent, grey-haired and bespectacled, the Reverend Robertson looked at first sight like a typical, bumbling C of E vicar, but over the cupcakes a different figure emerged.

'I work in a Coloured parish in Capetown, with a Zulu curate,' he explained. 'The Coloureds are now making common cause with the Blacks; they no longer want White status. They won't work as servants, they go to the factories.'

It transpired the couple were reluctantly on their way to Rhodesia to convalesce after he'd been knocked off his scooter by a hit-and-run motorist. 'I won't be able to talk to my friends, they're one hundred per cent for Smith, who is a disaster, and there'll be a bloody clash there soon. If I preach I'll probably be in trouble with the authorities. If I talk about human relations and the love of God for all people, this involves treating the Africans as equals which inevitably becomes political.'

His wife explained that in Cape Town they worked closely with Reverend Theo Kotze, of the Christian Institute, and this brought all sorts of trouble. 'After Theo preached in our church the hall was burnt down. I even think my husband's "accident" might be connected with our

---

[37] The African National Congress, formed 1912, was the main political party leading the struggle for Africans to obtain equal rights. Banned in 1960, at the time of our visit it was working underground and many of the leaders were in exile.

knowing the Kotzes. Their house has been shot at more than once.'

Bewildered, I asked: 'What about the police?'

'Oh, we told them, but they never do anything.'

Seeing her sitting there in her twinset and pearls and looking every bit a county lady, it was difficult to imagine anyone less likely to be subject to alarming fantasies. Four weeks later we were staying in the Kotzes' house ourselves, probably under Special Branch surveillance, and meeting more charming old ladies with revolutionary Christian ideas.

We felt more secure with our next contacts, though they belonged nominally to the other 'white tribe,' the Afrikaners. Felicity and Colin Van Vuuren proved enormously generous with their time, contacts and practical help, as well as helping us sort out our ideas. 'Come to supper on Saturday,' said Felicity over the phone, 'we're having a *braai*.'

A braai is a barbecue. In their small but exuberant garden, Colin towered over the stone fireplace, glass in hand, booming a welcome to everyone. 'The steaks are ready,' he shouted, heaping a couple of huge T-bones onto each of our plates. 'I'll have the lamb chops done just now,' ('just now' is South African for 'in a minute').

I chewed my way through some of the meat, wishing there was more bread or salad to ease it down, but the plentiful red wine oiled a conversation with Koos and Lucia, who were almost certainly National Party voters. 'Ag, man, the Africans are quite happy,' said Lucia. 'We all used to play together on the farm. They're just like children really and don't want to take responsibility.'

'Well, that's certainly not true of Nigerians,' I began hotly. 'Ag, you've been to other African countries? For us, we'd rather go to Europe. ...' No interest there, so I tried education.

'I teach in an Afrikaans-medium school,' Lucia told me. 'The discipline is very good – no one ever cheeks a teacher like I hear they do in the UK. There aren't any more dual medium schools. If you speak English at home you go to an English school and vice-versa.'

'So even the white communities are being separated now!' I muttered.

'Come and have some of our wonderful *boerewors*,' called Colin, thrusting a great plate of coiled, pale sausage in front of me. I gulped and decided to become a vegetarian.

Felicity, fair, petite and an accomplished hostess, lamented she had not had time to talk to us. 'Come to breakfast tomorrow,' she said, 'and we'll show you round a bit.'

The Van Vuurens lived in a more modest suburb further out from the city centre than the Unterhalters, with denser housing, but there was the same careful planting to screen each house from its neighbours and always a swimming pool. They had a large bouncy dog called Muzzle and a young daughter Katharine who rode on its back.

Colin was a slightly off-beat Afrikaner; reputedly a radical in his youth, he was now a sober lawyer and an ironic observer of political folly. Felicity, of English heritage and a lecturer at Wits[38], worked on a more intuitive level, though with a sociologist's awareness of social complexities. She genuinely enjoyed encounters across the colour line and listened carefully to the stories she heard. 'My gardener, it's true he works less the more he's paid. He's got a farm in his "homeland" and he doesn't need any more cattle at the moment, so he'd rather spend time with friends and relatives. But that doesn't mean he's lazy.'

She thought that people's attitudes towards their servants were changing. 'They realise that they may be people of status in their own societies and respect them accordingly. They pay them better too.'

Was this just a personal view? Later I found that Felicity had developed a real friendship with Dora, her cook, and with her family; far into the as yet indiscernible, unimaginable future, in 1994 they would walk together to the polling station for the first free election. Meanwhile they gave us a huge breakfast, with more sausages, and drove us round the older parts of the city. In Parktown the first mining magnates had built their massive mansions along a steep-sided ridge in the 1890s, in styles that mixed Victoriana with Cape Dutch. Most of the great houses had been taken over by institutions but the Oppenheimers still lived on their eighty-acre estate in the middle of it all, accessed by their own underpass under the motorway.

'This is Vrededorp,' Felicity pointed out of the window. 'Here Indians, Coloureds, a few Africans and even some Whites are still living side by side and quite at ease with each other. But this is embarrassing for the

---

[38] Common name for the University of the Witwatersrand.

government and it is to be cleared for "road building and redevelopment" – in other words, for Whites only.' The process of separating people was more difficult in the cities.

Johannesburg had some very pleasant spots if you could get away from the politics, and for recuperation we spent a couple of afternoons in Melrose Bird Sanctuary, ticking off twenty-two new species in our book. But politics kept on intruding.

'If you want to understand Afrikanerdom you must go to the Voortrekker Monument outside Pretoria,' Felicity advised us. So one morning we took the motorway north from Johannesburg, trying to imagine what it was like to trek over this vast, dry landscape, now browned with winter frost, desolate and monotonous. There would have been teams of oxen under cracking whips, women and children rattling in the wagons along with basic household goods, the men riding out to hunt for game or to spy for hostile tribes.

For these Boers living under British rule in Cape Colony, the abolition of slavery in 1833 was the last straw among the regulations they found so irksome. More and more took their cattle and their families over the coastal ranges and up on to the vast unsettled spaces of the high veld, until it swelled into the 'Great Trek,' spreading over the Drakensberg into Natal. Here they clashed with similar pastoral farmers, the Zulus, whose spears were no match for the Boers' guns.

The Voortrekker Monument commemorates this epic, fateful, movement of people. It is set on a low hill presenting a huge square stone face to the world, half a fortress and half a church. Around it is a wall of circling wagons modelled in stone representing the defensive *laager* from which they fired on their foes. The guidebook calls it 'a *sacred Temple to the Volk* (people)' and as you approach a notice warns: '*Ladies must be properly attired and gentlemen should remove their hats. Please desist from eating, drinking or smoking. Keep firm control of all children.*'

Inside the building is a marble frieze depicting the main events of the Great Trek, and in the centre, on a lower floor, is a stone altar with the words in Afrikaans '*We for thee, South Africa,*' cut into the top surface. Through a hole in the roof a ray of sunlight strikes the words at noon on December 16th, the Day of the Covenant or Dingaan's Day, which celebrates the Boers' conclusive victory over the Zulus at Blood River in 1838. The guidebook quoted evidence that this victory was a miracle, an act of God, showing favour to the 'People of His Covenant.'

As we left Patrick said grimly: 'Psychologically, many of them haven't left the laager and still believe they have a God-given right to rule over this country in the way they choose. Their ideas are as set in stone as these wagons. What can possibly change them?' I thought it was rather like Hitler's Art Gallery in Munich and wondered why Fascist architecture has this terrible aura of stern certainty. We found little comfort in the Voortrekker monument.

Arguably the strength of modern South Africa rests less on a heavenly covenant and more on geological happenstance. It was not the grassy plains but the mineral-rich rocks underneath them which brought other adventurers to the high veld and to Johannesburg, City of Gold, so we took the tourist trail to West Driefontein, said to be the richest gold mine in the world.

Dressed up in hard hats and yellow jerkins, we entered a mocked up mine-face, to be deafened by the horrific noise of compressed air drills. In real life the men would be working a six-hour shift in this noise thousands of feet underground in temperatures of ninety degrees Fahrenheit, with an hour-long journey each way.

'On arrival,' said our guide, 'the new recruit is given leadership and aptitude tests to determine whether he will be a team leader, skilled or semi-skilled worker, or just a labourer.' But we knew that white trade unions denied Africans the chance to rise any further even if they were capable.

'He is given a health check to see if he can stand the heat and then training and safety instructions. Alongside this, he must learn Fanakolo, the pidgin *lingua franca* made up of English, Afrikaans and Zulu words. In three days, he can understand enough to follow basic instructions.'

With pride the guide showed us the great kitchens. 'This is always open: you can get mealie porridge, beans and vegetables any time. The men get 2lbs of meat a week, raw so they can cook it on their own stoves, and two quarts of beer. Quite often they'll put on 12-15lbs in the first couple of months. And if they're ill, we've got a hospital with fifty beds. It's so much better than what they get at home.'

In one sense perhaps it was. We wondered what the men thought as they filled their plates and took them outside – there was no dining room – to sit on benches under thin grass roofs in the chilly winter wind.

Although it was off schedule, we persuaded the guide to show us a room in one of the long hostel blocks. It was about 22ft square and twenty men lived here, sleeping in double-decker bunks along the walls, a shelf above the only place for personal possessions. There was a coal stove in the centre where they cooked their meat and a bicycle hung from the roof. Out of 10,000 workers only 104 – senior instructors, hospital staff – had family accommodation, though of course white staff lived with their families in the nearby town. This separation of men from their families, which pre-dated but was intensified by apartheid, seemed inhuman and we were to see the other side of it in the so-called 'homelands', where the women and children lived.

What could persuade men to do this? Poverty, of course, and the lack of other opportunities to earn such relatively good money. But there was perhaps also a certain sense of machismo and pride; for young Africans it could be a rite of passage to manhood, as described vividly in one of the first non-white South African novels, Peter Abrahams' *Mine Boy*. His picture of resilience in the face of personal struggles and unfair laws, however, gave us a different slant on the mines.

Lastly we went to see the final stages of the gold production process, where molten gold was being poured into moulds. When the red hot crucible was tilted the stream of metal cascaded dramatically down a staircase of rectangular basins, crackling and sparking as it went. After cooling, the bars were turned out, polished and put in the safe. 'Pick one up and take it with you,' our guide joked and we tried, but it was almost impossible to lift this brick-sized bar, worth at the time around R110,000. We were looking at the economic heart of South Africa, for the price of gold still largely determines the strength of the rand.

However, there was, of course, one place where black families could live together, not *in* Johannesburg but close enough to service it – the South-West Township, or Soweto. After Sunday lunch Mr Henwood had said: 'I'd like to show you Orlando High School, where the Oppenheimer

Trust has sponsored new buildings. No, I don't have any permits for you but I can argue my way out if necessary. My office, Tuesday morning, OK? I'll drive you into Soweto.'

Where was this huge shadow city, probably a million strong, umbilically linked to Jo'burg, yet invisible, un-signposted? The wide road, tarred and often a dual carriageway, wound through mine dumps, headgear, white employees' housing, waste land and a few farms. This area formed an eight-mile wide *cordon sanitaire* cutting off Soweto from its mother city, making it easy to ignore, but also easy for police and troops to access.

As we came over the last hill we saw a vast expanse of identical box-like houses, row upon row laid out in the sunshine under a thinning layer of cooking smoke. Each low, rectangular box sat in its own plot, often with a well-kept vegetable garden, the toilets standing like sentry boxes at the end. Wide roads divided the city into sections, often with open spaces and waste ground where the social amenities were still to be built. There were some rough football fields, even a scrubby golf course, with just one stadium and one swimming pool for half a million youngsters. No Whites could invest here, so the few cinemas and dingy shops were run by Blacks.

There seemed to be many kids on the streets, some barefoot, kicking tin cans or scrunched-up paper in lieu of footballs. 'Shouldn't they be in school?' I asked.

'Well, most do start primary school, but teaching and facilities are not good. Often the schools have to run two three-hour shifts a day because of lack of buildings. Many children can't pay the fees.'

We were seeing the results of the tenfold disparity in the funding for white and black education. While almost all white children could expect to reach high school level, only about 6% of black children did and, even if they passed matric, few could afford to take up a university place.

However, Orlando High School existed for those who could pay and Mr Kambule had been its headmaster for seventeen years. His firm but easy manner with the students impressed me as he showed us round the sparkling new domestic science room and the superb laboratory, built by the Oppenheimer Trust.

'We named the library after Sir Robert Birley (ex-head of Eton) who helped us immensely when he was professor of education at Wits,' explained Mr Kambule. 'The authorities didn't like it, they said he was a communist, but I insisted!' It was well-stocked with English novels, but they looked second hand, probably donated.

'Nearly all my staff are graduates,' he continued proudly, 'even though they could earn better money elsewhere. We have about 1,000 students, mainly boys since girls peel off to do nursing or train as primary teachers. They want to meet you – would you like to talk to them?'

The classroom was crowded with wooden desks and benches, its walls almost bare, but the students began at once:

'What are English schools like?'

'Is there a colour bar in London?'

'Why is there fighting in Northern Ireland?'

'What causes all your strikes?'

I was astounded. The questioners were as articulate and informed as an English Sixth Form, their questions and comments just as challenging. These students were a culture's breadth away from the respectful African students of Lagos or Dar. How had they survived Bantu Education in this way? They wanted to KNOW, they didn't want lies or reassurance, they wanted to talk politics and they wanted to change the system. I was left wondering: if I was teaching here how could I deal with their demands and not get involved – would I be brave enough to face the sinister consequences?

They proved they had that courage. A year later the Soweto students marched to protest against the enforced use of Afrikaans as a teaching medium, among them probably some we talked to that day – and some died from police bullets.

Our next visit was arranged by Beryl Unterhalter. 'Are you interested in early childhood development?' she asked. 'The Bernard Van Leer Research Foundation has an Early Learning Centre in Soweto.' Of course I said yes, so we met Glynis Armstrong, the supervisor, outside Wits at 8 am in driving rain and she drove us into the township, again without passes. Glynis could see potential everywhere, once the oppression was lifted.

'I have a staff of thirty, all African,' she explained. 'We have a black psychologist, teachers, social workers and some local mums. I let them decide how to run things and they soon start using their own initiatives.

I just ask questions, sometimes make suggestions. You'll see more control here and rather less free play than I'd like, but that's part of their culture.'

In her view, the relationship between the races had been skewed by years of separation. 'Blacks, both adults and children, respond in a particular way to Whites, a sort of cringing. You can see why! I watch the government inspectors treat my staff as though they were total imbeciles, so they tend to act the part. No one has ever asked them what they want; they're just told what the Whites think they want. We've got to break this pattern if we are ever to get peaceful change.'

I chatted to one of the senior social workers, who was interested in how I had liaised with social services when teaching in London. 'No, our teachers leave the problem families to us. Would you like to come with me to some of my clients?'

We visited two of the little brick boxes – identical outside, but housing two different human stories. The first belonged to a 'problem family'. Dirty children sat on the rough concrete floor, sucking their thumbs; others kicked a tin can outside in the bare yard. There appeared to be little food or furniture in the house and it smelt.

'The man is a recovering alcoholic,' she said, 'and the wife probably mentally defective. There are nine children, and the eldest daughter now has two illegitimate ones, who live here too.' Thirteen people somehow fitted into three rooms and kitchen in a house which measured overall approximately 16ft by 20ft.

In the second lived a clerk, his wife who was in domestic service, their three children and a live-in girl help. The sitting room was smartly furnished – tables, sofa, chairs and a cabinet – though there was a large damp patch on the wall. In the kitchen there was a fridge – this was one of the few houses with electricity – and an aga-type stove, but the only water supply was a tap in the backyard next to the outside flush loo in the corner of the garden. There were two small bedrooms for six people. The aspirant middle class live in cramped conditions, next door to a slum, because there is no way out of Soweto for them.

We nearly got stuck there too. Back at the Centre we were told: 'There's roadblocks on all the entrances! I suppose you've got passes?' Beryl had told us not to bother. Now what were we to do? We thought of all sorts of scenarios and excuses but apparently the officers were focussed on stolen cars and waved Glynis through, with us sitting nervously on the back seat.

CHAPTER 24

Exploring Johannesburg with Black Friends

In which, pursuing all leads, we become involved with the Churches and visit Soweto again, this time as friends of a good doctor.

Getting hold of our black contacts was trickier but eventually we reached Dr Motlana by phone and arranged to meet him *outside* the Carlton Hotel at 9 am. In such an 'international' hotel the races may eat or drink together but, as a black South African, he couldn't go in until we arrived and escorted him.

Dr Motlana was a slim, lively man, with a direct gaze and a look of confidence about him. He had chosen to stay in Soweto, working as a doctor and keeping a low political profile, when many of his contemporaries had gone into exile. We gave him news of his friend Rakhetla Tsehlana whose son had been among my students in Brixton.

'I'm so glad he took the boy with him,' said the doctor thoughtfully. 'We're not allowed to educate our children outside the Republic, though some slip over into Swaziland to Waterford, which is mixed and has international standards. Our new Dean of Johannesburg, Desmond Tutu, has said publicly that he won't have his children educated under Bantu Education. That man is going to stand up to the government!'

We told him something of our trip so far, who we had talked to and how confusing we found the situation. 'I have a meeting to go to now,' he said, 'but if you'd like to come and have supper in my home in Soweto, I'll get my friend David Thebahadi to drive you in.'

We made a date. This seemed to us an enormous privilege.

The trails from Nigeria and Dar were also leading us into interesting places and not always where we expected to go. When I rang Ann Sebati, a friend of Mr Hononu in Dar, she suggested we meet her at the big Baragwanath Hospital, the only one serving the black community. A senior nurse, Ann was tall and smiling with an air of authority, and we chatted happily away in the junior doctors' office which she had blithely commandeered for the occasion. While the nurses were black, most of the doctors were white but they seemed to consider Ann as a colleague. A quick internal call and there was Mrs Binda, very happy to have first-hand news from Ibadan of her sister Todd Langa. She was anxious to open up more possibilities for us.

'Next time you come, I'll introduce you to some teacher friends of mine. We could meet in St. Peter's, that's a safe place. Have you been there yet? Oh, you must go and meet Father Erson.'

So we made an appointment and drove to St Peter's Anglican Community in Rosettenville. When we arrived the brothers were at their mid-day service, so we waited in the warm common room, a refuge from the bitter cold outside, till a rather mousy little man appeared.

'I'm Father Erson, forgive me for keeping you waiting,' he said. 'May we offer you a simple lunch in our refectory?' Over excellent sausages, this time with plenty of avocado salad and bread, the brothers were happy to gossip.

'Did you hear our new Dean, Desmond Tutu, has been fined for speeding?' said one with a smile. 'Do you think that's symbolic of how he is going to run Cathedral affairs?'

'Well, he will certainly stir things up a bit,' said another. 'Have you read his message to the Diocese? I have it here '– he pulled a paper from his habit, put on his spectacles and began quoting passages: '*Division and separateness in South Africa is a direct contradiction of the Scriptures… I am deeply committed to reconciliation but I am certainly not committed to cheap reconciliation. Real reconciliation cost God the death of His Son and if we are to be instruments of His Peace, then we must know what we are about… I shall be living in Soweto, not the Deanery in white Jo'burg.*'

'One day he might be Bishop, they say[39] – that will ruffle some white feathers!' He turned to us. 'Desmond Tutu was a student here, in the days when we could be open to all races. When the Group Areas Act[40] came into force we had to close down our seminary; it's now in Alice in the Transkei and only us Whites are left to do what we can in the community.'

After lunch Father Erson took us into his austere office to give us his message, all clerical politeness forgotten. If we had mistaken him for a mouse, he now resembled a tough and extremely angry rat.

'The white community is almost totally ignorant about the situation of the Blacks. Either people just don't care or they deliberately try to remain in ignorance. They have no idea what it is like to live in Soweto or other townships, or the depths of resentment that people there feel. There is now an enormous gulf separating our two communities, far worse than when I was a young man. On the white side you have this ignorant, unchristian complacency. On the other, rising anger among the young and the development of this new 'Black Consciousness.' Combined, this must lead to an explosion.

'Do you see any path to peaceful change?'

'Perhaps through the white women. They are beginning to see black women as women with needs and problems similar to their own. Some are beginning to understand what the reality is and are changing their views accordingly. They tend to be five years ahead of their husbands! Maybe their menfolk will follow them. But it's more difficult in the Afrikaans-speaking community. Any Afrikaner who steps out of line is subject to total ostracism and it is only the very brave like Beyers Naudé who can accept the sacrifices resulting from radical political activity.'

It was becoming increasingly clear that, although at home we had long stopped going to church, here we were finding common ground largely with active, committed Christians and that the Church was almost the only bridge left between the races. We went back to the South African

---

[39] Desmond Tutu did indeed become Bishop of Johannesburg in 1985. He fought fearlessly against apartheid and in 1984 received the Nobel Peace Prize. After Liberation in 1994 he headed the Truth and Reconciliation Commission to try to heal some of the wounds left by the violence. His contribution to human rights is recognised world-wide.

[40] The legislation which in 1950 assigned different racial groups to different residential and business sections in urban areas.

Council of Churches to see what arrangements Harry Makubire had made for us.

We met in a small room with dusty windowpanes, the yellowing walls covered with notices, minutes and newspaper cuttings. 'This is June Chabaku, Chair of the Black Women's Year Committee' – he introduced us to a large ebullient woman with a great gruff voice – 'and this is Lindi Myenza' – indicating a slighter but still dynamic lady. 'They work with women's groups attached to the independent African Churches. Adult literacy mainly, and June's very keen on drama in education.'

June was keen to educate us too. 'We provide literacy classes for domestic workers. But one of the main aims is for them to recognise their own worth and face up to their employers. Like asking their madam why she hasn't yet learnt Zulu when her maid can speak both English and Afrikaans. And we encourage the domestic workers to learn new skills.'

'Mrs Henwood told us she runs a "Centre of Concern," where they give classes to their servants,' I said.

'Oh, but those are so patronising,' retorted June. 'We want to empower black women, not just train them. That's why I teach drama. But there are no theatre facilities for the black community, only bare halls, and those are controlled by Whites so they can censor anything we put on. I want our drama groups to work on black group identity and political consciousness.'

'What about the position of black women in the country?' I asked.

'In the cities they're really active. They've set up trade unions, for example in the textile industries, and they run all sorts of self-help activities, from childcare to sewing and finance classes. It's the "homelands" that are worse. Most of the people living there are women but everything's run by the chiefs, who are all men and very conservative.'

'What do you think is going to happen in South Africa?' ventured Patrick.

June became grim-faced. 'I hate the idea of violent revolution. But I don't think the Whites will ever share real power, voluntarily. So I'm afraid nothing will change substantially until we fight. Meanwhile our job is to prepare the African community for the time after the revolution.'

June and Lindi were facing the future with lots of energy, whatever their fears. Now an elderly man came over to us slowly, stooping over his cane.

'I am Mr Ngakane,' he said. 'I'm now seventy-three and I've supported the African National Congress all my life, but these ladies are right. If the Whites don't give way there will be violence. And if the two communities are ever to meet as equals, we need to develop Black Consciousness and greater self-respect among us Blacks.'

We asked him to tell us his story.

'I started off as a school master. In the 1930s I was appointed to run an experimental reformatory. I only had twenty-five boys and I used to treat them as my children rather than my prisoners. Have you heard of Alan Paton? He was one of my governors and we worked well together.

'I began chairing political meetings – that's when the police started coming round – and eventually when I became deputy-president of the Transvaal ANC I was arrested. We were found not guilty but immediately I left jail I was "banned" for five years. That meant I was confined to Orlando Township and not allowed to meet with more than one person at a time. So I was very lonely; I couldn't work – what was I to do? Finally I got permission to move to the family farm in one of the "homelands" where I organised the building of a school for the local village. But once it was built I, a teacher, was not allowed to enter – because I was a banned person!

'Finally, in the last month of the five-year ban period the police escorted me back to Orlando for Christmas with my family. "Report to the station later," they told me. When I got there the officer in charge said, "Here is a Christmas present for you," and threw across the desk a new banning order for a further five years. No reasons given, no appeal! So that was ten years out of my life.

'I'm a farmer at heart. When I was a child my father's family worked part of a white farmer's land as paying tenants. Once the owner acknowledged publicly we produced far more than his white tenants did. My, did he get into trouble! Of course, in those days with far less expensive machinery Europeans and Africans competed on a more or less equal basis; we had cattle and knew how to plough, we worked hard.

'The real problems started when the rural Boers, who weren't well educated, came to the new cities looking for work in the offices and factories run by the English. We young people came too, competing with those Boers, and often beating them for jobs because we'd been to mission schools and spoke English. That's when they started bringing in the race laws to keep us out.

'What about the "homelands"? Ag, there's no future there. Yes, it's the only political base available, but it won't take us far. I fear we shall have to fight.'

Having started talking at 11.00, we left the SACC offices at 3.30, wiser and sadder. Yes, we remembered Alan Paton's novel *Cry the Beloved Country*. At the end the black priest says: '*When they come round to loving, they will find we have turned to hating.*' Was this prophecy about to come true?

The next time we visited the SACC June took us over to the Inter-Church Aid offices to meet Mrs Constance Koza, an introduction from the British Council of Churches. She was another large, ebullient lady, wearing a long African skirt under her thick woollen cardigan and several layers of African beadwork. Her hair was combed out in an 'Afro' style and she exuded enthusiasm. 'Elliott told me about you,' she said. 'You've been to other African countries where I can't go. Come and have some tea while you tell me about them.' She pulled papers off a couple of chairs in her crammed office and made us some instant coffee.

We asked about her own projects. 'I run Inter-Church Aid,' she explained. 'We channel aid —mainly from overseas – to projects initiated by Churches. The criteria are that the schemes must be oriented to developing people's skills and well-being, they must be relevant to the people's needs and capable of being sustained over a period of time, and they must have a Christian purpose. Our projects range from handing out soup and blankets in emergencies to financing home industries and paying the running costs of health clinics.'

As she sensed our interest she paused and looked at us. 'Would you like to come and see for yourselves? I need a holiday from the office. You've got a car? I can get one too. We could all go down to the Transkei together with some friends of mine.'

This seemed almost too good to be true. We arranged to meet her in Maseru at the end of May.

It was the evening of our supper in Soweto. David Thebahadi turned up late and obviously nervous. 'Please sit in the back, it's darker there. I'll drive slowly up to any red robots (traffic lights) so we don't have to sit there under the glare.' What we were doing was illegal.

In the township we could see little in the smog and the tall arc lights lit up the mist rather than the road. Once David pulled into the side 'I don't like that car following us,' he explained, but it passed by and vanished. A large white residence lit by a wreath of coloured lights loomed up. 'That's Richard Maponya's house, richest man in Soweto. Owns a supermarket here.'

Dr Motlana's house was less imposing but it was a comfortable family-sized home with modern furniture in the lounge, including a large stereo, and a brand new automatic washing-machine in the kitchen. Dr Motlana worked as a GP in private practice in Soweto and his wife was a nurse at his clinic. David Thebahadi was an insurance broker in a white firm, one of the very few to break the black ceiling, while his wife taught English in a junior secondary school. To our delight Mr Wilkinson Kambule, head of Orlando High School, was also there.

We were offered drinks – none of the others touched alcohol – and after the usual grace sat down to a wonderful meal of soup, better steaks than at the braai, with heaps of vegetables and salad, followed by stewed apricots from their own trees.

The conversation was rather dominated by Mr Kambule, who seemed a different man here among his own kind, with a wry sense of humour. Mentioning the 'homeland' policy, we asked which group he belonged to.

'I'm a Xhosa-speaking African,' he cried. 'I'm not a Xhosa, I belong to the whole country. These "homeland" leaders, they're wrong to accept such positions in such a bad system.'

David Thebahadi, who sat on the Soweto Town Council, disagreed. 'We must reject the principle, of course. But let's use the power we're given to benefit the people as best we can.'

'Your town council doesn't even control its own budget,' said Kambule contemptuously. 'Twenty million rand and all you can do is "advise" how it should be spent. That's why I have to go cap in hand to the Oppenheimer Trust for a new lab.'

'Nothing good can come out of this government,' agreed Motlana.

'Look at the Bantu Investment Corporation. It's supposed to lend money to Africans to set up businesses. A friend of mine got a loan from them, putting his own savings into the pot as well, to set up a workshop in one of the "homeland" towns as they suggested. What happened? He lost the lot! They're trying to ruin any Blacks with saving by enticing them into hopeless situations.'

'Oh, you just have to outwit them,' said Kambule grinning. 'My brother got a loan from the BIC and followed his own business instincts. He's made plenty of money.'

Motlana was still angry. 'We put our money into white building societies and where does it go? To finance white housing! Even the BIC gets more from us in deposits than it lends out.'

We asked these educated, intelligent Africans, who could move among the white community as equals when allowed to, where enlightened white leadership might come from.

None of them saw any difference at all between the white political parties. 'The Progressives, they're just like all the others. No, there are very few enlightened Whites around now. The older campaigners have been banned or gone into exile. The younger ones no longer have any contact with their black peers because our students now have to go to the Bantu Colleges in the "homelands" instead of the proper universities.'

'Do you know what the law called "Universities Extension Act" really means?' Kambule teased us. 'It means "segregated and second rate". The famous old universities like Wits, Cape Town and Rhodes, where we studied, are now reserved for Whites only; Indians have to go to University of Durban-Westville, the Coloureds get something called University of the Western Cape and Blacks are sent into the "homelands" to former teachers' colleges like Fort Hare, or new ones like Venda and Boputhatswana, with no libraries and second-rank teachers.

'In spite of this, or perhaps because of it, the next generation of black youth are much more radical than us, he added.' I thought of the students who'd challenged us.

'Do you tell Mr Henwood this?' I asked.

'Not quite. He'd get very defensive, like all the so-called liberal Whites. They don't really understand. We can say it to you because you are not

South Africans. You must go back to the UK and tell them what it's really like.'

It was becoming clearer: one of the reasons black South Africans were so ready to talk to us was that they hoped we'd give their message to the outside world. We felt rather humble and very responsible.

On our last evening, we went to the popular new musical *Ipi Tombi*, billed as an 'exhilarating spectacle of African life'. The curtain rose on nubile black dancing girls dressed mainly in beads. Then came the sturdy miners stomping and slapping their gumboots to the drumbeats. A thin storyline developed tracing the tale of a young African who left his 'native reserve' against his father's advice and his girlfriend's tears. We saw him arrive in Jo'burg – this bit seemed quite realistic – and then watched his trials and tribulations unfold. Simple and incompetent, he was bullied by his boss, tricked by thieves and betrayed by a woman. The musical accompaniment wasn't the wonderful township jazz played in Soweto, nor West African highlife, but plagiarised, vaguely African, pop. Finally our hero returned to the Reserve, was forgiven by his faithful girlfriend and declared proudly: 'This is where I belong; here I can be a man.'

We spent the rest of the evening re-drafting it as the 'Anti-Tombi' show, with a final scene in which the Zulu warriors lay down their shields to reveal the city people: the clerks, drivers, miners and industrial workers on whom the whole of Johannesburg depends. But after our trip with Constance Koza to the 'homelands', our version would have been much darker than that.

CHAPTER 25
Swaziland

In which we pay a short visit to another independent country where we are welcomed by an old friend and make a new one.

Always ample in girth, Francina almost smothered me in her embrace. 'Welcome to my home,' she cried. 'Here is your room. Mandla, take up their bags. Will you have coffee? A hot bath after your long journey?'

Seven years earlier I had become friendly with Francina Mamba when we were both doing post-graduate education courses at Leicester. She was now lecturing at William Pitcher Teacher Training College in Manzini and had enthusiastically invited us to stay in her staff house.

Hardly had we finished supper when visitors started arriving and we began to feel we were on display as trophies from her time in the UK. Yet during our week there she was enormously generous to us and insisted on giving us a tour of the country – in our car – introducing us to as many friends and family as she could. Although many of these turned out to be interesting people – from a banned politician to a subsistence farmer and yet another radical priest – we felt rather stifled, partly by the country itself, which seemed drowsy and humid in contrast to the invigorating high veld, and partly by its politics which we found confusing, if less toxic than those of apartheid.

Swaziland is a tiny country nestling on the eastern escarpment of Southern Africa, the land falling in steps from the cool mountains to the sub-tropical plains. It is landlocked, cut off on one side by the Republic and on the other by Mozambique, which was just about to win its independence from Portugal after a ten-year war led by the Marxist Freedom Movement known as FRELIMO. Their success was sending shudders down white South African spines.

Like the Basotho, the Swazi chiefs had managed to preserve their independence long enough to emerge after the Boer War as a British Protectorate. At independence in 1968 they had received the usual Westminster-type constitution but now the King and his National Council were rewriting it to make it reflect the traditional role of the King in Swazi society – a more authoritarian one than ever Moshoeshoe had claimed. While the Basotho saying went: '*A chief is a chief by (consent of) the people*,' the Swazi kings had ruled for a century in the more autocratic style of Shaka and the Zulus. The King was openly polygamous; each year the most beautiful Swazi maidens were paraded so he could take his pick.

Francina and her kin were not admirers of the royal family or their way of life. 'My husband took another woman while I was in England,' she explained. 'We'd been married in church too. So I wouldn't take him back. My daughter Iris stays with me; the boys, Kenneth and Mandla, spend some of their time with their Uncle Ambrose.'

Dr Ambrose Zwane had once led the principal opposition party, the Ngwane National Liberatory Congress, but now the Constitution was repealed he had no role to play. He had been arrested on trumped up charges and spent some time in exile; when we had supper with him we found a sadly frustrated man, an orator looking for an audience. 'Good people, let me say just this...' he would begin as he expounded the doctrines of liberation and democracy. His walls were hung with framed letters, pictures, quotations, clippings by or about himself, and speeches by his great heroes, Nkrumah, Sobukwe and Nyerere; his house had been a meeting place for many revolutionaries.

Different in outlook but equally radical was Francina's cousin Father Zwane, a Catholic priest who combined impressive dignity with an impish sense of humour. Widely travelled in Europe and America and well known for his religious broadcasts, he was seen as a potential successor to the present Italian Bishop of Swaziland. We sat talking to him over coffee in his book-lined study in the capital, Mbabane, and found him caught up in the tension between ideologies.

'Unfortunately you won't hear me on the radio these days,' he smiled. 'The Swazi government and I differ on what "religious affairs" can cover.

When I say capitalist development is dividing us into rich and poor or that by inviting super-rich tourists we're creating attitudes of envy, they say I'm talking politics!'

We found common ground in Nyerere's ideas of 'fair sharing.' 'But so difficult to put into practice,' the priest commented. 'We're trying a kind of villagisation here, but without the compulsion and political indoctrination.'

So what did he think would happen in South Africa?

'The students and other militant youth groups are taking a very hard line; they refuse to sign any document that is also signed by the "homeland" leaders and they shout down moderate speakers. It's not just bloody-mindedness; they think it's the only answer to overthrow the present regime and its system.'

'Do you agree with them?'

He hesitated. 'I can sympathise with their frustration; I understand their bleak assessment of the future. But first you need a more intense political awareness amongst the whole black community to create a common front against apartheid; I'm not sure where that could come from.'

'What is your church doing?' I asked, remembering Father Erson, and knowing that Father Zwane had also trained at St. Peter's seminary in Johannesburg.

'The Catholic Church in Southern Africa is far too worried about Marxism! I told them at a meeting of the Bishops of Southern Africa they ought to take a more positive attitude towards FRELIMO in Mozambique, who have been fighting for justice and human rights. I'll lend you the confidential report.'

We read it with fascination. The bishops were clearly worried about the developing situation in the Republic of South Africa on the one hand and Marxist influences on the other.

One quote from the Archbishop of Durban stood out for us: *Whites in South Africa stand where the Whites in Mozambique stood about ten years ago – threatened by a resolute liberation movement but almost totally unsuspecting. In my opinion our hopes of winning people over to the acceptance of meaningful social and political change are tenuous because we have only five years before the crisis will be upon us in all severity.*[41]

Would it really come to civil war in South Africa in five years' time?

As we drove back to Manzini, the road curved downwards with ever-lengthening views over the valley, the evening light emphasising the sharpness of the rocky ridges and the twin peaks known as Sheba's Breasts. The scenery, climate and freedom from apartheid drew in tourists both black and white – there were strings of hotels and the Royal Swazi Casino – and the country served also as a more permanent escape route for some educated black South Africans, like Mr and Mrs Mokgokong. He was a senior inspector of maths and she was working on a new primary school mathematics curriculum for Swaziland.

'It sounds excellent,' I enthused. 'Will the ideas be used in South Africa itself as well?'

'Of course not,' she retorted. 'Their minds are closed to new ideas. That's why we left.'

Her husband explained. 'We are Swazis by descent, but we lived in the Republic until the Bantu Education Act of 1954. I was a headmaster, but I resigned and moved to Swaziland so that my children would not have to attend the "Bantu" schools. Now my eldest daughter is a doctor, my son an architect – he designed this house for us. The next-born is an engineer, and the others are all doing well at school. I hope they'll study overseas.'

Then he offered a fascinating insight into the 'homelands' policy. 'I still own land in Lebowa, the "homeland" designated for the Northern Sotho people. My father bought land there from the missionaries. Then under the apartheid legislation this land was declared a "black spot", so all Africans had to move out and allow Whites in. My father negotiated hard with the government – or perhaps we were just lucky – and we got some reasonably good farming land in exchange, in Lebowa. Now it belongs to me and my two brothers.'

He smiled. 'I went there recently on farm business and the Lebowa government official, who was an Afrikaner, actually was quite polite – he even asked me to sit down! Perhaps it was because of the "homelands"

---

[41] Ambrose Zwane was consecrated as the first black Bishop of Swaziland in 1976 and provided support for many young refugees after the Soweto school riots. He died in a road accident in 1980 but was honoured posthumously by Mandela for his anti-apartheid work.

policy; they think we are independent and must treat us better. But we'll never live there; I may not agree with all of Swaziland's policies, but we're now Swazi nationals, for good or ill.' We wondered how South Africa could afford this brain-drain of its energetic and educated Africans.

Swaziland with its tiny population of half a million was not short of land. The big sugar estates and pineapple farms were still mainly owned by Whites, but there was also 'national land,' which anyone could apply to use for farming. However, this was not an attractive career for most young people, as Francina showed us.

She had taken us down to the eastern Lowveld, partly to see the sugar plantations, partly to visit a retired colleague who had become a good artist, and on the way back she suddenly exclaimed:

'There's an uncle of mine here, I haven't seen him since I was a girl. Let's go and visit him.'

We drove into a small village of about fifteen to twenty huts. Here lived a grandmother, her two sons, their wives and those of the grandsons who had stayed, married and set up their homes here. The huts were framed with wood, as in Tanzania, filled in with stones, and plastered over with mud; the roofs conical and thatched with reeds. Beside the village was a stoutly fenced *kraal*[42] and a large herd of cattle was being let out to graze, driven by small boys dressed only in skins hanging down front and back. Goats wandered through the nearby maize fields.

The conversation was all in Siswati but soon we were invited into one of the huts and served fizzy orangeade by the grandmother, who hobbled about wrapped in a sacking shawl. 'Her grandson works in the civil service in Mbabane,' explained Francina. The hut was very neat, tidy, comfortable and cool; it had two good beds, a table, chairs and a glass fronted cabinet full of crockery and glassware, all standing on a concrete floor. A pleasant weekend home for a commuter?

Outside some old men were sitting in the sun drinking beer, taking snuff and eating roast meat. They wore European shirts with skin skirts like the boys. Nearby, two teenage girls in short dresses danced by themselves to pop music from an expensive portable radio.

'May I take some photos?' I asked. A small fee changed hands and I

---

[42] Enclosure into which cattle are driven for safety.

snapped away.

'Have some meat. Do you drink our beer? It's made from our own sorghum.'

We took several generous swigs from the pot; it was very good and tasted just like the beer in Kwassam in Northern Nigeria.

There was money coming into the household, but little would be invested in farming. The youngsters wanted a modern job and Western life-style while the elders were content to carry on in traditional ways, but family ties were still important to all them and were being maintained. Francina, like our black friends in other independent countries, accepted all this and moved comfortably between the two worlds. In South Africa, by contrast, this gradual process of social change was deeply constrained by the pass laws and by the attempts to push would-be modern families back into the 'homelands'. As a result, huge pressures of unfulfilled economic aspirations and eager intellectual energy were building up. How come the Whites couldn't see this? How long could the pressures be contained?

One evening Francina gave a supper party for us, inviting some relatives together with Bongile Putsoa, a young headmistress from a nearby school. The conversation ranged over inflation, house prices and then discipline in schools, upon which Bongi invited me to visit Mjingo Secondary Girls' School next day. She came to the door to welcome us, a slim figure in a fashionable long skirt and platform soles, her hair braided in the latest style, and full of enthusiasm.

'This used to be a white school, so we've got nice modern buildings,' she bubbled. 'I've got 240 girls, just Forms 1–3. They board here; many come from far away and others might not have good facilities for study at home. Of course when the missionaries first started boarding schools they wanted to indoctrinate us with Christianity, but I'm a science graduate and I'm preaching careers for women!'

'What do they do at weekends?' I asked.

'On Saturdays there are organised games and activities,' she replied. 'On Sundays they do what they like.'

'What's your biggest problem?'

'Sex! Nearly one in ten of our girls get pregnant!' I wondered what really went on during those Sundays.

Bongi was the first woman appointed by the government to a secondary headship and her pioneering career later took her to Britain for postgraduate study, where she spent New Year with us in Norfolk. 'The sun really does stay low on the horizon!' she exclaimed when we took her to the northern coast. 'As a scientist, I knew that fact, but I never really understood it; just shows how children must experience science for themselves!'

Such views led her on into teacher education, and she became the first woman Dean of Education at the University of Swaziland. Over the years, we met periodically at conferences.

After Patrick's death she was visiting her married daughter in the UK and rang me up: 'I'm coming to Brighton,' she said. In Africa, you don't send a card or even a letter of condolence; you go all the way down from London by train, just for an hour, to express your sympathies. I was deeply touched.

CHAPTER 26
Nqutu and KwaZulu

In which we remember some history, experience an appalling
'homeland' and visit an uplifting hospital.

We drove south from Manzini through upland pastures scattered
with small settlements, many with 'modern' houses among the
thatched *rondavels* (circular huts) and kraals. But once over the border
into South Africa the people and their villages disappeared from the
landscape, which was covered instead with huge eucalyptus plantations,
interspersed with broad fields of maize or dry brown pastureland.

In the few clean little towns – Piet Retief, Paulpietersburg and Vryheid
– we saw some people again and noticed that all the pedestrians were
black and all the people in cars were white. The white children were
being bussed from their whitewashed bungalows to their gleaming white
school, dressed in white uniforms, with shining flaxen hair. We didn't
know where, or if, the black children went to school but when we stopped
for a picnic lunch at Blood River, sitting by the stream in the hot sun, a
crowd of African kids stood idly watching us from the bridge.

Were they perhaps the descendants of Dingaan's impis, killed in 1838
not far away in that myth-encrusted Battle of Blood River commemorated
in the Voortrekker Monument, where 470 Voortrekkers under Andries
Pretorius had defeated several thousand Zulus? The Boers fastened their
wagons together to form a circular *laager*; firing repeatedly from behind
the wagons they mowed down the waves of Zulus, never allowing them
to come close enough to use their spears, till many lay dead and the rest
retreated. This heralded the end of the old independent Zulu kingdom;
Prince Mpande made a treaty with Pretorius and Zululand became a

client state. Now, under the 'homelands' policy, it was supposed to become 'independent' again, under the name 'KwaZulu.' Was this possible, we wondered?

There was no sign to tell us that we were entering KwaZulu but as the tarmac surface ended suddenly the land was inhabited again. Clusters of little brown huts like mushrooms were spread densely all over the landscape; some were beehive-shaped and built of grass and reeds; others stone-walled with thatch, like in Lesotho, while modern breeze-block shanties were grouped haphazardly along the roadside. Between them the pasture lands were badly eroded, yet full of thin cattle searching for grass; small patches of maize grew here and there with goats grazing on the stalks and chickens pecking at the roots. Women walked along paths, often carrying headloads; the elders sat outside the huts and children played everywhere. There were no younger men and no commercial activity. This was a landscape from another planet.

We'd written to Dr Larsen at the Charles Johnson Memorial Hospital asking if we could visit and he'd replied that he would book us a room at the local hotel since we would need a government permit to stay at the hospital itself. Nqutu (pronounced *N-click-utu*) is only a crossroads with a couple of garages, two stores, a hotel and the hospital. We went into the hotel bar.

'Do you have a room booked for Stuarts?'

'No.'

'Could we have a room please?'

'No. We're full.'

'Could we have a couple of beers please?'

'No ladies allowed in bars in South Africa. You can sit in the lounge, madam.'

Grrrrrowl! But did I really expect gender equality in the land of apartheid? Sullenly I sat down in the dim and stuffy lounge while Patrick brought me two glasses of 'America's Lively and Lusty Beer!' Feeling sleepy and cross instead, we walked over to the hospital and were shown to the Staff House where everyone was having tea.

Dr Larsen had decided to ignore the permit rules. 'You are most welcome. I want you to stay in the guest room and eat with us so you can get a feel for the community.'

The Charles Johnson had begun as a small clinic funded by the Anglican Mission and grew rapidly after the charismatic Dr Anthony Barker and his wife Maggie arrived in 1945. Now they had just left because the government was going to take it over and they could no longer run it on their own liberal principles. The hospital had grown to over 500 beds, two operating theatres and a nursing school with 150 students – but it had also become a vibrant, caring, non-racialised community that was now well known outside South Africa. This brought them into conflict with the government and to the attention of Special Branch who were keeping files on several of the staff. There was a feeling of proud defiance in the air as well as fears for the future.

The hospital compound was centred on the chapel; the wards were on one side and on the other a garden dotted with attractive white-washed rondavels and cottages all thatched in local style, while the larger Staff House contained lounges, the community dining room and our guest room. A young German doctor, Hendrik Reuter, invited us over for a glass of wine before supper to meet his wife and young son, to whom they had given the Zulu name Mandla.

'I come here for three months as a student and come back because I was so happy. I am a child doctor, how do you say, a paediatrician, and now we have nearly finished building the new children's ward. There will be play facilities there, as well as nursing ones, like we have in Germany.'

'What health problems do the kids have?'

'I can tell you, it is kwashiokor! That is bad malnutrition. Then some have intestinal infections, and some have TB. I tell you a story about how bad it is. There was this child, he died of kwashiorkor. I know the parents are farmworkers, so I go to the Afrikaner farmer who is their boss. I find he has a dairy farm! He was very polite, but when I ask why the child did not get the milk from his cows, he tell me he does not concern himself with the domestic affairs of his workers! Then he tell me his workers are just like children and he must always watch over them! This man has a private plane and the children die of malnutrition! Now, shall we go to supper?'

The doctors – all white – and the senior nursing staff – all black – were sitting together at long tables, sharing curried stew, rice, and beans. After supper we had coffee with the Larsens and asked him what he saw as the main problems.

'I think it is the migrant labour system, which is leading to the complete breakdown of the traditional strict Zulu family way of life. Do you know, in this area 70% of the men are more or less permanently absent working in the white areas – mines, farms or factories in the urban areas? So the children are growing up with absolutely no idea of what a normal family life really means – neither in the traditional Zulu way nor the Christian way. Permanent marriages are becoming the exception.'

'How do you see the future?'

'There have been great changes of attitudes in the white community in the past five years. Perhaps the government can generate sufficient reforms to avert an explosion. The problem is, can the electorate be persuaded to move fast enough to meet the demands of the politically aware and increasingly resentful and suspicious Africans? Sometimes I am hopeful, sometimes I am filled with foreboding.'

At breakfast next morning in the communal dining room Greg Wells came over to us. 'I'm going out on a clinic visit, would you like to come?'

There was thick mist as we hurtled down the dirt road behind the hospital Land Rover and when we emerged into sunshine we found ourselves among rolling eroded hills, again thickly dotted with scattered huts and cattle. In the porch of the low white-washed building women waited with their babies and the elderly sat looking into the distance.

Greg was young, South African and full of enthusiastic visions. 'Clinics like this are staffed by a resident senior nurse, who deals with everything except the very serious cases. One of my projects is to train "family health agents", rather like the model of the Chinese "barefoot doctor". Typically, she would be a local woman, chosen and paid by the community, dispensing first aid. That's what the *people* want – curing. However, the hospital adds to her salary if she also dispenses advice on hygiene, nutrition, etc, which is what *we* want – preventing disease.

'But the worst problems,' continued Greg, 'are just down the road, in Mondlo. It's a resettlement township of 10,000 people and it's about to be doubled in size. I can't take you there because you don't have permits and at the moment we're trying to keep on the right side of the authorities.'

'What's a "resettlement township"?' we wanted to know.

Greg was usually a calm man but we sensed the anger and passion in his voice. 'When they started moving Africans off white farms, they brought them to such places. There were no huts, no amenities. At first they lived in tents, destitute. Not until a typhoid epidemic broke out did the government do anything, such as building privies and a clinic. Now some people have built their own houses, but there is still a perennial shortage of water; no dams have been built and people scoop water up from puddles – and we still have typhoid. Worst of all, there is no work. Yet the government plans to send another 12,000 people there. What is the sense of establishing a sizeable town in a rural area with no water and no employment?'

It made sense under apartheid: the 'homelands' were labour reserves to supply black men and some women to work in the mines, factories and homes in the white cities.

What this can mean in human terms, I found out from Liz Clark, the social worker. While Patrick took our car off to Vryheid for repairs she showed me round the hospital. In the children's wards there were rows of apathetic, limp and stunted little bodies, often two to a cot, victims mainly of kwashiorkor, while the adult wards contained mostly TB and typhoid cases. By contrast the new post-natal maternity ward was bright and cheerful. The expectant mothers were all sleeping on the floor in another large room; many would not have had beds at home either and they enjoyed each other's company.

Liz looked strained and tired but she spoke also with great passion and a deep understanding of the context. She told me how little she could achieve here. 'Occasionally we can intervene. For example, last week a man came to my office who wanted to look for work in Jo'burg. Before he can get a work-seeker's pass he must show his tax receipt. But he can't pay his tax till he gets work. What a vicious circle! So we paid off his tax arrears and he's gone to look for a job. If there is one… I was trying to start up chicken-rearing among the local women. But now I can't go out of the hospital compound – I've lost my permit to move about in KwaZulu.'

Her recent book *Women Without Men*, based on a study of 150 families in the area, had infuriated the government and she was now restricted. 'Among the families, only seven of them had an able-bodied man at home; the others were all away in the urban areas,' she summarised. 'A typical household here would need R104 (£70) per month to cover their basic needs but I found the average income, in cash and kind, was only R15! OK, some sent money home. But others acquired another "wife" in town and the payments stopped. No wonder the children have protein deficiency illnesses. And the men come back from those over-crowded hostels having picked up TB or VD which in turn they pass on to the family.'

I spent the rest of the afternoon reading Liz's book till Patrick came back and we got talking to Kate Hutchings, the office typist, who was part of a young troubled generation.

'I'm an apartheid baby', she confessed. 'I've never known what interracial mixing is like. Most of my age group are apolitical, but me and some of my friends, we're all hung up about the race issue. I left uni to work here in a multiracial group. The trouble is, we feel so guilty that we overdo things in our efforts to relate to the Africans and they resent it! I may end up going to Europe to get away from it.'

Kate took us to see the local Bushman rock paintings, a beautiful half-hour walk across the veld: along a flat ridge and over some rocky outcrops to a small overhang where two or three little painted figures could just be discerned. Then we sat on the warm rocks and looked across the peaceful landscape. Below us was a wide valley cut up badly by *dongas* (erosion gullies). On the further side a sweeping ridge rose into a rocky buttress, with more such ridges going off into the hazy distance. Golden light lay over it all and haze mingled with the smoke from the nearby huts. A visually beautiful land, productive enough for a small number of farming families, but unable to support the great masses of people who had been pushed back into it.

After supper we had coffee with Greg and Mary Wells in their rondavel. Both were doctors; they had a small child and Mary worked part time. They had become interested in the problems of community medicine in developing countries but had been unable to travel elsewhere in the continent.

'Other African countries don't accept South African passports, so we couldn't go, for example, to Tanzania to see for ourselves,' Greg explained. 'So we got sponsorship from the Christian Fellowship Trust to spend three months in Europe talking to people who knew about Third World medicine.'

Their report had been published as *Health, Healing and Society.* 'We wanted to show what an enormous gap there is between the medical provision in white South Africa and that provided for the "homelands", and we came here because the medical profession needs to re-orientate its training towards community health issues.'

They took us off to 'journal club', where the staff met weekly over coffee and biscuits to keep themselves abreast of medical news. We all sat on the floor of someone's rondavel while each doctor read aloud an article that they felt useful. The medical conversation was way above our heads, but it was very cosy and at the end we had an opportunity to thank all those who had made us so welcome.

The hospital had an amazing atmosphere where everyone seemed to be accepted. Of course most members did share a basic set of values, though it was not obtrusively Christian and those of other faiths were welcomed; the Unterhalters' daughter Elaine spent some time there. We invited the Wells to visit us in London on their next trip for a 'breath of fresh air'; they eventually emigrated to England and became life-long friends.

Before we left Greg took me to see the local school. We walked down a sandy path to where a little white church stood among pine trees, the Catholic primary school beside it.

'We have 350 children enrolled,' Sister Romualda, the Principal, told me. 'But we only have five teachers. So we do double shift; one lot of children come in the morning and the others in the afternoon. But the same teachers have to teach both lots.'

'May I talk to the class?'

'Of course. This group is the top class, a mix of Standards 5 and 6. Some are as old as seventeen because they started late or had to repeat many times.'

They weren't quite up to the level of the Soweto students, but there were some bright and articulate ones.

'Are there any Bantu in England?' asked one. I tried to explain about

West Indian immigrants, and asked them to show me their history and geography textbooks. These all promulgated the South African Nationalist ideology, with such statements as: 'The Hottentots who lived in South Africa were very lazy. When the Whites arrived, slaves had to be imported to do all the work'...

The children were writing essays about 'my daily life'. The girls typically wrote: *When I get up, I make the mealie porridge. I help my mother clean the hut*, while the boys recorded: *I eat my breakfast. I take the cattle to the veld...*

As far as the South African government was concerned this was the only future they deserved.

The only other place we'd seen such poverty was the Dodoma region of Tanzania but at least there the government sent in famine relief; the TANU flag flew in the square, the local cadres scurried round rallying people into cooperatives and Nyerere would pay a visit; meanwhile UN bodies were in evidence with aid and expertise. Here one looked in vain for such signs of development. There were apparently no government extension or welfare services and the voluntary ones were being restricted. Just over the 'border' was all that money but it didn't flow here. It was hard to remember we were in the same country as Johannesburg.

But then the government was busy trying to pretend we weren't. Under the policy of 'separate development', this was a 'homeland'; a mini-state destined for eventual 'independence.' In reality this would never be possible because there wasn't enough land. Even back in 1951 the 'native reserves' could only support, agriculturally, 40% of those living there and since then natural increase and the resettlement programmes had hugely enlarged the population, while the recommended industrial development on the borders had been minimal, so to feed their families the men had to seek work in the big cities. In other words, the 'homelands', instead of being places 'where the Bantu nations can develop separately' were reservoirs of cheap labour whose internal development was stultified. And KwaZulu, even after consolidation, still comprised ten separate areas of land! Chief Gacha Buthelezi, the designated 'Prime Minister' of this mini-state, had accepted some self-government, but refused to accept formal independence under these conditions.

We were to see more 'homelands' later on.

CHAPTER 27

Second Interlude in Lesotho: May

In which we come home to Lesotho, finding some more history on the way and ponder about education.

Some battles are quietly forgotten by the history books, others are celebrated with medals and films. At the Battle of Islandlwana in 1879 a Zulu army of some 20,000 carrying assegais and knobkerries almost wiped out an armed British force one tenth of its size. Under the rocky buttress rising from the wide empty veld, a Zulu schoolboy solemnly showed us the white-marked graves and a display of relics, while his younger brothers strummed their home-made guitars hoping for pennies. We gave them our last oranges.

What happened the following day was remembered better. When some Zulus swept on to the outpost at Rorke's Drift, some eight miles downriver, 140 men kept 3,000 tribesmen at bay until reinforcements arrived, winning eleven Victoria Crosses in the process. The small cluster of houses from which they fought had been preserved, along with a letter from one of the survivors describing the action. Patrick, who'd seen the film *Zulu*, looked in vain for the mountain backdrop but it obviously wasn't shot in this open, wooded valley – the Drakensberg escarpment was more photogenic.

Ruminating on historical accuracy and selective colonial memories, we drove out of KwaZulu, through Dundee via Bonny Doon and Glencoe, then past the Newcastle Collieries. No need to ask who settled and named this rolling land of maize and cattle farms. In Ladysmith we saw Indians in the streets for the first time; they had been living here in Natal since arriving as indentured labourers in the nineteenth century but were forbidden to move up to the Orange Free State. Then we swung westwards towards that great photogenic wall of the Drakensberg, now dark against the evening sky, beyond which lay Lesotho and the high veld. As we climbed 2,000 feet up the winding road to Van Reenen's pass, we looked on one side back over the misty hills of Natal and on the other into deep, dark gorges crowned with buttresses glowing blood red in the sunset.

We spent the night in a damp, cold and expensive hotel in Harrismith which only offered tough steak and greasy chips for supper. But at least we were better off than the Coloured family who had to stand on the steps and have their food brought out to them because of the laws against mixed eating.

Next day the hills accompanied us on our left hand side: isolated mesas, ridges of little buttes and further south the blue massed peaks of the Golden Gate Highlands on the border of Lesotho. When we turned towards Fouriesberg the hills thickened around us, the tar ended and we entered Lesotho through a dramatic cleft in the hills. The South African police were bored and gave us a perfunctory farewell; the Basotho frontier officials were playing Monopoly on the veranda and, all unasked, gave us ninety-day residence permits.

We felt we'd come home! People in blankets and conical grass hats smiled and waved at us. It was Saturday; there were whole families shopping together, laughing together, riding bicycles and driving beat-up cars. Yes, some men were away in the mines; yes, others were unemployed and others drank too much *joala* – that sorghum beer again – but that gave women an income which paid school fees. Yes, there was poverty and too little land, but most of the available fields had been ploughed and were growing maize; not as tall as that of the Republic but after harvest the cattle would come down from the mountains and feed on the stalks. There was at least some energy around, unlike the hopelessness of KwaZulu.

When we stopped in Leribe for a picnic lunch a stray conversation with a passing curate sent us to the Anglican Community of the Holy Name, where four elderly English nuns came out to greet us.

'You live in south London? Good heavens, our mother house used to be in Vauxhall! Beside the Marmite factory – is it still there?' This was a good start. Their Superior, Sister Marjorie, was a great character: cheerful, bustling and a practical leader as well as spiritual.

'I started a weaving school for girls,' she explained. 'We used the local wool and mohair from the angora goats. Now we've got a big craft centre with over forty women. They knit and crochet as well as weave. We help them market their goods – shawls, belts, rugs, hats and so on for the tourists and stoles for the priests. I even sell horse-girths to farmers in the Republic!

'I was an engineering draughtswoman in the war,' she recounted. 'I designed our new buildings here and showed the local builders what I wanted; they are good at working with stone but we had some fun installing the flushing loos and a septic tank!'

She told us about her training centre for home economics, now government-recognised. 'When I first came out I lived on an African diet and got malnourished, so I know what changes they need to make. Christian Aid gave us money for equipment, but I made sure they learn to cook on open fires and kerosene stoves as well as electric ovens, to match whatever they have at home.' So much better than the ultra-modern domestic science centre in the Lagos slums!

We bought a delicate crocheted shawl and scarf and they pressed us to stay for tea, obviously pleased to have visitors, so it was 4 pm by the time we left. It was impressive, but where were the Basotho women to take over and run it for themselves? We drove on fast down the newly tarred road as the mesas turned golden and then red in the sunset, reaching Maseru as it got dark. Anna was out; we settled down with brandy and the fire to read our enormous pile of mail – including some lost Christmas post – before falling into bed.

Over Sunday lunch Anna decided we should behave like proper tourists and visit the National Mountain, Thaba Bosiu. 'Why not today? I have to go to a funeral but Hlomi will go with you.'

Hlomi was a young relative living with Anna while finishing off her education. 'She's been so well brought up in our African traditions,' Anna enthused. 'She never interrupts her elders.' In fact, Hlomi had hardly ever dared to talk to us but she obediently got into our car and guided us to

Thaba Bosiu, a small flat-topped mountain which had been the nation's refuge in time of war.

A long stretch of sandstone crags some 200 feet high lay along the road, glowing gold in the afternoon sun. At its foot nestled a cluster of thatched rondavels, their walls painted red or ochre and decorated with curving patterns which had been finger-pressed into the mud before it dried. The official guide, Dickson Rafutho, had just come back from church but insisted on walking us up the rough road still wearing his black suit and tall hat. Relieved perhaps to have a rest from English, he told the whole story in Sesotho to Hlomi who translated it back to us.

'When the Basotho were attacked Moshoeshoe took all the people with their cattle up here where there was pasture and water. There were only two narrow paths then and the men rolled down stones, so the enemies were killed. Now they've built this road so the ministers can drive up in their jeeps to pay their respects. Some are too fat to walk,' she added laughingly.

Moshoeshoe's grave, marked by a stone cairn, lay in the middle of the wide grassy plateau, those unscaleable cliffs dropping away all round. Ponies grazed peacefully on the bleached pasture, while long blue shadows spread over the valleys towards the Maluti mountains. It was hard to imagine the place thronged with refugees hurling defiance to their foes encamped below.

When we got back to the village the sun was setting and the cattle were being brought back into the stone-walled kraals for the night. Their bellowing mixed with the shouts of the herdboys and greetings from the villagers while the smoke and smell of the cooking fires drifted across the open doorways. Some small boys came running up asking us for sweets and were promptly shooed away by a self-assured young woman in a red jacket, who turned out to be Mr Rafutho's granddaughter, Alice. Her parents were, like many others, working in the Republic to earn money to support the family. She and her friend Grace wanted English pen-friends so we spent a happy half hour taking photographs, exchanging addresses and eventually being invited into her rondavel. There was a bed and bookshelves, while primus and cooking utensils hung on the wall and everything was kept neat and tidy. With just one small window in the thick walls it felt very snug on a winter evening.

When we reached home, under another wonderful apricot sunset with the hills etched black against the sky, Anna was still out. We persuaded Hlomi to share our traditional Sunday night supper of scrambled eggs and she at last came out of her shell, telling us about the holiday job she had collecting census data.

'It was difficult,' she recalled. 'What do you write down when someone says: "I was born the year Chief So-and-so died"? And I know they didn't tell me how many cattle they had in the village, because the cattle were supposed to be up in the mountains!' We began to see why no one was quite sure how many citizens belonged to Lesotho or how one might reckon up the national wealth. Certainly most of it came in as migrant remittances, and an expatriate advisor suggested much of the rest arose from smuggling *dagga* (cannabis) over the mountains. There wasn't much else Lesotho could export.

Next evening when Anna, unusually, was at home, we got talking about bringing up children. She feared the modern children of Africa had no self-control and argued with their elders. 'In my day children learnt not to do something because it was the custom – no reasons were given. For example, there was a taboo on girls eating eggs; this helped them learn self-control.'

'Surely,' I retorted, 'it is better to discuss things with kids and lead them to understand the reasons for behaviour so they can take responsibility themselves? And Anna, I'm surprised that you, a nutritionist, approve of banning eggs!'

She laughed. 'That was just an example! Let me say, then, if a visitor came with food the child of the house never dreamt of touching that food unless given it by his mother. Now they just grab!'

Beyond the jokes, this was for us and our expatriate friends a serious issue. Some worried that traditionally African children are brought up in loving but often authoritarian relationships, mixing with their peers rather than with adults and so might lack mental stimulation at appropriate times. We wondered how social culture and cohesion could be maintained while equipping youngsters for a world of change and individual responsibility.

Schools were obviously the place to look and so I went visiting, though on this trip I found few answers. I knew that Lesotho had one of the highest literacy rates in Sub-Saharan Africa, largely thanks to Moshoeshoe I's enthusiasm for missionaries and in particular to the Protestant ones. They quickly developed Sesotho into a written language, primarily as a vehicle for translating the Bible, but in 1863 they also started a newspaper *Lesilinyana* (the Little Light) which was Africa's oldest extant vernacular newspaper.

I spent a morning with Jasper Selwyn at the Lesotho High School, *alma mater* of both Anna and Mary Hlalele, with a good headmaster and a high reputation. He was teaching maths using modern teaching materials and group work, to which the pupils responded well.

When I described the Nigerian enthusiasm for schooling, he shook his head. 'I think maybe they are a bit disillusioned with it here. Men can earn more in the mines than as primary teachers. And my pupils tell me: if we want government jobs, it's not what we know, it's who we know. But His Majesty is keen – go and talk to the Sprays.'

The current king, Moshoeshoe II, had just founded a large new high school in the Royal Village at Matsieng. The school was to have a vocational focus; the students would study agriculture, woodwork, sewing and so on, alongside development studies, that mixture of sociology, politics and economics that Don Taylor was pioneering at the university. Paul and Wendy Spray were teaching the subject and showed me round the school.

'It's all a bit shambolic,' Wendy explained, 'since His Majesty is rather under-employed and interferes all the time in the school. He's driven a couple of headmasters nuts already, as he doesn't quite get the point. The students, for a practical exercise, built a chicken house and fattened broiler chickens. The King found it "untidy" and has set up a large capital-intensive broiler unit which spoils their market and doesn't teach the kids anything!'

I thought it all fascinating and fun; four years later I was to find myself facing all these contradictions in my role training teachers of development studies at what had by then become the National University of Lesotho.

CHAPTER 28
Through the Ciskei

In which we go where we should not have gone, visit missions and townships and meet a banned leader.

There had been no message from Constance Koza when we got back to Lesotho, so we wondered if her invitation to tour the 'homelands' had been serious. A telegram brought an immediate call back.

'Yes, of course I'm coming, with two friends. It's really a work trip but we want to have some fun as well. Meet me at 9 am on Wednesday at the Maseru Holiday Inn.'

'Having fun' meant, in part, being treated as 'normal' guests in a 'normal' hotel, so we found them dawdling over a huge breakfast buffet set out South African style with cheese and cold meats as well as fruits, cereal, bacon and eggs. Connie, as usual resplendent in a colourful long skirt and matching tall turban, introduced a younger, more soberly dressed woman with a quiet, smiling face. 'This is Elda Olifant; she's blind but trained as a telephonist and I'm hoping we can find a job for her with the Ciskei government. This is Joe, market development officer for Inter-Church Aid. He'll drive us.' Joe was a cheerful practical man with a good sense of humour and a way of fixing everything without fuss.

We set off in separate cars till we got past the border posts – we were waved through the barrier but the Africans had to get out twice – and then Connie joined us in the Beetle. As we drove south through the empty, wintry landscape we listened and she talked.

'I won't let the government put me into any tribal box! I feel African and I dress like an African. My grandmother was Sotho and married a Pedi catechist. My mother grew up in an Afrikaner farming community and as a child she used to sleep in the old white lady's bed to keep her feet warm – oh yes, there was a personal content to the master-servant relationship then! My father was a Zulu chief as well as a Christian Minister and I married a man of mixed Swazi-Shangaan parentage. So that covers five of our so-called tribes and I speak most of the other languages too. My daughter has left the country; she's studying nutrition in the States. My son? Well, he joined SASO[43] and was detained for a while, so he had to leave university and can't get work.

'I went to an all-African girls' high school but we had matches and debates with white schools, even residential courses together. I've still got so many white friends that people say I'm a "diluted African", or even a sell-out! The next generation hasn't had the opportunity for such personal contacts and they are bitterly anti-white. My son scolds me: "Why do you talk to them? Three hundred years of talking has got us nowhere." My generation offers the last chance of a peaceful compromise – the next generation will fight!

'But the white liberals – bah! They are worse than the Nats[44]. They say they "want to do things for the Africans" but we want to do things for ourselves. Those liberals and the Jews, they are trying to divide us, to get the black middle class on their side so they can go on making money! The Nationalists have done us this one good turn: they've forced us into a more radical consciousness and now we Blacks stand solid.'

All this time we were driving through the eastern Free State. In the distance, constantly changing shape, was the frieze of blue hills, made up of rocky flat-topped ridges broken by the occasional peak, none very high, forming a backdrop to the wide maize fields and the flocks of sheep and cattle. This open country with huge farms looked so empty that Connie kept saying, 'Why do so few people need all this land when the "homelands" are so overcrowded - this must be changed!'

'You're taking us into the "homelands" – is there any virtue in this policy?' we ventured.

'No! They simply divide Africans from one another. They give the

---

[43] The South African Students' Organisation recently set up for non-white students.

[44] Members or supporters of the mainly Afrikaans-speaking Nationalist Party, which was then in power.

shadow of power without its substance. Gatcha Buthelezi, Chief Minister of KwaZulu, is the only one who is trying to use his position to help all Blacks; he even belongs to the ANC[45]. But the others – pah! I don't trust Matanzima in Transkei. In fact, the Nats are downright wicked to manipulate our leaders in this way. We used to respect our chiefs, but they are often not the most educated in Western ways and now they've been made to look like fools.'

In Queenstown we stopped to buy supper provisions and wine. Supermarkets were integrated but bottle stores (the equivalent of the British off-licence) had separate entrances for Blacks and Whites.

'You go in your queue and I'll go in mine,' Connie ordered, 'and we'll meet at the top!' At the counter we poked our heads round the barrier and there she was. 'Tassenberg Red?' she suggested and we bought two large bottles. We felt rather embarrassed but Joe just made fun of the system.

'I know how to get good meat,' he boasted. 'When I go to the butcher's I write down what I want on a piece of paper, scrawl a signature and hand it over the counter. They think I'm buying for my boss and give me the best, otherwise I'd get any old scrag end!'

Lumko Mission

We doubled back northeast over a pass where the great cliffs were glowing amethyst and garnet in the sunset and into the Ciskei, one of the two 'homelands' designated for the Xhosa people. The road became rough dusty gravel, making driving slow, and it was practically dark when we turned into the gates of Lumko Mission. The square church tower looked very European; chimes sounded and nuns came walking through the dusk. There were brief greetings in gutteral English from a German priest. 'No, we have not got your telegram but that is OK, we make rooms for you in the hostel.' We were swept into the warmth and light of the refectory for supper. Soup, beans and bacon stew with *samp* (maize kernels), hot tea, tinned pears – it was all very welcome.

'Lumko began many years ago as a German Catholic Mission Station,' Father Lobinger told us. 'Now we are four priests together with five

---

[45] Buthelezi later split with the ANC and set up his own Inkatha Party.

African sisters. We run courses for lay preachers and catechists. But the village is part of the "betterment schemes" and we feel we should be doing more development work there. So we invited Mrs Koza to advise us.'

After supper we settled down with Sisters Ursula and Bridget in the recreation room. Both Joe and Connie were very curious about the religious life and their 'vocations'. Celibacy is unthinkable in traditional African society and Sr Ursula had great difficulty in explaining why she ran away from home to join the Community of the Precious Blood. Two of the priests joined us, delightfully relaxed in scruffy old clothes and, being Catholics, happy to drink our wine.

At 9 pm Connie suddenly said: 'Please turn on the radio. The commission investigating the Christian Institute was to report today.'

The newscaster's voice was clear. 'The Christian Institute has been found to be working for change of a radical kind… At their bible and study classes they discuss social and political themes instead of religious ones… Some of the ideas of the Christian Institute are influenced by the British and American Left…'

We'd heard about the Christian Institute, ironically, from our Jewish friends in Johannesburg who had lent us their publications. It was an interdenominational group of churchmen inspired by the charismatic Dr Beyers Naudé, an Afrikaner who gave up his high position in the Dutch Reformed Church to lead this ecumenical 'think tank' which believed apartheid to be fundamentally wrong and said so. They set up the *Study Project on Christianity in Apartheid Society* to collect facts about the inequalities in their society and then published a series of excellent reports, setting out the facts soberly and outlining ways in which Christians could work for peaceful social change. Any reader from a Western democracy would judge them as social reformers, politically somewhere on the right of the UK Labour Party, or perhaps Liberals, not violent revolutionaries. But here they were seen a serious threat to the government.

The work of this remote mission in Lumko was unlikely to be affected but Connie's Inter-church Aid and the South African Council of Churches itself were vulnerable. More beacons of hope and sanity were being threatened; we shivered slightly as we sat among these dedicated folk and talked on till the wine was long gone. 'Lights out in 20 minutes,' said our host, meaning that the generator would be switched off, and so we had to write the diary by candlelight. As there was no heating Patrick suggested I should emulate Connie's grandmother and sleep at the end of the bed to warm his feet; the ensuing tussle with the bedclothes made them even colder.

Breakfast was early; the porridge and bitter wind brought back memories of Morambo Hut on Kilimanjaro. Connie was negotiating hard but seemed disappointed. 'Their facilities are badly underutilised and the priests don't seem very dynamic. Still, we've agreed to station a fieldworker here and possibly we'll run a health education conference in September. Let's go and see the village which is supposed to have been "bettered".'

In the past the Xhosas, like the Zulus, lived in small family clusters scattered around the veld, the men watching over the cattle as they grazed and the women tending the maize plots. Here the government agricultural advisers had moved the families onto a single ridge and made them rebuild their huts in straight lines on a village pattern. Some land had been fenced off for ploughing and the hillsides divided into 'camps' for rotational grazing. In places, stone barriers had been built across the dongas to prevent further erosion. We remembered the ujamaa villages and asked Father Lobinger if it was working.

'Well, there have been some protests. The promised water supply hasn't arrived and as for electricity – wait fifty years! I do think the hills are greener now and the boys go to school instead of herding. But they can't grow enough food to live off so still most of the men become migrant labourers. The people don't trust the government officials because they try to impose cattle culling.'

Connie interrupted angrily. 'You can't meddle with our cattle. I knew a project where the Church persuaded everyone to put their cattle into a well-managed cooperative farm; the beasts grew fat, were sent to the abattoir, and the villagers got a cash dividend. But that didn't work: they wanted to tend the calves, they wanted their own beasts to slaughter for feasts, or to pay bride price with. It's too much part of our culture for rationalised stock farming.' A clash between culture and economics!

After lunch with the friendly talkative sisters we set off again. When

Johannesburg from the Carlton Tower.

Felicity Van Vuuren.

Molten gold being poured into moulds.

Soweto mass housing.

Orlando, a middle-class area of Soweto.

Bongile Putsoa at her school.

Francina Mamba and her son.

Swazi homestead where Francina's cousins lived.

Charles Johnson Hospital, Nqutu.

Zulu homestead.

The high veld with white farmland.

Constance Koza at the South African Council of Churches.

Tandi Thebahadi in Soweto.

Cape Town central area with Table Mountain behind.

Elaine Bhettay.

Theo and Helen Kotze.

Cape Flats: women outside their shanties.

Cape Flats: transitional housing for families.

Cape Flats: new blocks replacing the shanties behind them.

Barkley Pass at the southern end of the Drakensberg.

Mist around Cape Point, where
two oceans meet.

A sign saying 'Whites Only on this beach'.

I stopped to photograph the 'bettered' village, Connie came with me, saying, 'They just might be suspicious. The Lesotho number plate is a blessing, they respond more warmly to foreign Whites than to ours. But your visit will have been reported – there are bound to be informers here.'

After that Connie fell asleep wedged in the back of the Beetle. We were left to ponder the huge problems of 'development' and 'betterment' in these rural areas. For the villagers to come together and to change their whole way of life, giving up their cultural customs, there would need to be visionary leaders, huge incentives and a deep trust in the future for their children. None of those existed in such a depressed, oppressed, impoverished community of women, children and old men. What solutions might there be?

We stopped at the tiny village of Whittlesea to buy petrol, which had to be hand-pumped as there wasn't any electricity. 'Look at that!' I exclaimed. All along the nearby hillside were rows and rows of drab white boxes.

'That's Sada,' said Connie. 'It's a new township for Xhosas being resettled back to their "homeland", the Ciskei. Twenty thousand have been moved there. But there's no work; only three small factories have been set up since white investment in the "homelands" has been allowed.'

Shiloh

But Shiloh Village was amazingly different. We turned off, bumping over dirt roads through an untidy village where mud houses were being replaced by brick or cement ones; there were several tractors and farm implements; nearly every plot had pigs, chickens, cattle, donkeys or horses in their back yards and small gardens fenced off. There was a river and a borehole and some of the fields were irrigated. This was an organic village, alive and thriving as much as any place could on agriculture alone.

'Begorrah, it could be pre-war Ireland without the bog,' muttered Patrick.

'It's like some of the Nigerian villages we visited,' I remembered. 'You've got poverty but prospects of development as well; people are getting on with their own improvements with their own resources.'

'What you're seeing here,' Connie said, 'is a rural village as it was before the Group Areas Act moved millions of people across the country.

Coloureds and Africans are still living together here.'

And how had this pleasant anachronism survived? Because when the Moravian missionaries came to South Africa in the eighteenth century they were not salaried; they bought land from the local chief and settled down to farming alongside their converts, teaching them to become independent peasant farmers. The comparative prosperity of this village was the result of an agricultural emphasis and a tradition of cooperation between African and European, showing how the rest of the countryside might have looked if apartheid hadn't stopped rural development in its tracks.

Pastor Martin Eberle was a large, jolly German living with his family in the old rambling mission house. They'd moved on from farming to industry and he was very proud of his new factory, which employed 140 women from Sada earning about R40 a month and was turning out crimplene dresses to sell in local stores. It had to be built on Church land because Whites couldn't own property in the 'homelands'.

Over a good German supper of meat and vegetables with more red wine we discovered that Martin had run the German Churches' relief operations in Biafra.

'I was completely on the side of the Igbos when it started,' he said. 'But so many died! I had 1,000 children in my camp and only food for 500 – the rest died and it still haunts me. And I wonder – if there is revolution in South Africa, is that the kind of price they'd have to pay?'

'So what do you think about the "homelands", living here inside one of them?'

'The Ciskei is very tense. The government was elected with a bare majority and is sensitive to criticism, although Chief Minister Sebe is doing his best, especially for education. We Moravians have been criticised for putting up schools in segregated areas like this – they say we are supporting apartheid. We're not; we want to educate people at all costs and provide work where we can. Our factory is doing well, lots of orders, but it's a drop in the ocean compared to what's needed to provide jobs for all. The "homelands" need far more investment but where will it come from?'

The next news bulletin brought the announcement everyone had feared:

the Christian Institute was declared an 'affected organisation' and thus prohibited from getting funds from abroad. As 75% of their budget was from overseas they would have to curtail their activities. Would the South African Council of Churches be next? Would Naudé be banned?

'I don't think Beyers Naudé will be banned,' said Eberle. 'He is held in great admiration in Germany and we are such an important trading and investment partner for South Africa. They will hesitate before doing anything to him.'

This made Connie angry. 'I'm sick and tired of Whites being set up as martyrs and becoming famous because of Blacks while Blacks do all the suffering and go unnoticed,' she burst out. 'We must free ourselves; our struggle is not to provide a romantic destiny for Whites with consciences. Mandela and Sobukwe are in prison on Robben Island – why so much fuss about Naudé?' With that, she swept off to bed.

The next day didn't exactly go according to plan as African time kicked in. We were expected in King William's Town by mid-morning to visit the famous old college of Fort Hare and the infamous township of Dimbaza. But Connie felt on holiday and wanted to go shopping. The factory women ran a sideline in traditional beadwork – tiny orange, white and black beads made into intricate necklaces and bracelets or sewn onto tops and skirts.

'Wholesale prices for you, ladies!' Connie, Elda and I decided buying here was actually saving us money and went on a spree. I bought some jewellery and a long traditional orange Xhosa skirt, decorated with black and white beads, and a fringed orange shawl to match, which I was to wear in the final scene of this story. More productively, Joe was organising shipments of these attractive things to the Inter-Church Aid shop in Johannesburg for the tourist trade. Patrick sat on the veranda reading about the banning of the Christian Institute, watching the midday procession to the river to wash clothes and stalking the occasional hoopoe. Presently lunch was served.

Finally Joe and Connie leapt into the Volvo and drove off so fast over the bumpy road that our Beetle could hardly keep up. When we reached King William's Town the Rev Tembo Sibeko was on the point of leaving as they had been waiting for us since noon and our planned tour was in ruins. 'But you must see Dimbaza,' decided Connie and drove us off in the gathering dusk.

What was so bad about Dimbaza? A few years previously this bare patch of veld had been designated a resettlement township for the families being sent back to the 'homelands' from the white areas where they had lived for generations. The government officials were mostly rural Afrikaners who assumed all Africans lived in mud huts, so they built one-room wooden shacks for them. But these were urban families, quite well off, and they brought so much furniture and goods with them that it had to be piled up outside. There were no amenities and no work. Typhoid broke out.

Then the Church got to hear about it and Father David Russell arrived. For six months he lived on the near-starvation rations handed out to the destitute families and he wrote about how he deteriorated, mentally and physically, on this diet. In 1973 they made a film, secretly, called *Last Grave at Dimbaza*.

When this was shown private and public funds poured in. The government built improved houses to replace the shacks and some schools, the Churches appointed Rev Sibeko – whom we had just met – as community worker and a few factories were set up; these employed about 200 women in all out of a population of over 15,000.

'The Church donated seeds and trees and offered prizes for gardens to encourage vegetable growing to supplement the mealie meal diet,' Connie told us. 'Morale has improved at bit but basically it is still an impossible situation and you need to see it for yourselves'.

We could see rows of tiny pale houses stretching away into the dusk as Connie took us to the home that won the first prize for its garden. The man was lucky enough to have a government job, so they had bought good furniture and re-plastered the walls; the three well-dressed children sat quietly watching us. The garden was indeed full of vegetables and the township had given them a private water tap as their prize; otherwise there were only street taps and bucket-type privies at the end of each garden. There was just one store and the church hall was the only social centre for the hundreds of youngsters who were wandering around with nothing to look forward to.

'In some ways Dimbaza has become a model for visitors to admire,' commented Connie grimly. 'There are much worse resettlement areas off the beaten track which didn't get the publicity.' We remembered Greg Wells' account of Mondlo in KwaZulu, which we'd been forbidden to visit. How many other horrors lay hidden in these wild, beautiful lands, out of the public eye, away from the public conscience?

The political geography of this peculiar society dictated that King William's Town – an old-established, thriving centre – was to remain part of white South Africa, while most of its poor arid hinterland was to become part of the new 'country' of Ciskei. Therefore the only place we could meet our black friends was in the church community centre but its interracial nature had attracted unwanted attention.

'Our new truck is a burnt-out wreck,' Moses Moletsane, the social worker, told us. 'Last week someone broke into the offices and smashed the furniture – look, you can see it. The police can't or won't protect us.'

What to say to this evidence? We were tired and the rest of the church workers rather shy, but the feelings of fellowship grew over supper and two bottles of Connie's favourite wine. A car-load of young people turned up from Umtata and invited us to visit them at the Transkei Council of Churches. Then a tall, good-looking African came in.

'This is Steve Biko,' said Connie. 'Steve, these are friends of mine from England. They are trying to understand what is going on in South Africa. Can I bring them to have breakfast with you tomorrow morning at the clinic?'

'Of course,' said Steve, before being swept away by the youngsters from Umtata.

'Now we have to separate,' said Connie. 'We can't stay together in a white town. I've booked a room for you at the hotel and we'll stay in Dimbaza. See you tomorrow at nine.'

It was only a few hundred yards but suddenly we were back into the other world where the only black people were those scurrying round to carry your suitcases. It felt odd.

Zanempilo Clinic and Steve Biko

We weren't at all sure why Connie wanted us to meet this Steve person. We knew only that he was some sort of student leader and that he was officially banned, which meant he had to live in a particular area, could not travel and was only allowed to meet with one person at a time. We realised that his appearance at supper the night before had been a deliberate flouting of the law, so he clearly was not cowed by authority.

We followed Connie's Volvo out of town along the dirt road leading to one of the old 'locations', a black area where the workers lived who serviced King William's Town. The Zanempilo Clinic was a simple white building run by Dr Mamphela Ramphele, one of the very few black women to have graduated from the only non-white medical school. Over breakfast, Steve and Mamphela were pleasant and polite but reserved, and we felt that while Connie had been effusively trying to win us on to her side, well-intentioned foreign Whites were irrelevant to this couple. While Steve talked funding with Connie, Mamphela gave us a quick tour of the clinic.[46]

'It was built by a black architect,' she told us proudly, 'with funds raised by the Black Community Programme. Thanks to Mrs Koza the running costs are now covered by Inter-Church Aid. We have maternity beds and an outpatients' surgery because the government doesn't provide any medical facilities round here. I have five nurses but I try to see all the patients myself at least once; they have the right to see a real doctor.'

'What are the biggest problems you deal with?' I asked.

'I'd say the biggest is malnutrition and of course that comes from poverty. But for the children, it's aggravated because the mothers have to give up breast-feeding. That's because working women aren't allowed to take their babies with them to the farms or to the houses where they work. The white ladies are so ignorant, so thoughtless!'

I remembered in all the other countries we'd visited the babies on their mothers' backs, safe in shawl or blanket, ready to be fed in a quiet corner. Even in the UK some alternative lifestyle couples were wearing baby-carriers. What an extraordinary thing that South Africa should forbid it!

'Can't you get any white women on your side? What about the Black

---

[46] In 1976 Dr Ramphele was detained without trial and then 'banned' for several years. She then moved into academic work and was VC of the University of Cape Town in the 1990s; later she became very active in both business and politics, including a stint as a director of the World Bank.

Sash movement?'[47]

'Oh, they get publicity for their actions but they don't change anything. Their protests assuage the consciences of the wealthy, that's all.'

At this point Connie, Elda and Joe had to leave for Johannesburg and we sat down with Steve in the winter sunshine. In his late twenties, even in jeans and open-necked shirt he carried with him an air of authority, emphasised by his short, curling beard and direct gaze. As the conversation developed we asked him to explain to us about 'black consciousness'.

'It began when we were at university,' he replied. 'The National Union of South African Students was multiracial and went about proclaiming ideals of natural justice, even protesting against apartheid laws. But nothing much was changing for Blacks because the student leadership was mostly white and it felt paternalistic. We felt that ultimately the leadership of the non-white peoples in this country must rest with us.

'So in 1968 we set up the South African Students' Organisation – SASO – for non-white students. At first the government approved as this seemed a vindication of their apartheid policy! We saw it differently: we wanted to boost up the morale of non-white students and heighten their own confidence in themselves. Only then could the different communities enter into dialogue as equals. When the government understood we were fighting for our rights they stopped us and, as their president, I was expelled from medical school.

'I started working with black community projects in Durban but two years ago I was banned. I had to come back to my home and stay here.' He got up to walk around the room and we felt how restricting it must be. 'I cannot visit schools, factories, or printing offices; I cannot attend any gatherings, make speeches or write books. This was to stop me doing my work in community development, but it has not done so, not completely.' He smiled. 'I should not be talking to you, nor should you be in this area!'

We knew that already and guessed our presence was being reported by some government spy but we didn't care; this was a new and fascinating voice whom we felt we could trust with open questions. Patrick asked:

---

[47] The Black Sash began in 1955 with white women demonstrating publicly in silence wearing broad black sashes to symbolise the death of the constitution under the Nationalist Government. By this time they also had a large social action programme and were running advice centres to help people navigate the consequences of the pass laws.

'Can you tell us, if black people came to power, what sort of government would you set up?'

'Do you mean are we Marxists? Many of our leaders are suspicious of Marxism because the white Communists in the old ANC manipulated the Blacks for their own ends. The Black People's Convention, our political party, is definitely socialist in orientation and any enterprises we set up would be 50% worker-controlled.' He paused to gauge our reaction.

'But that's for the future. Right now we're more concerned with grass-roots activity than political rhetoric. That's where the Black Community Programme comes in. We are working in black areas all over the country. Our long-term aim is to start enterprises to generate funds, but we have a problem in that we will not call ourselves Xhosa or Zulu, or any other tribe. We say we are all "Africans" and because of this we cannot qualify to set up a "homelands" business. But we have many projects, ranging from literacy programmes, crèches, home industries, cooperative buying programmes, to this clinic. Our whole emphasis is on self-help and self-respect; as well as giving material things we aim to make people proud of being black. This is the Black Consciousness Movement in action.'

He smiled again, shaking his head. 'It is ironic. Since I have had to stop making speeches and focus on practical projects, I am now accepted by more conservative black people who did not like the militant rhetoric. At least I am still here; I have not run off into exile like some of those who shouted loudest!'

'You're doing all this in a "homeland"', Patrick said. 'Does this give you a political base from which to operate?'

Steve became very definite here. 'In no way! These so-called Bantustans are a trick, they actually work to oppress black people and divert their attention from the real problems. The elections are rigged, so the conservative parties, led by the chiefs, are always going to win. No fundamental change is going to come out of the "homelands"! When there was a strike in the textile factories over the terribly low pay the Ciskei government actually helped to put it down.'

Steve did not look like a man who would lightly resort to violence, but we had to ask the other question that was haunting us: 'Would the Black People's Convention join the armed struggle?'

'Not at the moment,' he answered firmly. 'We do still think there is an alternative; we believe that there is a way of getting across to where we want to go through peaceful means. We Blacks must articulate what we want, and put it across to the white man from a position of strength. That is the purpose of the BPC – to gain a majority of black support so that it can be the authentic voice of black people and speak on their behalf.'

He asked us politely to stay to lunch, but we felt we'd taken up enough of their time so after photographing the clinic – but not Steve, for security's sake – we left.

'That was by far the most interesting conversation we've had so far,' said Patrick as we drove away.

I agreed. 'If South Africa had a normal democratic system he would be running for parliament by now and be prime minister within a decade or two.'

Tragically, South Africa did not have such a system. Two years later Steve died from brain damage in a police cell. He would indeed have been a worthy successor to Mandela; he had the breadth of vision, the balance and the charisma to lead the country – but they killed him first.

CHAPTER 29
White Settlers in the Eastern Cape

In which we experience culture shock on a farm and are only partly restored by Grahamstown.

It was perhaps unfortunate that our itinerary took us directly from the world of Steve Biko and Black Consciousness to the world of the white settler – a couple of hours driving south-westwards across rolling, dry and rocky hills, but light years apart in attitude.

We had been invited for the weekend by farming friends of Patrick's father – let's call them the Strongs. We drove up to a large solid bungalow, tin-roofed, with wide verandas. The lawn spread out to brilliant bougainvillea bushes, spiky aloes and even a banana tree; tall bluegums to the north kept off the midday sun. Dorothy welcomed us warmly and offered a cup of tea. Inside the house was dim and cool with dark old furniture, English country house style. Dorothy's hobby was weaving and her pieces covered both walls and chairs.

Peter took us out in his *bakkie* – the ubiquitous South African pick-up truck – to see the farm. Half Afrikaner, he retired years ago as professor of animal husbandry at Pretoria University and said he was now putting his theories into practice. He explained how the bush could be turned into good pasture and we admired the fat contented cattle with their strange horns.

'Indigenous Afrikander crossed with Hereford and Devon. Plus I've got sixty Friesian dairy cows and some sheep. It's too dry for arable but I grow some winter feed crops.'

We asked about the workers and Peter told us he employed twelve men. 'They've each got about ten dependants. They build their own houses, over there.' Sure enough, there was a cluster of low shacks, built of wattle and mud with thatched roofs, hidden well away from the bungalow. 'They get R14 (£9.50) a month, and free rations as well – mealies, cowpeas, sugar and coffee and of course milk. They can keep chickens but no pigs or dogs. They can run their own cattle with mine – up to six head – but I charge them 50c a beast per month.'

Patrick did a quick calculation – that could be 20% off their wages. 'Do they grow vegetables?'

'Well, they used to have garden plots, but they let them get too weedy, so I stopped that.'

I asked whether the women could earn anything. 'Oh yes, they work in the house or they ask for contract work, like weeding or cutting down trees, but we pay them practically nothing for that. I can always get workers because of the school. We have a farm school here with a government teacher – it goes up to Standard 2.[48]'

'And after that?'

'Well, nothing really, there's no boarding facilities at the school in town.'

Along the path came a stately African woman with a baby on her back and a load of wood on her head. Peter's dogs rushed up to her barking loudly; she clutched at her load and shrank into the bushes.

'Ha! Ha!' laughed Peter. 'My dogs like giving Kaffir maids a fright.'

At that point we decided that the gulf was too wide for dialogue and we would leave as soon as we could.

However, we were stuck for at least one night and had to make the best of it. We earned Peter's approval by drinking his brandy neat and helped them plan a trip round England, still seen as the Motherland. Over a good supper of bush buck stew, shot on his own land, we took another of those deep breaths and inquired about the political situation. As United Party supporters they were firmly against the Nationalists.

'The Nats gerrymandered the rural constituencies after 1948 to keep their majority. We think apartheid is wrong; we don't like mixing but we'd let the Blacks own their houses and have families in the white areas if they work there.'

He thought the Bantustans were a big mistake both ecologically and

---

[48] Second year of primary education.

politically. 'Firstly, they've taken over some white farms under consolidation agreements and they've gone to rack and ruin under the Blacks. Secondly, you'll see, Russia and China will move in, like in Mozambique. They'll turn Communist!'

It wasn't to be expected that white South Africans would be able to distinguish between different brands of socialism and our description of Tanzania was dismissed. How did they see the future?

'I'd like to see an evolutionary process – not one man one vote, but to let a black middle class emerge. It'll take a long time – the Africans are five hundred years behind us and that's being generous! Do you realise the Bushmen were like animals when Europeans arrived? The Hottentots are just lazy. The Bantu – they've got some honour and some pride but it will take them at least a hundred years to catch up.'

They pressed us to stay on for a few days but we invented an invitation in Grahamstown and retired angry and depressed. 'They are really just as racist as the Nats and apartheid serves their interests very well but they won't say so,' I fulminated to Patrick in our chilly bedroom where the plumbing was as antiquated as the attitudes.

Next morning was Sunday so we accompanied Dorothy to the local Methodist church. The young student who took the service was obviously practising his preaching but the theme – about blobs and dry trees which developed with God's grace – seemed to us to have little relevance to practical Christianity in a society urgently in need of it.

The congregation was entirely white and we asked Dorothy if services could be mixed. 'Last year's President of the South African Methodist Church was an African, yet people hereabouts feel affronted by mixed communion services.' Then she went on: 'I went on a church leadership course last year with Africans to see if I could take it. It was very hard and one night I nearly came home, but I'm glad I stuck it out.'

Suddenly I felt compassion for her but I couldn't ask her just why she found it so hard; they were a lot older than us and I felt it would be rude to persist. In some ways they were kind and well-meaning folk, but their lives were structured so far apart from those of Africans that it was very hard to see how the gap could be bridged.

We headed for Grahamstown in a depressed mood. The first hotel was too expensive so we took a room at the one-star Victoria. After multifarious problems with the African maids over keys, geysers, hot water and alternative rooms, we got very bad tempered with them, each other and the absent boss who was sleeping, and carried all our luggage downstairs again, to end up in the three-star Cathcart Arms. At least the water was hot and the beds comfy but it was too late to have a snooze before dinner. So we rang up James and Sara Christie, contacts from Felicity in Johannesburg, who not only invited us round for supper but restored our confidence in rational dialogue.

James lectured in sociology at Rhodes University and Sara taught primary school part-time. The flat had trendy décor, with low seats and posters in Russian on the walls and we immediately fell into the sort of conversation one might have in London in similar circles, exchanging reminiscences of travel round Europe and comparing notes on teaching multiracial classes in England. It transpired that James had been at LSE concurrently with me. We started on large bottles of local wine and were shortly joined by a nervous asthmatic divorcee and Rob Davies, a long-haired bearded economics lecturer of Rhodesian origin. The divorcee talked a lot, and not always to the point. James apologised in an aside that she had come uninvited and was 'apol' – i.e. .non-political. The Rhodesian was rather silent until we spoke about our meeting with Steve Biko.

'I'd like to have met him,' he said. 'Two of my students worked with him on the Black Literacy Programme. But our students at Rhodes are largely apolitical. I know just four who are trying seriously to analyse the society on Marxist lines. But then not many lecturers talk about politics either.'

'Three actually – you, me and that guy in history,' said James. 'Last week I gave my sociology students a lecture analysing economic trends. They wrote it all down and said oh yes, they agreed with me. When I told them that was a Marxist analysis their eyes popped out of their heads with horror!'

Sara told us she was currently involved in organising a petition against the removal of twenty Indian traders from the town under the Group Areas Act. 'Over 50% on the municipal voters' roll have signed it – out of about 4,500. We got a few African and Coloured signatures too. On Tuesday we shall present it to the Minister of Community Development but he will probably ignore it.'

'That's an example of South African "doublespeak" where words mean the opposite,' chortled James. 'The "Minister for Community Development" is tasked with breaking up mixed communities to resettle them somewhere they can't develop. The "Universities Extension Act" restricted Blacks to the "University Colleges" in the "homelands" – they can't come to places like Rhodes any more.'

'And what of the future?' we asked yet again. They had no clear answer but their analysis was mildly hopeful. 'There are changes – insignificant perhaps from a world perspective but considerable by our standards. There may still be time for a peaceful evolution. There is such a long history of repression in South Africa that the Blacks will have to recondition themselves before they can start initiating violent change. That's what Black Consciousness is about and that takes time.' [49]

Next day we felt more at home, finding Grahamstown reminiscent of an English market town with its wide central street leading down to the Gothic-spired, grey stone Cathedral. The plain-fronted houses jutted out over the street on delicate wrought iron pillars to shade shops and people from the heat. Patrick found a European barber while I replenished our supplies of food and books, then we sat in the winter sunshine under the leafless trees, drinking bad coffee and eating delicious scones, while students flowed in and out of the unpretentious university buildings in the adjacent streets. All white, of course.

On the edge of town stood a monolith to the '1820 Settlers' who in the early nineteenth century were given land in this area, both to stabilise the frontier against the Africans and to counter-balance the Dutch speakers in the Cape. Their first farming efforts were pretty disastrous – they didn't have Peter Strong's expertise – but the settlement survived and Grahamstown developed a distinctly British atmosphere, with debating societies and cricket matches, English-language newspapers and a college which morphed in 1904 into Rhodes University.

'Fingo Village – that's under threat, isn't it? Let's go and look.' Back

---

[49] Rob Davies went into exile shortly afterwards, pursing an academic career in the UK and Mozambique. In 1994 he was elected to the new South African parliament and later served as Minister for Trade and Industry.

in the 1850s, the Governor of the Cape granted Africans some land to settle on just across the valley, no doubt so they could become reliable labourers for the British. It had indeed a settled look, with bungalows and cottages replacing the huts, and large gardens with vegetables and livestock. Like Shiloh it was unpaved and untidy but full of individualism and signs of growth. People were laughing around the street taps when I asked to photograph them.

But under the Group Areas Act the Village was a 'black spot', soon to be demolished and the people moved to Committee's Drift, a desolate place thirty miles away where there were neither jobs, services nor houses. Fingo would be redesignated a Coloured Area. The villagers were protesting vehemently at this gross and stupid vandalism and so was the Town Council; they valued the villagers' labour and buying power in spite of their skin colour. British pragmatism versus Afrikaner ideology: which side would win?

We turned back south-eastwards towards the coast. After our trip with Connie we couldn't look at the landscape in the same way for although there were no signposts we could see the geography of apartheid imprinted on it. The land here was dry and little grew among the rocks except thorn bushes, aloes and red-hot pokers, but this had to be Ciskei again, for there were clusters of drab new houses along the ridges, wave after wave of them. You couldn't grow crops, or even graze cattle, so what were these people living from? Migrant wages?

We stopped by the Great Fish River where it cuts dramatically through the sedimentary rocks of the plateau to watch sand martins, pied wagtails, and a giant kingfisher. Hoping to swim, we found our way down to a 'Whites Only' beach of marvellous white sand with not a soul about. But a strong cold wind swirled around our feet and when, after two sandwiches of bread and grit, we went down to the breakers' edge this part of the Indian Ocean felt as though it had come straight from Antarctica. We walked out to the point and back, adding black oyster-catchers and black-backed gulls to our list, and wondering if it would be easier after all to study the habits of birds rather than people.

CHAPTER 30
East London and Transkei

In which we explore the contradictions around border towns and Bantustans.

For the next five days we were immersed in the world of business, media and government. We interviewed manufacturers in East London and journalists in Umtata, which was just becoming the so-called capital of the so-called independent Transkei. We met with an embattled priest, a cautious bishop, a liberal lawyer and another radical student. We broke the law by eating in mixed company in a public hotel. And finally we visited another sad rural hospital before taking a beautiful, if problematic, way home to Lesotho.

In East London we chose a sea-front hotel and unpacked with relief – we'd moved on for six nights in a row. Cargo ships were creeping up into the Buffalo River and dolphins were playing in the waves as the setting sun turned their crests into pink crinkles. To affirm our European heritage we ate *fondue bourgignon* at a Swiss restaurant called Mowenpick, with Black Forest tart and half a litre of Sangria. We felt we deserved it after all that stew and samp.

From his stockbroking days Patrick knew the directors of Hoover UK and we had a personal invitation to visit their subsidiary in East London. I was intrigued to see Patrick in his role as research analyst: the friendly preliminaries, the ever-more focussed questions, the polite but firm requests for written evidence: Why had they moved from Johannesburg? What were the market prospects? Whom did they employ, and at what wages? How would they describe their labour relations?

We had the guided tour and lunch in the directors' dining room with the (largely British) managers, at which the conversation was allowed to roam over sport and culture and – lightly – political change.

Patrick then wrote up a 1,200 word report as though he was recommending the company for clients, but with a political slant. Because, of course, the biggest question of all was: would overseas investment in South Africa help or hinder black development and political change?

An Executive Summary might have read something like this:

1. East London is a white 'border' town, between Ciskei and Transkei, scheduled for industrial development, so Hoover have moved there to take advantage of both tax breaks and a more stable workforce; the Blacks live in Mdantsane, a big new township away inside the so-called 'homeland', while the Whites enjoy the warm climate and unspoilt (no Blacks) coast.

2. The company assembles washing machines, vacuum cleaners, etc, and is beginning to manufacture some of the parts, for a mainly white market, since only a few Africans can afford such things.

3. They pay above average wages (see detailed comparisons with the so-called Poverty Datum Level), and provide fringe benefits in the form of pension rights, subsidised food and transport to the township and educational loans or grants. They insist that they are developing the skills of their black workers and allowing them to rise to more responsible positions; the highest so far is the senior payroll clerk, but they mentioned bringing in black engineering apprentices at some future unspecified date. A consumer spending survey revealed relative prosperity among the workforce, with 10% owning a car.

4. On the surface, inter-racial relations seem friendly enough, though Blacks must of course eat separately, and only the one Indian uses the white canteen. Unions are outlawed, but there is a Works Committee which is regularly consulted and – they claim – listened to.

Certainly the management were much more liberal than the Strongs, but Steve Biko would probably label them as paternalistic, luring the workers on to their side with promises of more material goods as long as they accepted their subservient place in the capitalist system.

So what was the answer to the big question? Investment can bring change, but very slowly, and there was no guarantee that political development would go along with industrial growth. It was partly this that persuaded Patrick when we got back to the UK to support the disinvestment campaign and to work for a group called 'End Loans to Southern Africa', which put pressure on banks like Barclays not to support firms like Hoover building factories, whether in the 'homelands' or anywhere else.

Just to complete the picture we drove out to see where their workers lived and found a pattern that was becoming only too depressingly familiar. Duncan Village, the old African location in a suburb of East London, was being cleared and all the families were being moved to Mdantsane, a new township a dozen miles away over that invisible bureaucratic border into the Ciskei. Like Soweto, rows of drab little boxes stretched in dense, neat lines across the hillsides. At least 100,000 people had been moved there out of the white areas, while Duncan Village had been re-zoned for Coloureds and Indians, with slightly larger houses replacing the old slums. Thus the housing policy was creating a caste-like society.

Next morning our coffee arrived at 6 am complete with rusks – thick crumbly fingers of dried bread to dip into your cup. That's breakfast unless you're extravagant, which we were not, so by 8 am we were on the N2, a ribbon of dual carriageway leading up to Durban. As we swept down onto the bridge over the Great Kei River we were suddenly confronted with a posse of black police in unusual uniforms. We realised this must be the new 'border post', but we were not stopped – like much about the 'homelands', the border was a fantasy.

So we were now in the Transkei, the biggest of the so-called Bantustans, set aside primarily for the Xhosa people and scheduled to be independent in a year's time. Could it become like Lesotho, politically if not economically independent?

The borderland was a rough country of steep hillsides scattered with thorn bushes; the usual drab houses stretched along the tops of the ridges where there was a ribbon of dry grass. But as we moved into an area of grassy rolling hills the land had a more prosperous look. Each group of whitewashed rondavels had a fenced patch of garden and maize was growing in contour-ploughed fields. This area had been 'bettered' some time back and perhaps with the consent of the people; the houses were all gathered together and the arable was carefully separated from the pasture lands; with comparatively little sign of erosion it was the best bit of 'homeland' which we had seen.

Later I learnt that Nelson Mandela's clan lived in this Xhosa heartland, where traditional leaders had maintained their authority while moving by stages into the modern world. Of course at that time in South Africa Mandela was a non-person as far as Whites were concerned, though to Blacks he was still a potent symbol. We never heard his name mentioned in public; imprisoned on Robben Island, he might as well have been dead, which was exactly what the government wanted.

The skies were dull and a cold wind blew as we arrived in Umtata, a nondescript little town as yet unsure of its new status as capital. At the post office, where Blacks and Whites still stood in separate queues, Patrick deliberately chose an African to ask where we could find the offices of the *Daily Despatch* newspaper[50]. He was giving us a perfectly clear answer when an officious white man bustled up and told us all over again. Obviously this was still South Africa.

At the *Daily Despatch* Arthur Rose welcomed us into his office and went through our list of contacts, saying which needed to be approached with caution. He recommended a hotel and we invited him to lunch there. 'May I bring a colleague, Patrick Lawrence?'

Patrick Lawrence was a thin and gentle giant of a man, with a receding hairline and bushy beard, his sharp, combative eyes belied by his friendly manner. He worked for the *Rand Daily Mail*, one of the very few 'liberal' newspapers, and he was to become one of its most famous and doughty writers, tireless in reporting the indignities and stupidities of apartheid. Far away on Robben Island Mandela was cheered by his articles and long afterwards was able to tell him so. We told him of our trip so far and how

---

[50] The *Daily Despatch* was at that time edited by Donald Woods, an outspoken critic of apartheid and a friend of Steve Biko. He led the outcry over Biko's death, for which he was himself banned. He escaped into exile and published an excellent memoir, *Biko* (Paddington Press 1978).

shocked we had been by the wretchedness in the 'homelands'.

'Yes,' he said thoughtfully, 'the Whites are isolated in their laager of privilege. They don't see the malnutrition and poverty or the crime and social dislocation; it's so far away from them. They have become desensitised. This laager mentality means they reject the Christian values of love and compassion; instead they preach toughness, obedience and conformity.'

We asked him whether he was allowed to write in this vein and he smiled. 'The editors of the English language press see themselves as having a duty to "light the way for the new South Africa", but when push comes to shove, they err on the side of caution. Recently I quoted Chief Gacha Buthelezi, Prime Minister-designate of KwaZulu, saying that the non-violent approach has failed and it is time to consider other tactics. My lawyers told me to drop it, saying it could be interpreted as being an incitement to racial strife. That would bring down penalties on Buthelezi as well as on the paper.'

'And on you, I suppose?'

'Me? Oh well, I've already been convicted! Three years ago I got an interview with Robert Sobukhwe and sent it to your *Observer* newspaper in London. They gave me a suspended prison sentence under the Suppression of Communism Act and I'm still going through the appeals process. Actually that's why I'm here. His brother Bishop Sobhukwe is in Umtata and I'm due to interview him on Friday.'

We invited this congenial second Patrick – both over six foot, they could look each other in the eye – to supper the following night and went off to find St. Bede's Anglican Seminary, where we had an appointment with its director, Reverend Bax. We stopped to ask some schoolgirls for directions and as it lay near their school we gave them a lift. They told us enthusiastically that they were studying commercial subjects at a private school and would we like to visit it?

'I'm a teacher and I'd love to. We'll come later this afternoon,' I promised.

When we reached the seminary we gasped: all the driveways and courtyards were full of caravans and there were even tents in the gardens, under pouring rain. A tall, gracious man, wearing clerical robes and with a rather distracted air, came out. Doubtless Rev Bax had more important things to do than talk to itinerant Brits but he made us feel welcome.

'Do you drink *roibos* tea? It's made from a local shrub and is good for colic and hay fever.' We accepted eagerly although Patrick had been fever-free since leaving England.

'Sorry, I forgot the scones my wife prepared for you. You saw the people outside? The Federal Seminary has just settled on our doorstep; they were next door to the University of Fort Hare and the government requisitioned their buildings, ostensibly for university expansion. Actually, the seminarians are very radical and most belong to SASO – you know, the South African Students Organisation which is influenced by the Black Consciousness movement. The authorities fear they will infect the university students!'

'Much of the SASO leadership has been arrested,' he went on, 'and thirteen are on trial. Today we heard that the trial was put off again because the prosecution again failed "to supply particulars of the charges to enable the accused to know the case against them". One of those released without trial told me he had lost the hearing in one ear after being interrogated while standing with a noose around his neck and being slapped in the face when the answers were wrong. These youngsters are very brave.'

'We know about SASO; a few days ago we met Steve Biko…' I began.

'Shssh!' Rev Bax held up his hand. 'My telephone has recently been mended. They told me there was an external fault but I think it is now bugged. Let's not mention names. I know of the young man you met. He has a remarkable way with people. Let's go outside.'

Once out on the terrace he told us the following story. 'There was a student who was being pressurised and offered money by BOSS[51] to become their agent at the Federal Seminary. He was desperately worried about what might happen to his family if he refused, so he kept prevaricating. Then he went to a meeting at Steve's house. When the police came in and accused him of breaking his banning order, Steve defied them to prove that he had not been studying in his room on his own. Then when the two policemen entered his room to question him he openly taunted them, saying: "Only

---

[51] Bureau of State Security, an extremely powerful and greatly feared intelligence service, charged with defending the apartheid state against both internal and external threats. It became involved in spying, detentions without trial, and even murder.

one at a time please or you will be contravening my banning order!"

'When the police wanted to arrest one of the young men for being without his pass, Steve shouted, "You don't have to go with them, you are allowed to produce your pass within seven days," quoting the relevant part of the act. The police released the man. Encouraged by this example, the student, when next he was approached by black agents of BOSS, refused to work for them and the threats stopped. Biko can give people the confidence to stand up for themselves.'

Unlike many South Africans, Bax seemed to have a real concern for other parts of the continent and wanted to know about our experiences in Nigeria and Tanzania. Returning to the future of South Africa he mused: 'I won't pretend I can foretell the future. I've been pleasantly surprised by the easing of some of the restrictions and I'm not too pessimistic. There could be a realignment of white politicians. But the main problem remains that there is so little contact between black and white people. Even in my congregation, Africans are there on sufferance, and some white families left. This is unchristian and a tragedy!'

Leaving Bax to deal with the seminarians squatting on his doorstep, we went back to the girls' school. The headmaster, Mr Ghu, was a tall, elderly African gentleman, who had the same accent and turn of phrase as Mr Hononu. With great courtesy he explained his project, saying he wanted us to see what the black man was doing for his own people. 'First I registered a charity for the rehabilitation of paraplegics and was granted this block of land. But it was difficult to raise money for the facilities we needed and so I invited this commercial school to use the land instead. There is a desperate shortage of trained office staff in the Transkei but the school doesn't get any money from the government.'

There was one brick-built classroom block with four rooms, plus a long mud and wattle building which was a dormitory for about thirty girls; it was neat, stark and cold.

'We cook for ourselves on primus stoves,' they said. 'Yes, there in that little room. We have no toilets. We fetch water from the borehole down at the end of that street but it doesn't taste very good.'

Peeping into a classroom, we could see the questions set out on the blackboard and Patrick laughed. 'That's a bank reconciliation exercise, but it's based on an ill-kept cash-book! Still, the questions are challenging; the school's probably doing a good job.'

We reflected sadly on the stupidities of a system which held back and excluded such people as Mr Ghu and these intelligent young women. It seemed so obvious that Transkei needed a crash programme of education if it were ever to succeed. Back at our hotel, we noticed that all the guests were still white and planned how we might challenge this.

Next morning the hotel disappointed us in another way; there was no hot water. 'Why can't you join the modern world and use an electric razor?' I grunted as I heated Patrick's shaving water on our little stove. Thus smartened up, we visited the Diocesan Offices to lunch with a black lady named Sybil Plaatje whom we'd briefly met in King William's Town. She introduced us to Peter Mtetwa, the local officer for the 'Dependants' Conference,' an organisation that looked after the families of political prisoners and detainees.

'They are often living in extreme poverty,' he explained. 'The wage-earner is in prison and they may have lost their house. We get money from overseas through the Churches. We do what we can and pray for their release.'

Peter was a devout Christian and a compassionate man but all he could do was to stick plasters on open sores. As we sat talking a much younger man came over with very different ideas in mind; he turned out to be a student from that radical Federal Seminary encamped around the Rev Bax.

'What are you doing here?' he asked suspiciously. 'What can you achieve? You've got racial problems too. Isn't British society just as sick as white South African society?'

I told him I taught in multiracial schools in London and that we had laws against discrimination, even if not always effective. Then Patrick asked him what he thought the British could do for South Africa. 'You must support Peter Hain,'[52] he replied, 'and keep up the sports boycott. Then you must boycott all trade with South Africa and stop all investment.'

---

[52] Peter Hain was the son of South African liberals who came to the UK in 1966 to escape persecution. He was at this time prominent in anti-apartheid activities, arguing against sporting contacts with South Africa.

'But investment brings jobs,' argued Patrick. 'Wouldn't it be more useful if Britain invested in the "homelands"?'

'Not at all,' came the angry answer. 'These "homelands" will not help the black cause in South Africa because they are designed to keep us in an inferior state.'

It was his belief that in the end guerrilla warfare would be the only answer. 'Meanwhile we are working to teach the people self-reliance and to raise their consciousness. They must not accept handouts from the government. I tell them not to vote for these black stooges.'

'But then you are condemning the people to yet more poverty and perhaps a long armed struggle.' Patrick was determined to force the issue but the answer came clear and defiant: 'For the sake of an ultimately fair and just society they can bear ten years of hardship.'

We were impressed. Once he got over his suspicions he responded constructively to our challenges, developing his argument logically. Clearly these positions were well thought out; whatever Steve Biko had said to us about peaceful change, Black Consciousness was leading others towards violence.

At that point Bishop Sobukwe himself appeared; the student nodded an apology and left. The bishop seemed pleased to be talking to visitors, albeit in a very different vein, so we asked him to have supper with us and the journalists. He accepted and we went back to the hotel to try to organise it. There would be Patrick Lawrence, Arthur Rose, his (black) assistant Sidney Moses, and now Bishop Sobukwe. Our conversation with the management went something like this:

Hotel Manager: 'No, I cannot serve you. It is against the law to entertain black men in this hotel.'

Us: 'The Transkei is becoming independent. It now has a black government. Surely its people can eat here. Particularly the bishop.'

HM: 'Anyway I would get into serious trouble if I served them with drinks without a police permit.'

Us: 'Fine. We'll have soft drinks.'

HM: 'Both my kitchen stoves are not working.'

Us: 'OK. We'll have cold meat and salad.'

HM: 'Well, I suppose you could have the upstairs private room.'

And that's what happened. We went out and bought a large bottle of wine in case, but in the event the waiters brought us all the (hot) dishes and drinks we wanted without any fuss.

Patrick Lawrence dominated the conversation, telling us about his recent interview with Matanzima, the nominated leader of this new statelet. 'He's a very wily, very capable politician, and at heart an African Nationalist.'

'He has little popular support and he is very corrupt,' put in Sidney quietly.

Lawrence went on regardless: 'He insisted that the future Transkei would be a non-racial state and thus a model for the rest of South Africa. Both Blacks and Whites should be able to buy any property they like – providing they are Transkei citizens. They can't have dual citizenship, they must opt for one or the other. Or sell up and get out.'

'It doesn't sound encouraging to me,' said Arthur gloomily. 'I wouldn't mind taking out Transkeian citizenship but not if it stops me working in South Africa; I couldn't make much of a career here. What about you, Sidney?'

Sidney smiled politely. We couldn't tell what he was thinking and he didn't want to enlighten us.

The bishop seemed rather different from his firebrand brother Robert and was worried about the radical clergy in Johannesburg who kept getting deported.

'The current bishop is even more radical,' he lamented, 'I'm not sure where it's all heading.'

'Bavin's a bachelor, so he won't have to worry about his family,' said Patrick L. grimly. 'And he'll have Desmond Tutu breathing fire down his back, who does have a family and is sending his children to school in Swaziland to keep them out of Bantu education. Changes are coming in your church, Bishop.'

The wine went round again and Patrick L. was now well away, telling South African stories. Many featured Van der Merwe, the archetypical stupid Boer. For example: 'Van der Merwe has fallen into a well but the rope with which they are trying to pull him out is too short to reach down the well and go round his enormous girth. So they shout down "Van der

Merwe, you've got good strong teeth, hold the rope in your jaws and we'll pull you up that way." All goes well until Van der Merwe is near the top when some helpful soul says "Van der Merwe, is it going alright?" The reply of "Yes" is heard diminishing down the well. That's one of Vorster's favourites because the moral is to keep your mouth shut.'

But our favourite was about Hendrik Verwoerd at dinner in England. When he is asked how he would like his coffee he smiles: 'Strong and sweet, please, like our South African girls.' Waiter, straightfaced: 'Black or White, sir?'

We fell exhausted into bed. In two days in this disputed 'homeland capital' we had gathered a whole spectrum of views from conservative to radical, from traditionalist to change-makers.

It was Friday and we headed for home. Petrol restrictions meant you could not fill up between Saturday lunch and Monday morning so we had to plan our route with care. At Connie's suggestion we visited St. Lucy's mission hospital on the way home, which was in a very similar situation to that of the Charles Johnson hospital in Nqutu and we heard similar heart-rending statistics. Although on the surface Transkei had looked more prosperous, it still could not support the population living there and migrant labour claimed most of the active men. Malnutrition and TB were rife among the families left behind.

The hospital had many out-clinics like those Greg ran around Nqutu, but St Lucy's also put much emphasis on teaching about nutrition. They had a special kwashiokor unit and while the children were being nursed back to health, the mothers were taught how to feed their children and how to make vegetable gardens. At the hospital demonstration plot the gardener explained: 'You dig a long, deep, wide trench. Then you put in long grass, then earth, then grass again and more earth till it is full. Too little rain, so this way the bed keeps damp.'

It was clearly a good idea but with the men away in the mines how many women would be able to carry out this task on their own, even though the hospital offered subsidised seeds and fencing?

We sat in the pale sunshine eating our sandwiches and consulted the map. We had come northwards and there were roads marked to the Lesotho border at Tele Bridge, but from now on it would be mostly gravel.

Should we go on or return to the tar the way we had come with Connie?

'That way more adventure,' quoted Patrick and we headed into the heart of the Drakensberg. It was difficult going, with the rough road climbing over steep passes and the low sun shining straight into our eyes. Finding a good stretch of tar, we decided to go on to Elliot but the road deteriorated and the sun set behind the hills. In the rapidly gathering gloom we welcomed the sign *oompad* (detour), often a sign of improvement. But this one was a very long and rough *oompad* and we almost lost the road in a maze of ruts, potholes and white painted drums. Once past these we found the new tar, but without white lines it felt like driving on a sea of blackness spreading out beyond the feeble rays of the VW's lights.

When we finally made Elliot we staggered into the Stamford Hotel which was very comfortable, but *cold* – any sort of space-heating seeming un-South African. However, we had an excellent dinner with huge steaks nearly the size of our respective shoes.

'In some ways this is a right-thinking country,' mused Patrick, comparing his steak with mine. 'Men naturally get given the best and largest of everything.'

'Well, at least that is one point on which both African and Boer can agree!' I retorted. By this time I had a bad headache from a combination of too much talking to too many people in too short a time and travelling over rough roads, so we went early to bed. At least the hotel supplied hot water bottles and I didn't have to warm Patrick's feet.

Next morning we filled up with oil and petrol and set off towards the Barkly Pass, climbing to over 6,000 feet with dramatic views back over the farmlands below and of the cliff-topped mountain ridges above. Great grey outcrops of rock cut square like castle walls, or pointed like giant teeth, were silhouetted against the sky, while the slopes fell in brown and mauve shadows into the far distance. Over the pass we dropped into wintry valleys with frost lying in the shade and unidentifiable eagles perched on the leafless trees.

We began to worry about petrol. We took a wrong turn and had to retreat; we enquired for petrol from some tennis players – this was still a white, if poor, farming area – but the nearest pump was twenty miles in the opposite direction.

Lundean's Nek, at 7,400 feet, was the last pass, with a magnificent view of the southern Drakensberg where they merged into Lesotho and became the Maluti. Those steep-sided cliff-bestrewn mountains rose to over 10,000 feet and as we descended new peaks and crags were revealed at every turn as different valleys opened to our view. We dropped nearly 2,000 feet in about 16km to the Tele River on the Lesotho border. There was little land beside the river and the tiny patches of cultivation backed by the massive mountains reminded us strongly of the Atlas Mountains in Morocco.

The needle on our fuel tank swung lower and lower and the time was getting on for 1 pm. Suddenly we came upon a country store and outside it was an ancient petrol pump, one of those where the petrol is pumped up into a gallon jar and then released into the car's tank. The store-owner came out.

'Can you sell us some petrol?' we asked.

'Ja,' came the answer in guttural Afrikaner English. 'But only by the gallon,' he added.

Four gallons made our little tank overflow but at least it got us over the border at Tele Bridge and back to Maseru. The roads were still bad since Lesotho had run out of money for their upkeep halfway through the previous financial year. As we reached the tar the sun, spilling through the rainstorms, bathed the mountain ridges in purple, pink and gold – a dramatic ending to our journey.

When we arrived at Qoqolosing Road Anna was out at a meeting and she returned only briefly, on her way to another and then on to a party. We admired her stamina, made ourselves large brandies, cooked a quick supper of soup and scrambled eggs and sat down to a wonderful bunch of mail from friends and family. Perhaps most usefully there was a negative response to my enquiry about teaching jobs so I didn't need to be back in the UK before the end of the summer term.

CHAPTER 31
Third Interlude in Lesotho: June

In which we hear expatriate views on Lesotho and tour the
mountains to see for ourselves.

'You do the washing, I'll rinse in cold water,' said Patrick manfully as
we faced a mammoth pile of travel-stained clothes. These returns to
base in Lesotho were times for rest, relaxation and reflection but also for
practical and household tasks – to wash and repair clothes, service the car,
answer our mail, check the money supply, write up the diary and think
what to do next. Anna was always busy, so for much of the time we had
their spacious comfortable house to ourselves.

Now, in early June, planning was paramount as the odyssey was drawing
to a close; we made a final commitment by booking a flight home for July
25th. This would give us time for a couple of weeks in Cape Town, a last
visit to Lesotho and a final fortnight in Jo'burg. There were more than
thirty letters to write – from 'Please may we come and stay' to 'Thank you
so much for your hospitality.'

Inspired by our visits to South African missions, we decided to use
an introduction given us by a church group in Romsey, Hampshire, and
visit St. James' Hospital at Mantšonyane, 125km away in the Lesotho
Highlands, to see if things were any better than in the 'homelands'.

On the way we stopped at Thaba Khupa, an agricultural school run
by John and June Durrant whom we'd met through the Selwyns. In the
arid, broken foothills it lay like an oasis, with fields of cabbages, dams for
irrigation and fish, and rondavels for the students.

'We take twenty-five students a year,' explained John. 'In the first year
they combine theory with practical work on the farm here, growing all

sorts of vegetables and soft fruit, even asparagus, and helping with the livestock. In Year 2 they have to create and manage their own projects, like raising chickens. They keep 75% of their profits as start-up capital when they leave.'

'Girls as well as boys,' added June proudly.

Patrick elicited that the funds came from Oxfam, Christian Aid and other church groups. 'Keeping track of the money takes up a lot of time,' John admitted. 'There aren't many good bookkeepers in Lesotho.' Patrick commiserated, unaware of what lay in our future.

'Where do your students go afterwards?' I enquired. It seemed an excellent scheme, but commercial farming in Lesotho must be tough and I'd heard that most youngsters wanted to go into safe white-collar jobs.

'Our first lot have just graduated and most have gone to work on mission settlements, growing food in partnership with the hospitals. I'm off to visit some of them in the mountains next week. Would you like to come along?' We hesitated, we were leaving soon for Cape Town and anyway we were bound for the mountains right now.

'Thanks, we'll think about it,' we said and set off up the mountain road, our little car loaded down with provisions. 'Sharp curves and steep gradients' warned the notice just beyond Roma. In spite of the bright sunshine icicles from the overhanging rocks dripped across the road, freezing as they went. The Beetle began to splutter and stall. At the top of Bushman's Pass, at 7,400 feet, we stopped for photographs of the endless ridges of mountains and valley spread out in the haze before us and consulted the guidebook. 'This is the lowest of the four passes between us and Mantšonyane,' I read out loud.

'We need the car to get to Cape Town; we can't risk it breaking down here,' Patrick admitted. We bought a Basotho hat from the smallest herdboy we'd ever seen and turned back. On our return to Thaba Khupa the Durrants' two-year-old twins were having a birthday party with a couple of solemn little African boys and some farm students. 'What's the matter?' enquired June, handing us some gaudy, sticky cake.

'Our car isn't up to it. Can we join John's trip next week? But please come and have supper with us first.'

As Anna was away for the weekend singing in Germiston, South Africa, with her church choir, we were free to entertain. On the Friday evening we invited Dr Pascal Ngakane, son of the old man we met in Jo'burg, with his wife; both were doctors working at Queen Elizabeth II hospital in Maseru. Pascal was a younger version of his father but taller and stronger and with an even more serious air about him. We told him how his father had impressed us.

'Yes, and he brought us up to be politically active too! We trained at the black medical school in Durban – yes, Biko went there too – and afterwards I used to help people escape over the border. The police caught me and I was jailed for two years.'

'It was a hard time,' recalled his wife, 'but Amnesty International took him up as a prisoner of conscience.'

Pascal frowned. 'We appreciated their support,' he said thoughtfully, 'but Amnesty doesn't attack the systems that cause the problems. After I came out we were still harassed, so we left for England, children and all. We worked there for five years in Croydon hospitals.'

Remembering a fruitless encounter with local medical staff when I had backache, I asked him how he found working here.

'It's a challenge! Badly equipped, badly organised! But at least we're nearer to home and I hope my father can get a passport to come and visit his grandchildren.'

'Has South Africa changed since you left?'

'Not really, but perhaps Afrikaner attitudes are shifting. When I meet them here, they start justifying the system and asking for patience. But I don't think there is time for political evolution. Some of the "homeland" leaders may push for gradual change but the people won't wait. I'd give it five years before there's a violent outbreak.' Was this an illusion of the frustrated exile?

His wife put in: 'The Afrikaners are so naïve sometimes! I overheard them in the Holiday Inn, saying in Afrikaans, "Why is it we don't mind eating in mixed company here in Lesotho?" The answer came back: "Ag man, these are gentle and civilised Blacks here, not like ours!"'

Pascal smiled at last. 'Enough of our politics! Tell us what is happening in Britain! You know, we got involved there and we even voted in local elections!' So we recounted our differing views on Harold Wilson and the evening passed pleasantly away.

On Saturday it was the turn of the Durrants and the Selwyns. Ambitiously, I'd cut a recipe out of the *Rand Daily Mail* for the famous South African *bobotie* – a dish of spiced mince with chutney and eggs. I started cooking at 3 pm, put too much curry in and kept sending Patrick down to the shops for things I'd forgotten. Too late I found the avocados were all unripe. However, hunger was satisfied, we washed it down with good red wine and found much in common.

The Durrants had worked in Nigeria and Uganda, having to leave hurriedly when threatened by President Amin, while the Selwyns had taught in Zambia. We swapped travellers' tales and moved on to the brandy, glad to have found kindred spirits.

John was basically pessimistic about Lesotho's agriculture. 'Less than 12% of the country can be ploughed; the soil is poor and easily washed away. Land is allocated by the chiefs to families for their use but with rising population the fields gets smaller; they can't grow enough to feed themselves, so able-bodied men go off to the mines and production falls still further – it's a vicious circle!'

'Traditionally Basotho counted their wealth in cattle', June put in. 'The more cattle a man has, the richer he feels, even if they are small and skinny. Yet modern stock rearing is impossible; one scheme tried fencing off grazing areas in the mountains, but they all got pulled down – it was seen as selfish and against the culture. That's why only the sheep and goats flourish – there's some money in wool and mohair but no one gets rich by farming in Lesotho.'

We talked of Tanzania and poverty. 'The African traditions lay much more stress on the community,' I offered. 'They can build on that.'

Jasper disagreed. 'I think the community spirit is a result of poverty, not its solution. People who have the opportunity to get education and earn a good salary find they are expected to share it with the extended family. People who go abroad to study are reluctant to come back, partly because of this, and partly because the government sees them as a threat and is unlikely to implement their ideas or even give them rewarding work.'

'There's a development issue here,' put in Patrick. 'Capital has to be created. The claims of the extended family restrict the creation of wealth which is needed for investment.'

Bridget pointed out that there was another dimension in Lesotho: although there was no tribalism, since the people were all Basotho, the Protestants and Catholics supported different political parties, so it was difficult to achieve national unity.

We talked on into the night, rehearsing all the problems of Africa and the world. 'You know,' said Bridget as they left, 'When we get home no one will really be interested in what we've been doing. We'll have to meet up and talk together.' And that's what we did.

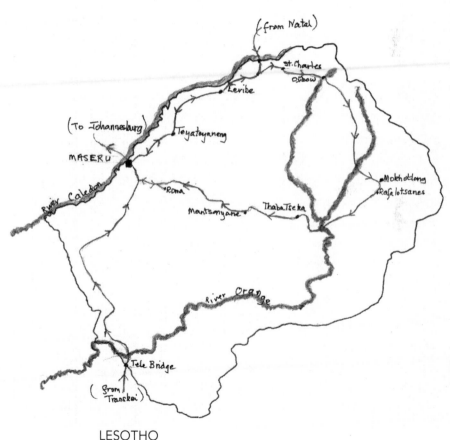

LESOTHO
Places visited by car, with two major rivers.

Meanwhile on Monday morning John picked us up in a big four-wheel drive Chevrolet. 'This is the plan,' he explained, the map spread out before us. 'We're going to visit all the clinics supported by Catholic Relief Services. They want us to set up demonstration gardens at each clinic, run by agricultural extension officers – like my students will be. They will teach the women how to improve the family diet by growing vegetables, raising chickens and rabbits and so on. I need to see how feasible this will be in the various sites. Dave here is a volunteer from Canada. And this is Paul Jackson from the States.'

Paul was a tall African-American with a bushy Afro haircut and gold-rimmed spectacles, dressed in college-type slacks and shirt. 'Hi,' he said, in a Yankee accent. 'I've taken a year out of Yale to work on this project for CRS. It sure is interesting stuff.'

We spent four hectic and exhilarating, if at times cold and uncomfortable, days in this company, visiting a dozen Church-run clinics, some attached to large mission stations staffed by expatriates and others to small parishes, one being run from a garage by a cheerful Mosotho nurse.

On the first afternoon, as we stopped off near Leribe on our way north, an elderly man approached our group and greeted us in English. Then he turned to Paul and said inquiringly: '*Ntate?*' ('Father': the local form of address to men.) He touched his cheek, looking at Paul, and then laid his brown hand alongside Paul's, matching it. Paul smiled: 'I'm American!'

'Then you are a Negro?'

'No, I'm an Afro-American. Are you a Bantu?'

'No, no!' the man was shocked.

'Then I'm not a Negro. Where is Bantuland?'

The man grinned. 'Nowhere.'

'Then where is Negroland?' asked Paul.

'Nowhere!' came the answer and we all laughed.

Paul seemed oblivious of colour and although shocked by the poverty and violence in South Africa – he had stayed illegally in Soweto – he was no radical, just a nice American middle-class, upwardly mobile guy. Wherever his ancestors might have come from, he belonged now irretrievably to another continent, another culture, and it showed.

That night we stayed at St Charles Mission, a large Catholic settlement in the rocky northern corner of Lesotho. The French-Canadian priest, who had been there for twenty years, had built an imposing complex of hospital and schools – partly with his own hands – out of the local sandstone. He showed us round with pride, telling us: 'The way I raise money is with the Montreal telephone directory!' To prove it he had an well-furnished office and a Mercedes parked outside. 'But we do not have doctors,' he lamented, 'our nurses take care of all,' which was perhaps why we got a private hospital room to ourselves. His latest gadget was solar-powered heating and though my bath water was tepid, we were snug enough.

Next morning the road wound up through a great rocky amphitheatre where flecks of snow lay among the peaks and stopped for coffee at Oxbow Ski-Lodge. 'Yes,' the owner said enthusiastically, 'if it snows enough in June we'll have South Africans skiing up here for three months.'

Further on were diamond diggings, another potential source of revenue, if not yet very productive, and the going got rougher and slower. We picnicked on the topmost plateau beside something that looked like a stone igloo. 'That's a herdboys' hut,' explained John. 'They live up here in the summer with the sheep and goats. That's why they don't go to school with their sisters.'

We buckled on our seat belts as the Chev lurched down the next steep descent, bouncing from rock to rock, doing perhaps five miles per hour. At one point a stream crossing the road had frozen solid and we had to spread out gravel before the tyres could grip the ice. Our Mosotho driver Francis was unconcerned. 'I've done the Roof of Africa rally over these roads many times,' he explained cheerfully. 'I know them all.'

Then we met a worse obstacle. A large lorry had gone to fetch the wreck of one of those rally cars and had broken down on a narrow piece of rough road, with a steep drop on one side and the hillside on the other. There was not quite room for us to pass. Attempts to hack away the hillside were abandoned when the driver reappeared and rolled his vehicle perilously near the drop and we squeezed through.

It was getting dark. It took us an hour to prise some petrol out of the suspicious guardians of the government pump at Mokhotlong, and then it came in jugs transferred by hand. Finally we reached St. James' Mission at Rafolatsane's to a warm welcome from yet another group of French-Canadian sisters, who had been radioed from St. Charles to expect an important party. After a large dinner we were shown to a modern block of bedrooms with paraffin heaters, candles and Victorian washbasins. 'The electricity, she is not here. We bring you water,' apologised the nun in broken English.

But good agricultural practice there certainly was. Next morning John was exuberant as Francis interpreted, using Sesotho, between his English and the Sister's French. 'She is one step ahead of me! She has a small demonstration plot and for two years she's been running agricultural shows! Last year over two hundred mothers entered vegetables they'd grown at home! Isn't that fantastic!' It was good to know that John's vision was entirely realisable.

Having nearly reached the eastern border with Natal, close by the highest point in Southern Africa, we were now heading back westwards through yet wilder and lovelier country. At 10,000 feet we ground our way over the first pass and dropped into a high valley where wheat, not maize, was grown on terraced fields. Women were threshing and winnowing by hand and men were ploughing with oxen yoked to iron ploughs. Then cloud cover spread over most of the sky and the mountains sank into a sombre purple-brown, relieved only by the pale yellow strips of stubble.

Towards midday we could see one of the tributaries of the Orange River snaking along 3-4,000 feet below us, the sun came out and we stopped for lunch with a grandstand view of deep curving gorges. As we shared our meagre tins of sardines and cheese, the wily Francis produced some bread and meat he'd had in reserve all the time, saying that once he got stuck up here for three days. The last of the wine washed it down and the last apples too.

The next stretch of road was one of the most magnificent, along a vast promontory with the gorges on each side, clear in brilliant light with shadow patches adding touches of blue to the brown hills, until we finally descended to cross the river. Over the Orange the landscape changed and we drove for an hour or so through an open rolling plateau fringed with high peaks; the nearby land was patterned again with terraced wheat fields. This was why so many people could live in the mountains; with good grain and plenty of milk and meat from the herds, people were better nourished than in the crowded, maize-growing lowlands.

Thaba Tseka, at the centre of this beautiful highland valley, was an unpleasant surprise. The Swiss doctor in charge of the hospital was not interested, and for once even the missionaries were unwelcoming so, after a cold supper and even colder beds, next morning we pressed on to St. James' at Mantšonyane, which we had been trying to reach when our car refused the pass and which was supported by Romsey Abbey. After the big Catholic hospitals this Anglican one seemed small, but all its thirty-five beds were full and there was a real doctor in charge. John was delighted too. 'Gabriel, one of our graduates, has got his poultry unit up and running. The hospital is teaching nutrition already.'

Close to the hospital was a chapel and a few staff houses, while a small herdboy watched a flock of sheep. Sturdy Basotho ponies were tied up at the hitching rail, for over the mountains most people travel by horse and there were particularly splendid strings of passing riders. I spent a happy half hour taking pictures to show the Romsey supporters of oxen ploughing, women threshing, horsemen riding and some nice teenagers who told me how they couldn't afford to go to secondary school. 'My parents are farmers; we grow mealies, wheat, vegetables, and we all help on the farm.'

The drive back was still more dramatic. Between Mantšonyane and Maseru the road descends into three deep valleys between blue-shadowed peaks and climbs over four high passes. But in places it was rough and steep; we were glad we had not gone further in the Beetle. On the last summit I stopped to photograph the horsemen riding into the sunset. Surely that must be the end of my film? But it rolled on ... and on ... till I discovered it had never caught at all and there were no pictures in my camera to send to Romsey. It was almost more than I could bear!

✳

And what of our comparison with the 'homelands'? We didn't see or hear anything about kwashiorkor. There was certainly poverty in Lesotho but, as in Tanzania, there was also hope and people were, to some extent, in charge of their own destinies and free to discuss alternatives. Whatever the arguments around development aid, funds and well-intentioned outsiders arrived to help and offer new ways forward. No, thanks to Moshoeshoe and Queen Victoria, Lesotho was better off than any Bantustan.

CHAPTER 32
Exploring Capetown

In which we drive through beautiful landscapes, meeting many different shades of colour and as many different opinions.

In a cold, red midwinter's dawn – June 20th to be precise – we set off for Cape Town, 1,150 kilometres away. While I photographed the brilliant cloudscape Patrick scraped thick ice off the windscreen. At the border post the 'Whites Only' window was free and while our forms were being checked – we wondered if we were on their 'suspect' list since our excursions in the 'homelands' – we saw Paul Jackson, the Afro-American, standing patiently in the long queue of Blacks at the other window. Was it solidarity or had he been refused honorary White status? What a strange country!

The arable land fell behind us as the countryside got flatter and drier and farming activity was confined to grazing – first cattle, then sheep – as the land got poorer and we neared the Great Karroo. The flatness was only broken by irregular pimples and weals of koppies and from each small ridge miles of empty road stretched to the next rise. As the shadows lengthened the kopjies took on a more romantic hue in the purple mist of evening and we were treated to a gorgeous sunset over the distant outlines of the Nuweveldberge. The sky turned amethyst over a yellow horizon, with rays in the mist dancing like Northern lights; then the yellow changed to orange while the purple sky deepened and darkened. Finally the orange became a luminous green which faded slowly away leaving an intense red line at the horizon. Above, the stars and moon glistened in the dark sky.

After a night in a motel at Beaufort West we left the hills behind and for a time travelled through the Little Karoo, semi-desert with only sage-brush growing, until the land rose again and became greener. We began climbing up mountains buttressed with ridges of harder folded rock, while cloud came crowding up to the top from the west and sliding over the ridge. Suddenly we were through the pass and there below us was a valley hidden between the grey slate mountain-sides, a patchwork of red and green squares dotted with little white houses. What at first looked like ploughed fields of red soil was transformed into rows of vines whose leaves had turned to crimson, and the green was winter wheat. This was the Hex River Valley and the first of the Cape vineyards – an unforgettable sight.

From Worcester the road ran straight across the valley to what looked like an impenetrable mountain wall but as we zig-zagged up and round a shoulder we saw a pass between crags towering two thousand feet above us, with long waterfalls tumbling down the precipices and dark forbidding clouds swirling around. Over the pass the road twisted and turned down the side of the ridge and suddenly, dropping below the cloud, we could see miles across a green and friendly land, farmed and densely populated. We couldn't have entered the Cape by a more dramatic route.

Arriving at Cape Town we were directed to the Seapoint area, where we found a room in a boarding house for old ladies. 'Just like my old flat in Belsize Park,' sighed Patrick. 'Look, a bow window, and the ceiling moulding has been cut where they subdivided the rooms!'

Unpacked, we went out to explore. We could hear the sound of surf and against a wild, west wind we staggered down to the Esplanade where the air smelt of salt and Atlantic tang. Huge waves were breaking in clouds of spray on the rocks, withdrawing and coming crashing in again and again. We watched, fascinated, as a thin watery evening light lit up the stormy sea like a Turner painting. Welcome to the Cape on Midwinter's Day!

We felt rather uncomfortable being scrutinised by the old biddies in the boarding house, so next day we found a more congenial flatlet at the Capri Residential and settled down to telephoning our contacts: White, Coloured, the university, Reckitt and Colman again and, most importantly as it turned out, the Church.

We began in the white English community where my mother had given me, through the Girl Guides' Association, the name of Mrs Greenshields.

We were warmly bidden to tea and while I helped her in the kitchen, Patrick started talking to her sister, visiting from England.

'How do you find the country? Is it what you expected?' he asked.

'Oh, the English papers have got it all wrong! There's no exploitation in South Africa! I've just been out shopping, and all the Coloured people are buying things just like us.'

Patrick described our visit to the 'homelands', telling her how Africans had been pushed into these areas where there was no work so the men had to become migrant workers, leaving their families behind. 'A lot of children are dying of malnutrition,' he added.

'Well,' she retorted, 'people starved in Britain during the Depression. And in the war, when all the men were off fighting, our women kept things going. Why can't the Zulus?'

Fortunately I came back with the sandwiches in time to avert an explosion and moved to the safer topic of Girl Guiding, which I'd been brought up to believe was a very moral institution. How did it fare under apartheid? I was assured that, although companies were still segregated, they had started integrated training for Guiders. 'And when the Chief Guide came to visit,' she assured us, 'the officials looked the other way and allowed us to have a multiracial event, so everything is fine. Some of my best friends are Coloured: you must meet the Fouchés.'

'They're well-meaning but so complacent!' I fulminated as we left. Patrick pointed out, logically, that the 'homelands' were far away, the press was restricted and most people were just getting on with their lives. Thankfully we found some with a wider vision.

Next day we sent our hard-working Beetle to the local garage for a check-up and took a race-divided bus into the centre of town; as Whites we had to sit downstairs and so missed the best views.

According to the Nationalist version South African history began here in 1652 when Jan Van Riebeck, on behalf of the Dutch East India Company, established a provisioning station for ships en route to Java and the Indies. There was good water; the mediterranean climate allowed them to grow familiar fresh fruit and vegetables and the local Khoikhoi would barter their sheep and cattle. Settlers were not encouraged, though after 1688 French Huguenots were given assisted passages, bringing with them the bonus of viticulture. Since the Khoikhoi refused to do agricultural work – although they made good herdsmen – and the Europeans found manual labour beneath their dignity, slaves were imported from East Africa and from Malaysia. Out of these fairly brutal conditions there arose in the Cape a 'mixed' population – from European, African, Asian and Khoikhoi – which later became known as the 'Cape Coloured.'

Cape Town has surely one of the most dramatic sites of any city in the world. The town itself lies facing north, penned in between the great cliff of Table Mountain and the edge of Table Bay, now rimmed with railway lines and docks. To the south-west, along the rocky shoreline, is a narrow belt of expensive flats, hotels and homes, running from Sea Point – where we were lodging – down to Hout Bay, beyond which is the preserved wilderness of the Cape Peninsula. Eastwards are the attractive suburbs of Claremont, Rondebosch, Newlands, towered over by the shady, mysterious, broken side of Table Mountain. Farther east stretches the dead flat sandy expanse between False and Table Bays to which the African and Coloured communities were moved – often forcibly – under the Group Areas Act. Some of the housing estates were quite pleasant, others depressingly monotone and poor, and beyond were the horrifyingly squalid squatter camps.

Although it is the legislative capital Cape Town has no space for wide boulevards or broad vistas. The Parliament buildings hide their classical red brick and white columns behind the trees in the Company's Gardens, a pleasant park with the old Dutch Tuynhuis at one end and a statue of Queen Victoria glowering at it across the grass. In the grid of narrow streets there are some older buildings with white pilasters and attractive wrought iron arcades where we browsed among the bookshops. The city had a very different feel from Johannesburg, more relaxed and more diverse. Faces on the street could no longer be clearly defined as black or white but came in many shades of brown, with many different features and hairstyles. Given the more liberal British traditions here, perhaps the apartheid race laws were less easy to enforce, the barriers more permeable.

We certainly found no problem in meeting the Coloured people, though we were to find as many shades of opinion among them as shades of skin. Before the Group Areas Act many had owned their own houses and lived peacefully among white neighbours in the suburbs. In particular, District Six had been a vibrant multiracial area full of jazz musicians, writers and political activists, living in cheap lodgings mixed with family homes. This affronted the Nationalist Government who rezoned it for Whites in 1966; it now had a desolate look with decaying houses and few new buildings.

Elaine Bhettay had trained as a doctor alongside Mary Wells (of Nqutu) at the University of Cape Town in the days when a very few, very bright non-Whites were allowed in. Her husband Ebi was tall with light skin and dark hair and could have passed as British, especially when he opened his mouth, for he had acquired an impeccable English accent at – of all places – Dublin medical school. But most of the time Elaine spoke for them both in a strident South African accent.

'We just avoided being in District Six – this area's been re-proclaimed Coloured,' she said, as she served coffee and cakes in a beautifully furnished, very modern living-room with a view over the business area and the docks.

'Does that mean you can stay here permanently?' I asked.

Elaine laughed. 'Only if we are careful. You see, Ebi is classified as Indian, his family has lived in Port Elizabeth for generations. We're married under Muslim law which isn't recognised by the state. If we had a civil wedding I would cease to be a Coloured and become an Indian, in which case I'd have to give up the house which is in my name and go to an Indian area. We made a mistake with our daughter; we registered her as Indian, we should have made her Coloured, as then she'd have a few more rights.'

'But I thought people weren't allowed to marry across different groups?'

She laughed again. 'You mean are we in breach of the Immorality Act? No, that only applies to sexual relations between Europeans and Non-Europeans, they don't care what the rest of us get up to as long as they can keep their own white purity untainted. Which they haven't, of course. There's heaps of white families with darker-skinned relations whom they've packed off to live in non-white areas!

'I was born in Alice,' she told us, 'in the Ciskei where my father was a schoolteacher. We were so lucky; we lived in a multiracial community with Whites and Africans. Right next door lived the family of Professor

Z.K. Matthews, the famous African academic, writer and political leader. There were great possibilities in those days which have faded away – no, they've been destroyed. These new so-called "homelands" – they won't allow Coloureds to live there at all now.'

We asked Ebi why he'd come back from Dublin where he could certainly have got a good job. 'I feel things are improving for us and we can make a good life for ourselves here. All that we need is the restoration of the franchise and then we can begin to redress the injustices. We'll get it in the end – though there may be violence first.'

Elaine broke in again. 'Yes, there are real injustices. Would you like to come with me round the Cape Flats area? Then you could come back to supper afterwards.' Delighted, we made an appointment for the following Friday.

Patrick was becoming increasingly concerned about whether British investment in South Africa was contributing to social change or propping up the status quo so, using his father's introduction, he arranged to visit Reckitt and Coleman in Cape Town. He came back full of doubts.

'The chairman of the South African Group is a complete nonentity! He doesn't know what goes on in his factories and he doesn't know how far they are developing a non-white market! There's no prospect of them investing in the "homelands" either – far too risky, he thinks. The managing director was more impressive but very dogmatic. His workforce is mainly Coloured now and even the office staff are mixed, but of course they are paid less than Whites. He says they are following university guidelines on minimum pay levels but their rates seem lower than Hoover's.'

'Does he allow unions?' I asked.

'Oh no! They have a works' committee but it doesn't initiate anything. His latest innovation is to have an integrated "works and staff" party next Christmas; his words were: "When they will dance with our wives and we will dance with theirs." Big deal! He also made a couple of really racist remarks like: "Africans and women are content to stand and do the repetitive work which men could not tolerate!" They're not interested in changing government policy,' Patrick concluded sadly. 'So I don't think inward investment is of much benefit.'

On our fourth day in Cape Town we met the man who was to transform our visit and give us a far deeper understanding of how some Christians at least interpreted their role of 'bearing witness' in the face of apartheid.

Theo Kotze was the Cape Province Director of the Christian Institute, which we had already heard mentioned so many times, and invited us to lunch at their offices. We met a man of medium height, bespectacled and balding, with deep-set thoughtful eyes and a warm smile – a gentle, kind, perhaps slightly puckish, figure. After a few moments' talk we realised he was a man of great courage and deep convictions, both spiritual and political, and also that he was hugely stressed.

'Two and a half years ago, he told us, 'the government set up the Schlebusch Commission to investigate the Christian Institute, as well as the National Union of South African Students and the Institute of Race Relations, to see if they were involved in political activities and were receiving finance from overseas. Of course we were and are. So last month they declared us to be an "affected organisation". That means we can't any longer receive funds from the churches abroad which have been sustaining us and we're into a major financial crisis. We also worry about our student friends in NUSAS, who may well be banned.'

'How about yourself?'

'I'm not banned yet! I refused to testify before the commission because the hearings were held in secret and proper legal procedures were not being followed. I was sent for trial months ago, found guilty of obstruction, and I'm still waiting to be sentenced. There's been a campaign of harassment against all of us; our offices have been fire-bombed and shots fired at our houses. It is not surprising; anyone who is committed to change in South Africa must expect government action to be taken against him. From a Christian point of view, that becomes a privilege.'

'Could you tell us something more about the work of the Christian Institute here in Cape Town?' I asked. 'Is it as political as the government claims?'

His eyes twinkled. 'The Nationalists make everything political! We are first and foremost Christians. We believe the commandment "love your neighbour as yourself" was meant seriously. But in this country it is not being taken seriously. Relationships between the races are not at all loving. We want to change this; we want to reach out to all communities and improve their lives.

'Can you guess why our office is here in Mowbray and not in the centre of Cape Town? It's between the bus terminus for the Coloured people coming in from the Cape Flats and the railway station, where the Africans arrive from the "homelands". Everyone can find us. We intended to create a place where all people can feel at home, a building that will be a centre of vibrant ecumenical life.' He looked into the distance in search of his vision. 'But it's not the building that matters. I call it a "church without walls", open to everyone, no matter what they believe.'

We'd only asked him for a brief interview and we were completely bowled over when he said at the end of lunch: 'Your present lodging doesn't sound very comfortable. My wife and I are going away for a week; would you like to make use of our house in our absence? We leave tomorrow.'

When we got our breath back we accepted most gratefully. He then asked his secretary, Gwen Witbooi, to set up a series of meetings for us. She told us she had a travel grant to visit London soon and we invited her to stay with us in there, which she duly did. We could now begin refilling the lake of hospitality.

Later Theo took us round to meet his wife Helen, an equally impressive lady with greying hair and a firm but friendly face. Their house was in Rondebosch, one of the many middle-level white suburbs on the eastern side of Table Mountain; a pleasant bungalow set in a small garden with a splendid view of Devil's Peak. It was full of books, original paintings hung on the walls and to our delight there was superb hi-fi and a stack of classical records. Because of the financial crisis at the CI they were having to sell the house and, we suspected, some of the paintings too.

As he took us to the gate in the warm afternoon sunshine, Theo stopped and looked searchingly at us. 'I have to warn you. Special Branch has at times been watching this house and there have been incidents. That's one reason we don't like leaving it empty. Are you OK with that?'

We felt a slight shiver for a moment but this also made it easier to accept his offer; it was a service we could do for him.

Next morning we moved all our bags and baggage round and settled in, revelling in the luxury of comfortable beds, functioning machinery and a proper kitchen. For once we didn't have to do our own washing since they had a live-in helper, Vinah, who also worked weekends as a nurse. Once, when we gave her a lift to the hospital, she introduced us to a friend and I unthinkingly held out my hand. There was a long pause before the lady grasped it. 'I'm not used to people like you shaking my hand,' she laughed and we all became good friends.

It was time to meet Elaine Bhettay again for the promised tour of the Coloured townships. We went first to the private medical centre where she worked and to a showcase children's library, where her friend Vincent told us how much he had enjoyed London. 'I was able to buy a Communist newspaper from a street vendor,' he said. 'Then I met another street vendor who told me that newspaper didn't have the right Communist viewpoint – "Here, buy mine instead for the true interpretation of events!" That made me feel I was really in the free world!'

She gave us a whirlwind tour: there seemed a wide variety of housing, from Soweto-type cabins through slum terraces to individual freehold plots where the Indian community had built large eccentric houses. There were also areas of council-built, but pleasant, houses for Coloureds to buy over a period of thirty years. 'What happens if you want to move during that time?' Patrick asked naively.

Elaine looked confused. 'Well, if you are transferred then I suppose you can sell them back.' We realised this was a country where, if you weren't white, you had to stay in your allotted economic and geographical place unless 'they' moved you. For many, this was a totalitarian state.

At supper we met Richard Rive[53], author, academic and opponent of all segregated institutions. Dark-skinned, with curly hair and a very set jaw, Richard was not one to compromise. 'I won't go and teach at their new University of the Western Cape,' he thundered, 'because it's for Coloureds only and I won't be part of their system. I'd like to teach at the University of Cape Town, which is still open to all races, but meanwhile I've taken a post at Hewat College of Education. It's Coloureds-only, of course, but there I feel I'm being useful and although the students are quite radical

---

[53] Richard Rive stayed on at Hewat College and though he later became visiting professor at Harvard and gave guest lectures at many overseas universities, he remained committed to working for change within South Africa, publishing many short stories and three novels. Tragically, he was shot dead in 1989. As political tension grew in the 1980s, many young Coloureds threw in their lot with the Africans as he had done.

they don't regard me as a sell-out.'

'As for me,' declared Elaine, 'I won't use the Coloured bank, we don't go to Coloureds-only theatre and we won't vote in the elections for the Coloured Representative Council. It doesn't represent me!'

Patrick challenged them: 'This policy of rejection that you've all endorsed, how do you think that will bring about change? Is there anything positive you can do?'

They seemed less clear about this. Richard again: 'I think they'll reinstate the Coloured vote. Why? Because most of them are Afrikaans-speaking and 90% of them will vote Nationalist to keep the Blacks out! It's only the educational fringe like me who think we must make common cause with Africans.'

But we got a different view from Dick van der Ross, the new Rector of that new University of the Western Cape – aka 'Dick's Bush College'. Using Beryl Unterhalter's introduction we made an appointment at his very expensive house in the very superior Coloured area of Belleville – like the near-by campus it had recently been carved out of the sandy bush. We parked in his wide driveway alongside his two Mercedes. He was a short stout man, eager to tell us what he thought. I began by saying we'd met Richard Rive and asked him what other South African novelists he could recommend.

'Oh, so much of it comes from the pens of the extremists these days,' he said dismissively. 'And most of them have left the country anyway. They should stay here now we have been given a stake in the country and Africans have got their own areas.'

'But don't you think the "homelands" are fraudulent?' Patrick asked.

'Well, yes, of course, but in a way, this means that we Coloureds, and the Indians too, will be able to take our place alongside the Whites in the community.'

'The Black Consciousness Movement suggests that Coloureds should show solidarity with Blacks,' I mentioned cautiously.

'Those people are just aping the Americans! We are not like the Blacks! They have only one high school in the whole of the Western Cape, so how can we meet them on an equal basis? Our new university here is going to give the Coloured people great new opportunities for training and development.'

We understood why so many people called him a sell-out, and did not find his views or personality appealed to us. But on the other hand he was, in his own way, trying to do the best for his community. Lots of Coloureds were quite happy to see Africans shut away in their 'homelands', so they could be left alone to take all the jobs in the Western Cape and to move gradually up the social ladder towards White status.

The Fouchés were among these. 'They're a wonderful family,' said Mrs Greenshields. 'They're all Scouts and Guides and contribute lots towards their community. Mrs Fouché and I both sit on the committee for the Leilebloom Home for Coloured Children. You must go and see them.'

We did and we were given a great welcome, with a huge spread of biscuits, cakes and piles of dried fruits, before being whirled off to see the Home. There were six houses, each with twelve children under a house mother; it was well built, beautifully kept and seemed to have a good atmosphere.

In some ways, we felt we were back in Nigeria. The Fouchés chatted away about their lives and activities, photo albums were produced and they burst out laughing at every opportunity. They were full of self-confidence and seemed unconcerned about race or class.

'Yes, I've been to England,' said Mrs Fouché. 'I think we've got a higher standard of living here. I went to a wedding in Manchester and they could only afford to invite a hundred people – everyone here would be able to have many more guests, such a shame! Yes, we were moved out of Wynberg nine years ago when they changed the laws, but we bought this plot and built our own three-bedroom house and now we're building an extension. We've got a proper bathroom since the council put in a sewage system. The house is worth nearly three times what we paid for it!'

Mr Fouché was a qualified joiner working in a small furniture business where he was the senior on the shop floor. 'We're a mixed bunch of workers and we all get the same wage rates,' he said. 'The foreman is Coloured and he and I run it together, we can give orders to the Whites, no problem.'

Mrs Fouché worked as a machinist for Wonder-bra, but her daughter had trained as a pattern-maker. 'Five years ago I wouldn't have got such a job,' she said.

Patrick gently tested the political water.

'But you've lost the right to vote. Do you think you'll ever get it back?'

'Probably not. But the Nationalist party have treated us well; we're all getting better jobs and making more money!'

'Do you ever fear there'll be an explosion one day?'

'Oh no! We don't have earthquakes in this part of the continent. But they do have serious explosions in the mines…'

They showered us with more boxes of dried fruit and as we drove home we concluded that the Nationalists could indeed rely on this group as long as they offered economic advancement in lieu of political freedom: a policy familiar in all fascist regimes.

We had become so absorbed in the human landscape that for much of the time we paid little attention to the scenery – yet it is magnificent. The jagged toe of Africa divides two oceans and where they meet billowing clouds drape themselves over the pinnacles of the Twelve Apostles and the steep sides of Table Mountain.

At the weekend we took the coastal road which snakes southwards along the peninsula, continuous surf pounding on our right, the battlemented mountains rising sheer on our left with heavy winter clouds enfolding their tops in a grey shawl. Where the land allowed, white settlements were dug into the rocky hillsides, like the glistening new blocks of Camps Bay on the west and the older colonnaded streets of Simonstown on the east. The main Coloured township was over the mountain, well out of sight of the sea though in true South African doublespeak it was named 'Ocean View'.

Driving into the nature reserve we entered a strange landscape; among the litter of grey stones grew weird tough-leaved bushes, mostly dusty green or brownish, with occasional bursts of bright flowers. This was the *fynbos*, a unique South African vegetation, and the flowers were the famous proteas. Under the lowering winter sky it was not inviting and as the clouds were hiding the famous lighthouse we drove down a rough road to the beach. We were sitting on a rock eating our sandwiches and trying to identify the gulls when a voice behind us enquired: 'Excuse me! Isn't that a Maseru registration plate?' He looked like a Triton arising from the sea, wearing a wet-suit and carrying a fishing spear, oblivious of the icy currents and whistling wind, but introduced himself as Paul Malherbe. 'My wife and I have recently been in Maseru. She's writing a book on Lesotho for secondary schools…'

This started an animated conversation which clearly needed more time and a warmer place. 'I've done my water-skiing but I'm just off to dive for crayfish. Why don't you come and have supper tonight?'

Over a delicious supper of fresh crayfish Cindy Malherbe and I happily compared notes on school textbooks – we found much in common – until politics again took over. Paul was a chemist working for Mobil Oil and had tried unsuccessfully to win a parliamentary seat for the Progressive Party. Now he expounded his solution for the country's dilemmas.

'What we need is a "Multistan" alongside the "Bantustans". Let us set aside an area of South Africa which will be open to all races but where Blacks will be in a majority; to be economically viable it must contain both industrial and agricultural land. There will be equality for all, including freedom of movement and ownership of property protected by a Bill of Rights, and it will remain part of the Republic of South Africa. This will be a pilot project: people living in the Multistan will become used to living and working together and it will allay so many of the white fears that they will come to accept a rapid transition to a non-racial state as long as individual rights are entrenched. The whole Republic will learn from us and became liberalised!'

What a vision! And what a welcome antidote to the pessimism of the last few days! But could it ever work?

'The Progressive party has only got one MP at the moment, Helen Suzman,' I pointed out. 'What makes you think you've got enough support for such ideas?'

'We're poised for a breakthrough! We can offer a real alternative to the Nationalists now that the contradictions of apartheid are making themselves apparent. We Progressives are attracting activists now from both Nationalist and United Parties. We have to develop a strategy for change which won't threaten white interests, and I believe the Multistan will do that.'

'How long do you think it will take?' Patrick asked.

'I believe our situation will be resolved within ten years!'

'Peacefully?'

'Yes, through political reform. International pressure will be important but I don't see a breakdown in law and order, let alone guerrilla warfare. Our next election will be in 1979 and I believe that will be the last under white domination!'

He was only out by fifteen years before South Africa did indeed become one huge Multistan but at the time it seemed an impossible pipe-dream.

At the end of the week we visited a fruit farm near Elgin run by Andrew Browne, a retired English naval commander, and his South African wife Ann, friends of the Kotzes and CI supporters. We drove across the Cape Flats on a bright sunny morning and as the clouds lifted they revealed a huge panorama of unbelievably high, steep, blue-grey pinnacles ahead of us, rising from the plain like a child's drawing of Tolkien's 'Misty Mountains'. These were the Hottentots Holland Mountains, through which wind deep clefts laced with vineyards and little white farmsteads. Sir Lowry's Pass took us up fifteen hundred feet and then down again into a broad fertile valley.

The Brownes had returned to South Africa from England to run Ann's family land but they felt uncomfortable here. 'I find my position as a large landowner in an unjust society very difficult,' said Ann. 'Things have got to change and soon. Otherwise we will go back to the UK and leave our son to run this place.'

Andrew seemed more cautious and conservative than Ann but he too spoke out against the government. 'They have become totalitarian,' he declared firmly. 'They are no longer concerned with the rights of the individual. We want to be part of the Western capitalist world with its vision of personal freedom but the regime is destroying that vision. The Special Branch came round here to ask us damned impertinent questions – I soon sent them packing! The democratic world needs to realise what is going on and disassociate themselves from South Africa until things improve.' This was music to Patrick's ears and here he found strong support for disinvestment.

After lunch we walked up to the storage dam through acres of apples and pears, bare-leaved and close-pruned in this winter season, while we asked about their workers.

'We have about fifty Coloured families living permanently in our estate village and then we have black migrant labourers at harvest time; they live in those rondavels away from the village as they can't bring their families. We pay each worker about R6 per week to cover food, clothing and entertainment and we help out sometimes with school fees and doctors' bills. We'll show you round.'

The houses were of brick, with kitchens and bathrooms recently added, and electricity everywhere. 'Three years ago,' said Ann, 'we appointed a community development officer to help our employees begin to organise things for themselves. After generations of subservience they found it hard at first. Now the mothers are running a pre-school playgroup, there's a village library and they have dances to raise funds! We focus on the children in the hope they'll grow up more pro-active and the local headmaster says yes, our kids are doing better in school now.' This was a far cry from the Strongs' lack of concern.

We could easily imagine the Brownes and their farm in the English shires. He would fit in as the retired naval man, benevolent though not much interested in ideas; she could pass for one of the county set, if a bit more radical and widely read than most. Indeed, here were the 'kith and kin' that the English gentry claimed supported apartheid. But the Brownes opposed it because of the self-same English values. We felt we had a message to take home that even our parents would understand.

CHAPTER 33
The Underbelly of Capetown

In which we are drawn into the work of the Christian Institute and become reporters of the darker side of Cape Town.

Now we had become, accidentally, part of the Christian Institute network we found ourselves being drawn deeper and deeper into the political situation and at the same time gaining a new perspective on Christianity. At home we had both long ago given up going to church, regarding Christian theology as incompatible with a modern scientific outlook even though we agreed wholeheartedly with its values. But here in South Africa Christianity was different. The Church was one of the few places where we could meet and talk freely with people from other racial groups; it was maintaining the bridges that apartheid was busy pulling down. These wonderful, sympathetic, interesting people who were standing up for democracy and human rights, for our own values, were mainly Christian – wielding that same theology as a weapon against apartheid.

For the next week we scurried about in our Beetle, following first one contact, then another. We asked questions, we listened, we watched and I took photos. In the car, over supper with our new friends, or on our own in Theo's house, we discussed endlessly what we had seen and heard. In the evenings, we – mostly Patrick – scribbled long accounts into the notebooks comparing, contrasting and trying to draw conclusions, mostly rather grim ones. We became social and political reporters, first to satisfy our own interest, but later because people said to us: 'You will tell the outside world what it's *really* like, won't you?'

So what was it *really* like? That depended first on the colour of your skin and secondly on how much you cared, how much you wanted to know. At times we got very depressed: there was so much that was wrong by our standards, so much poverty, such a powerful government, so little hope they would listen, so few levers to pull.… Yet we kept meeting people who believed in trying in their own way to make a difference to someone nearby, here and now, whatever the future might hold.

There was, for example, Jill Wenham who worked at SACHED – the South African College of Higher Education. As so often in South Africa the name was misleading. 'No, it isn't a normal college,' she explained. 'Since the Universities Extension Act closed down educational opportunities for non-Whites instead of extending them we've been tutoring African and Coloured students who've dropped out of high school or been forced out. Some do matric (school leaving certificate), others take degrees by correspondence.'

Jill was trying to stimulate the teachers to be more imaginative in their pedagogy and saw this as part of necessary change. 'All the time in all the schools here it's just rote learning. Honestly, how any African or Coloured students can achieve high levels of education, what with the poor quality of teaching and having to pay fees, I just don't know! It's going to take violent revolution to get any real change here.'

In the Christian Institute office building there was a large hall which had become a non-racial meeting and eating place known as the 'Open Door.' They served good cheap food to anyone who turned up, be they domestic servants or foreign diplomats, Christians, Jews or agnostics. At lunch there one day we talked to Dr Margaret Nash, a well-known theologian.

'This is one of the few places where Blacks can sit down to a meal instead of picnicking on the pavements,' she said. 'Yet even this was opposed by some of the white parishioners who felt that church property is for church people.'

She had published a book on the ecumenical movement and was pessimistic about the prospects of peaceful change. 'We aren't moving fast enough. White people still expect to be the leaders of the Church councils. They are still endlessly patronising and condescending! We really need the Black Consciousness movement down here – the Coloureds need to learn to stand up for themselves too.'

'What of the future?'

'I can't see how we can avoid an explosion. Like in Rhodesia, as the pressure for change builds up our leaders will get progressively less liberal. In today's papers they report an 8% swing among white voters from the Nationalists to the Herstigte Nationale Party – that's the extreme right-wingers.'

We heard similar views from the Cleminshaws, who lived round the corner from the Kotzes and entertained us one evening with coffee, ten-year-old brandy and good conversation. Harry was a technician at Groote Schuur Hospital and for this reason couldn't actually join any political organisation. Dot, with her calm eyes and friendly face, seemed in many ways just like any ordinary little grey-haired old lady but she was deeply involved with the Christian Institute – we later discovered she was working on a report on prison torture at the time – and like others she had refused to testify before the Schlebusch Parliamentary Commission.

'They just fined me R25,' she said, brushing it aside. 'Now tell us about Tanzania. We've just been to Mozambique. Ah! We got a glimpse of what our future might be: there were all these Africans doing all the things they could never do in South Africa!' Her eyes shone with excitement. 'It was even good to be stopped by black soldiers carrying guns who had no trace of subservience in their brisk approach to their task.'

'Did you think people accepted FRELIMO and its socialist regime?' we wondered.

'Yes indeed. There was a great sense of excitement and hope throughout the country. We met some Anglican missionaries who were really enthusiastic about the way FRELIMO works at the grass roots, educating and encouraging self-development. There are appalling difficulties, of course, as the Portuguese had done so little and then there was the civil war, but it's a very hopeful beginning.'

'Do you think there'll be a civil war here?'

'We're not optimistic,' said Harry. 'We support the Progressive Party as the only possible force for change. But the white community just won't face the facts; people ignore what Church leaders say and many of the parish priests are apathetic.'

'Part of my work with the CI,' said Dot, 'is to develop a "white conscientisation programme". I'm like a missionary among the Whites, trying to convert them before it's too late – though I'm an agnostic myself, not a Christian. They could start by treating their servants better. Have you talked to Maggie Oewies?'

Maggie was a dumpy brown-skinned lady wearing the usual urban African's winter outfit of woollen beret and a blanket over her jacket and skirt. She had a devilish sense of humour and irrepressible energy; her story was punctuated by laughter.

'My father was Coloured and my mother was Xhosa; I wanted to be African, but I'm quite light-skinned so they made me Coloured; my brother was darker and he got himself classified as African although this meant giving up the advantages the Coloureds have over the Africans. It's all rubbish – for me both Africans and Coloureds are Blacks.

'For years I was a domestic servant. Now I'm working full time under the Young Christian Workers' Union to organise the domestic workers in Cape Town. Take Sea Point where you stayed. They are rich there: on average each household has two servants, so there are about 20,000 in the district. We appoint local representatives who encourage them to stand up to their employers. When employers want a servant we make them come to our organisation; they won't get a servant unless they pay properly.'

Patrick asked about wages. 'Very low, somewhere between R12.50 to R35 a month, while the churches say they should be getting R54 for those long hours they work.'

'But they get board and lodging as well?'

'Yes, but you should see the food – it's terrible! One girl I know got a cup of boiled carrots and a piece of bread without butter for her evening meal; another was given a very old egg which was too old for the employers to eat and a piece of bread! And they have no social life at all! Visitors are not allowed in their rooms and there are no places in the white areas where they can gather or go for entertainment. So they just walk about the streets in their off-duty hours; the residents complain and the police harass them. And the accommodation is unbelievable. Would you like to see?'

We would. Next day she took us back to Seapoint where we surreptitiously entered the servants' quarters in a block of flats. The room, measuring about 7ft by 9ft, opened directly off a dark courtyard full of bins and puddles of water. It smelt of damp and had no windows, just a ventilator brick clogged with filth. There was a bed and a wardrobe which the police had damaged when they suspected she was hiding an illegal resident inside it. A single low-watt light-bulb hung from the ceiling – which she could only use at certain hours – but no heating of any sort was supplied. The final straw was the decrepit bathroom and lavatory, used by all seventy servants in the block, since the 'madams' didn't allow the servants to use their loos or even draw hot water from their taps.

How could such a situation exist right inside the building also occupied by their prosperous white employers? The rural slums in the 'homelands' were hidden far away, but here these Dickensian conditions were right under their noses. Truly, we thought, white South Africans just chose to be blind.

'So what can you do?' we asked Maggie.

'Well, I help them stand up for themselves! I've even been to Jo'burg to help organise servants there, especially the older ones. I met a woman of about fifty who had worked for the same employer for over twenty years and whose wages had barely risen as she was afraid of losing her job. Her employer was a doctor so I pretended to be a patient. At the surgery she said to me, "We don't usually treat Coloureds, but we will if you have the money." I said, "There's nothing wrong with me but there is something very wrong with the way you treat your servant," and I gave her a good lecture, till she cried. Then I brought up pensions – Africans get tiny pensions – and asked the doctor to put a considerable sum on one side to buy a pension for all the past service. I said: "I have seen your house, illegally I know, and you can have me arrested if you wish, but I have seen the valuable furniture your servant looks after every day and I know that you can afford it." I wasn't arrested.'

We were bowled over by this small brave woman who put her own fate on the line to help those at the bottom of the social scale.

The Athlone Advice Centre was set up to handle some of the most intractable problems facing local families and we spent a couple of mornings listening to the cases brought. Most were about 'passes' – those precious, dog-eared documents that every non-White must carry, to show who they are, where they were born, where they may live, what jobs they have had, whether they have police records and so on.

Under the apartheid system, Africans were not supposed to live in the Western Cape – that was for Coloureds. But since Africans had been brought there as slaves three hundred years earlier and many Xhosa had moved west over the years, this was like un-mixing a fruit cake. The government was trying to sort it out by imposing strict 'influx control' on any new immigrants, and 'endorsing out' anyone who had no work and appeared to belong to one of the tribal 'homelands'. However, if one had a job – and therefore the right passbook – he or she might stay and in the past this had included one's family too. These partial contested rights gave rise to much confusion and bitterness.

One of the cases went something like this: 'I thank you for helping me last year to get my right to stay here with my husband but he has now passed away. I have a job and so does my son; we have a house here, my two youngest daughters are in school and my other daughter is looking for work. But the people at the Bantu Administration say we must all go back to the "homeland" now my husband is dead. Only my son can stay here, as a migrant worker, and he must send all his wages to keep us alive in the Ciskei.'

The Advice Centre people were confident of winning that one but they showed us a letter which said (in departmentalese) that it was policy to apply the law as strictly as possible to reduce the African population in the Western Cape regardless of the merits of any particular case.

The next applicant was a man. 'I was working on the roads and I have strained my back so they sacked me. Thank you for arranging a doctor's appointment for me and helping me make a claim for Workmen's Compensation. I can do light work now. But they say I must go back to the Transkei and apply for work from there. But all the jobs they offer to us in that place are heavy work like mining and I can't do that so I will never get another job. I think I will starve; I have no family in Transkei.'

What a Catch 22 situation! This looked tricky so it was handed over to the lawyers.

This was definitely a morning to bring on despair. Later we met Mrs

Qunta, an African social worker who was no more hopeful. She was a beautiful person with a manner which reflected her composed saint-like but sad face. Talking to her became increasingly depressing as we felt her hopelessness overwhelming our spirits.

'I have quite a good white boss at the Department for Bantu Affairs and we can do some things which are technically illegal but, in general, things have deteriorated – less money, stricter rules.'

'What do you mean, illegal?'

'Well, I bring in white volunteers to work in community centres. It is so important that young Blacks meet the better Whites and realise that the Whites are not all animals. I believe in reconciliation between Black and White; I don't agree with the Black Consciousness talk. Whites will always be with us, and we must learn to get on with them, not withdraw. The young black radicals attack me for saying this. Even my children don't agree with me – two have fled to Botswana now.'

Despite her moderate views, however, Mrs Qunta had no real hope for the future and warned that it had become too late for peaceful change. She saw little possibility of a successful revolution being generated within South Africa, feeling that the change might well eventually be imposed from outside by the liberation movements or others.

'You will tell the truth about South Africa to the outside world, won't you?' she said as we left.

The most depressing places of all were the Cape Flats, a vast area stretching east towards Gordon's Bay and those beautiful Hottentot Hollands mountains. On a damp cold morning we were driven out through dense fog to visit the shanty towns. No one knew how many lived out here – 60,000? 200,000? – such was the housing shortage. Single migrant workers were supposed to live in hostels but they wanted to have their families with them so they moved out and squatted anywhere they could.

Tommy Pearson was a Catholic social worker, a brown-skinned man with a big black bushy beard and a hearty laugh. 'Have you heard of *pondok* farming? Come, we'll show you.'

He and a Muslim colleague took us to one of the original unorganised shanty sites where, for a rent, the farmer had allowed the homeless to set up their shacks – a highly profitable business as he didn't provide any facilities at all. These shanties were built principally out of battered old corrugated iron and the tiny little rooms were held together with any materials which came to hand. The whole area was low-lying and very wet in this wintry weather; there was mud and puddles everywhere, yet there was an active feel to the place.

'Shanty dwellers are creative,' said Tommy. 'If they can have a bit of land they'll put up their own shacks and improve them as they get money. But they've got no security. Recently a farmer told them all to leave. When they asked where they should go, they were told: "Ag, just walk to the crossroads." So they set up a whole new shanty town which is now called Crossroads. The local council is trying to evict them but we've giving them support.'

The government had by now recognised the problem but it was taking a long time and their first efforts seemed rather half-hearted. We saw an official 'site and service' area, with pit latrines and water taps provided, where people were allowed to build their own houses, mostly of old corrugated iron on a square wooden frame, desperately cold and damp. Yet all round people were busy getting on with their lives; washing was strung out on lines waiting for the sun to appear; women were preparing food and chatting; children were playing on the muddy ground.

'It's better than the site they moved us from,' one lady told us. 'But it's very cold and my rent is R.7.80 a month. I only earn R.60 and I have to feed my family and everything.' She invited us inside. Her furniture – tables, chairs, beds – was crammed into the one room. Many of these people were not destitute; it was housing they needed.

Our final visit was to the transit camp supported by the Church, where people went for about a year when their site was cleared for building or while waiting to be allocated government flats. The camp had rows of long huts built of corrugated iron – a bit like a prisoner of war camp – divided up into family units.

'It looks dreary,' said Tommy, 'but they are waterproof and there's water and sanitation. This is where we do a lot of our work: we try to get them organised and develop a sense of group identity. The council has promised to try to keep these communities together when they are finally settled.'

'And where will they be settled?' we asked.

'I'll show you.' The new housing areas consisted of drab blocks of flats placed very close together – worse than any council housing we had ever seen with no social amenities for either children or adults. We felt we were looking at the slums of the future.

Against this scenario of political and economic frightfulness the Christian Institute offered both practical and psychological help. In this 'church without walls' there was also a weekly service without a priest, known as the *Agape*.

'It is like a family meal,' said Margaret, inviting us to take part, 'but it points us to the wider community. We use it for spiritual sustenance but it is also a forum for discussion, a way of sharing experiences and of coordinating action. It is, I think, unique, though Theo learnt the new version of "Our Father" from the civil rights movement in the States.'

About twenty people – White, Black, Coloured, men and women, some young, some older – sat round a table set with glasses and little plates, with a loaf of white crusty bread and bottles of wine in the centre. Mrs Perez stood up, a lady of about fifty, dressed in a neat dark dress and jacket with pale brown skin and African hair under her beret; a kindly, sensitive face but the eyes were sad.

She bade everyone welcome by name and led us in prayers for peace and for reconciliation, for those in prison or in mourning, for those suffering hunger and illness. Then each person in turn took a piece of bread, poured a glass of wine and offered them to their neighbour, saying: 'May God bless you and yours this day.' When all had taken part in this simple communion Mrs Perez asked if anyone wished to share their story today.

Harold, a young black man, spoke first. 'They have let me out for four weeks, a kind of "leave",' he said bitterly. 'Either they think this will make me turn state's evidence or they are hoping I'll go over the border. I was detained last September. I was in solitary for most of the time. No, I was never taken to a court. They didn't give me any books or writing materials till I made a statement, then they let me have some but just novels, nothing political. I was lucky; other detainees told me about being interrogated under bright lights, being made to sit in stress positions, being deprived of sleep and food.'

Mrs Perez turned to a young white girl who was sitting hunched in her chair, but she shook her head and wiped her eyes. My neighbour whispered to me: 'She was arrested and kept in solitary for sixty-four days, being interrogated harshly, and had no idea why. Only after her release did she discover they'd arrested an African friend of hers whose name was among her papers. She still can't talk about it.'

Meanwhile Mrs Perez was saying quietly: 'Two of my children are in Botswana to escape having to give evidence in the SASO trial. I have little news of them. The children are full of hate and bitterness now but I know that as a Coloured woman and a Christian I have to bear this cross. I live one day at a time and I know anyway that here on earth we have no permanent dwelling place.'

We left deeply moved by this experience. Perhaps the early days of the Church were like this, when Christians met secretly in each other's houses knowing they might be thrown into prison, facing torture and possible death. Theo's version of the Lord's Prayer had replaced *'Lead us not into temptation'* with *'Do not bring us to the breaking point'*. For many of the people here the breaking point was too close for comfort.

How could it be that these quiet, gentle, kind people were regarded as 'enemies of the state'? Father Erson in Johannesburg, Dot Cleminshaw, Maggie Oewies and Grace Qunta: they seemed the most unlikely protagonists of radical change until their anger came bubbling to the surface and they were moved to act against the injustices they saw and felt.

The next day the Kotzes returned from Johannesburg bringing their son Stephen with them. I had prepared a three-course supper to welcome them home, but by then their daughter and son-in-law had also turned up and a couple of friends had popped in. Everybody whirled about and Theo, uncontrollably kind, sent out for bottles of this and that in anticipation of every possible taste; my roast chicken was stretched out for nine and washed down with plenty of red wine, brandy and laughter. They were a tremendous household, full of fun as well as serious purpose.

Saturday was our last in Cape Town. We had been too busy for much sightseeing and the weather had not been conducive; a trip in the cable car up Table Mountain had ended in a wet, windy walk through ragged bushes with no views at all. But today the sun invited us out and we went first to the botanical gardens at Kirstenbosch, which are situated a little way up the south-eastern flank of Table Mountain. The site and the views almost outshone the plants, but we could admire the stiff flowers of the proteas close up and delight in spotting the originals of many English garden plants like geraniums and plumbago.

Nearby stands Groot Constantia, built in 1685 and famous as an example of Cape Dutch architecture with its broad white gables and simple interior. A wide avenue of evergreens led up to the house and its small garden while all around stretched the vineyards, legacy of the Huguenots rather than the Dutch. We bought some wine to take back to the Kotzes.

After supper Mr and Mrs Perez called round. They were a delightful couple, both intelligent and dedicated to serving their community and beyond. Mrs Perez had led the Agape service and she had now come to give us letters for their children in Botswana. 'We can't write direct to them, it would be dangerous,' she said. 'Please will you post them in London?'

Mr Perez was a tall handsome man of mixed Spanish-Mauritian parentage who looked Italian. 'I'm classified Coloured,' he told us, 'but my brother managed to pass for White and we haven't seen him for years. I think he's dead but I know his son married a niece of Villiers de Graaff, the Leader of the United Party! So they wouldn't want to acknowledge us!'

I asked him tentatively how much he minded. 'It's sad for the next generation,' he admitted. 'As a child I benefited a lot from visiting both my White and my Coloured families. I learnt to know both worlds – now that's not possible. And yes, my life could have been different. I've worked for thirty years for this paper factory and now probably I more or less run it. If it were not for my pigmentation, I guess I'd be called the managing director! I remember twenty years ago, before the social laws were so strict, I was working with an Englishman and I took him out for a drink. He said to me: "Look, old chap, I thought you were to be the next boss, but they say you can't be because you're Coloured – what does that mean?" If we'd emigrated, I could have bettered myself and my family, but we stayed to help our people here.'

After they had gone Stephen prevailed on his mother to play one of

Donald Swann's recent records – he was a personal friend of theirs – and we talked about British attitudes to South Africa, while Patrick asked Theo whether investment could have a positive effect on social change, hoping to get some clarification for his own views which were moving from believing it could to fearing it could not. 'I'm no economist,' said Theo eventually. 'But I'd support an international ban just to put pressure on the government for change.'

Just before we all said good night Theo asked us if we'd had any trouble with BOSS.

'We haven't noticed anything,' we replied cheerfully, for in truth we had dismissed his warning. Theo took us to the front door. First he showed us the bullet hole – which we'd never noticed before – and then pointed across the road. The curtain in the front room opposite was carefully arranged with just a chink open.

He told us: 'A security policeman sat there every evening for three months checking our comings and goings. We never knew until a neighbour told us afterwards. He said he'd been too frightened to say anything earlier. Today,' he went on, 'I met a recently released detainee. He told me the interrogators had played him recordings of conversations that took place here in my sitting room.'

We stared at him aghast. Had the watchers returned? Had BOSS been listening to us all this time?

'Probably not, as they knew I was away,' Theo reassured us, 'but we know the CI is bugged. Once at a Board meeting I said something like, "Death does not matter so much to a Christian because we believe in life after death." Next thing was a wreath of carnations arrived here with a card saying: "Theo Kotze RIP". They sent it COD so it cost me R15! We think it was Scorpio – an extremist organisation – but they must have been told by the Security.'

How like Theo not to worry us with all this until the end of our stay! As bedtime reading he gave us their book of press cuttings covering the last few years – a tale both horrifying and inspiring. As we had come to know them, the Kotzes and their friends were not narrow-minded puritan revolutionaries – they were just committed Christians doggedly defending what they believed to be a Christian way of life against an anti-

Christian state. In fact South Africa seemed to us not unlike the picture of Russian society portrayed in Solzhenitsyn's novels: a police state. It must have given Theo quiet if ironic satisfaction when, while he stood on the Cathedral steps with the students, a senior police officer (a brigadier) asked him to leave, saying 'you are too important to arrest.' Theo, naturally, stood his ground and was eventually arrested; the publicity did the government no good at all.

✳

Two years later, in October 1977, the CI was banned and so were its leaders. This meant Theo could not leave his home district nor meet with more than one person at a time, so he could no longer continue his work in any form, not even as a minister.

He did not want to abandon South Africa but the Christian Institute directorate asked him to go to Europe to continue its work abroad. Late one evening in June 1978, Helen Kotze appeared unannounced at our London house looking sad and exhausted; she was uncharacteristically uncommunicative and left early next day. A month later, Theo was smuggled across the border into Botswana in the boot of a car and so escaped to Europe. They spent some time teaching in the UK and were eventually able to return to Capetown after Liberation in 1994. Theo died in 2003 and at his funeral the eulogist said of the Kotzes' home: '*It was a dwelling place for friendship, a home of faith for the fearful, a centre .... through which streamed the surrounding community of life.*' We felt very privileged to have experienced this place.

CHAPTER 34
Goodbye to Lesotho

In which we stay in a different house but enjoy the same warm friendship.

'When you get back we'll be living in the old African location,' Anna had warned us. 'We're renting this house to diplomats.' So for the last few days we found ourselves staying in a crowded suburb at the other end of town, where modern bungalows jostled with mud-walled huts, where some people grew cabbages while others kept a cow for daily milking; one yard might be full of junk cars and the next hold a shiny new Mercedes. Children played in the unpaved streets, women gossiped alongside their chores and chickens or even ponies searched for food. In the evening a thick pall of smoke, reminiscent of Soweto, blanketed the area as the fires were lit for food and warmth. It was rather like that first week in Lagos, so long ago, but less tidy – and a lot colder! Coming back from Cape Town over the Sneeuberge mountains we had indeed driven through snow.

The Hlaleles' house was bigger than most, with running water and electricity and an anthracite stove; I soon learnt to cook on it. We slept in the servants' quarters with a paraffin heater and a table for writing up the diary of Cape Town, struggling to express what we had experienced there.

It was time to go shopping, pack up and say goodbye to friends. I sent a last huge parcel home full of sheepskin slippers for all the family. We bade farewell to our expatriate friends, not sure if or when we would meet again. A couple of South African exiles holed up here in the safety of Lesotho gave us letters for their friends in London, which we stowed carefully at the bottom of our suitcases.

On Saturday, our last day, the Hlaleles took us to Ha Ntlama, their countryside base where Wilson spent much of his time. After the 1970 coup Wilson had resigned from the civil service as his name had appeared on the blacklist even though he was not politically active. He became first manager and then lessee of one of the big trading stores that the British firm Frasers had built all over Lesotho and he now hoped to buy it outright, the first Mosotho to do so.

These stores functioned as commercial centres for rural communities. In the big red-painted corrugated iron shop girls were selling all the basic necessities: from groceries and clothing to hardware and paraffin, from patent medicines to Basotho blankets. Peanuts were being roasted and packeted. Nearby were a borehole and a mill where women queued to grind their maize and sorghum, their patient donkeys standing ready to carry the sacks home again. Behind lay warehouses, originally to store grain and wool but now full of building materials; miners returning from the Republic with wages in their pockets would buy cement and iron for new homes. The manager's large stone house stood surrounded by orchards of peach and apple with a large vegetable garden and two rondavels.

'When you buy it,' we suggested to Anna, 'those would make perfect holiday homes for us to come and stay in!'

They made it a very special day for us. They knew our tastes by now and offered us beer and brandy though they were teetotal, even peanuts to nibble, before laying out a large lunch on the veranda where we had a magnificent view across to the snow-bespattered Maluti. Afterwards they showed us round the village of sturdy stone-built houses with traditional reed-thatched roofs. Shepherd boys with their flocks of Angora goats posed for my camera and then round the corner came two heavily laden sleds, each drawn by six cattle. Wilson, much more at home here than in Maseru and wearing his special Seanamarena blanket in our honour, swept his arm around the scene. 'We are not rich,' he said, 'but it's been a good harvest this year. People are improving their homes, the children are going to school and we are developing our country. It's not like South Africa.'

And indeed it was not; this was what the rural areas such as KwaZulu might have been like: men and women working together, facing challenges and changes together under leaders of their own choosing however imperfect they might be. Would South Africa ever be able to change course?

On the way back we visited Anna's family compound at Teyateyateng: three houses set round an impeccably swept yard with a great pile of shelled maize cobs in the middle and a productive vegetable garden at the side. The oldest house, with thatched roof over thick mud walls freshly plastered in ochre, had been built by Anna's great-grandfather. Her father's house was of brick with a sloped tin roof and the third was built with concrete blocks – marking the family's increasing wealth and status. The sitting room walls were hung with family photographs, including one of the Bath students in Anna's final year – and there was Aunt Mary, the originator of our voyage, sitting among them!

We accepted a glass of *joala*, the sorghum beer that we had first tasted in Kwassam, pronounced it a good brew and drank to Aunt Mary's health. They presented us with a chicken as a 'thank you' for visiting them and as we left the youngest sister broke into singing '*Nkosi Sikelel' iAfrika*[54] before walking with us a little way down the road as a gesture of courtesy. In the darkness the stars were very bright and a new moon lay low in the sky.

At yet another sister's house we were treated to yet another large meal ending with an elaborate farewell cake. Then we rushed back to Maseru as Anna had invited several of her friends, at this eleventh hour, to see our Tanzanian slides. We were so late that most of them had given up waiting so while I struggled with an antique projector there were hasty telephone calls all round. Some were interested, others too full of joala to care, but the children enjoyed the animals in Arusha Park and the adults laughed at us dressed as mountaineers on Kilimanjaro. It was midnight before they left, one saying in farewell: 'You're not expected to sleep on your last night.'

It had been a very African day at home in Lesotho. Now for the complexity of Johannesburg again.

---

[54] 'God Bless Africa'. This hymn was linked to the ANC and the liberation struggle. Although not technically banned in the Republic, we could not find a recording of it there. People would only sing it secretly or to make a political statement. Because of its inspiring words it became one of the two national anthems of the new South Africa.

CHAPTER 35
Final Return to Johannesburg

In which we pick up old contacts, make a few new ones and visit Sharpeville.

At the Hawthorne Residential Hotel Mr Finlayson seemed pleased to see us. Originally from the UK, he told us he'd gone back in 1964. 'But soon I'd had enough, what with the socialist government and all those black immigrants taking all the jobs. I'll never go back again.' We decided not to explain why we'd taken the flat instead of the bedsit: we were planning to break – if not laws, then conventions – and invite our black friends to meals here.

After the exhaustion of the Lesotho farewells we needed time to catch up. As usual Patrick settled down to turn his diary notes into a more readable form of journal to send home while I went shopping to stock the fridge with our favourite foods and then to take advantage of the laundrette, a luxury after all that hand-washing in cold water. We read a book on the evils of migrant labour, the report on the Christian Institute and even a copy of the *Financial Times*, though Harold Wilson's latest pay policy initiatives seemed rather far away from the urgency of poverty wages in South Africa.

We took our ironing to the Van Vuurens and were invited to stay to supper. Their daughter Katharine had fallen and needed an X-ray; their cat had had its hip replaced after being run over and was hobbling around, but Muzzle the ridgeback was as bouncy as ever and Colin was still offering snifters of brandy at the first opportunity. Patrick began on politics.

'People are saying to us that things are changing. The Progressive Party seems to be making great strides. I hear Helen Suzman's been joined by seven more MPs.'

'That's just a flash in the pan,' replied Colin gloomily. 'And I think Vorster's changes are cosmetic, just to keep the international community at bay.'

When we told them about our flat and our plans to try to repay our black friends' hospitality, Felicity broke in: 'But we'd like to meet them too. Would you like to give a party for them here on Sunday? That would be an opportunity for us as well.'

How typical of the generous, open-hearted and unorthodox Van Vuurens! Together we planned who might come: the Motlanas, and the Tebahadis from Soweto, Connie Koza and Harry Makubire from the SACC if they could get transport, some liberal white neighbours....

But before that we went to a different sort of dinner party. Next day I collected five boxes of slides from Kodak and settled down to label them while I could still recall all the faces and places, while Patrick went off to visit John R., the research partner in a firm of stockbrokers and thus a counterpart from his old life. Meeting him in London, Patrick had thought him a politically aware, liberal sort of guy, but seen through our new South African eyes he was no such thing. Patrick came back sputtering.

'He knows nothing at all about Africans. He told me that twenty-five years ago none of them could drive a car! Then he boasted that South Africa spends twice as much on black education as all the rest of Africa. I told him Nigeria has 24,000 university students, while here there are only 5,000 Blacks at college. This must be the only country where one can hold a job as a financial research analyst and be so ignorant about the political situation! Anyway, he's invited us to supper – do you want to go?'

We went. Our host was drunk when we arrived but after some futile fumbling in the drinks cabinet he managed to find us some wine while his wife played the perfect hostess. 'This is my sister, Rosemary, and her husband Mike. He's from Rhodesia.' Warning signals were flashing, but we started off on the safe ground of the beauties of the Cape and our adventures in Nigeria. Even Tanzania was relatively innocuous, as Mike allowed that socialism might suit their circumstances, but further south he became adamant.

'Smith is the first Prime Minister to truly represent the views of the Rhodesian people,' he declared. 'Britain must not interfere with the affairs of Rhodesia or of South Africa. It's unfair!'

'What about fairness towards the African population?' Patrick asked.

'Separate development is the only answer! They want to develop in their own way.'

'But separation is impossible if everyone is to flourish. There's too little land for the Blacks and white South Africa needs their labour. Even the Nationalists are beginning to see how impractical it is.'

'That's ridiculous! Above all we must maintain European standards! Africans are ungovernable and violent. They smile on you one minute, and kill you the next.'

By this time both men were arguing in circles and had become too emotional to listen to each other.

At the other end of the table John was telling me how the standards of everything had gone down in Britain – 'they even have regional accents on the BBC!' When I suggested that standards of living had risen greatly for both working and middle classes since the end of the war he seemed disbelieving.

Towards the end of the meal, having drunk more wine than I should, I asked him: 'Tell me, John, suppose an educated black middle-class family – say teachers or accountants like you and Patrick, who also liked nice houses and tidy gardens, moved into this street, what exactly would you object to?'

'Oh my dear girl,' he replied patronisingly – white South African wives don't usually talk about politics at dinner parties – 'such people don't exist.'

'Well they do, we've met them. But say in five years' time?'

'I can tell you, young lady: the value of my house would fall, right? More Blacks would move in and standards would go down, right? And women wouldn't be safe on the streets at night, right? Anyway, the whole idea is ridiculous; if you allow a black middle class to emerge, all the others will get frustrated!'

'But there is already even more frustration because all avenues are blocked to them. If you give Blacks a real stake in the country, with opportunities to rise, you'll secure their alliance and your own safety at the same time.'

'It's impossible! If Blacks lived amongst the Whites we would always be afraid that one day they would turn round and stab us in the back.'

It was time to go. As we put on our coats, his wife said thoughtfully: 'It would be interesting to meet some Blacks, but of course it's illegal to invite them to our house.'

'It's not,' we said and left. When we got home I was violently sick. Perhaps it was just too much rich food and that last brandy… perhaps not.

For our first attempt at illegal entertaining we'd invited Ann Sebati, the senior nurse at Baragwanath (and a friend of Mr Hononu's in Dar). She asked to bring her sister and a Mr Rathebe. The sister turned out to be Mrs Mangope, wife of the Chief Minister of Bophuthatswana, the large[55] 'homeland' designated for the Tswana people. Educated, poised, articulate, these relatively privileged black ladies nonetheless seemed inordinately pleased to be invited to a meal at our place, cramped and makeshift as it was. 'We no longer have the opportunities to meet white people like we used to,' said Ann rather wistfully.

Connie had said much the same about the growing gap between White and Black but had advocated a different solution. These ladies belonged to a rising black political elite rather than to a revolutionary movement and for the first time we heard some support for the government's policies.

'The "homelands" policy is a great step forward,' said Mrs Mangope. 'It gives us a platform where we can present our own policies and demand the authorities listen to us.'

Mr Rathebe told us he was a self-employed contractor. 'Black people are running their own show in the "homelands", doing things for themselves. We have a normal non-racial society there. The only problem is that we need much more land and we need industrial growth points.' We remembered the colour bar in the Umtata hotel and thought he was being rather optimistic. But we also thought of Paul Malherbe; here were black people who would fit well into his Multistan.

Mr Finlayson didn't notice that they'd been there. Good! Our next guests were June and Lindi. 'It is so good of you to invite us,' boomed

---

[55] Bophuthatswana was actually divided up into six separate pieces of land, scattered around the north-western area of the Republic, so it was particularly meaningless as an 'independent' entity.

June, and Lindi added: 'It's so very special to be made welcome by white people in their own home.'

'Well, it isn't exactly ours and by the way we've just discovered there are cockroaches in the kitchen but not as big as those in Benin,' I confided to more guffaws.

We shared our experiences of Cape Town and the CI. In turn they told us of their latest assignment. 'We were invited to talk to a unit of the Women's Army,' said June. 'A huge crowd turned up. We couldn't get away till two in the morning. They asked so many questions. They were fascinated by what black women have to say. We've now been invited to lots more Women's Army groups. This must be significant, eh?'

Johannesburg nights are cold and our flat had no heating, so I offered our guests my shawl and a blanket from the bed. Lindi wrapped herself up, caught June's eye and started to laugh. 'Are you sure you won't have to wash it? We smell, you know!'

'This is a true story,' June told us. 'A black person was invited to tea at, of all places, the Bantu Affairs Office, you know, where they rule our lives from. After he'd gone every single cup had to be washed in bleach just in case!' We agreed we wouldn't tell Mr Finlayson about the blanket.

June recorded a short talk for British schoolchildren on my tape recorder and then Lindi asked if she could send a message to her brother in Bristol in the same way. After the recording session when they stood up to go, they took our hands and standing in a circle June led us in prayer for peace in South Africa and a safe journey home for us.

To thank Dr Motlana for his hospitality, we took him and his new partner Peggy to dinner at the 'international' Carlton Hotel. Over the meal, he opened up and told us something of his personal struggles.

'I was born into poverty at Marapyane up in the north,' he recalled, 'what they now call Bophutatswana. I herded the cattle and I went to the Lutheran mission school, it was light years better than what is offered under "Bantu Education". Yes, it was strict and I got beaten, but that never hurt anyone,' he added laughingly. 'I studied at Fort Hare and then got a medical bursary to Wits, open to us in those days. Of course, I joined the ANC Youth League, and in 1952 became its Secretary General. We helped organise the Defiance Campaign that year; we were detained, and stood trial alongside Nelson Mandela and Walter Sisulu. I was given a five-year suspended sentence, and then banned. I might have run away, but I stayed; there are things one can do to make a difference.'

This doctor thought of himself as a businessman and a politician as well as a healer. 'In 1954 I opened my clinic in Soweto. I started up a medical business, selling uniforms for nurses. I'm now looking for capital to open a private hospital in Soweto.' At the same time he had successfully fought for black doctors to be paid the same as white ones.

We were impressed both by his concern for his community and his high expectations of them. 'You know,' he insisted, 'we can't just sit down and play the victim, bad as things are. We've got to work hard and prove we're just as good as the Whites. I've done it in spite of all they throw at us, so can others. I'm glad you met Steve Biko; he's a fine young doctor, and an inspiration to others. I helped him set up the Black Community Programme. In such youngsters lie our future and we must support them in the struggle.'

We took a letter back to our mutual friend in London. 'Tell him my letters still get intercepted even though I keep my head down these days.'[56]

In order to hear some white voices for a change we attended a political meeting where the local MP for Yeoville, Harry Schwartz, was trying to explain to his constituents that although they had elected him as a United Party member, he'd recently left it to set up the new Reform Party, which might merge with the Progressives. He was moving, very cautiously, leftwards. There were about three hundred people in the hall, a wide age range and seemingly a mixture of social classes – but all, of course, white.

Mr Schwarz explained he was leaving the United Party because it was moving towards the Nationalists. 'We need a party presenting a real alternative to apartheid and providing a real opposition. We must learn from Mozambique and not allow socialism into the vacuum.' He went on in this vein, saying they would encourage 'responsible black leaders,' maintain law and order, uphold free enterprise and ensure change

---

[56] Nthato Motlana didn't keep his head down for long and played a central role in both political and economic liberation. After the student riots of 1976 he set up the Black Parents Alliance and then became Chair of the Committee of Ten which led the community struggles in Soweto. He also encouraged Africans to follow his example to set up businesses on capitalist lines and become rich, as he himself did.

happened in a controlled way.

He ended: 'The new party will provide a bridge between Black and White. We aim to build a country where all can live in peace, to build a just society, in which there is opportunity for all people and an end of all discrimination.' It was not quite a clarion call to the Whites to rise up and set right the major injustices of their society but it seemed a step in the right direction.

In the question and answer session that followed, the limits to that step became clearer.

Q. 'Do you stand for integration?'

A. 'I stand for freedom of choice with whom I associate.' (Loud cheers!)

Q. 'Do you support the qualified franchise?'

A. 'You must wait for your answer till after the policy of the new party is announced.'

Q. 'Will you be able to prevent Yeoville from being overrun?'

A. 'No one will force you to go and live in a mixed society.'

He concluded: 'What we put forward, we put forward as representatives of the white community; other groups may have different ideas.'

And that was exactly it. Where was the black voice? In jail, banned, exiled or dead, some still living in the interstices underground, unable to give their views. Most of the Whites were frightened of mixing at any level. All these debates began to seem like shifting deckchairs on the *Titanic*.

It was our last Sunday when we went to Sharpeville. On a sunny winter's day the Johannesburg air has a brilliant tang to it and one can almost smell the snow from the Drakensberg away to the east. But driving south-westwards we could see the dense smog over Soweto and catch the acrid whiffs of coal smoke.

There being no signposts to townships and no maps, we made rendezvous with the Ukwes at a certain junction. They took us through the industrialised area, past the colossal ISCOR (Iron and Steel Corporation) works and other factories, including the depot of the trucking company where Mr Ukwe and his friends worked as drivers. They were clearly proud of their jobs, pleased to be settled in the urban areas, however problematic they might be, and intending to be a full part of the industrial future.

The depressing township areas stretched on into the distance, rows of identical box-like houses with few trees or open spaces, until we came to Sharpeville itself. We stopped beside the church, a large, simple, brick-built structure looking out over the infamous open space. Here on 21st March 1960[57], some 6,000 people converged on the police station, deliberately offering themselves for arrest for not carrying pass books – a move organised by the Pan Africanist Congress as part of a campaign against the pass laws. The police panicked and began shooting. Sixty-nine people were killed, and 180 injured, including women and children, many shot in the back as they fled.

It was a turning point in South African history. Around the country there were marches, strikes and riots. The government declared a state of emergency, arrested nearly 20,000 people and banned both ANC and PAC. As a result they went underground and began to plan for armed struggle since passive resistance now appeared futile. Internationally, Sharpeville woke up the world. With Resolution 134 the United Nations called on South Africa to abandon apartheid; the country became increasingly isolated and left the Commonwealth a year later.

'Yes, that's where the shooting took place,' said William Gabuse. 'We'd all stayed off work that day demanding a wage rise, but I wasn't part of the demonstration.'

'I was here,' Mr Ukwe told us. 'The crowd was quite peaceful, just standing and waiting. The police station is over there, you can see it behind the chain-link fence. Then someone started throwing stones and the policemen came out. They were scared and one fired – perhaps he got jumpy – and then they all started shooting. My brother was hit by five bullets but he lived, thank the Lord.'

Fifteen years later people had not forgotten but were getting on with their lives. Julia Gabuse and Diana Ukwe gave us coffee and biscuits in Father Mohale's house – he was taking a service elsewhere – and then took us into the church. 'It's a community service today,' they said, 'so there will be lots going on.'

---

[57] March 21st is now Human Rights Day in South Africa, and President Mandela chose this site for the signing into law of the Constitution of South Africa on 10th December 1996.

The church was large and plain and some of the windows were broken. Rows of chairs stretched down the nave, filling up throughout the service, perhaps three hundred in all. As guests we were ushered into the chancel where we felt both honoured and horribly exposed, but we managed to follow the service, a form of Anglican matins delivered in Setswana. When the sermon came it was translated swiftly into two other languages by the interpreters below the pulpit; a good bridle on lengthy discourse! But everyone sang in their own language: 'The next hymn will be Ancient and Modern 197, Setswana 306, Zulu 220, Xhosa 343.'

There were many hymns; they sang them in that wonderful four-part harmony that seems to come naturally to African voices, until Fr Mohale arrived, processed up the aisle with his white-robed choir and the service proper began. Communion was taken by virtually all the congregation in the high Anglican style with bells ringing and incense billowing round the church.

After that all became much less formal and not a little moving. First a child was brought to be christened; Fr Mohale laughed and joked with the parents while he splashed water from the glass bowl that served as the font. Then a very shy couple came up holding hands; they had been married by traditional rites in some rural area and now wished a Christian blessing on their union. Finally an elderly lady appeared attended by two young men, gave a prayer of thanks and laid money on the table. We were told she had recovered from a serious illness and her two sons had just come out of prison. The priest blessed them all and the congregation sang in response. Then he turned to us and made a short speech of welcome – fortunately no reply was needed as the collection was about to start.

No shuffling around with bags in the pews – this was an opportunity to dance and sing and show your generosity! First came the True Templars – a men's charitable organisation like the Lions – dancing up the aisle singing and beating out a rhythm on their briefcases, all wearing broad red sashes adorned with their badge of office. As each reached the table at the chancel steps they slapped down their gift of money and danced back down the other aisle. Then came the women's groups in matching blue skirts and white capes with white kerchiefs, dancing and ululating. As one tune faded another started up, echoing through the church which was now full of movement, musical chat and laughter, as line after line of people came up, stamping, twisting and singing, to put down their R1 note or their 5 cent coin, whatever they could afford. They collected nearly R80 that day – about £50.

We didn't stay till the end. Fr Mohale beckoned to us and we slipped out with our friends. As we entered the vicarage he stopped and said: 'Welcome to my house! You are the first white South Africans to come to our church!'

'Oh, we're from Britain,' we explained and told him what we were doing.

He was disappointed. 'I've had white visitors from Holland and Germany before; I had hoped the times had changed and our own people were coming!'

He was a tall, jovial man with a great sense of humour, but he seemed also deeply frustrated that he could do so little to improve the life of his parishioners. We asked him about the future.

'I think there is real change on the way but whether it will be fast enough to prevent a violent explosion – who knows? I am so sorry I have to leave now, I have a third service to take. People here look to the church for comfort and there are now so few priests to look after them.'

So we sat down with our friends and their friends at tables covered with cold meats and salads. Sweet sparkling wine was served and the atmosphere became cheerful and relaxed. 'We wish we could invite you to our houses,' said Julia, 'but then people would start asking questions and the police might come.' We sensed their nervousness; they were not politically involved at all, and they just didn't want to attract attention. When we left they escorted us back to the main road.

'We'll see you again. When do you leave?'

'Friday evening, about seven, I think,' said Patrick casually. 'So we won't have time to come again. But thank you all so much for your kindness and hospitality. It has been a wonderful experience.'

We never thought to see them again but we did.

That same evening we drove out to the Van Vuurens. Felicity produced a superb supper of chicken and lasagne and Colin ensured we washed it down with plenty of wine and brandy. Tandi Tebahadi found her way there; Joe had brought his wife Martha, Connie had brought Elda. 'I've been accepted by a white employment agency as a telephonist; they said my qualifications were what mattered!' she whispered, her blind eyes seeming to sparkle. How ironic that she couldn't even see the colour of anyone's skin! Felicity had invited Professor Drew Archibald, a sociologist from Wits, and his wife Carol, so we were six Whites and five Blacks. For the first time since coming to South Africa we felt we could relax as in a normal society, not worrying about colour but responding to each other's ideas and jokes and even making plans for working together in the future. Patrick was arranging for handicrafts from Inter-Church Aid to be sold in London through Project Hand.

Connie said to Felicity, 'Don't you ever think of emigrating. We need people like you to work together with us.'

'We will,' Felicity replied, 'but we look to your Black Consciousness movement to make this country worth staying in.'

CHAPTER 36
Farewell to South Africa

In which we try to make sense of what we have learnt and decide
what to do with it.

In that last tumultuous week we reported back to old contacts
and followed up new ones, trying to fill in some of the gaps in our
understanding of this strange fractured society so that we could explain
to people back home what was going on – and perhaps do something to
support what we now felt was a burning issue and a righteous cause.

In Cape Town we'd seen the Christian Institute as compassionate
politics in action, but its intellectual force came from Beyers Naudé. Of
impeccable Afrikaner heritage, he was ordained minister in the Dutch
Reformed Church and for years preached its religious justification for
apartheid. But his doubts grew and after Sharpeville he founded the
Christian Institute to promote reconciliation between races through
dialogue, research and publications. For this, he was ejected from his
parish.

We met a tall, bustling, energetic man with a forceful personality and it
seemed to us that where Theo would gather respect and affection, Beyers
commanded respect and admiration. He was, however, a good listener as
well as a very able communicator and understood where we were coming
from. 'You are saying that South Africa seems the very antithesis to Western
ideals of democratic capitalism? Yes, that's partly true. Disinvestment, you
suggest? I think it is unrealistic to ask for a complete cessation of British
investment. For one thing, there are many other countries queuing up to
invest here and of course withdrawal of all investment would have a major
impact on black employment. I would tell foreign firms they should only

invest in South Africa if they will train their black employees, allow them to rise to responsible positions and give them all the normal rights of a modern workforce, including trade union rights.'

We wondered how, as an Afrikaner, he judged the position of the Nationalist Government and his reply seemed to offer some hope. 'The leading Nationalists continue to support apartheid in public,' he said, 'but now they are beginning to appreciate that separate development cannot succeed. Some, I believe, do accept the inevitability of black majority rule, but dare not say so for fear of rejection by white voters. That is why we put so much emphasis on educating the white electorate.'

The SPRO-CAS materials, so illuminating for us, had originated here: did he think they had made a difference? 'They have made a difference, yes. People at last are wanting to know what Africans really think. I am still amazed by how ignorant Whites are about Blacks! Sometimes they just don't want to know, but often it's because they don't meet any Africans except their domestic servants, who of course tell them what they want to hear. We are focussing on helping Blacks to speak out for themselves, in particular the black pastors.'

Finally we asked what he thought we could do from outside to help. 'How can you help? You must inform people through the press and other media; you must educate the business community; you must encourage the Church in the UK to support the churches here as we try to bring about change.'

One of my unanswered questions was: what might be the role of trade unions? In Marxist theory the workers would rise up against their exploiters, and in our own history the Labour movement had indeed successfully spearheaded social and political change. In South Africa, as ever, things were different. The white working class jealously guarded job reservation which denied Blacks access to skilled manual jobs. The Trade Union Congress of South Africa had expelled non-white unions because, although not illegal, they could not be registered.

However, in 1973 there had been a wave of strikes by black workers in Durban with over 60,000 taking part. For once the government had not used force and the demonstrations were all peaceful. Public opinion was shocked at the low level of wages revealed, often below the Poverty Datum

Line which researchers had set as the minimum for family subsistence. On their side the white business community recognised that, for good or ill, they could not do without a more skilled and stable black work force. Wages were gradually raised and some limited concessions on the right to organise and strike were made, grudgingly, to black trade unions.

By 1975 there was a new feeling in the air, stimulated in part by the Black Consciousness movement. Rejecting offers from the Trade Union Congress of South Africa, TUCSA, to reincorporate Blacks, activists set up the Black Allied Workers' Union to represent their own interests, and in a dingy top floor office in mid-town Johannesburg Mr Mbeo explained their philosophy to us.

'We want to run our own affairs. There will be no white interference in this BAWU. We organise weekend courses for our members where all the lecturers are Blacks. In factories where we are strong, we use the works committee system to confront management. We learnt in Durban that the sky will not fall on our heads if we strike! The Durban townships lie within KwaZulu and Chief Buthelezi was the only "homeland" leader to call for African trade unions.'

Patrick was still pursuing his questions about overseas investment. Peter Randall ran Ravan Press, which published progressive literature from the Christian Institute and some black writing and Theo Kotze had suggested his views would be sound.

'It's a difficult question,' Peter began. 'Here in South Africa if you call publicly for a trade boycott or withdrawal of investment you are guilty of terrorism as defined by the Terrorist Act, which can carry the death penalty. I believe it is unrealistic to call for a boycott of trade or a cessation of investment but to advocate one, even if you know it will never happen, is a good way of maintaining pressure on foreign companies operating in South Africa. I don't think white attitudes can be easily changed but I do think the industrial area is one where pressure could fruitfully be applied.'

It certainly seemed difficult to change white attitudes and my next contact, Horst Kleinschmidt, seemed close to despair. An earnest and rather distraught young man, he had been running the Programme for Social Change (PSC), set up by the CI to raise consciousness in the white community as a counterpart to the Black Consciousness movement.

'We tried to set up structures where Whites would be forced to meet and accept Blacks as equals. But it didn't work; the Whites kept trying to "help" Blacks, not understanding they want to stand on their own feet.' He paused, staring into space. 'So we're closing it down. We're just doing small scale practical projects – investigate conditions in firms, publish reports on them and mobilise pressure to get them to improve pay and conditions. We found a German-funded school which paid its workers an average of R34 a month. Pressure from West Germany in response to our report doubled the wages. Now I'm doing casework with detainees' families – there are so many of them, and it's really important.'

He paused. 'But for me personally it's bad. Really, I can't find a satisfactory role. My own community won't listen, the Blacks don't want me. I'm going to train as a lawyer and reform some of the abuses within the system. I will join an Indian firm.'

People outside the country, he thought, should focus on making overseas businesses understand what was happening and tell them to train their black workers for positions of responsibility. But he added from his own present desperate concern: 'For God's sake, get the press to remind the world of the detainees! Get people to write to their families! Get churches to send funds to the Black Community Programmes!'[58]

We'd had no contact at all with government, but one faint ray of hope popped up when Patrick visited Dave Jackson of the Institute of Personnel Management. First he spoke of his earlier plans to pack up and leave. 'But this year,' he went on, 'in the wake of changes in Portugal and its ex-colonies, I find attitudes are changing fast. I'll give it three more years and see if I can help persuade business it's in their long-term interest to support a programme of significant social change.'

Dave became almost conspiratorial. 'Now this is off the record. I am convinced now that the government has had a real change of heart. It's like they are standing on the back of a spirited stallion galloping in one direction and are trying to work out how to turn it through 180 degrees without falling off – and they are worried about who might climb on if

---

[58] Two months later Horst Kleinschmidt was detained without trial for seventy-three days. He then fled into exile and found a role with the International Defence and Aid Fund, set up by Canon Collins to help political detainees and their families in South Africa. He was its director from 1983 until it closed in 1991 when the ANC was unbanned.

they did! I heard a senior Nationalist say that apartheid has created such a tense and divided society that it must be dismantled and another way sought.

'Confidentially, we've been offered a chance to develop with government the next steps on worker representation, provided we don't bash on in public about black trade unions. We do believe that the government is genuinely trying to find ways to bring about major changes. Once they have made up their mind they will offer incentives to business to adopt more progressive policies.'

Patrick became very excited about this – perhaps there really was a peaceful way forward?

'No,' said Beryl Unterhalter when we went round to say goodbye. 'An explosion is inevitable. So many of our liberal friends have moved out of the country; only the hardliners are left. And they will fight to preserve their way of life.'

Jack was less sure. 'I think they may shift in time to prevent a civil war. But it will take strong action, perhaps from guerrillas within the country or perhaps or a trade boycott. The dockworkers of the world could throttle South Africa's trade.'

But for us it was the Church who was giving the lead. Connie Koza had invited us to the Annual General Meeting of the South African Council of Churches at Hammanskraal, north of Pretoria. Three months earlier we had approached the SACC tentatively, unsure of who they were, what they did or whether we would find them sympathetic. Today we felt among friends - here were the familiar faces of those who had taught us so much and made our time in South Africa so memorable: Harry Makubire who was our first contact, Lindi Myeza the Johannesburg social worker, Mr Ngakane who told us his life story, Constance Koza who took us through the 'homelands', Rev Bax from Umtata, Dr Margaret Nash from Cape Town, Dr Beyers Naudé of the Christian Institute, Themba Sibeko from King William's Town, among others.

It was the second day of the meeting and there was a feeling of embattlement. That morning's edition of *Die Transvaaler* had banner headlines: *The Night of the White Man in South Africa*, implying the SACC was working for a black-dominated South Africa in which Whites would have no place. The chairman asked the reporter to apologise for such inaccuracy. He refused.

A face like a medieval icon took the microphone. Now we understood the charisma of Rev Bax and why the government feared him. 'I move that the reporter be excluded forthwith,' he thundered and he was.

Bax went on to propose a motion saying that 'the Churches shall commit themselves to a radical programme of social and political change', in order, he added, 'to stop people turning from Christianity to Marxism in pursuit of social justice.' This was eventually adopted but with dissenting voices from the more conservative elements. Not everyone was a radical.

The last speech was from a professor of theology, David Bosch. Only in South Africa had we ever found theology so dramatic and exciting; some of his words went on ringing in our ears long after we had left the country.

'Some Christians,' he declared, 'emphasise the *horizontal* elements of our faith: those that relate to man, to loving our neighbour. Others stress the *vertical*: the aspects of worshipping God. But there should be no conflict: the Church can combine the dusty with the divine. We must take action, humbly and with trembling hearts, to do what we believe to be right in both directions.' His conclusion was a very fine defence of the Christian Institute's position: 'We believe in God not because we despair of the future; rather we believe in the future of man and the world because we believe in God. Precisely because we hope for the eternal and final things we also hope for the temporary and provisional. Hope manifests itself in taking the next step. Hope is action and only as such is it genuine hope.'

We left after a final round of handshaking and hugs, feeling that this was a group with which we could identify more fully than with any other political or religious group we had ever encountered.

It was our last evening in South Africa and the Thebahadis had at last made it to our flat. We had invited them the previous week but they never arrived. The following day Tandi had explained that they'd got the wrong flat number and had knocked on the door of No.14. It was opened by a white man who shouted and swore at them in such a fashion that they simply retreated, got into their car and drove back to Soweto. We were totally shocked, not only that a professional couple could be so treated but also that they had allowed themselves to be put off. This time they brought with them Richard Maponya, the richest man in Soweto, and we very soon decided that no one could have sent him packing.

Richard was a massive man in all directions with self-confidence to match, a loud, cheerful voice, sharp eyes and a penetrating intelligence. He sat sprawled in the easy chair, still muffled up in his overcoat in spite of our attempts to warm the flat with Mr Finlayson's electric fire.

Here was another man, like Nthato Motlana, who had the confidence to take on the Whites at their own game. He told us he started as a primary teacher as that was the only route open. 'Then I took a job as a stock taker for a clothing company and we did so well in my department, both me and my white manager got promotion! In gratitude, he sold me the offcuts and "seconds", which I then resold in Soweto. I got together enough capital to start up my own company, but the government refused to give me a licence.' He unbuttoned his overcoat, happy to have an audience and warming to his theme.

'So I put the money into milk – the Dube Hygienic Dairy. Me and my wife Marina, we hired a fleet of boys on bicycles to deliver fresh milk to customers in Soweto every day, since they don't have fridges. Then we opened a couple of stores and now we've built this supermarket, but I can't expand any more; Blacks may only own one business and we may only sell the necessities of life.'

He sat upright, sharing his vision with us. 'What I really want to do is to open a black bank, and utilise black savings. The government tells me I can only do that in the "homelands", but that's no good, it must be in Soweto and other townships, where people are earning money.

'I have founded the African Chamber of Commerce to bring together like-minded black businessmen. Now we can talk with white business, we speak the same language.[59]

On my single gas ring I'd made some soup to warm everyone up and then Tandi and I slipped out to buy a bucket of Kentucky chicken. When we got back David and Richard were discussing their work as urban

---

[59] Maponya continued to expand his commercial empire, culminating in the Soweto Mall, a shopping complex with over 200 stores, which Mandela opened in 2007. While some radicals were suspicious of him, when he was the first Black to be granted horse-racing colours he chose green, gold and black – the colours of the ANC and a significant political gesture at the time.

councillors. Patrick challenged them to say what they felt they could really achieve since these positions were only advisory.

'We must use what platforms we have to reach the grass roots and politicise them,' declared David. Richard added: 'One of the main problems among us Blacks is our lack of unity. Here in the urban areas we can bring all the tribal groups together.'

'What about the students, SASO and the Black Consciousness movement?' demanded Patrick. 'They seem to be moving things forward.'

This older generation thought the young were on the wrong track. 'Those students, away in their ivory towers, they are out of touch with the man in the street or the herders on the veld. They are in too much of a hurry and they are unrealistic in their aims. I told them the government would come down on them if they formed a political movement and they wouldn't listen, that's why they are in jail.'

For one last time we asked: 'What of the future? Will there be a revolution?'

Richard didn't answer directly but it was clear that he hoped things would not get to that stage. 'I meet with white business people and politicians,' he said, 'and I do believe there is a real change of attitude at the very top. The nationalists have accepted the urban Blacks as permanent residents in the white areas of the country.'

David disagreed. 'It hasn't got that far. In Parliament last week they repeated the mantra about Blacks being "temporary sojourners" in white areas. I read it in Hansard. But perhaps attitudes are changing; at work I now share the white secretary with my boss!'

Richard chuckled. 'Anyway, I'm not planning to move out of my Soweto house!' We remembered the mansion we'd glimpsed. These people were buying into the Western capitalist system; they were natural allies of the white upper classes, who couldn't or wouldn't see it. As we washed up our borrowed crockery Patrick remarked: 'In a normal country, Richard Maponya would by now be chairman of a nation-wide business quoted on the Stock Exchange. I wish we'd had John Rogers sitting round this table tonight; these are the people he doesn't believe exist!'

That night we set the faithful alarm for 7 am so we could make an early start on our round of goodbyes. First we drove to the Van Vuurens to return the plates and cutlery we'd borrowed for our unconventional entertaining and to present them with some plants for their beloved garden in return. In the sunshine the weaver birds were beginning to build a nest and the first peach tree was in bloom; spring was coming.

Felicity waved away our thanks. 'It's been great. The supper was a success and I'm already in touch with Elda about a job for her.'

Then we delivered our little blue Volkswagen to the Christian Institute; it had taken us 10,000km over tar and gravel, to the homes of the elite and into places where we should not have been. Its innards were not in good shape but they could sell it for a few rand or use it, with its Lesotho registration, to make unobtrusive trips, perhaps to smuggle someone over the border. They gave us letters to post in Britain for security's sake; we circulated our London address and invited anyone to come and stay for as long as they liked to refill the lake of hospitality. Lindi burst into tears and June gave us both great bear hugs.

We walked back to Hillbrow and packed our permitted 60kg of baggage. To save weight, I decided to wear my heavy Xhosa skirt over my trousers and my Lesotho hat on my head. We posted a last parcel of books and papers and gave everything else to Stephina the maid. In return, she showed us her room, which was just as bad as what we'd seen in Cape Town. She told us she got R30 a month, working six hours a day seven days a week, and she went home once a year to see her children. We gave her the address of the Black Allied Workers' Union.

We bade goodbye to Mr Finlayson and told him about the cockroaches but not about our supper parties. The taxi took us to catch the airport bus; a full moon hung over gloomy suburbs and glinted on the mine dumps. In rather doleful mood we queued up at the check-in. We felt we were going out with a whimper – but, suddenly, bang! – there was Father Molale and the whole Sharpeville crowd; they had borrowed a minibus and made the journey from Sharpeville just to see us off and wish us Godspeed!

The airport bar was 'international' so we all went off to drink boisterous toasts in several languages, including the Stuart Christmas toast which goes:

Here's to all those who we love
And here's to all those who love us
And here's to all those, who love those that love those, who love
those who love those that love us.

From now on, it would reach out internationally. A group of young Blacks was sitting nearby, looking at us all. Finally one came over: 'Please, may we take your photograph?' The biter bit at the eleventh hour!

They gathered round us and pop went the flashes; they just wanted to be photographed drinking with white people. Such a universal social activity, so difficult to achieve in South Africa! The departure was announced; after hugs and handshakes all round we stood on the escalator to go down to security while the white fellow passengers stared at us disapprovingly. I was dressed in a long African beaded orange skirt, Patrick had my Lesotho hat on his head and they saw us waving to – could it be those black faces smiling at us through the barriers which we had, after all, broken through?

AFTERWORD

Our 'journey of self-education' reshaped the rest of our lives. At first we tried to tell our story to the church, but although our local vicar was enthusiastic our illustrated talk to his parishioners fell flat. So I helped Christian Aid write some teaching materials for on *Family Life and Migrant Labour in South Africa* and completed my book for schools, published in 1977 as *The Unequal Third*. Then I went back to teaching social studies in a London comprehensive school, being sure to include Third World development in the curriculum. Though we had lost touch with many of those who helped us on our journey we used to have an 'open house' evening once a month where African friends both old and new would pitch up – one way of refilling the lake of hospitality.

Patrick decided not to return to the City and joined ELTSA (End Loans to Southern Africa), a group campaigning for the end to apartheid through the imposition of financial sanctions; he would probably have moved further into 'ethical investment' if new pathways hadn't opened up for us in Lesotho. When the National University of Lesotho wanted a replacement for Don Taylor he sent me the advert, I applied and was offered the job. So June 1979 saw us back in Lesotho and living on that beautiful multiracial campus in Roma in the shadow of the Maluti mountains. For five years I taught development studies there: training secondary school teachers for the subject, running in-service workshops, developing the curriculum, writing school textbooks with teams of local teachers and enjoying myself enormously.

Meanwhile Patrick worked for a firm of accountants in Maseru and then branched off into freelance projects, including training bookkeepers for the Thaba Khupa Agricultural Institute. Quite possibly his work contributed more usefully to Lesotho's development than did mine. His most satisfying job was running the accounts for Scott Hospital at Morija – the headquarters of the Lesotho Evangelical Church – and during our final year, when I was doing the classroom research for my D.Phil, we lived in an old sandstone mission house on the hospital grounds.

On our return to the UK in 1985 Patrick found work with the Centre for Employment Initiatives and later with the Institute of Chartered Accountants to monitor 'sole traders' while I wrote up my research thesis. In 1988 I joined the Centre for International Education at Sussex University, where we ran post-graduate degree courses for Third World students and carried out research and consultancy in education and development. We moved to Brighton and Patrick, keeping a careful eye on the stock market, decided he could afford to retire. He looked after our house, garden and cats, helped people with their tax returns and, until he fell ill, pursued his interests in wild flowers and butterflies. I often returned to sub-Saharan Africa, especially to Lesotho and the new South Africa, as part of my work but never again to Nigeria or Tanzania.

South Africa

In spite of the dire warnings we'd heard, apartheid ended relatively peacefully though not without twenty years of turmoil. P.W. Botha, who led the country between 1978-89, believed passionately in 'separate development'; he granted limited political rights to Indians and Coloureds, but none to Blacks outside the Bantustans, whose status he tried to enhance. He built up the army and police, using them for internal repression, for armed raids on ANC offices in neighbouring countries – Lesotho suffered twice from such incursions while we were working there – and for intervening in the Angolan civil war against left-wing forces. As civil unrest grew he responded with ever-stricter laws against free speech, detention without trial, and torture, which led in turn to increased violence.

This vicious circle was broken when F.W. de Klerk succeeded him in 1989. He unbanned the ANC, released Nelson Mandela and set up constitutional talks with all groups. In 1992 a 'Whites Only' referendum voted overwhelmingly to abolish apartheid and in 1994 free elections brought the African National Congress to power with Mandela as

President. The country had a new name ('republic' was dropped), a new flag, a second national anthem (the formerly forbidden *Nkosi sikilel' iAfrica*) and eleven official languages. The artificial borders of the 'homelands' disappeared within the nine new provinces, though the geography of apartheid is still imprinted on the land in terms of who farms what, how and where.

What caused this relatively benign outcome? We had seen the first signs of some of them. External pressure in many forms, including economic boycotts and disinvestment, spearheaded by ELTSA, weakened the rand. Internally Church leaders like Naudé, liberal politicians like Malherbe, and pragmatic Africans like Motlana and Maphonya, as well as many others, appealed to common sense and fought against ideology. But the end of the Cold War was also a key event; in 1988 Reagan and Gorbachev agreed that Soviet and Cuban troops would withdraw from Angola and that Namibia should become independent in 1990. Most white South Africans understood at last that the 'wind of change' could not be resisted and, free of the fear of communism, decided to make the best of it.

Although the legacy of apartheid remains, today the problems of South Africa are now mostly the 'normal' ones of development – poverty, schools, health, sanitation, rural and urban imbalances, industrialisation – rather than the 'extraordinary' ones of apartheid.

Lesotho

Lesotho's story is less positive. It had enjoyed status as a 'frontline state' in the fight against apartheid which brought much economic and political support from the West, while educated Basotho stayed at home and tried to develop their own resources. After 1994 the borders became permeable and Lesotho lost some of its raison d'etre, to the extent there was talk of it becoming the 'tenth province' of South Africa. Unemployment is worse, since South Africa now prioritises its own workers in the mines, though educated Basotho can find jobs over the border and many have emigrated.

Political instability has followed. Chief Jonathan was ousted by military coup in 1986 and, after both King Moshoeshoe II and his son Letsie III had tried to interfere with the constitution, democratic elections returned in 1993. Since then splits within parties and contested elections have characterised the political process and in 1998 the South African Defence Force was called in to quell disturbances, resulting in much of Maseru being burnt down. A new electoral system gave more weight to smaller parties and the General Election in May 2012 – when I was on holiday there – passed off peacefully, with power being transferred from one coalition to another, yet the stability of successive governments seems somewhat precarious. Lesotho remains poor and marginal, its fate bound up with that of its neighbour; its stalwart people playing as best they can the hand that geography and history have dealt them.

ACKNOWLEDGEMENTS

My gratitude spreads out in many directions. First of course, to all those who made us so welcome on the trip: by inviting us into their homes, taking us around, or just sharing their knowledge and views with us; they shaped our journey for us and are in a sense co-creators of this tale. Almost all are named in the book and I hope that those I have not been able to contact will remember what they did and accept our thanks in this form.

Secondly, I am grateful to all those who supported and encouraged me in writing the story so many years later. Before Patrick died we met David Arscott who showed us possibilities and introduced me to the Sussex Authors' Society, a useful forum for discussion on many topics. The Writers' Group at St. George's Park – Penelope Bennett, Lisa Button, Geoffrey Pink, Alan Robertson and Maxine Vlieland – listened patiently to many episodes, read some of them, and gave encouraging feedback.

I learnt a great deal from two Arvon Foundation courses on travel/memoir/life-writing from the participants who shared their work and in particular from the tutors: Rory McLean and Jay Griffiths in 2011 and Rachel Holmes and Hannah Poole in 2013. Between them they helped me find a suitable 'voice', a suitable length and varied ways of writing.

My brother-in-law Rory Stuart offered me a writer's garret in Italy when I needed isolation to get started and read the final draft. I also found welcome writing refuge while housing-sitting for Eleanor Watts and for Mary and Martin Lewis. Others who read various drafts include Jenny Boden, Jill Eddison, Antonia Lister-Kaye and Greg Wells. Ola Uduku advised me on the Nigerian section, Andrew Coulson and Judith Scott helped make my account of Tanzania much more accurate, Mary Hlalele commented usefully on Lesotho and the Selwyns added some ideas; Bongile Putsoa and Bhadala Mamba enhanced my understanding of Swaziland and Elaine Unterhalter gave valuable feedback on South Africa. Phil Beauchamp helped me digitalise and improve my slides for the illustrations. I thank them all whole-heartedly. All mistakes and interpretations remain my responsibility.

I am most grateful to my editor Karen Holmes and to the whole team at 2QT who have brought the book into existence.

ACRONYMS

ANC	African National Congress
BIC	Bantu Investment Corporation
BAWU	Black Allied Workers' Union
BCP	Black Community Programme
BPC	Black People's Convention
BOSS	Bureau of State Security
CCC	Christian Conference Centre (Dodoma)
CI	Christian Institute
ELTSA	End Loans to Southern Africa
FAO	Food and Agricultural Organisation
FRELIMO	Frente de Libertação de Moçambique
ICA	Inter-Church Aid
IMF	International Monetary Fund
LSE	London School of Economics
NUSAS	National Union of South African Students
NUL	National University of Lesotho
NNSL	Nigerian National Shipping Line
PAC	Pan African Congress
PSC	Programme for Social Change
RSA	Republic of South Africa
SACHED	South African College of Higher Education
SACC	South African Council of Churches
SASO	South African Students Organisation
SB	Special Branch
SPRO-CAS	Study Project on Christianity in Apartheid Society
TANU	Tanzania African National Union
TUCSA	Trade Union Congress of South Africa
UN	United Nations
VSO	Voluntary Service Overseas
YMCA	Young Men's Christian Association

THE AUTHOR

Janet Stuart is a teacher and teacher-educator with a particular interest in Third World development. She taught in secondary schools in London and then at the universities of Lesotho and Sussex. She has published academically and produced textbooks for students both in the UK and southern Africa. She now lives in a retirement village in Sussex.